Political Economy in Haiti

Political Economy in Haiti: The Drama of Survival

Simon M. Fass

Transaction Publishers
New Brunswick (U.S.A.) and London (U.K.)

First paperback reprint 1990

New Brunswick, New Jersey 08903

Library of Congress Catalog Number: 89-25532
ISBN: 0-888738-158-8 (cloth);
0-88738-855-8 (paper)
Printed in the United States of America

Library of Congress Cataloging-in-Publication Data

Fass, Simon M.
Political economy in Haiti.

Bibliography: p.
Includes index.
1. Haiti--Economy policy. 2. Haiti--Economic conditions--1971- . I. Title.
HC153.F37 1988 338.97294 87-25532
ISBN 0-88738-158-8

CIP

I dedicate this book to my mother and to the memory of my father.

Contents

List of Figures

List of Tables

Preface

This book originates in a 1974 conspiracy to send me to Haiti against my will. That summer John Herbert, then vice-president of PADCO, Inc., was desperately seeking an architect or engineer. He needed someone to serve as urban infrastructure planner in a United Nations technical assistance project with the Haitian government. At the same time, I was busily complaining to the chairman of my doctoral committee, John Friedmann, about the difficulty I had in securing a job offering opportunities for extracting a dissertation. Not surprisingly, soon after receiving a call from Herbert about prospective candidates for the job, Friedmann was hard at work undermining my general disinterest in developing countries, not to mention my complete lack of interest in Haiti, and convincing me that deep down in my soul I cared enough about poor people and a Ph.D. to justify a sojourn in Port–au–Prince. I arrived in the city with many misgivings a few weeks later.

Experiences during the initial months of my stay offered little to ease my anxieties. The job title, "infrastructure planner," was a sham—useful to PADCO only as a marketing ploy. My first assignment was to conduct a comprehensive survey and analysis of human waste disposal methods. The city had no sewers, and the tools of my trade as I randomly sampled shallow and deep holes in one neighborhood after another were a notepad, a pencil, and a long wooden rod. To be more precise, my job was to serve as the project's latrinologist or, sounding better in French, as its "latrinologue."

This start to a scholarly career in what I would later learn to call the field of development planning was hardly auspicious. But in confronting me with sights, sounds, and smells of universal human production of a fundamental type at levels below conventional delineations of the "lower depths" or the "grassroots," those first few months were important. Among other things, they helped shape my early thoughts concerning the conduct of certain human affairs on the surface—in particular thoughts about poverty, about policy, and about interactions between them.

One thought was that my search for understanding more about poverty and policy need not venture lower than where I stood. For my purposes at least, sludge required no disaggregation. The search could only move upwards in a methodical process of aggregation, from the outputs about which I was rapidly becoming expert to its source inputs, from waste to food and water, from food and water to the individuals and families that consumed them, from consumers to producers, and from consumers and producers to the makers of policies, programs, and projects that gave consumption and production their particular characteristics.

Another thought was that the path to understanding would take a long, long time to cover. The distance between the base of a cesspool and the basis of policy, though generally less than three meters in physical terms, was immense in explanatory terms.

My travel over this path is now well into its second decade. From time to time I would break the trip, take stock of progress, and then write about what I learned. The dissertation was done in 1977. The United States Agency for International Development circulated an abridged version of it in 1980. Thereafter I wrote a number of articles, chapters, and technical reports that advanced different themes contained in the original work. Although incorporating much of the earlier writing and adding new material, this book is not in any sense the culmination of a voyage of discovery. It is simply another step along the way.

Coming up on this and previous stations, I have had the honor to benefit from the support and advice of many colleagues. Irving Louis Horowitz was instrumental in convincing me that the various fragments of writing I shared with him several years ago constituted embryonic components of what could eventually become a useful book. He followed the course of my work from the first draft to the last, and provided me with constant encouragement and inspiration through difficult moments.

Harold Alderman, Leland Burns, Eric Chetwynd, Robert Denizé, Gerrit Desloovere, Margaret Dewar, Peter Easton, Michael Farbman, Robert Fischer, John Friedmann, Clothilde Manuel, Richard Massaro, William Miner, Linda Morse, Jo Ann Paulson, Lisa Peattie, Janice Perlman, Lenore Rasmussen, Lloyd Rodwin, Terry Roe, Vernon Ruttan, Rickie Sanders, Benjamin Senauer, Joseph Stern, Charles Waterfield, Aaron Wildavsky, and William Yaeger all read substantial portions of drafts of this manuscript and offered welcome criticisms and suggestions. James Berezin, Germilus Cadet, Dana Fischer, Roslyn Hees, Barry Heyman, Harlan Hobgood, Criss Juliard, Father Quirinus Muth, Robert Padberg, Carole Roy, Patricia Vermander, and James Walker, among many others, provided important information and insights at crucial times in the research process.

My research assistants, Sarah Dunning, Michael Lee, Smaragda Sazotou, and Peter Strzok were indefatigable in their searches through libraries for materials I wanted but could describe in only the most obtuse fashion. Michael also went to heroic lengths to verify my calculations and to extract statistical salience from data that I believed offered very limited scope for discovering numeric significance. And Smaragda worked tirelessly and painstakingly to prepare the maps, sketches, graphs, and photographs contained in the work.

Louise Straus, extending herself beyond the drudgery of typing one draft manuscript after another, was of inestimable value in correcting my prose and in making this book much more intelligible than it would have been without her timely interventions.

For their generous financial assistance at different times, I wish to express my gratitude to the Office of Urban Development, United States Agency for International Development; the Graduate School, University of Minnesota; and the Hubert H. Humphrey Institute of Public Affairs, University of Minnesota.

Finally, I must acknowledge the considerable debt I owe to the ordinary people I met in St. Martin and elsewhere in Port-au-Prince. With patience and good humor they took valuable time out of their daily routines to teach me things about the meaning of poverty and survival that I could never have learned without their active guidance.

Acknowledgments

Parts of this book extract materials from previously published works and I gratefully acknowledge the publishers and publications for permission to use them.

The first several pages of the Introduction paraphrase from CT Kurien, *Poverty, Planning and Social Transformation,* 1978, Chapter 1, pp. 1–6 (Allied Publishers, Private Ltd.). Used by permission of the Indian Council of Social Science Research.

Chapter 4 includes material from "Water and Politics: The Process of Meeting a Basic Need in Haiti," by Simon M. Fass. Reprinted from *Development and Change* vol. 13, no. 3, July, 1982. Used by permission of Sage Publications Ltd., London. Copyright © 1982 Institute of Social Studies.

Chapter 5 draws from two previous publications. One is "The St. Martin Project," by Simon M. Fass, pp. 231–256 from *Politics, Projects, and People: Institutional Development in Haiti* edited by Derick W. Brinkerhoff and Jean-Claude Garcia-Zamor. Copyright © 1986 by Praeger Publishers. Reprinted by permission of Praeger Publishers, a division of Greenwood Press, Inc.

The second publication is "Housing the Ultra-Poor: Theory and Practice in Haiti," by Simon M. Fass. Reprinted by permission of the *Journal of the American Planning Association* vol. 53, no. 2, Spring 1987.

Introduction

Most individuals and organizations that concern themselves with conditions in developing countries share a verbal commitment to eradicate the problem of poverty.[1] But their opinions vary on answers to questions about the definition of the problem, and about the meaning of commitment. Some believe that poverty can be remedied immediately through policy, program, and project actions. Others believe that only the processes of history will one day solve the problem. Whatever the nature of these opinions, poverty remains a concrete circumstance. There are people who cannot find enough work, who do not eat enough food, who do not drink enough water, who do not have roofs over their heads. Because this is the concrete problem of poverty, then solutions through immediate actions or through historical process will be in terms of identical categories: work for the jobless, food for the hungry, water for the thirsty, and shelter for the homeless.

This does not imply that understanding the problem is simple. Nor does it imply that solving the problem is a straightforward matter of moving from good resolutions to appropriate interventions. It suggests that no matter what the language of diagnosis may be, the problem of poverty remains one of people and their relationship to basic things. Because languages of diagnosis describe the people and things in so many different ways, it also suggests that there is no easy route from description to solution.

Poverty does not reveal itself to the student of the subject with the same concreteness as it does to a poor person. Description invariably passes through some procedure of abstraction, simplification, classification or other technique of explicit or implicit ordering. The problem of poverty for the student, and for the poor if a relationship exists between study and subsequent action, is therefore also a problem of procedure. If the procedure is to connect description with solution, if it is to do more than serve purposes like theoretical advancement that may or may not be pertinent to solution, then the procedure should assure that categories of analysis, the concepts, images, and languages created to assist diagnosis, are derived as much as possible from concrete circumstances.

An important challenge in this regard is the interaction between analyzed and unanalyzed categories. For example, to proceed on the assumption that analysis should be done entirely with the analyzed categories of one particular discipline or subdiscipline is to decide that the analysis should not extend further than the categories allow. Extending beyond the limits of disciplines (or science, for that matter) may not advance the state of formalized knowledge, but it may perhaps help in discovering some solutions to poverty.

A useful method of extending beyond limits, and possibly of attaining better understanding of the problem, is direct presence and involvement in the circumstances of the poor. To the extent that a student may find it difficult to distinguish between ascription and inference, and therefore between the theoretical and the real, immediate confrontations with the circumstances of the poor cannot yield "truths."[2] What they can perhaps provide are abstractions that more closely resemble the actual and concrete, or, to put it more idiomatically, new empirical data that can form bases for revised hypotheses.

Another challenge, in this instance internal to a discipline (or to science in general), relates to the large number of abstract categories that a student can superimpose upon what is presumably the same entity. With microeconomics, for example, an analyst can place individuals or households into the theoretical category of "consumer," and thereafter explain behavior in terms of the postulates of "consumer theory." Alternatively, the ascription may be to the category of "producer," in which case an analyst explains behavior in terms of propositions attached to the "theory of the firm." And then there is the category of "household–firm," which applies the properties and theoretical propositions of consumer and producer simultaneously.[3] Anthropology may fix the individual or household as part of a "kinship network"; sociology may place it in a class belonging to a metaphorical "structure" of society; and political science may ascribe to it the property of political volition and action. In reality, individuals and households are none of these things. In theory they are all of these things. But whether students do or do not distinguish between concept and that to which they have attached it, the world of theory, and also of assumption and opinion, is the only means by which they can create order out of the chaos of the real. The process of selecting from among the many available one or a combination of several abstractions to suit the purposes at hand may therefore be quite difficult.

If the purpose of an undertaking is to verify or develop a hypothesis, abstraction can come first and facts shaped by it will follow accordingly. If the purpose is understanding leading to intervention, which unlike hypothesis testing implies tangible effects upon people, facts should come first and abstractions should follow. But there are very few facts that are not already imbedded explicity or implicitly in theories of one kind or another. Interpretation of the simple act of eating, for example, will in microeconomics be an act of consumption. Under consumer theory it will constitute an act of "final" consumption explained in terms of utility or satisfaction that people derive from it. Under the theory of the firm, it will be an act of "productive" consumption, or more simply, "production," explained in terms of its function as a factor input, like electricity, in the manufacture of earnings. Choice between these two approaches is from a theoretical point of view dependent only upon relative advantages in terms of explanatory power. But explanatory power may often be inadequate as a criterion for intervention. In treating the question of how to link hungry people with food, ascription of final consumption and therefore no income–enhancing properties associated with food, might result in a policy focusing attention elsewhere in order to raise income and thereafter raise food intake. Ascription of productive consumption, and therefore a direct causal link from food to income, would have it that policy, wherever else it might stray, retain fixed attention on food as a method to increase income.

The act of eating is by itself a fact implying nothing. Choice between theories to interpret the act imply everything. Because criteria by which to make the choice are not obvious in either theory, immersion in the concrete circumstances can perhaps be helpful. If such immersion shows the act to be providing 3000 calories per day per person, perhaps consumer theory is appropriate. If it provides 1000 calories, perhaps the theory of the firm is more applicable. If it is between 1000 and 3000 calories, analysis and the interests of poor people may be better served by use of both theories.[4] And calories will say nothing about whether the outcome of the act of eating is somehow also associated with kinship, social class, or politics.

Adding to the difficulty of selecting from the list of concepts available to describe identical objects and actions is the challenge of integrating abstractions about parts with abstractions about wholes, the "micro" and "macro" perspectives. In much the same way as for theories of the consumer and the firm, micro- and macroviews can lead to divergent interpretations, diagnoses, prognoses, and prescriptions. A microview of the household yields one type of understanding of its behavior in terms of theorized internal motivations. The same household, viewed macroscopically in terms of the environment in which it functions, may lead to understanding of behavior in terms of its response to external forces. Returning to the theme of food, a microview may note that food preparation practices look suboptimal, might conclude that the problem is inappropriate knowledge about the practices, and could then point toward programs of nutrition education. A macroview, assessing relative market prices for different food items, may conclude that nutrition practices are perfectly suited to economic circumstances and thereafter propose policies to alter the prices and thereby improve nutritional intakes. A combined view might then posit that relative prices reflect a pattern of demand shaped by nutritional practices and that to some extent prices will not change unless the practices change, thus pointing action back to nutrition education. One, all, or none of these views could be accurate.

A fourth challenge, especially relevant to questions presumed to have policy answers, has to do with incorporating volition in social, economic, and political processes. In science it is sufficient for an analyst to describe for the purpose of describing. A scientist may say that people are hungry because they are poor, that they are poor because they are hungry, that they are both poor and hungry because they do not know how to prepare proper meals, or because price structures are such as to prevent them from preparing these meals. But it is quite another thing for a scientist to extend beyond the boundaries of an inquiry and address policy "implications" or "recommendations" to real or imagined "decision makers" whose actions were excluded from the inquiry. For policy purposes, there is the important practical matter of determining causality in current circumstances. A scientist may conveniently suppose, and might sometimes find it to be true, that an analytical discovery can influence policy. Often, however, the scientist will be on firmer ground if he or she assumes that to a greater or lesser extent the absence of policies that might help people become less poor or less hungry, like nutrition programs or food price interventions, has little to do with the absence of the discovery.

In either case, if the intent of analysis is to extend beyond science and into the world of policy, which it must do if the purpose is solution to the problem of poverty, then the analysis should contain within its boundaries one or more abstractions that can perhaps shape answers to questions like: Why are there no nutritional programs? Or, why are food price policies the way they are? The challenges here are exactly the same as those I have already enumerated: interaction between analyzed and unanalyzed categories, choice among theoretical propositions, and micro- and macroviews. A useful approach to dealing with the challenges at this level, as before, is direct immersion in the policy process as it pertains to poor people on one hand, and to jobs, food, water, shelter, and similar important things on the other. This approach also provides new data for revised hypotheses about the conduct of policy.

Related to this last, a fifth and fundamental challenge to the scientist is his or her appreciation of the implications of the movement of analysis from the scientific world of description to the world of policy prescription. This movement is an act of politics. It is a political act because it has the potential for causing poor people good or harm. It is not a scientific act because there is something inherently unscientific about proposing actions on the basis of conclusions that might have turned out completely different had fortune called upon one or another of several theories to shape interpretation. Nothing need prevent an analyst from making recommendations. As citizen of a community, country, or the world, he or she may say or suggest anything. What is important is the analyst's recognition that the proposal is not backed by "truth," and that it therefore cannot be more than one of a myriad of opinions.

This matter is especially important in developing countries, where poor people often have little capacity for political counteraction to argue about the conceptual categories used to describe them, about the conclusions derived from use of the categories, or about the policy opinions that flow from the conclusions. There is, for example, a large glossary of abstract categories that seem to circulate largely or exclusively in developing countries. Ordinary workers in rural areas are often "peasants" rather than farmers. Large numbers of workers in urban areas are supposedly "underemployed" rather than fully employed at low earnings because, at least according to one definition of the concept, output would not be affected if they were to cease working. The categories are doubtless useful for certain analytical purposes. But because most farmers with small land holdings in North America and Europe would object to being called peasants, because most social scientists would object to being labeled as underemployed (which is what they are according to the definition), because both would object to policies proposing to move them from their current "low- or non-productive" occupations to, say, "modern" factory jobs, and because the professional career of an analyst could be seriously impaired if he or she uses a politically unacceptable category or proposes an unacceptable course of action, democratic political process imposes severe limitations on both conceptual latitude and the extent to which singular opinion can influence policy. This process is largely absent in developing countries. The privilege of unconstrained analysis, of rendering opinion, and of shaping the policy process is the privilege of a small number of people, including scientists, who comprise a society's political class.

There are at least two implications of this challenge. One is acceptance by scientists of the possibility that some of the special abstract categories form part of the problem rather than part of the solution to poverty. Analysis is complex enough with the multiplicity of abstract categories available for use in developed countries, and policy is complex enough with the multiplicity of opinions that can result from each abstraction. Adding still more categories and opinions may sometimes make understanding of poverty even more elusive than it already is.

More important, however, is appreciation by scientists that the policy process is a struggle between competing self-interests, including the self-interest called "altruism." Analysts who venture opinions about the direction that policy should take, neither more nor less than anyone else of the political class, are political actors, actively or passively engaged in a political struggle for dominance of their particular opinions in policy. In developing countries they themselves are smaller or larger parts of the decision-making process and, to put it directly with a well-worn phrase, they and their opinions may be part of the problem rather than part of the solution. Because of the difficulty of knowing, learning, or accepting with certainty the possibility of personal or organizational culpability in the absence of a democratic political process to make the case, the least one may ask for is periodic reflection on the issue.

What the whole of the foregoing suggests is the improbability that analysis growing out of social science can do more than supply disparate fragments and strands of facts and abstractions that, combined in a sensible fashion, might shed light on a few particulars about the concrete phenomenon of poverty, and perhaps also venture a few restrained opinions about the characteristics of another concrete phenomenon called policy. And there are few guidelines to help define the meaning of "sensible." The objective is clear enough: to arrive at a useful body of descriptive propositions for an assumed reality. The method, a combination of practical opportunism, attention to detail, and recurrent prayer for luck, is somewhat less clear. But this is really not a difficulty. Some idealized suppositions about scientific practice might argue otherwise, but scientific practice, including creation of the supposition, is human practice, and it does not matter too much whether human practice strays far or remains close to the ideal. What matters more is the outcome of practice in terms of contributing in a useful way to understanding the problem of poverty, perhaps to understanding the problem of policy about poverty, and possibly also to eventual solution of one or both problems.

This book is about ordinary people and simple things in Port-au-Prince. It is about the tangible meanings that work, food, water, shelter, schooling, and credit might have for these people, about the internally motivated and externally directed reasons they may have for acquiring more or less of each item, and about the methods they seem to pursue in obtaining them. These ordinary people are extraordinary in only one respect. Their incomes are very low, so low that one serious error of judgment or one unfortunate act of providence can often threaten survival of a household as a corporate entity, and sometimes also threaten survival of its members as corporeal entities. What is extraordinary is not so much the poverty itself, but rather the ability of these people to survive in spite of it.

This ability does not reveal itself as a capacity to passively "subsist." They do not simply survive. They engage themselves actively and agressively in what seems to be a constant process of producing and reproducing, at minimum, a level of income permitting them to survive, and at maximum, a process of household economic growth and development. Nothing they do in this process is anything but a productive contribution to survival and growth, and the simple items they obtain have concrete functions as factor inputs to the production process.

This is, of course, an interpretation of what they do structured by the theory of the firm in microeconomics. What they may actually do is less consequential. From 1974 to 1976 I pursued a two–year confrontation with some of these people. The experiences included passing encounters with thousands in momentary interactions required for large–scale survey purposes. More important were longer duration chitchats with hundreds, often over coffee, to talk about science, business, life in general and, to the extent possible, politics. Most important were meetings with 145 families who lived on the streets, and 88 who lived in a neighborhood called St. Martin. These meetings combined the formal needs of survey work with the informal method of idle chatter, and each could sometimes last for several hours. The experiences all conspired to suggest that of the choices of abstract categories available inside and outside economic theory, the propositions attached to the firm often provided as close to an approximation as one could have about the concrete particulars of the people and their relationships to the things. Other categories having to do with kinship, social class, and politics were also important, but the central theme of production of survival presented a useful concept around which to organize these other abstractions.

The experience also suggested that these people were, like myself and the reader, quite ordinary. Many were illiterate and others not well–educated. But, making allowance for limited formal schooling, the particular range and composition of life experiences they could have in the city, and peculiarities that the presence of a foreigner of the political class imposed upon communication, most seemed to be intelligent, acutely aware of their circumstances, and eminently capable of making well–founded policy, program, and project recommendations. Other than the difficulties most of them faced in making ends meet with less than U.S. $0.32 per day per adult at a time when unit prices for food and water were higher than in North America and Europe—and the talent required to do so—they seemed to be little different from most urban residents in most developed or developing countries.

The book is also about the relationship between ordinary people, simple things, and extraordinary people of the city's political class. The class, a collection of Haitians and foreigners inside and outside government (and inside and outside Haiti) comprising a constellation of self-interests that form and reform around issues as circumstance and fortune dictate, is the world of policy. This world is as concrete as poverty, but because the direct problem of politics is one of people and people, more often than one of people and things, it escapes abstract categorization of the simple type offered by the theory of the firm.[5] My thirteen years of on–again, off–again immersion in this world (not to mention a lifetime of immersion in the routine political ethers of daily conduct), first through the United Nations Center for Housing, Building and Planning (now the United Nations Center for Human Settlements) and then in sequence through Haiti's Ministries of Finance and Agriculture, the Interamerican Institute of Agricultural Sciences, the World Bank, the United States Agency for International Development, and the Haitian Association of Voluntary Agencies, has yet to yield a sense of understanding that can be made comfortably consistent with one particular abstract category.

But in the same way that my experiences with the ordinary class yielded a sense that there was much to learn by ascribing the theory of the firm and by defining purposeful behavior in terms of survival and growth, my experiences in the political class suggested that there was something to learn in using similar theoretical premises and behavioral definitions for this class. Moreover, analytical consistency seemed to demand equivalent treatment of both classes. The distinction between the classes was arbitrary, useful only for a specific analytical purpose. Members of each class were of the same human species and therefore could not but share the same behavioral motives. If there were differences, they were in the things that helped members of each class produce survival and growth, and in the criteria they emphasized in measuring survival and growth.

Although both used similar measures, beyond salaries and profits members of the political class seemed to place heavier emphasis on more intangible benefits, such as recognized expertise, professional standing, political solvency, power, organizational repute, respect for "doing good," and so on. In this context, the things or basic needs that many in the class had to produce in order to obtain such outcomes included reports, policies, programs, and projects. That is, as I noted earlier, the behaviors of the political class, as for the ordinary class, were driven by self–interest, including the self–interest of altruism. Policy processes could have absolutely nothing to do with helping ordinary people. But as for any conceptual framework, there were limits to the explanatory capabilities of this approach, and in many instances there was a randomness in the flow of events that could find no clear cause.

This is not important. What is important is that the framework allows a separation between the political economy of survival of the ordinary class, which must bear the tangible consequences of policy, and the political economy of survival of the political class, which, for its own purposes, produces the consequences. The contents of this book are about the substance of each of these distinct political economies and the interactions between them.

Chapter 1 offers an overview of the evolution of the political economy of Haiti and Port–au–Prince, focusing first on the changing characteristics of the political class, and then in more detail on economic dynamics driving political change through the city's seven principal industries: government, foreign assistance, commerce, import–substitution manufacturing, assembly export manufacturing, travel, and labor export. With emphasis on more recent times, the overview covers the period from 1492 to 1986 and explores the mechanisms by which the political economy shifted from a system of armed foreign colonial governance oriented to extraction of consumer and producer surplus, to a more complex system. This newer system is armed auto–colonial governance joined with unarmed foreign assistance, which, through 1986, still devoted itself to the principle of extraction. Politics in the wake of the Duvalier departure in 1986 suggests that substantial change in terms of bettering the circumstances of ordinary people, while possible, is unlikely. The constraint is in part the difficulty that "progressive" elements in the political class are likely to have in gaining preeminence. More of a constraint is fundamental ignorance, even among progessive elements, of the circumstances of ordinary people. In the absence of means through which ordinary people can make themselves heard politically, ignorance among progressives is not likely to be replaced with knowledge in a near future.

Against this background, chapters 2 through 7 dedicate themselves to detailed explorations of the productive meaning to ordinary people of six simple things that individuals and organizations of the political class sometimes call "basic needs," of the complexity of the relationships between ordinary people and these things, of the parallel complexity of interactions between various components of the political class and the same things, and through these last, of the often hopeless and sometimes hopeful connections between the two classes. Discussions of political class behaviors in these chapters are more often about individuals and organizations of the foreign–assistance industry than about agencies of the Haitian government. This bias in treatment results, in part, from the greater volume of available documentation about the industry. The more important factor is that in recent years the industry has become Haiti's unofficial or shadow government, particularly with respect to matters of "development."

Chapter 2 is about the arts and sciences of making a living averaging

U.S. $42 per month per household, primarily through activities to which the political class attaches special labels, like "traditional," "marginal," or "informal," or that members of the class sometimes subsume under the general heading of "underemployment." Nothwithstanding the labels, and noting that $42 constituted what one would call *middle income* in the relative scheme of things in Port-au-Prince, the activities were essentially quite normal. They were of types, if one looked at the principles involved rather than their visual appearance, that are conducted by most people in most places in most developed and developing countries. The only thing somewhat unusual about them was their extraordinary labor-intensiveness. But to concerned members of the political class unwilling or incapable of distinguishing between labels useful for analytical purposes and the activities to which the labels applied, either as a result of belief or of political necessities demanded by their claims to expertise or other survival requirements, the activities could not but be perceived as abnormal. Although ascribed abnormalcy tied to ignorance did not prohibit all interventions that might one day prove helpful, it did contribute to a demise of a fundamental concept. If work activities were highly labor-intensive, then calories and other nutritional components were required as basic inputs to the production of labor. Therefore, questions of productivity, efficiency, and earnings could often revolve principally on the matter of food policy rather than employment policy.

Chapter 3 is about food. It begins with an examination of the reasons guiding the political class to ignore what looked like a growing food shortage, reasons stemming in part from government lack of interest in agriculture, and in part from the survival needs of technicians and others who presumably concerned themselves with the nutritional status of ordinary people. The chapter then turns to a detailed exploration of the meaning of adequate nutrition, in theory and to ordinary people, highlighting its importance to health, labor productivity, and income. Food, for families earning $42 or less per month and generally unable to obtain more than about 1500 calories per adult per day, was not a final consumption good. It was in every way a vital form of productive consumption that families went to considerable lengths to transform into nutrition as efficiently as possible. Unfortunately, largely oblivious to the meaning and importance to individual and aggregate economic growth of food consumption, and unable to conclude that data collection on the subject might be helpful, components of the political class primarily concerned with policy did little to provide relief. Only the breakdown of class control in 1986, and the consequent possibility of open smuggling, allowed a moment for domestic prices of basic commodities up to 70 percent higher than border prices to come down to a level where ordinary people could perhaps find themselves 20–30 percent less poor than they had been for a very long time.

Equally or more important than food, but a problem without the possibility of a similar solution, was water. As described in chapter 4, what was in principle supposed to be a "public service" was in fact a private industry of oppression and extortion causing families to spend more than 10 percent of income to obtain a daily average of 12 liters per adult, and in the process again making out of a simple act of final consumption a fundamental act of human survival. By available evidence, and notwithstanding concerted efforts by reform-minded segments of the political class to bring about change, the circumstance in 1986 was no better, and perhaps worse, than in 1976. The cause, as for most things, was politics.

Where there seemed to be relatively little progress up to 1986 in matters of primary importance like food and water, there was considerably more with respect to the less important matter of shelter. Although the discussion of chapter 5 notes that shelter could be important for certain members of the ordinary population who were not housed, space and quality attributes of housing for the population already housed were far less productive to families than members of the political class thought they should be. The class could not conceive of circumstances wherein constraints on food and water consumption might make of housing a matter of secondary concern to ordinary people. In the event, politics allowed relatively substantial institutional progress to be made on this matter notwithstanding the usual considerable difficulties of implementation. These efforts created some good and little direct harm, and therefore constituted a glimmer of hope about political class capabilities in an otherwise generally hopeless situation. More important for most people, as in the matter of smuggling, was the breakdown of control permitting one significant act that for 30 years had proven impossible: land invasion and squatting.

Chapter 6 examines the evolution of what by rights should not have been a matter of interest for a population consuming 1500 calories and 12 liters of water or less: sending children to primary school. But in the inverted manner in which circumstances of the ordinary class and behaviors of the political class expressed themselves in Haiti, schooling came to be a basic component of corporeal survival of no lesser importance than food—precisely because it was a mechanism to obtain food. For the political class, however, schooling meant something having to do with "education," and the politics of expanding access to schools and of improving the quality of instruction in schools presumed that they were formal learning facilities. As for shelter, the political class undertook substantial efforts to do what they believed were constructive things. Especially from 1976 onward, they engaged a political process that suggested that the political class was not necessarily condemned to remain ignorant. Within its boundaries, there were individuals and organizations who could define expertise as the capacity to listen and respond, and who did not necessarily need to dictate their opinions, assumptions, and theories in order to maintain corporate survival. In the near term, the process offered little of substance in matters of education to ordinary people. But it might yield helpful outcomes in the long term.

Last among the not so simple things, chapter 7 describes the various uses to which ordinary people put commercial credit. It notes along the way that if things like food and water were in such short supply as to convert final consumption into basic production inputs, and if the purpose at hand was to invest in corporeal survival, rates of return to investment could be quite high. Similarly, returns to additions of capital in work activities could be high when such activities were almost purely labor–intensive. For these reasons, interest rates of 25–50 percent per month were quite reasonable. For a political class incapable of understanding that such interest figures were consistent with statistics like $42, 1500 calories, and 12 liters, the rates seemed usurious and suggested a problem of credit warranting intervention. They could not understand, nor could they hope to understand, that the problem of credit was not a credit problem. Usury was not in the interest rate but in the political class, and the rates, like other statistics and observations that flow one upon the other from the first chapter to the last, were indicators of the past and present bankruptcy of the class.

Extending this theme, the Conclusion deliberates upon the source of this bankruptcy. It can be explained in terms of extraordinary bad luck. It can also be explained in terms of abnormal behavior on the part of many individuals and organizations in the class. But to the extent that production of corporate survival is a normal human trait, the bankruptcy of the class must be a normal attribute of the class. Indeed, a recapitulation of 500 years of class behavior suggests little difference between contemporary procedures and those in effect under the political economy of slavery. The reason the political class was, is, and will remain ignorant is not accident or abnormality. It flows as a logical necessity from the political economy that conditions it.

In this respect, returning to the matter I presented at the outset of this Introduction about the divergence of opinions on the definition of the problem of poverty and the meaning of commitment toward its solution, there would seem to be a dimension that does seem susceptible to rapid remedial action. But there is also a dimension that the slow political and economic processes of history, whatever they may be, must treat in their own time.

Still, dismal as the outlook appears in terms of bettering the circumstances of ordinary people in a near future, there is hope. This hope does not stem from indisputable evidence. It stems from an obligation to ordinary people. They deserve at least that much from the political class.

Notes

1. The sequence and substance of the initial portion of this introduction, as mentioned in the acknowledgments section of this book, borrows heavily from Kurien (1978: 1–6), to whom I owe my gratitude for providing a simple framework around which to organize an array of diffuse thoughts.
2. The question of whether there is or is not a "reality" that exists beyond the limits of the senses is the subject of much speculative debate among philosophers. By the nature of the topic, it has no obvious "empirical" answer. From the perspective of scientific inquiry, it is usually helpful to assume that the nature of the world is random and chaotic. Such a premise, coupled with a fundamental "belief" in order, encourages imagination, receptivity to new hypotheses, and a constant search for explanatory theory. Perhaps more important, the premise acts as much-needed proxphylaxis against the tendency to automatically shift from analysis to policy. The effects of action are "real" in their capacity to benefit or injure.
3. Readers unacquainted with theories of the consumer and the firm may find descriptions in any standard text on microeconomics. Useful overviews of the integrated "household–firm" concept as an extension of traditional consumer theory are provided by Nerlove (1974), and Evenson (1976), and as an extension of the theroy of the firm by Jorgenson and Lau (1969).
4. The reasons for this approach may be evident in chapter 3.
5. The people–to–people dimension makes the problem of politics more complicated because of the inherent difficulty of ascribing causality in such situations, a matter taken up in all its frustrating philosophical detail by Brown (1968). The people–to–things dimension is complicated also, but causality is sometimes easier to ascribe. For example, people eat food because (a) if they do not, they will die; (b) they do not want to die. This causal reasoning may be inaccurate in general, but it will apply in enough instances to make it a useful predictor of behavior. Politics is less predictable. For example, people will revolt against oppressors who starve them because (a) if they do not, they will not obtain food; (b) without food they will die; and (c) they do not want to die. Unfortunately, most people in such situations usually do not revolt. They die.

1

Politics and Economics

The only substantive political revolution that historical documentation accords Haiti is Columbus's establishment through force of arms of a colonial–mercantilist form of governance in 1492, and its subsequent spread to cover the whole territory by 1512. Exactly what types of indigenous political structures the new forms replaced is uncertain, but there is some certainty that suppression of the population for the purpose of profiting from export of the product of cheap labor to North America and Europe was not a significant component of the pre–Columbian political economy. Haitians did not discover the Old World until 1492.

Also uncertain is the course of history that the territory that later came to be known as Haiti might have followed if fortune had not conspired to unite together Italian mercenaries, Spanish investment funds, a particular wind direction, and the shattering of faith in a flat earth. But the fact remained that fortune willed many things, and in the matter of politics it decreed that the territory would, in perpetuity, have a large proportion of the population in an ordinary category or class having little control over individual or collective destiny, and a very small proportion with total control in a category that for convenience may be called the political class.

Political histories of Haiti from 1492 to 1986 are stories about the movement of people into and out of each category, but mostly about the dynamics of struggle within the political class. The story about the ordinary class is relatively straightforward. Its first members were the indigenous Caribs, and after their disappearance, membership in the class passed to African imports and their descendants. With respect to the political class, membership flowed among private buccaneers, Spanish colonists and soldiers, the British armed forces, and then formally to the French in 1697.

In the years leading up to Haiti's independence in 1804, the political class developed several factions. These included resident colonists; French army officers and civil administration officials; a group composed principally of mulatto families with commercial interests in towns; and another group containing senior black and (to a lesser extent) mulatto officers in the army. The effect of independence was to reduce the number of major factions from four to two—an urban–based mulatto commercial elite and a rural–based black military elite (which later moved into towns)—and to define the basis of class struggle as battle between the two factions for dominion over the administrative apparatus of government (Nichols, 1979:8).

Administrative dominion meant control of customs receipts, and with such control a faction captured monopoly profits on export taxes and import duties. These revenues financed accumulation of personal wealth and reproduction of power to control the faithful within a faction by rewards of money, other gifts, jobs, contracts, priority access to government services, and other favors. They also financed a large standing army to maintain authoritarian rule over the ordinary class.

With establishment in the late nineteenth and through the twentieth centuries of new, smaller factional groupings composed of Levantine, European, and North American immigrant investors engaging themselves in international commerce and manufacturing, dominion also came to mean power to build alliances with such groups through allocation of monopoly rents attached to export, import, and manufacturing privileges, and through fiscal and other policy measures designed to benefit specific group interests. Such alliances permitted further accumulation of resources useful for amassing wealth and maintaining political solvency.

Whether one faction and its allies or the other faction and its allies found themselves in charge of government, economic policy remained a constant search for extraction and concentration of producer and consumer surpluses in their hands. No government in the history of the territory from 1804 to 1986 (or from 1492 to 1804) did anything of significance to improve the circumstances of ordinary people or to leave them with resources sufficient to permit productive investment and economic growth. Allowing more resources to circulate within the economy of the ordinary class would not have been inconsistent with auto–colonial policies that sought growth of monopoly rents over the long term. But administrators, perhaps preoccupied with immediate concerns attached to the class struggle, perhaps for other reasons, did not have long–term perspectives.

Transient and resident detractors within the class sometimes used colorful phrases like "predatory state" or "kleptocracy" to cast aspersion upon Haiti's method of governance, particularly with respect to what they perceived as corruption associated with diversion of public resources away from intended purposes (e.g., Rotberg, 1971: 342; Lundahl, 1979: 357). Defenders counterclaimed that while such corruption was recurrent, instances of honest administrative practice vastly outnumbered instances of dishonest practice (Leger, 1907:342–43). Sensationalism, apparently, was easier to sell than truth (Early, 1937: 149). And then there were those who argued that detraction and defence of administrative practice was essentially irrelevant. A more fundamental issue in Haiti was the colonial structure in which the political class did not hear the will of ordinary people, and did not need to hear it in order to rule (Mintz, 1974). Corruption in Haiti was not about diversion of resources from intended purposes, but rather about intended purposes and practices that were themselves diversions from what the concept of "government" was supposed to be about. In Haiti it was a private industry.

Members of the class based outside the territory did nothing to alter the structure. In the nineteenth century, French and German gunboats demanding indemnity payments took from resident factions what the resident factions took from the ordinary class. United States occupation forces pursued the same policy with respect to foreign creditors from 1915 to 1934 and continued to do so without the forces through 1947. Later, foreign–assistance agencies demanded principal and interest indemnities on loans and local counterpart financing of recurrent costs for "development" projects of their own creation that collectively also did little of significance to improve the circumstances of ordinary people.

These projects of Haiti's shadow government, and demanding extraction of additional surplus, were also products of unilateral actions and factional struggles that at no time required hearing the will of ordinary people. Foreign assistance, perhaps because of the nature of government or perhaps for other reasons, was also a private industry. Dominion over some portion of it allowed Haitian and expatriate members of different agencies to reward themselves and others among the developmental faithful with jobs, contracts, the cloak of expertise, and other favors like career advancement. All of this found justification in good intentions. But at no time—not in 1492, not in 1804 and not in 1986—did any significant group find it necessary to attempt to join their opinions, assumptions or theories about the meaning of good intentions for ordinary people with the opinions, assumptions or theories of ordinary people in their various manifestations as aborigines, slaves, peasants, marginals, masses, or other inculcations of ascribed political powerlessness, like "the poor."

None of this implies that the actions or inactions flowing out of various groups within the political class were in some universal way morally reprehensible, or that all members of the class necessarily viewed the circumstances of ordinary people without interest, or that no member of the class ever made some serious attempt to understand the circumstances and to attempt serious remedies. Nor does any of this necessarily suggest that if the political class had extended itself to cover the entire population, the distribution of circumstances across the population would have turned out any different. And it does not suggest that Haiti is in any way unusual among developing countries. Other than having come early to the system of auto–colonization, the territory governs itself in much the same way as many other nations, with and without foreign assistance in their systems of governance.

The only matters of interest here are that the basic form of governance was and remains of a type that resembles the concept of "colony," and that the contemporary governors of the colony, the political class, are an assemblage of large and small, local and foreign groupings that together represent a very tiny share of the total population. In this context, what matters politically is not only the struggle among factions for greater degrees of influence over the direction of events but also the movement of people from the category of ordinary—not requiring hearing—into the category of extraordinary—warranting political attention as members of one or more factions.

On this second matter, the record suggests that such movement was negligible until after the U.S. occupiers relinquished control of the national treasury. Their departure permitted a more rapid flow of political events that had begun in the late nineteenth century and that were propelling economic changes permitting the development of new foundations for expansion of class membership. The basic change was gradual concentration of all nonagricultural economic activity in Port–au–Prince, leading, especially after 1946, to the rise of what some social scientists called a "black middle–class" (Wingfield and Parenton, 1965: 343–45).

This middle class was not a homogeneous social or political grouping, nor was it necessarily entirely of one pigment, nor did it contain households within a specific income range. The concept was more general and referred to a collection of individuals and households within the political class who drew their livelihoods from newly expanding sectors of the city's economy, who did not quite have the links required to attach themselves as parts of the traditional mulatto or black elites, who at the same time were not "ordinary," and who had certain social status and financial aspirations and expectations that encouraged them toward political involvement. Large segments of this class were instrumental in making François Duvalier president in 1957, and that date seemed to mark significant political change that, in combination with economic changes, might before the year 2500 prove more significant than the change of 1492.

The political process started off in standard fashion. After eliminating certain segments of the traditional elite with a thoroughness matched only by Columbus, the Spanish, the French, and a few military leaders during the war of independence, Duvalier rewarded many loyal supporters in the class by introducing them into the structure of colonial rule as a new elite.

The newly reconstituted administration, as all administrations before it, began to orient money, gifts, jobs, contracts, and public services toward the middle class that could now claim them as members of the political class.

Unable to use a standing army led by officers associated with traditional elites to create and protect the space required for a new one, Duvalier organized a new armed force, the Volontaires de La Sécurité Nationale, commonly referred to as the Tontons Macoutes (or bogeymen), to implement his policy of constructing new political realities. The Macoutes proved highly efficient, and by 1967 the need for visiting further uncontrolled terror upon the elites, other elements of the old political class, and opponents within the middle class was no longer evident. More evident was the need to spread dominion over the whole country, and the Macoutes were reassigned to this task.

Riddled with factional infighting, lacking focused leadership, and without funds to support the assignment, the processes by which Macoutes diffused control varied considerably. In some instances, especially among thugs recruited for direct political action between 1957 and 1967, the process was little more than diffusion of milder terror. More commonly, the process took the form of inviting middle–class leaders with social, political or economic standing in their various communities, and with unassailable political records, to join the organization. Only fools elected to graciously decline such invitations, and the number of individuals who could, if they wanted, lay claim to Macoute membership expanded from a few thousand in 1967 to a rumored range of 100,000 to 200,000 by 1986. In effect, the Macoutes created the rudiments of what looked like political party, with a membership that included government officials, business people, office and factory supervisors, priests and pastors, teachers, and other types of neighborhood and community leaders.

Membership rarely provided power to influence the course of events or to change the colonial properties of governance, but the spread of a nominal form of political representation had few parallels in Haitian history. A membership of 2 or 3 percent of the national population meant that 10 to 15 percent of families were somehow affiliated with the party, and through patron–client relationships linking each member family to nonmembers, that large numbers of ordinary people could have some connection to a political organization that, in theory, traced a path to centers of government. This quasi party was a radical departure from traditional mechanisms of control.

Establishment of a rudimentary political organization, even one delivering no direct benefits to most members, may partially explain the longevity of Duvalier rule (Nichols, 1979: 237). But this and the spread of party organization were not important by themselves. They became important in connection with significant economic changes that were taking place at the same time, particularly in urban areas. Basic sources of income from which members of the middle class could extract their livelihoods in 1957 were government and international commerce. Francois Duvalier's erosion of traditional elite control of these two sectors to make room for a new elite of the middle class tied its members to the system of surplus extraction. In 1967, import–substitution industry, an extension of commerce, provided a third source of livelihood. This sector was still closely bound up in the mechanism of extraction. After 1967, however, these three sectors came to be overshadowed by foreign assistance, assembly export manufacturing, travel, and labor export industries. These industries were not part of the traditional extraction system, and the growth in the size of the middle class resulting from their expansion did not lead to automatic allegiance to the surplus extraction process. Indeed, to the extent that members of this newly evolving component of the class derived little benefit from the process while being victims of it, they constituted a new and growing source of opposition to maintenance of several parts of the extraction system. Through these changes, the political class shifted its base from one in which most members believed that their self–interest was served by maintenance of extraction to one in which the range of self–interest broadened to include sizable opposition, and therefore a basis for intraclass struggle that might perhaps alter the future form of Haiti's traditional political economy.

In this context, the efforts of the Macoutes to create a political party served to accelerate the process of politicization that normally accompanies economic transformation. They did not create a party, although that is what their efforts looked like as long as all old and new Macoutes swore tacit loyalty to the Duvalier family. They hastened the evolution of an indigenous component of the political class that contained a wider array of competing factions than ever before. In a country that had not seen such diffusion of interests for five centuries, the change seemed important no matter where it led.

The political class, even with its recent growth in size, was still quite small in 1986, and still retained a great many colonial features. Ordinary people would contine to form little more than what Marx, commenting on political organization in Ancient Rome, called a pedestal for class struggle (Marx, 1847: 140, 195, cited by Nichols, 1979: 9). But with the introduction of new factions and sources of self–interest, there was some faint glimmer of hope that spillover or side effects of the combat could eventually prove of more benefit to ordinary people than had been the case for a long, long time. How the forces of history surrounding the city's seven major industries came to yield this hope, how they came to make the political economy of Port–au–Prince what it is today, and where they might lead, are the subjects of this chapter.

Government

In 1749, forty–three years after its founding as a safe harbor, Port–au–Prince became capital of the French colony of Saint–Domingue, the island of Hispaniola now shared by Haiti and the Dominican Republic. Until its designation as capital, the town's basic economic function, as was that of other ports dotting the island's coastline, was to export to France sugar, coffee, indigo, cotton, logwood, cocoa, mahogany, and any other items manufactured in the immediate region by slaves and to import from the metropole producer and consumer goods demanded by colonists. As the region was not exceptionally endowed with productive land resources, population growth was slow, with a population in the town of about 1200 people in 1749 (Haiti, 1974: 117).

Addition of an administrative function stimulated expansion to 3000 inhabitants in 1751 and to 7000 in 1804. Independence allowed the nation to retain a larger share of value–added, export taxes, and import duties, and the increase in economic activity pushed the city's annual population growth rate from 1.7 percent between 1751 and 1804 to 2.6 percent between 1804 and 1888, and to over 60,000 people by 1895 (Haiti, 1974: 119).

Most of this expansion resulted from concentration of public expenditure in the city. Other than a brief period of high world prices from 1885 to 1895, the value of Haitian exports increased at an average rate of 0.3 percent per year from 1821 to 1914 (Rotberg, 1971: 392–94). Public revenues, accordingly, grew slowly if at all, as did personal income and demand for imports. In addition, foreign debt obligations extracted 58 percent of the government's $1.4 million in annual receipts from 1839 to 1843, and 20 percent of $2.6 million in annual receipts from 1859 to 1875 (Rotberg, 1971: 307). Under these financial constraints, the city had little basis for sustained growth except through concentration of expenditures within its limits.

A 50 percent rise in value of exports during much of the U.S. occupation of 1915 to 1934 provided substantial increases in public revenues. But insistance by the occupiers that Haiti pay a share of American wages and salaries (about 13 percent of total public salary outlays), which the recipients subsequently repatriated, that it not only service debts to foreign (i.e., U.S.) creditors but also retire them early, that it accumulate large cash reserves for future debt service, and that it station a large standing army throughout the country, allowed only limited circulation of public expenditure within the city. Of $7 million in total receipts in 1927, 40 percent serviced the debt and 20 percent maintained the army (Rotberg, 1971: 131). In addition, the occupiers earmarked 21 percent for public works projects in the countryside and 8 percent for rural schools (Logan, 1930: 442). Under such policies, which dragged on for thirteen years past the end of the occupation because the United States supervised the treasury until 1947, public expenditures could not contribute to significant urban expansion. The city had a 1950 populace five times the size of its closest rival, Cap Haitien (pop. 30,000), but the growth rate from 1895 to 1950 had slowed to 1.5 percent per year (IHS, 1973: 33).

Several constraints on population growth remained even after departure of the Americans. Governments still expended large shares of revenue for rural public works, education, health, and agriculture. They maintained a large army outside the city. And they kept ports in other towns open to international trade, thus permitting some customs receipts to circulate at their points of collection. These constraints gradually disappeared. One government after another shifted expenditures back to the city by emphasizing urban public works, education, and industry. Under François Duvalier, unpaid Macoutes took responsibility for security matters and the army brought most of its soldiers to the capital. Lack of maintenance caused other ports to decay until they were unusable except for coastal shipping, and investments in harbor and airport expansion in the city concentrated almost all customs collections at that location (Rotberg, 1971: 342).

The result was a pattern of fiscal incidence wherein Port–au–Prince received 83 percent of all public expenditures, including 79 percent of salaries, 95 percent of other operating expenditures, and 80 percent of subsidies (World Bank, 1979: 166). That along the way the capital's population should have grown from 150,000 in 1950 to 640,000 in 1976 was not surprising (Haiti, 1976b: 9). Governments transferred resources from agriculture and other rural activities to the city, and people followed.

A consequence of taxing agricultural exports while returning little or nothing to the sector was removal of incentives and resources for investment in expanded production, sometimes even for continued production, and therefore in relative stagnation of receipts from commodity export taxes. Without growth in exports, there could be but small growth in imports, and without this last, little expansion of import duties. Rather than taxing export commodities into extinction, governments turned increasingly to internal sources of revenue. There being no sound justification for the political class to tax itself intensively through income, profit, or property taxes, governments sought higher receipts from specific excise taxes, service charges, and monopoly profits.

In 1972 government derived a third of its identifiable tax receipts from customs, and 7.5 percent from income, and property (mostly mortgage registry) taxes (table 1.1). Fifteen percent came from excise taxes on flour, sugar, cigarettes, and petroleum, and therefore from a more regressive type of levy on urban consumers. Also regressive was the service charge for identity cards. Most of the balance of $24.5 million derived from stamp duties, a solidarity tax, vehicle registration fees, passport and exit visa charges, compulsory insurance premiums, additional excise and export taxes, apprenticeship and literacy taxes, and at least thirty-five other taxes and levies producing greater or lesser amounts. Some of these items were relatively more progressive than others. Private vehicle registration, passport, exit visa, airport, hotel room, insurance, television, and similar fees, for example, exacted payment from wealthier residents more often than from lower-income residents.

In some instances the cost of collection, as in the case of a public market tax, was higher than the revenue received (Duplan and LaGra, 1974). By and large, however, the system of having a large number of small charges was efficient in terms of maximizing public tax collection employment, and in maximizing tax receipts without inconveniencing important factions of the political class.

Still, faced with internal pressure to raise receipts in order to do the things that needed doing for the class, like increasing public employment, and with external pressure by organizations like the U.S. Agency for International Development (USAID) and the International Monetary Fund (IMF) to desist from raising coffee taxes, excise taxes on basic consumption, or any of the small levies and service charges, government proceeded along the sensitive course of raising the share of revenues from import duties, income and property taxes, and nonbasic excise taxes on items like cigarettes. In 1982, after a decade of effort and inclusion of bauxite extraction and export revenues in the official budget, identifiable receipts rose to $150 million. But in real terms they were lower than in 1972. Two years later, after capitulating to IMF insistence that it introduce a value-added or general sales tax in order to offset fiscal losses from closure of the bauxite mine, from repeal of the flour excise tax, from unwise public investment in a sugar mill, fishing fleet, and cooking oil refinery, from disappearance of some or all of an IMF standby credit of $20 million, and from several other actions that caused the budget to drop into a serious and sustained deficit in 1980, real receipts rose to a slightly higher level than in 1972.[1]

While direct taxation seemed to be showing little growth, public monopoly enterprise profits and indirect taxation implicit in the profits made substantial progress. In 1972 net revenues of the five main public enterprises amounted to only 5 percent of total government revenues from domestic sources. By 1984 they contributed 22 percent and permitted the

TABLE 1.1
Government Revenues, 1972-84
(millions of dollars)

	1972	1976	1980	1982	1984
Taxes					
Customs revenues					
Coffee export	5.4	10.6	23.2	9.2	11.4
Bauxite export	0.2	7.2	8.6	6.8	—
Import duties	12.8	21.0	47.8	41.4	46.2
Internal revenues					
Income	3.8	12.0	17.6	24.6	28.2
Property	0.4	1.6	2.0	2.5	2.8
Flour excise	2.8	1.4	2.4	5.0	—
Sugar excise	1.6	1.6	1.8	5.4	4.8
Cigarette excise	1.1	1.6	3.3	8.4	11.8
Fuel excise	2.6	2.4	3.2	6.8	17.6
Identity card	0.6	1.0	1.3	1.5	1.7
Value-added	—	—	—	—	21.6
Other customs and internal revenues	24.5	26.4	26.9	38.2	37.0
Subtotal—in current $	55.8	86.8	138.1	149.8	183.1
—in 1948 $	36.4	32.4	37.2	35.0	39.0
Public Enterprise Net Revenues					
Flour mill	1.5	2.8	−1.4	8.6	14.6
Electricity company	1.2	2.2	6.4	5.6	9.0
Water supply (CAMEP)	−0.1	−0.1	−0.2	0.3	0.3
Telephone company	0.2	−1.8	6.0	11.8	22.4
Port authority	0.2	3.0	1.6	3.0	3.7
Cement plant	—	—	—	—	3.4
Cooking oil refinery	—	—	—	—	−0.4
Subtotal—in current $	3.0	6.1	12.4	29.3	53.0
—in 1948 $	2.0	2.3	3.3	6.8	11.3
TOTAL—in current $	58.8	92.9	150.5	179.1	236.1
—in 1948 $	38.4	34.7	40.5	41.8	50.3

Sources: World Bank (1978b, 1981a, 1982, 1985).

public sector to show an overall increase of 30 percent in real resources relative to 1972. Most consumers of electricity and telephone services were higher-income urban households and firms, and most of the revenue thus constituted something approaching a progressive income tax. The distribution of consumption of flour, cement, and cooking oil being broader, the revenues of these monopolies might have been more regressive. But whether progressive or regressive, the important aspect from a money collection point of view was that enterprises produced profits that government borrowed or otherwise transferred to the treasury if necessity demanded, as happened in 1982 with $15.6 million in flour and telephone profits, and with $23 million in 1984 (World Bank, 1985: 65–66).

Foreign assistance, described below, added less than 10 percent to public resources until 1973. Up to that year, budget expenditures were still constrained by the need to finance almost all recurrent and capital outlays. The share expended on salaries was therefore relatively low. Excluding the armed forces and public enterprises, 28 percent of the documented budget paid the wages of 17,000 workers in 1972 (table 1.2). With increasing devolution of the development or capital component of public expenditure to foreign agencies after 1973, domestic resources had room to expand recurrent outlays and salaries. By 1984 about 40 percent of revenues paid some 32,000 public workers. Adding the army and public enterprise employees, perhaps another 8000 people, the share of total revenues dedicated to salaries may have been around 65 percent. The spatial organization of public employment was unlikely to have changed since 1976, and therefore 30,000 to 32,000 of all employees may have lived in Port-au-Prince.

The largest addition to the public work force was in teachers, and, as I describe in chapter 6, growth in their numbers between 1972 and 1984 was an extension of a process that began in the nineteenth century. In order to satisfy urban constituents' demand for schooling for their children, to absorb as large a share of graduates as possible in order to lower the political

TABLE 1.2
Government Employment and Wage Expenditures, 1972-84

	1972	1976	1980	1982	1984
Employment (thousands of workers)					
Education	4.8	5.7	10.7	11.8	12.3
Public health	4.4	6.5	5.7	6.5	7.3
Public works, transp. and comm.	0.8	0.8	1.5	1.4	3.6
Agriculture and rural development	3.1	3.3	3.1	2.2	2.2
Other ministries[a]	3.9	5.3	7	7.9	6.9
TOTAL	17.0	21.6	28.0	29.8	32.3
Wages (millions of dollars)[b]	16.0	22.0	50.0	64.0	74.0
Wages as % of total revenues	28.0	25.0	36.0	42.0	40.0
Monthly wage per worker					
—in current $	78	85	150	180	190
—in 1948 $	49	32	40	42	41

Sources: World Bank (1978b, 1985) and author's estimates.
[a] Excludes 6000 to 7000 members of the armed forces, and workers in public enterprises.
[b] Excludes wage payments to armed forces, and payments and revenues of public enterprises.

inconvenience of having large numbers of educated people unemployed, and to reward the politically loyal with jobs, most governments devoted substantial budget shares to teacher salaries. The process received added stimulus in 1976 when the Interamerican Development Bank (IDB) and World Bank began to provide large loans to education.

Public health employment, disproportionately located outside the city, was more a response to foreign intervention that began with the U.S. occupation and continued through 1986 with additional support from agencies like the World Health/Pan American Health Organization (PAHO) and USAID. In general, rural public health programs were not priority activities of Haitian governments. They were, however, good providers of low-paid jobs for the faithful.

Rural development programs also had low priority, but provided a means of rewarding those of the faithful who lacked the education or skill to qualify as teachers or health workers. Filling the Ministry was strategically sound; particularly under François Duvalier, its ranks contained large numbers of Macoutes. The decline in employment after 1976, largely resulting from a shift of rural teachers from the Ministry of Agriculture to the Ministry of Education, was to some extent a reflection of the parting of company between the Duvalier family and their most loyal servants, at least until unrest in 1983 demanded that many of them be reintroduced to the public payroll, this time in the Public Works Ministry.

What remained to dispose of were university-educated and mostly young people attached to families somehow connected to ranking political figures inside and outside government. Not yet acculturated to processes of government, many of these individuals took their educations and professional careers seriously. They therefore required careful placement. With increasing demand by foreign assistance agencies after 1973 for trained counterpart personnel, meaning Haitians who could speak the same technological languages as foreigners, and with the willingness of some agencies to offer salary supplements, scholarships, and training trips abroad, they gradually filled key intermediary positions in important ministries like Finance, or in intermediary ministries like Planning, which beyond serving as the link between government and foreign agencies, absorbing trained people, and assembling statistics, served little practical purpose commensurate with its size.[2]

Unfortunately, although rearrangement of expenditure priorities permitted substantial public employment growth, the apparent stagnation of real receipts placed a ceiling on the total wage bill. Employment increases between 1972 and 1976, largely through hiring of teachers and public health workers who earned lower salaries than people in other ministries, resulted in a decline of average real monthly wages. The rise from $32 to

$40 between 1976 and 1980 was the outcome of a substantial increase in teacher salaries in 1979 and derived entirely from a 65 percent expansion of the share of revenues devoted to salaries. After 1980 the budget attained the ceiling, with total employment and real wages remaining more or less constant.

This ceiling was artificial. The budget did not account for all receipts and expenditures. Missing were amounts variously estimated at 20 to 25 percent of total public resources that went through or around the treasury and into the hands of the Duvalier family and its close associates inside and outside government. As long as this kind of corruption did not interfere with real income growth of public workers, it was tolerable. But in 1980 it had become so excessive that it was beginning to interfere with growth. After six more years of such interference, public employees were as ready as others to see change in leadership of the class.

Soon after the Duvalier departure, they made their priorities known. Teachers, health workers, and soldiers agitated for higher wages. The new government leadership was not in an immediate position to respond because budgetary sources to sustain a higher wage bill were not yet apparent. USAID came to the rescue with the first installment of a $55 million grant.[3] The grant sustained the government for a few months while it searched for the "Duvalier funds." It eventually found them, and by also eliminating from the payroll a large number of phantom workers, was able to come up with an additional $50 to $60 million in public resources with which to raise salaries.

Redirecting a large share of public resources back to their intended uses was an important action, but it did little to address a more salient issue having to do with the purpose of taxation. The apparent purpose in 1986, as always, was to provide income to a privileged group of people living in the city. Concentration of public wage payments in a capital was not unusual, but having 80 percent of it in a place containing less than 15 percent of the national population seemed excessive even in a small country.[4]

More important perhaps was the relationship between taxation and the newfound power that public employees acquired upon dissolution of the Macoutes. A collection of people that as a group had had limited political importance since 1957 seemed to hold significantly more power in 1986. If this influence proved more durable than transitory, Haiti would join other developing countries in having as a permanent political force the state's administrative apparatus.[5]

Unfortunately, if the primary purpose of taxation was to sustain the apparatus, it would continue to finance a very large number of people who were part of the apparatus simply because they had connections to people in positions to help them acquire legitimate methods of claiming a share of the public purse. Recalling the theme I introduced earlier, in some respects the more significant historical corruption of government was not diversion of funds away from their intended purposes, but intended purposes that were themselves diversions away from what official taxation was supposed to finance. Haiti had a taxation industry and an apparatus to collect and reallocate income. But even in comparison to other developing countries, what it lacked was an administration to use it for the purpose of general social and economic betterment. That function, for better or worse, would continue to be performed by Haiti's shadow government of foreign–assistance organizations using expatriate and locally hired personnel, and taxes and voluntary contributions from abroad.

Foreign Assistance

Haiti was an early participant in public and private foreign–assistance industries, but did not become a full–fledged member until 1973. The beginning of public assistance, a $4 million Export–Import Bank credit of $5 million in 1941, took the form of a fruitless attempt to promote rubber production. Following it from 1944 to 1947 came technical assistance on matters of education and rural development from the United States' Inter–American Education Foundation. Between 1949 and 1969, footholds in the country were established by most of the industry's main actors, including the United Nations family of organizations, the World Bank (with loans of $3 million), the IDB (with credits of $7.5 million), and the Export–Import Bank (with further loans of $12 million). The principal actor was the United States. It granted Haiti about $41 million for emergency relief, road construction, agricultural development, and government budget subsidies between 1949 and 1970. In these two decades, Haiti received an annual average of $4–5 million from all sources, with about half of it coming from the United States.[6]

Deterioration in the relationship between Haiti and the United States resulted in a halt to all but the most essential assistance in 1962, and with other bilateral and multilateral organizations keeping relatively low profiles at the same time, public foreign–assistance disbursements remained low through 1970. Upon Jean–Claude Duvalier's ascension to power in 1971, aid flows increased and the United States reestablished its "official" (i.e., government to government) assistance program in 1973 (English, 1984: 24). Thereafter the number of actors and the size of annual disbursements increased rapidly, reaching a first plateau of $75 million, or $15.85 per capita ($5.50 in 1948 dollars) in 1977 (table 1.3). With the signing of the 1981 Haiti–U.S. interdiction treaty designed to prevent the flow of boat people to Florida, the United States raised its contribution by $11.5 million to help push total disbursements to a second plateau of $26.35 per capita ($6.15 in 1948 dollars) in 1982.[7] Upon the departure of Duvalier, the apparent need to finance political stability prompted the United States to plan a rise in its support by an additional $55 million, pushing total disbursements towards a third plateau of $200 million, or $37.00 per capita. In 1948 dollar terms, this would amount to $6.70, or a 9 percent increase over the real value of disbursements in 1982.

Until the increase of 1986, Haiti did not have a privileged position with respect to public assistance. Relative to the average for ten other Latin American countries of similar size, it obtained 28 percent less per capita, and the growth in disbursements from 1977 to 1983 was 60 percent less (table 1.4). Also, compared to the average of eight very low income African nations, the country received less per capita, less in the form of grants, less as a share of income, and also had a lower rate of assistance growth.

One explanation for Haiti's below-average performance with respect to aid was limited absorptive capacity (World Bank, 1982: 32). Qualified personnel for analysis, planning, management, and execution of programs were supposedly scarce in government, and since multilateral and bilateral assistance sources usually oriented themselves directly to government, the civil service functioned as a constraint on expansion. This was not an entirely satisfactory explanation. Scarcity of high-level personnel in Haiti was no more severe than in most parts of Africa. In any case, most, if not all, preparatory analysis, planning tasks, and higher-level program management were carried out with the help of expatriates supported by technical-assistance contracts.

Perhaps a more salient constraint was that most assistance agencies demanded Haitian counterpart financing and personnel (English, 1984: 30). By definition, a technical assistant needed one or more people to assist, and an assistance agency required a counterpart local agency. Both requirements implied additional government resources to meet the needs of new projects, and except for USAID's Title I program, foreign donors were not prepared to finance these local recurrent costs, in part because it was not their habit or policy to do so, in part because it seemed to run counter to the purpose of pressuring government to increase revenues or use them more for "development" and less for public employment, and in part because such action might provide more space for raiding the public treasury or assistance project budgets.[8]

The notion that Haiti might not have a government but rather a private industry that called itself by that name, and that a foreign organization could therefore step into the vacuum and establish an autonomous agency to carry out various programs and projects on its own, was not widespread. This kind of approach was impolitic if made too explicit, and such foreign

TABLE 1.3
Public Foreign-Assistance Disbursements, 1970-84
(millions of dollars)

	1970	1977	1980	1982	1984
Multilateral Agencies					
Interamerican Development Bank (IDB)	1.1	20.3	17.9	18.1	18.9
World Bank	—	17.6	15.5	27.9	24.0
United Nations Capital Development Fund (UNCDF)	—	—	0.9	1.9	2.5
United Nations Fund for Population Activities (UNFPA)	—	1.3	0.6	0.9	0.6
United Nations Development Program (UNDP)	0.1	2.0	5.3	4.3	3.4
World/Pan American Health Organization (WHO/PAHO)	0.3	1.1	2.1	1.1	1.4
United Nations Int'l Childrens Emergency Fund (UNICEF)	—	2.0	0.4	0.7	2.3
Food and Agriculture Organization (FAO)	—	0.2	0.1	2.4	1.4
Organization of American States (OAS)	—	0.5	0.5	1.0	2.0
European Economic Community (EEC)	—	—	—	0.4	2.0
Other	—	1.4	1.2	2.9	1.2
Subtotal	1.5	46.4	44.5	61.6	60.7
Bilateral Agencies					
United States (USAID)	0.6	6.9	9.5	17.0	26.4
Germany	0.2	2.7	6.1	11.6	10.0
France	—	4.0	4.6	8.4	4.1
Canada	1.6	4.3	7.5	8.3	4.7
China	—	0.4	1.6	1.6	2.0
Japan	—	—	—	5.4	9.8
Other	—	—	0.4	0.6	—
Subtotal	2.4	18.3	29.7	52.9	57.0

Food					
World Food Program (WFP)	—	1.6	2.6	2.7	3.9
USAID—Title I	—	5.2	9.0	13.0	13.8
USAID—Title II	1.0	4.0	8.5	8.5	8.3
Subtotal	1.0	10.8	20.1	24.2	26.0
TOTAL	4.9	75.5	94.3	138.7	143.7
Per capita (in current $)	$1.15	$15.85	$18.75	$26.35	$27.40
Per capita (in 1948 $)	$0.85	$ 5.50	$ 5.05	$ 6.15	$ 5.85

Sources: English (1984), Walker (1984), World Bank (1985), Haiti (1985), and author's estimates.

TABLE 1.4
Comparison of Public Foreign–Assistance Disbursements Among Latin American and African Countries With Population Sizes Similar to Haiti

	Average Annual Disbursements Per Capita, 1977-83 (U.S. $)	Ratio of 1983 to 1977 Disbursements	Share of Grants in 1983 Disbursements (%)	Disbursements Per Capita as Share of Income Per Capita (%)
Latin America				
Jamaica	60	5.5	18	4.2
Nicaragua	48	3.3	61	5.1
Costa Rica	37	10.1	26	3.3
Honduras	31	3.3	51	4.6
El Salvador	28	6.4	58	3.9
Bolivia	27	1.8	74	5.7
Panama	20	1.3	50	1.0
Dominican Republic	17	3.0	26	1.2
Paraguay	16	1.1	48	1.2
Guatemala	10	1.2	51	0.1
Average	29	3.7	46	3.0
Africa				
Niger	32	1.7	74	12.6
Burkina Faso	30	1.7	76	16.7

Mali	29	1.9	61	18.2
Rwanda	27	1.6	79	10.0
Burundi	25	2.9	64	9.0
Benin	22	1.8	57	8.1
Malawi	20	1.5	63	9.4
Chad	17	1.0	97	6.2
Average	25	1.8	71	11.3
Haiti	21	1.5	58	6.6

Source: Haiti (1985)

colonization would not sit well with domestic class factions seeking to protect their own colonization privileges. In this instance, the constraint on aid disbursements could have been shortage of counterpart funds. It could also have been the effect of a disbursement technology that assumed, or that had no choice but to assume, that government was an actor in the process.

Governments of Belgium, Switzerland, and especially the Netherlands, that had the operational advantage of being able to choose between two types of assistance resources, one a portion of fiscal revenues and the other of funds made up of private contributions, did not face this difficulty. They opted to use the private funds to channel resources to private voluntary organizations (PVOs) already in Haiti or, as in the case of the Netherlands, to help create an autonomous PVO for this purpose.[9] Their official assistance funds did not go to Haiti regularly.

Even without the advantage of having two funds to work with, USAID developed a similar approach. When the United States stopped almost all official assistance in 1962, it nevertheless provided PVOs with funds and food for humanitarian and relief purposes, a practice that it still maintains for execution of its Title II program.[10] After resuming official assistance in 1973, the agency faced the problem of programs attached to government agencies often yielding negligible outcomes and wastage, and of vast urban (i.e., low-income) and rural areas where functioning state agencies were nonexistent. Gradually, particularly after 1980 when assistance to the private sector became an explicit component of U.S. foreign-aid policy, USAID resources increasingly circumvented government and went directly to existing PVOs or other nonpublic organizations, or were used for the creation of new ones.

After canceling its largest project in the country in 1982 amid accusations of widespread diversion and misuse of funds by public officials attached to it, Canada also shifted assistance from its official line to its PVO support line (English, 1984: 46–47). The drop in disbursements from $8.4 million in 1982 to $4.1 million in 1984 indicated in table 1.3 was in part a reflection of the shift rather than a drop in aid. Germany also pursued a dual assistance strategy.

Channeling of aid to PVOs may in some instances have resulted in lower reported disbursements and therefore in lower apparent levels of official assistance, but the sums in question were not large and would not have altered the country's relative position in table 1.4. Haiti may not have received as much as other comparable countries because of limited absorptive capacity, because of limited counterparting resources in government, or because of the inability of multilateral agencies and reticence of bilateral agencies to sidestep the state. But Haiti's long-standing independence was also a drawback in terms of extracting more resources from countries like France, that supplied a great deal of aid to ex-colonies. There was also the problem of the government's human rights record—not a particularly bad one after 1973 when compared to such countries as Nicaragua, El Salvador, Paraguay, Guatemala, or Benin—but the amplified image of it abroad was hardly the stuff that such countries as Belgium, Switzerland or the Netherlands would have liked to attach to their official aid activities. Nor would the image have appealed to Scandinavian countries that usually favored poorest countries. And then there was the matter of Haiti's lack of permanent strategic political or economic importance. Were it not for the Cuban revolution, U.S. official aid to Haiti would probably not have continued until 1962. And were it not for the boat people, the Grenada incident, and political instability following the Duvalier departure, U.S. government support would probably not have been as high. These fleeting moments of significance were helpful, but they did not have the kind of long-term value that internal insurgency, threat from a leftist neighbor, particularly scarce minerals, critical location, or an influential community of Haitians in the United States could produce.

But all these factors operated only on the supply side. Perhaps Haiti did not get more than it did because, lacking an economic development agenda, there was no particular reason for government to conduct sustained and aggressive marketing campaigns. Early support from the Export–Import, World, and Interamerican Development Banks were the result of marketing tours by Haitian officials, as were the early arrival of UN and U.S. assistance (Moore, 1972: 67–68). But after 1960, the government lost initiative in seeking out foreign support for items other than those of vital importance to domestic politics, such as urban and industrial infrastructure. In sectors such as housing, education, health, or agriculture, initiative often came from expatriate advisers and from foreign agencies operating in Haiti. The issue was not that government employees were incapable of producing project proposals for these sectors, such skills being in any event unnecessary when foreign assistance financed the import of labor for this purpose, but rather a widespread lack of interest in even asking for help in preparing proposals. In this context, government may have received more in assistance than it wanted.

The idea that marketing Haiti in the competitive market for assistance might have resulted in greater support had some evidence to sustain it. The Netherlands had no intention of providing assistance until a Dutch priest working in Haiti decided to make an appeal for help in 1969. The same held in the case of a Methodist minister with respect to Switzerland. More generally, the supply of assistance was responsive to the demand for it, and this was particularly evident in the growth of private foreign aid.

Private aid predated public aid by about one hundred–twenty years and came in the form of missionary services of the Methodists, Baptists, Wesleyans, and Episcopals, and then, with the Haiti–Vatican Concordat of 1860, the Catholic church. Aside from evangelical work, early assistance focused on education, health, and relief. The number of these PVOs grew steadily, as did the scope of their activities. A United Nations Development Program (UNDP) estimate in 1976 placed their number at 118, and the total amount of their expenditures for agriculture, community development, education, health, and social services at $9.6 million, or about 15 percent of the value of nonfood public aid at the time (UNDP, 1977: 19).

The UNDP figures may have been underestimates. In 1984 there were at least 400 PVOs operating in Haiti, and perhaps as many as 500.[11] Their disbursements totalled about $40 million, or 35 percent of the value of nonfood public aid, originating as follows:[12]

COHAN (Netherlands support)	$3.4 million
Foster Parents Plan International	3.2
Catholic Relief Services (U.S. support)	2.8
Compassion International	2.5
General PVO support from Canada	2.5
CARE Foundation (U.S. support)	2.0
International Child Care	1.4
Salvation Army	1.3
Methodist Church (Swiss support)	1.0
World Vision	1.0
FONDEV (German support)	1.0
Adventist Development & Relief (U.S. support)	0.8
Christoffel Blindemission	0.8
Other large PVOs (44 organizations)	7.5
Other small PVOs (340 organizations)	8.8

Although several PVOs had long histories in Haiti, most were relatively new. Of those in place in 1985, 32 percent established themselves before 1960, 17 percent in 1960–69, 34 percent in 1970–79, and the remaining 17 percent in 1980–85.[13] There were several reasons for their recent arrival. In some instances, it was displacement. A number of Catholic groups elected or were pressured to leave newly independent nations of Francophone Africa and moved to Haiti. At least one major Protestant group, losing its operation in Vietnam in 1975, followed the same path. But these cases were few. Another hypothesis suggested that interpretation of voodoo practice as "paganism," proximity to a large supply of Protestant missionary groups in the United States, and Haiti's desperate poverty provided an irresistible incentive for evangelical and relief work (English, 1984:26). These factors, essentially the same as the ones guiding public multilateral and bilateral missionaries to render developmental evangelism and relief, were plausible. However, the hypothesis did not by itself explain the sudden surge of interest after 1970 because the factors were quite old.

Marketing of Haiti's paganism and poverty may explain more. Major PVOs like Foster Parents Plan, Compassion International, and World Vision arrived in Haiti between 1972 and 1975 to establish foster parent adoption programs. These and a number of other organizations were local branches of multinational philanthropic corporations that generated funds through systematic advertising in North America and Europe. Once in Haiti, they promoted the one thing that assured overseas contributions: the plight of poor children. At the same time, the strong religious orientations of organizations like Compassion and World Vision allowed promotion of Haiti through various Protestant denominational church systems. Awareness of the country and of its poverty spread. This helped generate foster parent contributions, but it may also have provided the information upon which various missionary groups could assess the merits of actually establishing themselves in Haiti. Marketing of the factors, rather than the factors themselves, may have played an important part in bringing private funds to Haiti. And the process was far from over. The Christian Children's Fund, one of the largest adoption–oriented PVOs, and together with World Vision a heavy user of television marketing, began its Haiti operations in 1985. The Fund's preliminary plans called for an assistance level of $2–3 million by 1990 (interview with fund coordinator, November 1985). More obscure missionary groups were also continuing to show interest. In 1986 the Haitian Association of Voluntary Agencies was reportedly receiving fact–finding visits from them at an average rate of one different group every week (interview with Association director, March 1986).

Whatever the actual causes of below–average public and seemingly above–average private aid, expansion of foreign assistance was an important contributor to urban expansion. Of about $27 million in public foreign–assistance grants in 1976, $12.6 million was for technical services conducted entirely or mostly in Port–au–Prince.[14] After leakage out of the economy through repatriation of expatriate salaries and contractor profits, and imports of vehicles, fuel, and other supplies, approximately $4 million remained for circulation within the city. Similarly, out of $33 million in loans, $12 million were for projects in the city and $2.6 million represented local purchase of goods and services. Another $2.4 million may have entered circulation from purchases by permanent diplomatic and assistance missions not accounted for in aid statistics, and by households attached to them.

As regards food, USAID's provision of $5.2 million in Title I support had the effect of retaining within the urban economy approximately $3 million that might otherwise have left Haiti, and its provision of $7 million under Title II may have added $1 million to the level of local purchases of goods and services. And of the $9.6 million in estimated private aid in 1976, which tended to have negligible leakage compared to public aid, perhaps $3 million entered the city directly.

The total effect in 1976 may therefore have been of the order of $16 million, and an impact equivalent to establishment of 40,000 full–time jobs at the minimum wage. Because assistance levels were low in 1970, the rise through 1976 was a principal contributor to the noticeable rate of demographic expansion that the city seemed to be having at that time.

The habit of public foreign aid to emphasize technical assistants resident in Port–au–Prince and urban investment projects allowed the city to continue to capture a disproportionate 40 percent share of aid's immediate benefit through at least 1984.[15] However, stagnation of public assistance in terms of the real value of disbursements from 1976 to 1982 and again from 1982 to 1986 may have contributed to a slowdown in population growth. Expansion of the population from 640,000 in 1976 to 720,000 in 1982 was much lower than the 1971–76 growth rate. USAID's plans for the $55 million aid addition during 1986, and in particular for a $10 million component to provide 10,000 public works jobs in the city, might provide a small surge in growth. But, in general, without a much larger rate of real increase in assistance flows, the demographic and economic growth benefits of public foreign aid, if there were any, would present themselves at some future date.

What remained to contribute to growth was private aid. Although immediate leakage out of the economy was much less than for public assistance, a larger share of it went directly toward low salaries and relief outside the city than in 1976. Nevertheless, of the estimated $40 million disbursed in 1984, about $20 million remained in the city.[16] Private aid that remained in the city seemed to be growing faster than the urban population.

What would happen after 1986 was unclear. On the one hand, the departure of Duvalier and a few other individuals might encourage reticent bilateral donors to enter Haiti, or if already there, to increase their level of support. Similar results might obtain for some of the multilaterals. On the other hand, elimination of a handful of people was unlikely to have a noticeable effect on absorption capacities, on the propensity of officials and administrators to divert resources, or on the availability of counterpart funding.

The apparent dawning of a new political day might also entice more interest by missionaries, especially after the extensive media coverage given Haiti during 1985 and 1986. However, the fall of Duvalier was accompanied by a rise in the influence of the Catholic church, and many in the Church were less than enthused by the growth of Protestant missionary activity after 1960. In 1985 some of them called for discrete removal of Protestant teachers from public schools, closure of private schools run by "non-established" Protestant denominations (i.e., except the Methodists, Wesleyans, Baptists, Episcopals, Adventists, and others who had come to Haiti before 1960), and repatriation of North Americans whom they viewed as proponents of obscure cults.[17] Whether foreign assistance would increase or decrease over the medium and long term was difficult to predict.

Less likely to change was Haiti's status as an occupied country with a foreign administration consisting of several hundred multilateral, bilateral, and private assistants, advisers, and volunteers. In matters pertaining to food relief, natural resources, agriculture, industry, transportation, utilities, housing, health, education, and social welfare, policies, programs, and projects were often more the result of unilateral foreign initiative than of support for government initiative. Only in the area of finance had government retained authority over a sector of interest to several foreign agencies.

The IMF, World Bank, and USAID made numerous attempts to gain influence over financial policies and practices for many years. They managed a short-lived foothold in 1982 and helped introduce the sales tax of 1983 and a fiscal austerity program, but public finance remained essentially inviolate.[18] The sector was sacred to those in power because it was the basis of power.

But lying in shambles in 1986, the treasury needed repair work and the IMF, World Bank, and USAID were quick to respond to the job with resources, assistants, and a minister. And the minister, like his predecessor in 1982, a Haitian economist repatriated from World Bank headquarters in Washington, was quick to announce "rational" economic policy decisions. These included elimination of certain public and private monopolies in commerce and import-substitution industry, and other similar actions politically irrational for any minister wishing to retain the title for a long time.[19]

Prior to 1986, foreign agencies engaged government leaders on matters of finance. In 1986 they assumed the role of leadership, and as all leaders before them, they had to engage the other political factions of the country. These included government employees and workers in public enterprises and their demands for wages and job security. More important were the owners of commercial and industrial private taxation machines. These machines were as inviolate to them as the treasury had been to the Duvaliers. The Duvalier regime lasted thirty years. Several monopolist regimes under attack in 1986 had been in place for over eighty, and every government of Haiti, including that of François Duvalier, had come to agreeable understandings with them.[20] The disposal of one family in charge of one taxation machine may have been important, but the disposal of the other machines was potentially more important.

Commerce

While certain factions of the political class derived their subsistence and power from monopoly profits inherent in government taxation, other factions derived them from monopoly profits associated with restrictions on export and import trade, and on domestic distribution of certain locally produced commodities. The distinction between public and private monopolies was always blurred. Governments did not allocate commercial privileges without receiving something of political or economic value in return, and holders of the privileges did not usually allow government to modify allocation patterns without exacting a price. Commercial interests were often sufficiently wealthy that in alliance they could buy a segment of the official army, a private army, or crowds of demonstrators, and thereby unseat a faction holding control of government. Class struggle in Haiti was not only about control of public taxation, but also about protection of private taxation.

Another cause for blurring of the distinction, other than the evident fact that government was often just a convenient name attached to a private industry, was direct involvement by government in certain import and distribution activities that it traditionally would have allocated to nongovernmental factions. Historically, private commercial interests opposed this kind of involvement, among other things because it added to the wealth of whichever factions took control of government and thus tended to upset the balance of power within the class. But under François Duvalier, these interests did not have strength enough to prevent the initiatives, and from 1957 onward government extended itself further into what had been exclusive spheres for nongovernmental taxation. These extensions largely took the form of investments in import–substitution industry, a more complicated but nonetheless effective method of establishing a commercial monopoly, which I describe in the next section. A more recent dimension of the class struggle was therefore about the allocation of commercial monopolies between groups inside government and groups outside it. But however distributed, there was invariably an understanding that monopolies were vital to the survival of the class. A distinction between public and private was unimportant. They were all class monopolies.

With regard to exports, for example, studies on coffee and cocoa marketing through export licenses fueled constant debate about whether producer prices reflected market competition, or monopsonistic price setting, or monopoly, and on whether the share of world market value collected by export taxes was too high to provide adequate incentives for crop production or too low to provide adequate state revenues.[21] The essence of the issue was that while producers could receive 60 to 75 percent of final retail prices for most commodities destined for domestic consumption, for coffee and cocoa they received somewhere in the range of 45 to 50 percent of the export price. Also, in the few instances in which government grudgingly permitted rural cooperatives to market commodities directly to foreign importers, distribution of cooperative profits could sometimes raise producer revenues by 25 percent (World Bank, 1984c: 114).

Separate from these unresolved issues, an important aspect of the coffee trade was that it involved far fewer actors than did other commodities. Even with intense competition and low profits, the volume of trade per authorized actor was sufficiently large to form a basis for sizable accumulation of wealth. In any given year, ten exporting families retained profits on 80 to 95 percent of all coffee exports. If, as the World Bank suggested, their net margins were of the order of 5 percent of the export price, each one received a 1984 income of anywhere from $40,000 to almost $1 million before payment of office and telephone expenses (table 1.5).[22]

This income was political rent. To be an exporter a family needed to maintain agreeable political and financial relations with a president. Family A, for example, ceased to be an exporter within a year of François Duvalier's election. Family H found disfavor with Jean-Claude, while families N and O had brief periods of grace. In the case of family Q, it was useful to have a son-in-law as president. But outlasting all others were families B, C, D, and J. They were the country's principal exporters before, during, and after both Duvaliers. These four, and perhaps others, like K, L and P if they could withstand their direct associations with the ousted family, were major components of class power in 1986.[23]

Management skill, market knowledge, and financial resources placed obstacles in the way of entry to the coffee trade, but the frequency with which new exporters appeared and then immediately took hold of substantial shares of the market implied that these kinds of barriers were surmountable by more people than the ones with export licenses in hand. And the ability of small exporters, another twenty not shown in table 1.5 who shared what the ten large ones left to them, to maintain business year after year suggested that economies of scale were not major obstacles either. The only technical advantage to a government of allowing concentration of export licenses, as distinct from political realities and advantages, was that it simplified collection of taxes, not customs receipts, but rather personal levies. An open market with 100 exporters presented a much more difficult and costly personal tax collection challenge for a president or minister than

TABLE 1.5
Distribution of Income from Coffee Exports, 1957-84
(in dollars)

Net Margin Received	1957	1973	1977	1982	1983	1984
By exporter: A	930,000	—	—	—	—	—
B	870,000	455,000	1,260,000	336,000	407,000	456,000
C	870,000	525,000	810,000	360,000	518,000	532,000
D	580,000	630,000	1,180,000	336,000	555,000	532,000
E	348,000	245,000	370,000	—	—	114,000
F	348,000	—	—	—	—	—
G	290,000	140,000	—	48,000	111,000	38,000
H	232,000	105,000	—	—	—	—
I	174,000	—	—	—	—	—
J	174,000	175,000	444,000	216,000	407,000	304,000
K	—	210,000	444,000	240,000	333,000	304,000
L	—	175,000	370,000	144,000	222,000	228,000
M	—	105,000	370,000	—	—	—
N	—	—	592,000	120,000	111,000	—
O	—	—	222,000	—	—	—
P	—	—	—	72,000	111,000	114,000
Q[a]	—	—	—	360,000	703,000	988,000
Subtotal, 10 exporters	4,816,000	2,765,000	6,062,000	2,232,000	3,378,000	3,610,000

By all exporters[b]	5,800,000	3,500,000	7,400,000	2,400,000	3,700,000	3,800,000
(% of total to 10 exporters)	(83)	(79)	(82)	(93)	(91)	(95)
By wholesaler[c]	8,200	5,000	10,400	3,400	5,200	5,400
By government	22,400,000	14,000,000	25,700,000	9,200,000	13,800,000	11,400,000
By producer	200	82	151	47	72	74
(number of producers)	(222,000)	(317,000)	(336,000)	(380,000)	(380,000)	(380,000)

Sources: Author's estimates based on unpublished government statistics on coffee prices and exporter volumes, from World Bank (1984b) estimates of numbers of producers, and from World Bank (1984c) estimates of exporter and wholesaler net margins.

[a] President Jean-Claude Duvalier's father-in-law.

[b] Total of net margins received by all exporters, including the ten leading ones.

[c] Assumes 850 wholesalers in operation every year.

a market with 10. Wealthy Haitians paid income taxes, but not to the treasury.

Wholesalers, those who purchased coffee in rural areas for transport to the city, numbered about eight hundred and fifty individuals (Girault, 1981: 142, 146). Their net incomes from part–time margins of 6 percent of the export price were much lower than for exporters, $3400 to $5400 a year depending on coffee prices between 1982 and 1984, but still very high in relation to the national income average.[24] Technical barriers to entry here were also relatively low. More people could enter wholesaling than were actually in it. The politics at their level had to do with maintaining agreeable political and financial relationships with officials or other political figures in Port–au–Prince, and in the areas where they purchased in order to retain their licenses—on the odd chance that they themselves were not Macoutes or other persons of importance. Interestingly, the number of wholesalers operating out of each of the country's nine principal purchasing centers also averaged about ten. The number was perhaps an ideal for tax administration. In any event, wholesalers were also among the politically powerful, if not at the national level, then certainly at the regional level where they conducted business.

A similar pattern obtained with respect to imports. In 1985, nineteen families held almost exclusive rights to import eighteen basic consumer items (table 1.6). In cases such as family A, one family held licenses for varying shares of several items. In most instances, families had authority to import the lion's share of one or two items. Even if the presence of one or two establishments with the privilege of importing 80 percent or more of the nation's total import of an item did not yield impressive profit margins, possibilities for concentrating wealth were enormous, most especially when these and twenty to thirty more families had import licenses for another ninety–two items.

Marketing of commodities sold by government import and production monopolies had similar properties. Beyond the margins and taxes received by government for its monopoly distribution of imported or locally produced sugar, cigarettes, and flour, there was the matter of the number of individuals authorized to buy from government. The flour mill had 222 clients in 1983. Of these, 6 individuals purchased 38 percent of total sales, 9 purchased 12 percent, and another 17 purchased 16 percent (World Bank, 1984b: 32). Having 32 people share in the initial distribution of 66 percent of the flour mill's total sales of $65 million in 1984 could be quite remunerative (World Bank, 1984b: 45). Assuming a net margin of 5 percent over purchase price from the mill, each of the 6 major buyers could have earned $210,000, the next 9 about $43,000, and the last 17 around $30,000; less any political payments required to maintain market share.

TABLE 1.6
Allocation of Import Quotas for Selected Household Goods
March 1984–February 1985

	SHARE OF QUOTA ALLOCATED TO IMPORTER (%)																			Total Share (%)	Total Importers
	A	B	C	D	E	F	G	H	I	J	K	L	M	N	O	P	Q	R	S		
Household utensils, metal	7	92																		99	2
Household utensils, plastic	2	2	15	26	49															94	5
Shoes						70														70	1
Slippers	92																			92	1
Nails						65														65	1
V-8 juice	29							71												100	2
Vegetable and fruit juices	48							48												96	2
Toothpaste	3								62											65	2
Liquid disinfectant	11				14			14		39										78	4
Wrapping paper, cardboard	66							16												82	2
Paper and plastic bags	94																			94	1
Irons for pressing clothes		43		28			28													99	3
Paint											44	22	22							88	3
Hand soap	10		18						45											73	3
Candies	65							32												97	2
Textiles														31	12	37				80	3
Milk																	63	28		91	2
Spaghetti, macaroni, etc.	44																		56	100	2

Source: Reveco (1984).

The additive effect of restrictions on export, import, and certain kinds of domestic trade was to create and sustain substantial wealth and power among a very few families, perhaps numbering between 100 and 200, and lower but nonetheless important levels of wealth and local power among a few thousand. Such wealth required redistribution to individuals attached to government and to relatives within the extended family system, but what remained was not inconsequential.

Even if producers would not have received more and consumers not have paid less as a result of monopoly, the benefits to the urban economy of having a disproportionate share of wealthy people residing in the city were offset by capital flight. A difficulty facing the wealthy in Haiti was a basic lack of domestic consumption and investment possibilities. Such families could build houses, but beyond that there were few methods of disposing of income within the country. Conspicuous consumption required imports or travel abroad. Financial instruments like stocks and bonds were practically nonexistent. Term deposits until 1980 provided lower returns than in other countries (World Bank, 1985: 178). And there was always the political risk of keeping money in the country that they had to take into account. Such risks, and limited experience outside the field of political entrepreneurship, often made the notion of investing in agriculture or manufacturing unappealing. Wealth had few places to go except out of Haiti, and that meant less in circulation within the city.

In principle, concentration of wealth in the political class could find justification if this "mobilization" of resources transferred capital from less to more productive investments, and thence to long-term economic development. But taxes, as I argued earlier, seemed to transfer resources into consumption by government employees who were not particularly productive, and monopolies seemed to transfer a substantial share of resources from production and consumption by the many to production and consumption overseas by the few. The justification may not have applied. But some wealth did remain in the country, finding its way into manufacturing investment that by outward appearance looked productive. Much of that investment was of the import-substitution variety. Unfortunately, between restrictions on imports to protect the enterprises and gross inefficiency in their operations, the major ones succeeded in doing only one thing: increasing the rate of transfer of resources from the many to the few.

Import-Substitution-Manufacturing

Haiti's low level of disposable income provided a limited domestic market for imports of consumer goods or for the output of import-substitution industries that used high-capacity capital equipment to produce similar goods. The chances that substitution industries could operate efficiently without also tapping export markets were usually remote, and from 1948 to 1985 many expatriate advisers recommended that Haiti not base its industrialization efforts on them.[25] Others, especially from Latin American countries where import substitution was the basis for industrialization, endorsed the idea. The OAS, for example, generated a long list of substitution items suitable for local production, and firms to manufacture many of them followed shortly thereafter (OAS, 1972: 317–27).

From an investor's point of view, substitution was often an excellent way to increase profit relative to the level possible from import margins. Under industrial development policies established and modified from 1949 onward, any substitution industry that could produce enough to supply a substantial share of the local market was protected from import competition by stiff tariffs or outright import bans and from competition from other local producers by their inability to obtain operating licenses after one or a few firms took over the market (World Bank, 1979: 73–74). Also, second- or third-hand equipment had sufficient output capacity to meet much of total domestic demand for any one type of product. The cost of cornering the market, given that equipment and supplies could be had duty-free, was low. An individual with initiative, resources, and the necessary kinds of connections to assure that government would provide the operating license and then impose and maintain the protective clauses of policy could take control of supplying most or all of local demand. The first investor into a market therefore claimed the profits of other importers and of preexisting local producers too small to benefit from policy, and monopoly rents from consumers.[26] The only marketing skill required was that of selling the idea to the right people in the right places, not a difficult thing to do by definition if someone already had sufficient resources in hand.

Because the market could rarely absorb the productive capacity of more than a few firms per type of major product, the 1960s and 1970s witnessed a rush towards establishment of large import-substitution plants producing items like soap, detergents, shoes, cement, plastic and metal housewares, steel rods and corrugated sheets, textiles, paper products, cooking oil, flour, milk, matches, tomato paste, cigarettes, soft drinks, beer, and other goods. Having most of the national market captive to only a handful of plants owned by a handful of families and government provided a basis for significant further concentrations of wealth and a corresponding further loss in the resources available to ordinary consumers and producers.

With no penalty attached to the import of equipment and supplies, most large plants were highly capital-intensive, and the employment they generated through implicit taxation of the population was small. There was little gain in total earnings, only a transfer of income from consumers to a few thousand workers.[27] And with no competition to contend with, inefficiency in terms of underutilized capacity, weak management, and outdated equipment yielding high production costs were simply passed on in the factory price.

In the case of tomato paste production, for example, the firm's inability to use more than 32 percent of its capacity, its need to purchase high-priced cans from another monopoly firm, and lack of competition yielded a factory sales price of $0.70 per 8 ounce can in 1984, a figure that did not compare favorably with $0.20 in the Dominican Republic or $0.50 in the United States (World Bank, 1985: 15).

The government's flour mill was particularly hard on consumers. The combined effects of a low extraction rate of flour from imported wheat, a high price of credit for importing wheat (20 percent), high costs for other inputs like sacks and electricity, and twice as many overpaid workers as required (400 versus 200) were processing costs 20 to 30 percent higher than for imported flour between 1980 and 1984 (World Bank, 1984b: 28). After additional nonprocessing costs, port and freight charges, sales and other taxes, payment to a "special account" presumably belonging to the president, and a profit of 17 percent, the final sales price in 1984 to the mill's 222 clients was 100 percent higher than the import price for flour. Of total mill sales of $65 million, $32.5 million represented a subsidy of the mill by consumers. Of this subsidy, about $6 million went to official taxes, $2.5 million to the president, and most of the balance of $24 million to subsidize each mill worker at an average rate of $60,000 per year (World Bank, 1984b: 43–45).

Beyond the financial advantages inherent in a public monopoly and the simplicity of personal tax collection possible from a private one, import substitution offered other advantages to government. Payroll taxes, almost impossible to collect from thousands of small firms, were easy to obtain from large firms. The more workers covered by minimum-wage legislation, the more revenue a government could generate from the approximate 10 percent payroll tax. Also, raising worker earnings at the expense of the rest of the population had the useful effect of increasing the demand for consumer imports subject to high tariff rates, thereby raising public revenues still further. In effect, from government's short-term perspective there was much to gain and little to lose from expansion of industry, and so long as what looked like industrialization took place, it did not matter whether the basis was import substitution or something else.

The process of transferring income from rural areas to Port-au-Prince, from low- to high-income households, and then redistributing the income among the relatively well-off was an old process and usually worked quite well. This kind of "modernization" was simply a new procedure for carrying out a traditional activity. Unfortunately for many of the actors involved, the process began to fall apart in 1980.

Output of most large substitution firms, or at least of those with output estimates attached to them, began to decline after a long period of growth (table 1.7). Production of textiles, cigarettes, soap, cooking oil, shoes, soft drinks, matches, beer, and other products stagnated or declined after 1980. This may have resulted from the downturn of the world economy, but irrespective of cause, it was exacerbated by an apparently substantial rise in smuggling. Contraband always found its way into the country in limited quantities, but large-scale imports of this type were almost impossible without official sanction. Substitution industrialists and importers complained bitterly, and quietly accused the president's father-in-law of being the force behind this new competition.[28] As far as they were concerned, smuggling was a breach of the partnership between factions in government and in commerce.

To aggravate matters, government used up much of the central bank's foreign exchange reserves in 1980–81 to purchase a 34 percent share of the new cooking oil refinery I mentioned earlier (and more in 1985 when it took 100 percent control), the fishing boats, the sugar mill, and in 1982 and 1985, outstanding shares of the flour mill and cement plant. Confounded by rising collection rates in the "Duvalier fund," a drop in export earnings, and a rise in imports, Haiti's treasury and foreign exchange balance dropped precipitously, requiring government to request relief from the IMF and to eventually accede to the IMF's demand for fiscal austerity and foreign exchange controls.

That a faction in control of government had chosen to raid the public

TABLE 1.7
Output of Major Import–Substitution Industries, 1970-84

Product	Unit Quantity	1970	1976	1980	1984
Flour	thousands of tons	26	68	85	114
Cooking oil	thousands of tons	—	14	19	8
Cement	thousands of tons	62	232	243	230
Soap, wash powders	thousands of tons	4	8	13	14
Detergents	thousands of kilograms	—	—	578	936
Cotton textiles	millions of yards	4	2	2	1
Cigarettes	millions	420	718	1064	938
Soft drinks	millions of bottles	26	40	74	72
Beer	millions of bottles	—	—	5	4
Shoes	thousands of pairs	173	219	795	528
Matches	thousands of containers	—	—	39	44

Sources: IMF (1983), World Bank (1976a, 1978b, 1981a, 1983a, 1985).

treasury for questionable purposes, like buying fishing boats that never arrived or building a sugar mill that could not function, was not an important issue. Such behavior was acceptable as long as effects did not spill over into the private domain. Taking full control of such preexisting monopolies as flour and cement plants was also inconsequential. What commercial interests found harder to forgive was that the faction in government would take so much as to not only cause them considerable foreign exchange inconvenience, but also to result in imposition of new levies like the value–added tax in 1983 and stricter customs enforcement requested by the IMF.

Breakdown of the class alliance continued through 1985 as government apparently tried to drive four existing refineries out of business and thereby develop a complete production monopoly for its cooking oil plant (World Bank, 1985: 83). When in late 1985 and early 1986 circumstances dictated that votes be cast among the commercial interests in favor or against further support for the extended Duvalier family and its close associates, exporters, importers, domestic distributors, and industrialists who had suffered from government actions over the preceding five years, a sizable but not complete majority, opted for the latter course.

One of the earliest commitments of the new government was a promise that prices would be lowered, and it moved within weeks to announce diesel fuel, gasoline, flour, and cooking oil price cuts (Duchon, 1986: 1, 5). Protection of commercial interests remained intact for the moment, and the sales price of locally milled flour was still 65 to 75 percent higher than the price of imported flour, as was the price for locally produced cement and many other import substitutes.

Six weeks after the new government installed itself, one of the private oil refiners who had been under pressure from the government's enterprise in 1985 noted on radio and in the press that prices were 70 percent higher than necessary and that each of the 200 workers in the government's refinery was being subsidized by consumers in an amount of $64,000 per year (Madsen, 1986: 18, 38). The workers in question stormed the streets the next day demanding that government protect their jobs. They were vastly outnumbered by crowds demanding not only that government permit oil imports, which it did soon afterward, but also that it step down for breach of promise, which it did not do.

The first public monopoly seemed on the way out, and with restrictions on import of refined oil still in place, profits passed back to the four private refiners. The pace quickened with arrival of the new minister and his IMF, World Bank, and USAID allies. He shut down the public sugar mill and then moved against the private sector, eliminating protection for the steel mill and the milk plant. However, the most offensive industry, the flour mill, was to remain intact for a while longer. Quiet discussion in 1986 called for a strategy to eliminate the mill at some point in 1987 or 1988 and then to allow import with a flat tariff of 20 percent. There were several reasons for the delay in closing the mill, but an important one was the continuing need for public revenues. USAID's $55 million fiscal rescue effort envisaged sale of oil to refiners and wheat to the mill, with proceeds going to the treasury (USIS, 1986: 1). The mill would also generate profits from sale of flour at prevailing market prices, and thereby contribute even more to public resources. For a while at least, most of the 400 mill workers would keep their jobs, and the consumer, though paying less than before, would remain in the position of subsidizing the workers and the government. In this particular instance, a change in political actors changed little. Money was still the basis of government solvency.

At the same time, however, the newly formed government–foreign agency faction was in the process of attacking the commercial faction. By mid–1986, 80 of 110 items on the list of things requiring import authorization had been eliminated. There was also some talk of breaking the export monopolies at some future date, but this measure was uncertain. More certain was that a fundamental pillar of auto–colonial rule was under more pressure than it had been since 1804. This type of political foray would have never had the slightest chance of long–term success when opposed by a united front of commercial–industrial interests. In 1986 there was a small chance because the interests were not united. Under the Duvaliers Haiti had become a major exporter of manufactured goods. Many families of the traditional commercial faction, as well as newcomers and foreigners, had shifted from being mercantilists to capitalists by investing in the sector. The self–interest of many of the 200 families belonging to this relatively recent addition to the political class were best served by elimination of monopolies. They were the new government's closest allies. Concentration of wealth may therefore have served at least one productive political purpose as well as a productive economic purpose.

Assembly Export Manufacturing

When manufacturers from developed countries began to roam the world during the 1950s and 1960s in search of inexpensive contract labor to assemble machine–made parts, resources were readily available in Haiti for that kind of investment. How or why the country should have become something of a leader in this type of light export manufacturing (it ranked eighth or ninth among developing countries from 1969 through 1983) remains a matter of speculation (Grunwald and Flamm. 1985:3). Proximity to the United States, low labor costs, favorable domestic policies, and U.S. tariff provisions were certainly helpful factors, as was the availability of investment capital (Morrison, 1975: 27–29). But Haiti was not unique in these respects, and the size of investment, requiring little more than putting up a large building to protect workers, materials, and simple equipment supplied by foreign counterparts from the weather, was small. Having a 500–year tradition of exporting the product of cheap labor and a class of people with an equally long tradition of organizing labor and materials for the purpose of exporting for profit, may have been more important. To the extent that coffee and other commodities were manufactured with the use of land, labor, and capital, reorganization of these three factors of production to respond to demand for a new type of production service was perhaps a logical transition in a place where return to continued export of habitual products was stagnant or declining.

In any event, Haiti was an exporting country from its inception as a colony, and once relieved of the U.S. occupation and the obsession of the occupiers to view the purpose of the customs tariff exclusively in terms of revenue generation, it resumed its tradition of export promotion. With the postwar advent of industrialization as the direction developing countries were supposed to follow, Haiti incorporated industrial progress into its export philosophy. Fiscal measures in 1949, 1955, and 1959 exempted raw materials, machinery, and supplies from import duties; manufactured products from export duties; and all new industries from income and license taxes for five to ten years (Moore, 1972: 207). Periodic revisions and adjustments to these measures continued through 1986. From at least 1949 onward the country was open to investment in export manufacturing. Helping it along were advantages provided under the General Agreement on Tariffs and Trade (GATT) convention of 1949, the U.S. Offshore Assembly Tariff Provisions of 1965, amendments during the Kennedy Rounds in 1968–72, General System of Preferences (GSP) agreements in 1971 and 1974, and the Caribbean Basin Initiative (CBI) revisions in 1983 (Turnier, 1955: 319; Rotberg, 1971: 301–4). Export markets were available and growing.

To better link supply and demand, Haiti enacted labor legislation favorable to business; undertook periodic upgrading and expansion of power, water, harbor, airport, roads, and industrial estate facilities; and to a limited extent provided itself with such complementary services as investment and export marketing, vocational and management training, and long-term credit. Most of these things had the support of foreign loans, grants, and advisors. With nothing remotely comparable extended to agriculture for the purpose of increasing the supply of domestic raw materials, and with limited possibilities for new profit sources in commerce or import substitution, such wealth as might remain in the country had few places to go except assembly exports once pioneers showed the way at some point between 1950 and 1962.[29] And risks, both political and financial, were low. The only item at risk was the building if an investor chose to own one rather than rent space. Everything in the building—raw materials, inventories, and equipment (if there was any to speak of)—usually belonged to the foreign counterpart (Grunwald, Delatour, and Voltaire, 1985: 187–88). The difficult aspect was skill at managing a contract and making the connection to a buyer. Somehow or other these and other things conspired to yield growth in the net value of assembled exports (i.e., excluding the value of imported components and returns) from near–nothing before 1962 to $64 million in 1984 ($12.6 million in 1948 dollars). All of this expansion took place in Port–au–Prince, and the effect in terms of stimulating urban population growth was almost as great as the advent of foreign assistance (table 1.8). In 1984 there may have been 30,000 people working in assembly factories.[30]

But if the record of complaints over the previous four decades served as guides to the process, the expansion should never have occurred. According to the principal actors involved, a small number of government officials and technicians, local and foreign investors and expatriate short–term and long–term advisers, the metaphorical road of industrialization leading toward unrealized potential for growth was always cluttered with bottlenecks and obstacles in need of clearing.

The list of these was long. From 1949 onward items on the list included: inadequate numbers of qualified government workers, entrepreneurs, managers, supervisors, and skilled workers; inadequate or overpriced infrastructure services; insufficient investment, promotion, training, or credit; haphazard and arbitrary application of regulations concerning taxes, investment incentives, tariffs, and labor; inappropriate legislation with respect to these issues; inadequate coordination among government agencies, among businesses, and between government and businesses; insufficient data or research; inappropriate or irrelevant advice from foreign technical assistants; insufficient coordination among foreign–assistance agencies; too many foreign economists without business knowledge; too many local investors without sufficient economics; poor quality control; absence of clear or rational planning in either the public or private sector; excessive tax evasion by the private sector and graft in the public sector; minimum wages too high for international competitiveness or too low to maintain worker productivity, purchasing power, and stability; and, always, there was the inadequacy of the general investment "climate."[31]

Not atypical of the tendency to find some fault in affairs at any point in time was a 1985 World Bank report that presumed to recommend policies for economic growth to a government that, according to the report, had devoted too much attention to direct poverty alleviation (World Bank,

TABLE 1.8
Net Value of Manufactured Exports, 1951-84
(millions of dollars)

	1951	1962	1966	1972	1976	1978	1980	1982	1984
Assembled from imported components[a]									
Textile products	—	0.10	0.10	2.50	8.10	14.00	21.40	24.70	22.50
Electrical and electronics	—	—	—	0.30	3.80	4.60	12.70	14.40	25.60
Sporting goods and toys	—	0.30	0.20	2.10	8.60	8.50	11.40	14.00	14.10
Other products	—	—	0.10	0.20	1.00	1.60	3.00	1.70	2.00
TOTAL	—	0.40	0.40	5.10	21.50	28.70	48.50	54.80	64.20
(in 1948 $)	—	(0.38)	(0.30)	(3.34)	(8.01)	(10.30)	(13.03)	(12.40)	(12.55)
Made with domestic materials									
Textile products	0.90	2.09	0.08	3.07	3.84	5.48	12.70	14.91	9.90
Leather products	—	0.14	0.18	0.37	1.40	4.59	8.67	10.91	22.10
Wood products	—	0.07	0.09	0.27	0.90	1.78	2.84	5.83	7.10
Carpets, rugs, mats	—	0.18	0.06	0.09	0.93	0.37	0.70	0.50	0.30
Brooms, brushes, buttons	—	—	—	0.77	2.78	2.56	5.75	4.86	4.30
Other products	0.09	0.29	0.18	1.28	0.79	1.48	0.76	1.27	1.80
TOTAL	0.99	2.77	0.59	5.85	10.64	16.26	31.42	38.28	45.40
(in 1948 $)	(0.99)	(2.61)	(0.44)	(3.83)	(3.96)	(5.83)	(8.44)	(8.90)	(8.90)
% of total manufactured exports	100	87	60	53	33	36	39	41	41
Manufactured exports in total exports[b]	3%	8%	4%	21%	38%	33%	30%	63%	66%

Sources: Turnier (1955), Rotberg (1971), Latortue (1972), OAS (1972), Delatour and Voltaire (1980), Hippolyte-Manigat (1980), IMF (1983), World Bank (1978b, 1981a, 1982, 1983a, 1985), Grunwald, Delatour, and Voltaire (1985), and author's estimates.

[a] Excludes value of imported components.

[b] Total exports include merchandise (net of imported components) and nonfactor service exports.

1985: 1). The suggestions added little to the stock of ideas accumulated over thirty–six years. Similarly, and in excruciating detail, a white paper I prepared for the government and USAID in 1983 lamented all the headaches of investment life imagineable, including: delays in obtaining operating licenses; bribes required to reduce the delays; customs administration difficulties, delays, and bribes; random payments of personal political taxes; instability of holidays; quirks in the law biased against foreigners; an unreliable and heavily politicized judicial system; unreliable Haitian or foreign partners; incompetent commercial bankers; and disreputable lawyers (USAID, 1983).

Notwithstanding the lengthy list of complaints, Haiti became a major exporter. In a comparative framework, there was little basis for complaint. The only area in which Haiti had fallen behind other countries was in numbers of jobs, and the amount of disposable income left to circulate in the economy (Grunwald, Delatour, and Voltaire, 1985: 176–97). For reasons having to do with quality, price, timeliness, terms of sale, interpersonal relationships, and several other possible factors, exporting firms did not increase their purchases of available domestically produced inputs (other than labor) at the same rate as their exports. The corresponding need to import textile, cardboard, wood, straw, leather, plastic, metal, and other products resulted in a slower rate of growth of domestic value–added compared to other countries, lower demand for locally–produced materials, and hence fewer jobs and wage payments. This inefficiency, coupled with relatively high costs of factory overhead for land, buildings and utilities, management and transportation, and compounded by the high exchange rate of the U.S. dollar in 1983–85, also made it appear difficult for wages to rise quickly without compromising the competitiveness of prices.[32] In these and other respects, Haiti did not extract from assembly exports as much as some of the actors might have preferred. But the shortcomings were matters of constant discussion as well.[33] They were no different than all the other perennial items on the list of bottlenecks and obstacles, and events in 1986 would cause attention to them to shift from simple discussion to concrete action.

The points and counterpoints, and the actions and inactions of the few hundred actors participating in the process over time resembled democratic practice among political equals. Somehow or other, with the possibility usually open for anyone of significance to complain about this or that, for complaints with consensus to move into the category of things warranting action, and for local or outside resources to finance the actions, things that apparently needed doing were done well enough to maintain momentum. And at no time could the participants identify clearly which of the actions were more important than others.

An industrial estate built in the early 1970s with IDB financing lay virtually empty for many years while new companies established themselves on its perimeter. The problem with the estate, according to its critics, was high rent for industrial space and bureaucratic delays in obtaining space (Haiti, 1975: 21–26). Although the rate structure and red tape did not change significantly, by 1986 the estate was largely full and government was considering construction of another to compete with a private one rapidly expanding nearby. An action that looked dubious in 1976 looked much better in 1986.

Another issue of perennial concern was industrial finance. Long-term credit was apparently obstructing progress. A credit scheme financed by the IDB to address this concern also became the object of criticism. The scheme was poorly administered, leading to high overhead costs, to lending for unsound projects, and to lengthy delays in processing sound project applications (IDB, 1979: 137–38). On the basis of this criticism, the World Bank funded another credit scheme in 1980 to offer superior service. But by 1984 almost the whole of the fund had been used, squandered according to a new set of critics, in financing the foreign-exchange needs of existing enterprises rather than in financing new investments or expansions (communication from former staff of the World Bank project, 1985). Similarly, USAID and the local private sector collaborated to establish a development finance corporation in 1982 (USAID, 1982c). By 1984 the corporation had made loans to 14 enterprises (USAID, personal communication, 1985). Proponents of the corporation claimed that it had therefore created new enterprises and jobs. Critics countered that the only thing the corporation had done was to invest money in firms that had sufficient resources to launch themselves without formal credit and that the corporation was therefore a waste of resources.

Under the assumption that inadequate management skill was an obstacle to growth, USAID funded what it called a management and productivity center to provide training and consulting services to smaller enterprises (USAID, 1984d). It immediately ran into a problem of lack of demand for its services, and critics pounced on it as yet another example of irrelevant foreign assistance.

The World Bank credit scheme, the development finance corporation, and the training center did, in fact, look irrelevant. But that was also the case of the industrial estate a decade earlier. The more recent efforts might also eventually show themselves to be useful. It was hard to forecast their futures.

Relevant or irrelevant as the potpourri of policies, programs, and projects might have appeared at various intervals, the year that the World Bank finally accorded Haiti the dubious distinction of being absolutely the poorest country on earth in terms of food consumption, 1983, Haiti's company in the matter of assembled exports were Mexico, Malaysia, Singapore, the Philippines, Korea, Taiwan, and Hong Kong.[34] Haiti did not belong in this company in 1983 any more than it did in 1969. The process of rendering this achievement possible, whatever it was, could have generated more employment at higher wages. By the list of obstacles it should have yielded less. The accomplishment was in fact remarkable.

In 1986 a new set of actors entered the process: workers. For the first time in three decades, they could protest their working conditions by striking and demonstrating without fear of corporal reprisal, and in many factories they immediately exercised this option by demanding a purge of shop supervisors and low-level managers whom they believed were Macoutes, or more generally, whom they did not like. Factories with long-standing procedures for cultivating constructive labor-management relations suffered few ill effects. Factories without such procedures ran into immediate difficulties in finding replacement supervisors. Some foreign companies simply shut down and shifted their operations to branch plants in other countries.[35]

In the confused adjustment to a broader polity, many in industry worried about political ramifications of employment declines as factories shut down or lost contracts. The U.S. government, an important member of this export faction for over a decade, dispatched various experts to examine whether the minimum wage should be raised; to calculate how much subsidy would be required to lower certain input prices; to estimate how many public-works jobs the government might create to compensate for factory departures (i.e., the 10,000); to plead with foreign companies, particularly U.S. companies, not to close; and to call upon U.S. trade unions to assist in organizing factory workers—in order to reduce the randomness of strikes and to interfere with unionizing efforts of recently returned members of Haiti's communist party.

For those in the faction unaccustomed to dealing with such matters, the situation in 1986 seemed anarchic. For workers finding themselves engaged in political action as part of a new faction, it was a form of democracy in which their opinions caused government, investors, and foreign assistants to pay more serious attention to one of the most neglected factors of profit production, labor, and to listen to what they said they wanted: an improvement in the standard of living.[36]

This particular anarchy seemed to contain Haiti's, or at the least the city's, best hopes for a brighter economic future. It was introducing a political alignment and tension between factory owners and workers that had much more potential for yielding productive outcomes than any of the opposing demands within the political class that had pressed for policy changes in support of assembly export promotion. Until 1986, labor docility had been assured by the state, and owners had considerable latitude to fire and hire at will. Working conditions and the minimum wage had only to be high enough to keep labor turnover within acceptable bounds. Owners were rarely under internal pressure to raise efficiency. In 1986 they no longer had absolute power to fire. Workers were free to organize formally or informally and to strike against what they believed were unjust layoffs. Employers who were less able to fire, were also finding it more difficult to hire replacements, and the prospect of perpetual high turnover was not appealing to operators requiring stable work forces.

Owners were gradually having to come to grips with the political economy of "modern" labor relations and to view wages not only in terms of turnover, but also in terms of disruptions to production schedules. Caught between demands for higher wages that might make their production costs less competitive in the export market, and production disruptions that would have the same effect, profitability demanded that they align with workers in calling for price reductions from government, thus putting pressure on state and private import–substitution industries, import and other commercial monopolies, the oversized public sector, and the various regressive taxes required to sustain it. These all seemed like helpful politics.

It also helped that beyond putting pressure on forces outside their factories, they had also to put pressure on themselves to find means to lower nonlabor production costs in order to pay workers a larger share of the value–added in production, and to come to terms with the possibility that they might have to transfer larger shares of profit margins to wages. That kind of pressure was healthy for an economy.

How these new political arrangements might affect the future of assembly exports was uncertain. Some in the industry and in foreign agencies like the World Bank and USAID believed that democracy, such as it was, would put an end to Haiti's comparative advantage in cheap labor. Others believed that measuring the price of labor in terms of daily wages rather than in terms of contribution to output was unwise, and that the only method by which labor output could rise was through pressure on management to organize production for this purpose. In either case, the industrial development process would undoubtedly become less intelligible than it had been from 1949 to 1986, but since lack of intelligibility did not constrain past progress, there was no particular reason to doubt that it would continue.

For the moment, the only important thing was that workers were making a small mark on the process and on politics. For the most part educated, and with relatively high earnings, these workers were usually not ordinary people. But they were also mostly not of the middle class that depended on government and other monopoly privileges for subsistance. In listening to them, the concerned factions of the political class were not hearing ordinary people. But they were hearing some new things that might have benefits for ordinary people as well. Such benefits, like lowered food prices, were vitally important in 1986 because the two other important economic sectors that for many years provided flows of resources upon which ordinary people could earn their livelihoods, travel and labor exports, had collapsed.

Travel

The travel industry, drawing income from expenditures by foreign tourists, by other foreigners traveling on business, and by Haitian visitors residing elsewhere, was almost nonexistent before 1945. Construction of most of the city's major hotels between 1946 and 1956 and wide promotion of its Bicentennial Exposition in 1949 helped the country establish a small but important niche in the Caribbean travel market (Girault, 1978: 27). In 1945 it welcomed 4000 visitors (Moore, 1972: 217). By 1960 the number reached almost 80,000, and the net addition to the economy (i.e., less payments abroad by Haitian students and other travelers) came to $2.6 million (table 1.9).

The industry collapsed during the severest period of François Duvalier, but then slowly reconstituted itself, reaching a peak of 300,000 visitors in 1980, with net receipts of $44 million in 1981. This flow of resources was important in providing foreign exchange. It was particularly important for

TABLE 1.9
Travel and Tourism to Haiti, 1950-84

	THOUSANDS OF TRAVELERS ARRIVING		NET EXPENDITURES (MILLIONS OF $)	
	By Airplane	**By Cruise Ship**	**In Current $**	**In 1948 $**
1950	10.2	1.8	0.8	0.8
1960	25.6	53.7	2.7	2.6
1963	7.3	38.0	0.6	0.5
1972	67.6	92.3	9.2	6.0
1979	165.1	173.8	32.2	9.3
1980	138.9	162.6	35.9	9.5
1981	134.1	142.0	43.8	11.1
1982	120.2	94.7	39.5	9.3
1983	125.8	96.7	33.3	7.1
1984	117.4	93.0	28.0	6.0

Sources: Rotberg (1971), Moore (1972), Girault (1978), IMF (1983), World Bank (1985), and author's estimates.

the urban economy because most expenditures were concentrated in and around the city. Cruise ships stopped at the port for one day, and tourists on them rarely had the opportunity to travel beyond the immediate region.[37] Tourists coming by airplane and staying a week also spent most of their time and money in the city, as did business travelers and visiting Haitians. Port-au-Prince therefore captured a large share of direct hotel and restaurant employment resulting from the expenditures, estimated at 2000 to 2500 jobs in 1972, and also a large share of sales of art, crafts, and other goods and services (Girault, 1978: 39).

Growth in travel expenditures between 1963 and 1981 had relatively little to do with vacation tourism, however. Relative to other countries in the region, Haiti had nothing to offer of comparable quality in terms of beaches, hotels, or recreational activities. What it could offer, unique culture and art, was undermined by the constant sight and smell of gruesome misery.[38] To many Caribbean tourists, Haiti did not project the image of what a vacation spot was supposed to look like. There were foreign tourists among travelers arriving by airplane, but they were not the majority.

Most travel expenditures were reflections of the rapid growth of foreign assistance, industrial export activity, and emigration between 1970 and 1980. The combined effect of world media coverage of human rights violations in 1980, of accusations that Haiti was the source of "AIDS" disease in 1982, of political unrest in 1983, and of the world recession through this period was to lower but not eliminate the flow of resources, as had in fact happened in 1963. Still, the loss of $16 million in receipts by 1984, which in real terms put Haiti back to the same position it held in 1972, dealt a serious blow to the economy. Hurt hardest directly were hotel and restaurant workers, and producers of tourist-oriented arts and crafts.

Travel receipts seemed to pick up again in 1985, and for a few months late in the year and in early 1986 reached what might have been a peak when journalists filled hotels in search of stories, Haitians returned from exile, and U.S. officials and consultants commuted back and forth from Washington in search of solutions to the solutions that Haiti had administered to itself. The effect was short-lived. With recurrent disturbances on the streets becoming normal and no longer newsworthy, with exiles having come or gone, and with U.S. political and economic strategy formulated to the extent that there was something to formulate, travel dropped back to its previous level. In the absence of stability, travel and tourism were unlikely to return to 1980 levels for while. Ordinary people helped directly or indirectly by the trade would have to wait, especially after the minister of health gave tourism a "coup de grâce" in mid-1986 by announcing that perhaps 10 percent of all Haitians carried the "AIDS" disease.

Labor Export

Ordinary people had little choice but to wait. The alternative, exporting themselves to foreign markets, was difficult because the component of the labor export sector open to ordinary people also collapsed in 1981. Until that year, Haiti had done reasonably well in this industry.

It sent slaves to North Carolina for the Spanish in 1526, and exported about 30,000 colonists and their associates made superfluous by independence to Cuba between 1795 and 1805 (Buchanan, 1982; Lundahl, 1983: 95). In the free trade zone for labor created by U.S. dominion over Haiti, Cuba, and the Dominican Republic during the initial third of this century, many workers found productive use and higher earnings in sugar plantations of neighboring countries where indigenous workers were in short supply at the wage offered them by employers. From 1913 to 1931, some 450,000 people may have worked in Cuba as seasonal cane cutters, and perhaps 10 to 20 percent elected to remain there (Lundahl, 1983: 102, 106). A smaller number went to the Dominican Republic during the same period, and with annual increases and decreases associated with changes in the political relations between the two countries and in demand for plantation labor, the process continued through 1985.[39]

About 3000 legal, and perhaps 27,000 illegal migrants crossed into the Dominican Republic every year from 1957 to 1963. The number of legal workers rose steadily thereafter, to 16,000 in 1981. Many of them also chose not to return, and the permanent population of Haitians in the Dominican Republic was somewhere between 100,000 and 200,000 people in 1980 (Lundahl, 1983: 125–28).

Other important markets for exports were France, Canada, Martinique, Guadeloupe, and Venezuela (Allman, 1982: 11). After 1975, government made some lackluster export promotion efforts in Guyana, French Guyana, and Belize, but met with limited success. Expansion of tourism in the Bahamas during the 1950s and 1960s, however, created a new market for labor exports. Haitians in the Bahamas in 1980 may have numbered 30,000, with workers engaged primarily in nonagricultural occupations.

But by far the most significant destination, requiring little in the way of promotion or contract organization, was the United States. From 1956 to 1985 approximately 1 million Haitian visitors entered the United States legally with immigrant and short–term nonimmigrant visas. According to some estimates, half of the nonimmigrants chose to remain illegally, resulting in an estimated net migration of the order of 650,000 people.[40] In addition, especially in the decade after the Bahamas began serious efforts to deport Haitians in the 1970s, Florida received somewhere between 50,000 and 80,000 illegal entrants on its beaches.[41] Most of these Haitians were not repatriated, and the population of Haitians in the United States may have climbed to a level of 700,000 to 750,000. Including the first generation of children born to the migrants between 1956 and 1985, and the probable mortality rate, the current population of Haitian origin in the United States may be somewhere between 600,000 and 900,000, depending on the basis of estimation.

These exports, particularly the share destined for North American and European markets where earnings and therefore value–added were higher than in other places, became vitally important to the economy. Besides the increased material well–being of the 20 to 30 percent of Haitian society not required to earn their livelihoods within national frontiers, and a lessening of population pressure, a major benefit was substantial growth in remittances by emigrants to their families in Haiti. In 1960 the net documented flow of these funds represented less than 5 percent of the country's total exports of goods and services (table 1.10). Two decades later, the share was 26 percent. Making allowance for remittances through channels other than the banking system, such as commercial courier services from the Bahamas and cash carried by travelers, their value could well have been equivalent to a third of total exports.[42]

Penetration of foreign markets for other than agricultural labor being subject to rigorous quality control, the primary beneficiaries of remittances

TABLE 1.10
Remittances from Haitians Residing Abroad, 1960-84
(millions of dollars)

			NET REMITTANCES		
	Remittances[a]	Transfers[b]	current $	1948 $	Share of Total Exports[c] (%)
1960	n.a.	n.a.	2.6	2.5	4.8
1965	n.a.	n.a.	4.7	3.8	15.7
1972	25.0	4.1	20.9	13.7	40.2
1976	78.0	46.9	31.1	11.6	36.2
1978	76.0	47.3	29.1	10.4	21.4
1980	106.4	54.4	52.0	14.0	26.0
1982[d]	97.0	47.3	49.7	11.2	33.6
1984[d]	90.0	45.0	45.0	8.8	27.1

Sources: World Bank (1978b, 1985).

[a] Excludes remittances not channeled through banks.

[b] Transfers out of the country.

[c] Total exports include merchandise (net of imported components) and nonfactor service exports, and exclude remittances.

[d] Declines in these years may reflect increased use of nonbank methods of sending remittances to Haiti.

during the 1950s, 1960s, and early 1970s were higher–income families able to produce emigrants whose general education, marketable skill, and language proficiency was sufficient to pass inspection at Port–au–Prince consulates and immigration screening at foreign ports of entry, and who were able to finance the costs of migration. With increases in school enrollments and the possibility of circumventing quality control barriers through direct travel by sea, the range of beneficiaries expanded after 1975 to include almost all income classes able to finance travel costs. After the Haiti–United States interdiction treaty of 1981 allowed the U.S. Coast Guard to intercept boats and return their passengers to Haiti, accrual of direct benefits passed back to higher–income groups.

Capital flight and other private transfers offset the positive contribution of remittances, but what remained in the country for those who received them was an important basis for financing the costs of additional emigration, schooling, investment in land, construction, trade and manufacturing, and additional consumption.

The question of whether these export earnings were offset by loss in valuable "human capital" had no obvious answer. Some observers saw in the emigration of trained people like doctors, nurses, mechanics, electricians, and carpenters an almost catastrophic departure of skilled brainpower (Segal, 1975: 201). Although doctors and nurses were few and far between, the public and private resources required to sustain a large number of them did not exist. In addition, doctors and nurses were part of a curative infrastructure that did little to prevent illness. A principal cause of illness in Haiti was malnutrition, exacerbated by a low level of preventive health services. In this context, Haiti's loss of its best and brightest farmers to the Dominican Republic, the Bahamas, and Florida seemed much more serious than loss of medical personnel. And the loss of farmers who under the worst conditions earned three or four times more outside Haiti than inside, and who sent more to their families than they could have produced on their own land, was a net benefit. Similarly, emigration of trained mechanics, electricians, and carpenters could not have been much of a loss in an economy where demand for them was so low that their remittances from minimum–wage jobs in North America could exceed their annual earnings in Haiti. To the extent that the economic meaning of "skill" is that for which there is effective demand, as distinct from years of education or formally defined occupational expertise for which there may be no demand, Haiti may have lost only superfluous manpower with irrelevant training, people who perhaps often acquired the training for the principal purpose of exporting themselves.

There was also the possibility that by removing likely sources of dissent, emigration contributed to the maintenance of the Duvalier regime (Segal,

1975: 204). This may have been a factor as far as that one family was concerned, but not necessarily with respect to political organization of the economy by others. Until relatively recently, highly educated people were almost entirely the product of the privileged and mostly urban political class that supported itself through direct and indirect taxation of the majority and that transferred resources from production to consumption. Had they remained in Haiti, the pressure to raise taxes further might have increased and might have resulted in an even more oppressive political economy than the one administered by the Duvaliers. Viewed this way, emigration may have provided cause for relief rather than cause for concern. As for the 30,000 colonists who went to Cuba between 1795 and 1805 to use their know–how to create a thriving coffee industry, Cuba's gain was a loss to Haiti only if one could say with conviction that foregone coffee exports were not worth the price of reducing the severity of colonial oppression.

Relative advantages and disadvantages of labor exports with respect to economic and political development remain matters for speculation, but the process did serve at least one practical political purpose. It provided several additional sources of public and private taxation. Workers wishing to register for work in the Dominican Republic paid $5 to $10 to government (i.e., Macoute) contractors for the privilege between 1957 and 1963. Dominican planters paid $15 per head to the contractors, and half the workers' wages in U.S. dollars to special accounts of the Haitian treasury (Lundahl, 1983: 125–26). In 1981, the fee of $182 for each of the 16,000 legal migrants permitted almost $3 million to flow into the accounts, and from there to the Duvaliers and their associates.[43]

The fee for travel to the Bahamas in the early 1970s was $50 to $200 in advance, plus the first four to six weeks of cash wages after arrival or another $50 to $75.[44] Contractors receiving these fees paid local officials in both countries for export and import authority. Travel to Florida, costing $200 to $1500, yielded a similar distribution of commissions.

The treasury obtained nothing for permitting sea travel. After the Haiti–U.S. interdiction treaty, it finally collected a commission from the United States for permitting the coast guard to prevent such travel. Although receipts from the United States had to be accounted for, additions to the treasury allowed further substitution of foreign for domestic revenue sources and therefore more scope for pillage.

More important sources of official revenue were levies on air travelers. The $100 price for a passport and one exit visa, plus compulsory insurance, airport taxes, and other charges made possible official collection of $150 to $200 per traveler until 1979, and all manner of personal collections by administrators and other intermediaries from individuals wanting to obtain travel documents quickly (Allman, 1982: 11). Official levies in 1978 may have been between $9 and $10 million, but they fell to $4 million the following year when, under pressure from middle-class members of the political class, government reduced this progressive income tax by lowering the price of passports and visas.[45]

To ordinary people, however, the most important benefits of the industry were population relief and, of course, the remittances. The interdiction treaty was a major setback for them. Of the 50,000 to 80,000 boat people who managed to get to Florida between 1976 and 1981, 40 percent, or 4000 per year, were from the city or its environs (Stepick, 1984: 346). While they were leaving, the city's labor force was growing at a rate of 9000 per year.[46] Without emigration it might have expanded more quickly, increasing competition between workers for shares of limited urban income. And the flow of remittances to ordinary, low-income urban families of the order of $15 million, or about $120 per household each year, was very helpful.[47]

The slump in the economy after 1981 had many causes. The interdiction treaty was certainly one of them. The government's complicity in signing the treaty and in removing the last hope ordinary people had at the time for a better future added yet another reason to the already long list of reasons for change of political leadership. Unfortunately, the new government, tied much more closely to the United States than the previous one, was unlikely to abrogate the treaty. Indeed, it had every reason to meet treaty obligations scrupulously. The labor export industry, as far as ordinary people were concerned, was finished.

Politics in Prospect

With general elections scheduled for late 1987 or early 1988, political dynamics in 1986 looked like a race against time in which major and minor factions attempted to create new political and economic facts in a highly unstable environment. One major organizational effort, supported with U.S. financial, logistical, and technical assistance, was strengthening of the army, including the police, to fill the vacuum created by withdrawal of the Macoutes from political security service. Strengthening included higher salaries, an increase in the army's size, constitution of a new officer corps, and intensive training in bloodless crowd management techniques. From a strict operational point of view, the scale of the strengthening effort was an exaggeration. From a political standpoint it may have seemed essential in order to dilute the influence of ex-Macoutes and other disenfranchised individuals of the class scattered throughout the officer corps and the ranks, and also the influence of officers connected to traditional elite factions coming under antimonopoly pressure. The army was incapable of purging itself in 1986. If the objects of such action within the ranks did not organize to protect themselves in time, a quiet and gradual purge might succeed in creating a slightly repoliticized army in time for the elections.

Rapid transformation of the army was essential to block moves by diehards among the 5000 to 10,000 armed ex–Macoutes who had not given up their guns. Perhaps more important, a transformed army could better protect government and its IMF, World Bank, and USAID allies from serious challenge to their policy initiatives. The old army, besides being politically unreliable, had no mastery of bloodless protection techniques, a prerequisite for enthusiastic U.S. support.

An important immediate economic initiative of this faction, which had as its principal domestic components pro–U.S. members of the middle–class and export–oriented industrialists, was elimination of as many import and import–substitution monopolies as feasible in as short a time period as possible. To cultivate some modicum of popular support for the policies from middle– and lower–income consumers not dependent on monopolies for their livelihoods, the faction was trying to provide tangible evidence that consumer prices would drop significantly. Creation of this economic reality was of primary importance. Other measures, like breaking the export monopolies, trimming the number of public employees, shifting taxation from regressive to more progressive forms, and maintaining strict fiscal austerity, could wait. The issue of whether or not to raise the minimum wage demanded procrastination. Increasing it would erode industrialist support. Maintaining it ran counter to the purpose of cultivating popular support, especially after teachers, health workers, and soldiers received their substantial raises.

Although some civilian members of the provisional government might choose to run for political office, the essential purpose of generating popular support, besides treating immediate urban unrest, was to lay the groundwork for political parties and presidential candidates with election platforms that coincided with provisional government policies. In the summer of 1986, there were at least five such parties and presidential hopefuls. The parties and candidates varied somewhat in their ideological orientation with respect to capitalism, socialism, business, labor, the civil service, and deep penetration of Haitian affairs by the IMF, World Bank, and the United States, but they were all more or less "acceptable." An elected government led by one or a coalition of several of these parties would serve the purposes of the faction.

Such a government seemed an unlikely possibility if elections were to be held in 1987. The various parties were urban–based, led and organized by several members of Haiti's traditional elite factions and the newer "middle–class" elite. Their only distinguishing characteristics were opposition to Duvalier rule, and espousal of more progressive outlooks. And the politics being promoted on their behalf by the provisional government were of benefit largely to urban consumers, still a small minority of the national population. A year of preparation for elections allowed little time for these parties and the provisional government to generate national bases of support.

A second effort, financed in part by commercial and industrial interests still wedded to the principle of monopoly rents, involved organization of workers who lost or who were threatened with loss of employment, ex–Macoutes and ranking class loyalists dispossessed of their jobs or influence, and other middle– and lower–income urban and rural people who one way or another suffered setbacks in the turn of political events. This coalition, in addition to having arms, possessed sufficient resources and organizational depth (i.e., certain cohesive segments of the party–like structure put together by the Macoutes after 1967) to hire large numbers of demonstrators and voters who would not ordinarily involve themselves in politics, but who were more than willing to act as paid campaign organizers and lobbyists. This coalition had already flexed its muscles in organizing antigovernment demonstrations in the city, and through these practice exercises was accumulating essential experience for the elections.

In mid–1986 the coalition had developed several official political parties and official presidential candidates to address narrower factional interests within itself. Multiple parties helped set the stage for preformation of a coalition government after an election likely to have at least thirty political parties and presidential candidates. This group had no intention of inviting Duvalier's return, but it adhered closely to basic principles of traditional governance. Through its understanding of popular politics outside the city, the same kind of understanding that sustained François Duvalier, and through its financial and organizational capacity to rally large numbers of people to its side, it appeared to have several of the key attributes required to win a free election.

Other efforts, lacking funds, arms, organizational sophistication, or large populist bases, seemed of lesser importance. The Catholic church had influence in a number of towns and regions, but having returned to factional disputes between conservative and liberal elements after the departure of Duvalier, to disputes concerning whether the Church should take a pro– or antigovernment position, or whether it should even continue to engage in politics, its efforts were more a collection of dispersed activities than a unified undertaking.

University and secondary school students as well as government and factory workers were scattering themselves across a range of political parties offering a multiplicity of ideologies. Making some progress with these elements were the communist and transport worker organizations, but they too were urban–centered and relatively small. Some dispersed factions might congeal to build significant political fronts before the election, but without a tangible purpose around which to form a unified coalition, like ousting Duvalier, this seemed unlikely. Unless something dramatic happened before the election, like a postponement to allow more time for organizational development by additional parties and coalitions, the basic contest was likely to be between the army–backed pro–U.S. progressive coalition, and the traditional, middle–class populist and colonial–mercantilist coalition.

Ordinary people, except perhaps those paid or otherwise cajoled to show support, were still a pedestal for struggle within the political class. But because the class was larger and contained a broader variety of competing self–interests than in the past, political dynamics presented greater possibilities for production of side effects that might improve the circumstances of ordinary people, if not in 1987 or 1988, then perhaps later. There was even some chance that progressive elements might gain eventual dominance in the class and press effectively for helpful policy changes of the indirect types that had contributed to growth of assembly exports after 1949, and of the more direct types that were lowering regressive tax burdens in 1986. However, even with a shift of power toward the progressives, prospects for significant improvement of ordinary circumstances in the near future appeared unlikely.

The constraint on improvement was certainly not a shortage of words of concern about ordinary people, or about ideas for methods to make things better for them. Haitian thinkers, for example, had over the course of 100 years produced a long list of interesting suggestions. According to some of them, Haiti needed:

- secure land tenure for peasants, rural credit, universal education, mobilization of national savings to reduce foreign dependency, customs and fiscal reform, creation of a functional public administration, and "power to the most capable" (Janvier, 1885, 1886).
- to engage a program of social reform yielding a process of sustained economic development and permitting redistribution of wealth to meet work, food, clothing, housing, and other basic needs of the poor (Bellegarde, 1941).
- a progressive program that accords special actions for the most disadvantaged segments of society, democratization of the fiscal system, freedom of assembly and union organization, collaboration with all democratic countries, and, with respect to the United States, a subtle firmness in the defense of Haitian interests.[48]
- total revolution, which must penetrate all segments of national life to

shatter the political structure, transform social life, and completely remodel the framework of the national community (Lebert, 1966).

- participation of peasants in socioeconomic and political movements against hunger and capitalist exploitation (Pierre–Charles, 1967).
- to eliminate political and social privileges in society in order to bring about such structure change as is possible with available land, labor, and other resources under constraints imposed by international capital (Francisque, 1968).
- to create a new humanity based on the principles of fraternity, equality, liberty, and justice (Price–Mars in Preface to Mathon, 1969).
- a serious and scientific approach to managing economic production in a way that inhibits accumulation of wealth by extraeconomic means and can open a path to economic takeoff (Honorat, 1974).
- an egalitarian and self–reliant method of economic and social development that breaks away from the traditional relationship between social structure and economic structure, and from dominance by international capital (Manigat, Moise, and Olivier, 1975).
- to destroy the dominant historical ideology of maintenance or ascendancy to power for the sake of power (Luc, 1976).
- democratic participatory planning, a cultural revolution reforming the intellectual and moral traditions of the Haitian people, and an eruption of the masses (Aristide, 1978).
- a true, class–based popular revolution in the Marxist tradition that does not necessarily need the intelligentsia to guide it (Labrousse, 1978).
- to dispense with historical philosophy of political violence, to think developmentally in democratic terms and not in tyrannical terms of a social nature, to undertake a cultural revolution that breaks the belief that authoritarianism is historically necessary or that barbarism is part of Haitian culture, and to have a renaissance (Durand, 1979).
- a union of the progressive intelligentsia and the organized elements of the popular masses to battle for establishment of a national democracy (Joachim, 1979).
- reform of the army; administrative, fiscal, monetary, and banking reforms, land reform, and agricultural modernization; reform of foreign assistance to limit international investment, to protect the economy from exploitation linked to aid, and to work toward alternative methods of financing development; and elimination of the discriminatory characteristics of public education (Delince, 1979).
- to negate the hypothesis that Westernization will help (because it is the road of underdevelopment), to seek new forms of economic and social integration, to press for self–sufficiency in food production, to create an organized rural society working the land on a collective–cooperative basis, and to adopt the Hegelian thesis of creating a new future by pursuing a path of auto–development (Honorat, 1980).

One hundred years and more of published ideas by Haitians of the political class about what "ought" to be done or what "should" be made to happen may have left a few stones unturned, but by and large the ideas covered the full spectrum of generalities that a political class separated from the bulk of a national population was capable of producing. Published works by expatriate scholars embellished certain of the ideas. Foreign–assistance professional reports translated some of them into specific proposals for technical action, for example, provision of basic needs. But neither added substantively to the list of indigenous notions. Basic needs was proposed in 1941. Lack of good intentions was not an obstacle.

What stood in the way of improvement by well–intentioned progressives was ignorance masking itself under the cloak of "knowledge." The world of the political class was so far removed from ordinary people that few of its members, even the most altruistic ones, could hope to understand or even identify the meaning of improvement. Their world did not present them with information, and therefore with opinions, assumptions, or theories through which they could easily make sense of the world of the ordinary. Missing in the circulation of notions within the political class of Haiti, as in most developing countries, were ideas and suggestions put forward implicitly or explicitly in the published writings of the ordinary class. Works like the diary of Carolina Maria de Jesus, in which she spoke eloquently of the concreteness of basic things like work, food, water, shelter, schooling, and other issues of tangible importance to ordinary people in urban Brazil, and of the behaviors of the political class with respect to these matters, had no equivalent in Haiti (De Jesus, 1962).

However, the absence of a literature produced by the ordinary class, while having some importance, was not a principal source of ignorance. Such a literature could as readily serve the purposes of reinforcing preexisting opinions, assumptions, and theories as it could to undermine them. In the world of the political class, understanding of ordinary circumstances derived from thought about the circumstances rather than from tangible feelings of their effect. With understanding captive of thought, and with thought captive of a situation in which theory and reality are indistinguishable from each other, individuals could not see what they were not predisposed to look for in a literature.

Nor was lack of contact between members of the political class and members of the ordinary class a major source of ignorance. Although infrequency of contacts in rural areas could contribute to what one student of the phenomenon called a "cognitive problem" that allowed individuals of the political class to camouflage their ignorance and, worse, to prevent them from knowing what they did not know, such contacts took place every day in urban areas (Chambers, 1980: 2). In much the same way that individuals could not extract from writings what they were not conceptually prepared to extract, they could not see what they were not looking for in their daily experiences. The difficulty could have been one of cognition flowing from insufficient contact, but if the basis of the conceptual categories, and therefore ignorance, was the belief that they were "truths," no amount of contact could solve it.

Indeed, a more salient source of ignorance, and therefore serving as a more formidable constraint on prospects for improvement of the circumstances of ordinary people, was truth; or more precisely, the political economy of truth. Brecht's Galileo, believing in one truth about astronomy, thought he could share it with scholars of the Florentine court, who subscribed to other truths derived from Aristotle and the ancients, by having them peer at the stars through his new invention, the telescope (Brecht, 1972: 33–36). They chose not to look through it because, as they put it, such truth as this new mechanism for understanding might provide did not seem necessary, because their truth had such order and beauty that to disturb it seemed ill-advised, because it was impossible to decide beforehand whether the truth proposed by Galileo was actually in the stars or (painted) in the telescope, and because the effects of any new truth were sufficiently unpredictable that it seemed more prudent to explore with higher scholarly authority the consequences that the possibility of Galileo's proposed truth might have before proceeding further.

In this context, for both Galileo and the other scholars, the essence of truth was political. Beyond the direct opposition between two claims to truth, there was the inconvenience of rejecting two millenia of documented understanding that had served the purposes of occidental civilization quite well, and therefore the matter of the political repercussions of an alteration in "reality." For most members of the political class at that time, new truths could not serve their interests as well as old ones. Their individual claims to expertise, repute, professional standing and attendant salaries, and through amalgamation of individual interests, similar claims of the organizations to which they attached themselves (i.e., the court, the church, and the university), did not easily accommodate something new. In brief, ignorance dressed as knowledge was vital to individual and organizational self–interest, and therefore to corporate survival. Truth defined itself democratically by majority opinion in the class. The stars, however, remained unchanged.

More generally, the knowledge guiding thought and action within political classes is much less like a series of opinions, assumptions, and theories leading through constant revision toward an absolute kind of truth, than like an ever–increasing collection of mutually incompatible ideas wherein each opinion, assumption, theory, fairytale, and myth forms part of a collection forcing others into greater articulation over time (Feyerabend, 1975: 30). Driven by political and other forces, all of the ideas contribute through their competition with each other to something that might best be called "consciousness," and this consciousness of the moment is the truth of the moment. The difficulty for ordinary people in Haiti in 1986, although perhaps slightly less so than in 1492, was that in their inability to act politically and thereby challenge ideas within the political class, they could not alter the calculus of self–interest and survival of members of the class. By extension, they could not alter the consciousness of the class. In this respect the political class remained ignorant not because it lacked some absolute knowledge, but because this knowledge, derived from thought about ordinary people, excluded all forms of understanding that ordinary people derived from concrete experience. For the political class, ordinary people had as much to say about their own circumstances and about means to improve them as did the stars to discussions between Galileo and court scholars.

This difficulty was particularly acute in Haiti because ordinary people were not only poor, they were extraordinarily, excruciatingly poor even in comparison with other developing countries. Their poverty had meaning that often extended well beyond relative or absolute descriptive categorizations of living standards. It was an analytical category referring to a dynamic political economy in which outwardly simple and straightforward acts like making a living; obtaining food, water, and shelter; schooling children; and borrowing money were often extraordinarily complex activities essential to production of corporate and corporeal survival. This political economy was often incompatible with opinions, assumptions, and theories about it prevailing in the political class, including progressive elements of the class.

A political class of colonial governance did not need to hear, and did not hear, the will of ordinary people. A political class of what seemed to be postcolonial governance in 1986 did not need to hear it either. But even if it wished to listen, it often heard little but faint, unintelligible noise. The knowledge or truth that emanated from the political economy of the political class seemed often very different from the knowledge and understanding emanating from the political economy of ordinary realities.

As a member of the political class by definition, I cannot presume to understand the meaning of ordinary circumstances, or to speak on behalf of the ordinary class. With respect to the relationship between ordinary people and simple things, I can nevertheless point out what may be some of the important differences of thought and action between the two classes, and in the process highlight my reasons for suggesting that prospects for substantial improvement of ordinary circumstances in a near term are unlikely no matter how "progressive" Haiti's form of governance may become.

Notes

1. From 1976 to 1979 Haiti maintained a current account surplus. From 1980 to 1984 it ran consecutive deficits of $9, $31, $4, $6 and $10 million, and by 1986 accumulated a current account debt of almost $90 million (World Bank, 1982: 111; 1985: 159). The amount was small compared to the $800 million debt that Haiti carried in 1984, but any sustained level of deficit financing was a large problem in a small budget (World Bank, 1985: 153). The unexplained disappearance in 1980 of some or all of the IMF's standby credit to help the budget and the balance of payments made the problem worse (Southerland, 1984: 5).
2. Assembling statistics and serving as the central buffer between the government and foreign–assistance agencies was an important function of the Planning Ministry, but 600 employees were not required for this purpose. Similarly, the Ministries of Justice (1250 employees), Information and Public Relations (750), and Youth and Sports (400) seemed to have more than twice as many workers as required to fulfill their mandates. Data for employment are from World Bank (1985: 167).
3. Planning for a $55 million increase was in progress at USAID when I visited Haiti in March 1986. Most or all of this aid was to take the form of commodity donations to the new government, which would sell them at market prices and then use the receipts for budgetary support and other activities. Subsequent rumor placed the amount at $80 million (Fontaine, 1986: 25).
4. Fifteen percent of the population lived in the city in 1982 (IHSI, 1982: 2).
5. Horowitz (1982: 219–34) discusses the rise of state administrative power as an adjunct to the evolution of "post industrial" socioeconomic systems. In such systems, the apparatus must still be responsive to political leaders and taxpaying publics—if for no other reason than because the ideology of public administration demands it. The possibility of a rise in the power of a state apparatus in Haiti necessarily stems from a different kind of evolution. The apparatus is a network of extended families, friends, and followers who depend on taxation for their livelihoods, and with alternative sources of livelihood in short supply, the apparatus's members become politically active as a means to survive. As such, it need not be responsive to taxpayers or leaders. It is perhaps the most important political constituency to which leaders must respond.
6. Facts and figures about public foreign assistance from 1941 to 1970 come from Moore (1972: 65–104).
7. The treaty was less a cause than a catalyst for increased U.S. assistance. As with most USAID missions, staff in Haiti presented annual briefs to Washington seeking increased budget authorizations, and each year received more than before but less than requested. In 1979 they proposed a major increase, but according to the USAID mission director I interviewed in 1983, subsequent violations by the Haitian government of what USAID and State Department officials in Washington, and U.S. politicians (especially members of the Congressional Black Caucus) considered appropriate human rights practice, contributed to rejection of large–scale increases. But with the treaty allowing the U.S. Coast Guard to intercept boats and to return passengers directly to Haitian ports, and with calls by officials in Florida urging more aid, powers in Washington relented. The exchange for the treaty was a $4 million rise in annual commodity credits to the government under Title I (see note 8 below). Substan-

tial rises in nonfood support from 1981 onwards represented responses to requests of the USAID mission and Florida.

8. Under USAID's Title I program, government received a credit for market purchase of commodities such as wheat. It sold the commodities and used the proceeds for counterpart financing of specific development projects mutually agreed upon by USAID and the government. Terms of the credit were concessionary at a 2–3 percent interest rate over forty years, with ten years grace. This program was reviewed annually.
9. The PVO, Cooperation Haiti–Neerlandais (COHAN), was administered in Haiti by a Salesian Father, and in 1986 was one of the largest private organizations in the country.
10. Under USAID's Title II program, the United States provided several cooperating PVOs with dried milk, cornmeal, bulgar wheat, vegetable oil, and flour for direct distribution in support of school and preschool feeding, maternal and child health, and food for work programs. Cooperating PVOs in 1976 were the CARE Foundation, Catholic Relief Services, and Christian Service of Haiti. The Seventh Day Adventist World Service, also known as the Adventist Development and Relief Agency, joined the process later.
11. A Protestant mission telephone book listed 300 separate organizations in 1983, and a list of PVOs prepared by the Haitian Association of Voluntary Agencies, contained in a UNDP report (1983), showed 80 not on the Protestant list. Excluded from both lists were 20 organizations that established themselves in 1983 and 1984, after preparation of the two lists.
12. Disbursement data, which exclude the value of food received from USAID or the World Food Program (WFP), comes from UNDP (1983: 3–4), UNDP (1985: 10–11), World Bank (1985: 156), information I obtained directly from major organizations, and unpublished material collected by USAID in a 1985 PVO survey. Because some large PVOs provide support to many smaller ones, and because large and small ones receive grants from bilaterial assistance agencies and embassies, the USAID, UNDP, and World Bank data contain extensive double and triple counting. A straightforward addition of documented PVO budgets extrapolated to the whole community of organizations yields a disbursement figure in excess of $120 million. The $40 million estimate may therefore still contain some multiple counting.
13. Arrival dates are from a subsample of 60 PVOs covered by an unpublished 1985 USAID survey of PVOs.
14. Estimated from information in UNDP (1977).
15. A review of information for 1984 in UNDP (1985) indicated the same general pattern of aid disbursements as in 1976.
16. Based on unpublished data concerning administrative expenditures of major PVOs located in the city, and on their nonadministrative disbursements to urban beneficiaries.
17. Recommendations contained in a June 1985 newsletter produced by the Haitian Conference of Religious Orders.
18. The foothold, known as the "Bazin Affair," was the appointment of Marc Bazin as minister of finance in April 1982. Bazin, before his appointment a World Bank employee in charge of an industrial credit project in Haiti, cut the government's payroll, fiscalized several hidden treasury accounts, and according to Guest (1982: 24–25) began to encroach on hidden accounts of the president and his father-in-law. Bazin was removed from office within five months of his

appointment, and returned to Haiti in 1986 as leader of a new political party. This affair was just one extreme moment of intervention in a long history of effort by the IMF and World Bank to introduce what they believed would be better financial management and practice. The U.S. interest from 1915 onward concerned tax collection and financial management. It kept a fiscal administrator in Haiti until 1947, and then provided ineffectual advisory services from 1958 to 1962 (Smith, 1962). USAID tried again in 1982 with support of advisers to improve tax administration (Buck, 1982). The project apparently helped the government to increase internal revenues, but accomplished little with respect to customs receipts.

19. Fontaine (1986: 25) reported that Minister Delatour's announcement of the proposed end of monopolies was quickly followed by demonstrations calling for his resignation, supposedly financed by owners of the monopolies. That was possible since private financing of governmental change was a Haitian tradition, particularly from 1895 to 1915. Equally possible was a truly popular demonstration by workers in the monopolies, and by sympathizers noting the loss of employment. The minister's announcement did not emphasize the lowering in prices that would follow elimination of the monopolies, a relationship more obvious to an economist than to someone else, and this omission may have prevented counterdemonstrations of support by consumers. The need for demonstration management is more obvious to politicians than to economists.
20. Rotberg (1971: 254) noted that even during the period of Francois Duvalier's worst excesses, these families were treated relatively mildly. All trade and industry of significance was in their hands. Government needed them as allies, or at least not as enemies.
21. Lundahl (1979: 133–45, 1983: 171–89) and Delatour (1983), after synthesizing many prior studies about coffee, concluded that the market was competitive. Girault (1981) argued in favor of monopsony. Part of the discussion revolved around interpretation of profit margins. Lundahl (1979: 142), for example, interpreted an exporter net profit of 4–5 percent of the export price as not being excessive. It was not excessive compared to, say, 16 percent. Strictly speaking, however, a highly competitive market is supposed to yield profits quite close to zero, and in unrestricted large-scale trade profits of 1–2 percent would be more typical. In this context Lundahl implied that profits 400 to 500 percent above the typical range for competitive commerce were normal. Perhaps they were, perhaps not.
22. The World Bank (1984c: 78–79) estimate put exporter net margins, including office expenses, telephone, telex, risk, and profit, at 6.6 to 7.0 percent. The 5 percent figure I used for preparation of table 1.5 supposes that the risk component was 1.6 to 2.0 percent.
23. This public–private interaction conforms to Down's (1957) concept of a political market for policies wherein potential beneficaries demand policy interventions from which they can benefit (i.e., export monopolies), and the political leadership supplies it. In the case of Haiti, this has a temporal dimension. An initial investment is required to create the policy (i.e., few exporters), a second investment is required to benefit administratively from the policy (i.e., the export license), and then recurrent outlays are required to maintain the benefits over time. Bates (1983), Krueger (1974), and Srinivasan (1985) speak of such outlays in terms of the efforts by beneficiaries to collect political rents, with the

assumption that what political leaders obtain from the process of allocating rents is political support. This concept may apply in Haiti, but, as elsewhere, maintenance of positions of political power also requires money. In other countries, exchange for granting of political rents may take the form of contributions to party or individual political campaigns. There being no campaigns to speak of in Haiti, rents are purchased with cash down payments, and maintained with recurrent cash overhead payments. Since the political market is a cash market to some extent, rents are purchased by the highest bidders. The result is a political and financial partnership that ties political leaders and investors together for mutual gain over an extended period of time. Economists often make things more complicated that necessary, however. Political rent was the product of institutionalized bribery. And the bribes were collected by an institutionalized protection racket.

24. The World Bank (1984c: 79) estimate put wholesaler margins at 6 percent of the export price. This, presumably, was a gross margin and might therefore overstate net profits.
25. Objections in principle were raised by the UN (1949), UNIDO (1969), the World Bank (1976a, 1978a), and the IMF (1983). Objections with facts and calculations offering evidence that import substitution was unwise from an economic development point of view were raised by the World Bank (1981a, 1985).
26. The import–substitution industries in question were those large enough or modern–looking enough to qualify for industrial protection. Several hundred small firms, capitalized at usually less than $20,000, did not benefit from protection. The problem that import substitution created for them was sometimes unfair competition (e.g., soft drinks) but more often higher costs of obtaining supplies like flour for bakeries and textiles for clothing manufacture.
27. For an overview of the economics of import–substitution industrialization see Meier (1970: 402–9).
28. ADIH (1981: 8–9). The accusation with respect to the force behind smuggling came through in interviews I held with sixty–five factory owners and importers in 1983.
29. The exact point at which this kind of industry began is uncertain. Table 1.8 suggests a start in 1962, but since records showing the composition of manufactured exports before 1962 are elusive, it may well have started earlier.
30. The level of employment and size of payroll associated with export assembly remains elusive. An ILO survey in 1981 estimated the number at 35,000 (ILO: 1981). Others put the estimate at 60,000 for 1980 (Grunwald, Delatour, and Voltaire, 1985: 181). The census for 1982 suggested that the number could not be higher than about 30,000. Rumors in 1985 spoke of 80,000. If the net export value of the sector was indeed $64 million in 1984, then the average production worker salary of about $1000 per year would suggest a total employment of less than 30,000.
31. Such listings are contained in: UN (1949), Folsom (1953), OAS (1962, 1972), UNIDO (1969, 1984), UNCTAD (1976), World Bank (1976a, 1978a, 1979, 1980, 1981a, 1981b, 1982, 1983a, 1985), IMF (1983), ADIH (1981), and USAID (1982b, 1983). Actually, the components of the list had nothing in particular to do with Haiti. They were elements of a standard lexicon of complaints that applied everywhere all the time, and that followed logically from philosophies of growth and profitability in which it was inconceivable to suggest

that anything was good enough. The components were therefore standard packages for expert advice. They were nevertheless important because without their promulgation and discussion there was little basis for the constant taking of varied actions, and without a multiplicity of actions, probabilities for the right combinations to present themselves as further stimuli to the process of industrialization would possibly have been lower.

32. A study of production costs for shirts, automobile flashers, and power equipment in 1984 showed that direct labor costs for these items in Haiti were the lowest in the region, running between 50 and 60 percent of the regional average (USAID 1984c). What kept wages from being higher were primarily factory overhead, administrative costs, and freight charges. Dependence on imports was not a major contributing factor. Aside from managerial inefficiency, the additional costs of production in Haiti stemmed from high utility rates, primarily for electricity; high wharfage charges; and other similar services from which the government derived revenues. In other words, the government taxed assembly exports through peripheral service charges, and factories passed this tax directly to workers. Although exporters complained about these indirect taxes (e.g., ADIH 1981), workers found the minimum wage acceptable enough so that employers did not have to press their claims with too much vigor, and did not have to upgrade their own managerial efficiency. That is, cheap labor subsidized public and private inefficiency.
33. Grunwald, Delatour, and Voltaire (1985: 196) reported that purchase of local inputs was in fact beginning to take hold in 1980–83.
34. World Bank (1983b: 194) reported lower per capita food availability in Haiti than for any other country.
35. This description of happenings is from discussions, observations, and interviews I conducted during March–April 1986.
36. A small survey of factory women, the vast majority of workers in this sector, suggested that the longer a person stayed in a factory, the less satisfied she became with the job (USAID 1984b). Half the women were not satisfied. Causes for dissatisfaction were no doubt several, but the fact that the real wage had declined steadily since 1980 was not inconsequential, especially for women who had families to support. Real wages remained low through 1986, and they therefore had much to complain about when the opportunity for them to do so presented itself.
37. The figures for cruise travelers in table 1.9 include boats landing at Cap Haitien, Haiti's second city. The number debarking in Port-au-Prince was therefore lower than indicated in the table.
38. The port, for example, faced the central market and main garbage dump. The first impression cruise tourists obtained was not encouraging. Many would leave their ships, walk the length of the wharf, and then immediately return on board. They registered in statistics as debarked tourists but never set foot in the city.
39. Grasmuck (1982: 371–73) noted that in recent years Haitians have increasingly gone to work for small coffee growers in the Dominican Republic, where wages are higher than for sugar cane work. What is not clear is whether these Haitians are temporary migrants, or permanent illegal residents.
40. Allman (1982: 8) estimated the number at 450,000 people up to 1980. The figure of 650,000 in 1985 is my extrapolation of Allman's method, with slight adjustment to allow for stricter travel control measures taken by the U.S. government, and boat people flows, after 1980.

41. Buchanan (1982) reported the following recorded flow of illegal entrants: 3500 (up to 1975); 1700 (1976); 1700 (1977); 3900 (1978); 4500 (1979); and 24,600 (1980). Mixson (1981) reported 15,000 during the first nine months of 1981. The total from 1976 to 1981 was therefore 51,400. Illegal entrants were deported prior to 1979, and therefore the effective number of recorded arrivals was 44,100. The corresponding number of unrecorded arrivals is unknown. A guess of 50,000 to 80,000 total entrants could be too high or too low.
42. According to government statistics, remittances fell from a peak of $127 million in 1981 to $90 million in 1984. This decline was presumably only for the flow processed through the national bank (e.g., money orders, checks, etc). Starting in 1981, free conversion of local currency into U.S. dollars became more difficult, and the parallel currency market that developed as a result paid premiums ranging from 5 to 20 percent on conversion to local currency. These factors provided considerable incentive for more transactions to take place outside the regular banking system. But whatever the level of remittances through the banking system, a certain amount always came with travelers carrying cash.
43. The Duvaliers took the amount paid to them by Dominican planters when they left Haiti in 1986, but before their contractors had time to deliver workers across the border. The new government, unable to account for the payment, did not provide the services demanded by the Dominicans. In response, Dominican planters began to round up Haitians residing illegally in order to put them to work in the fields as substitutes for contract labor, which in turn led to all manner of protests by the Haitian government, demonstrations by students in front of the Dominican Embassy in Port-au-Prince, and denunciations by the Catholic church of both countries (Jean-Frantz, 1986). Chances were therefore improving that contract workers might in the future receive a larger portion of their earnings instead of sharing it with political leaders, or that the payment to the government might finally end up in the treasury.
44. See Appendix A, case 8.
45. IMF (1983: 68). The pressure continued after the fall of the Duvaliers with calls by the press for elimination of all travel charges except for passports and visas (Le Matin, 1986).
46. See table 2.1, chapter 2.
47. I interviewed forty-five essentially illiterate Haitians in Florida in 1983, and found that from their wages, slightly below the legal minimum in the state, each was able to send an average of $55 per month back to relatives. Therefore, if the total population of boat people in 1983 was indeed about 65,000, if 40 percent or 26,000 were from Port-au-Prince, and if 85 percent or 22,000 were working, their total annual remittance was approximately $15 million, or between 10 and 15 percent of their average earnings. The first 12 to 24 months of remittances were used to repay debts incurred for the financing of their travel. Subsequent remittances were for direct support of their families.
48. Reference by Barros (1984: 821) to article in *La Nation,* 19 March 1946.

2

Making a Living

Notwithstanding the emergence of an impressive quantity of writing on the subject over the last two decades, the arts and sciences by which ordinary people earn their livelihoods in cities of the developing world are not well understood by the political classes. This may result, in part, from insufficient data. But to the extent that such data as are available depend directly for their substance on the implicit or explicit theories adopted to produce them, inadequate understanding may also result from inappropriate theory. Data will only rarely reveal what their producers do not look for. And the effect of having no other kinds of data is to sometimes reinforce belief in the implicit relationships imputed by theory to the available data. Haiti was especially burdened by this phenomenon because the only sources of general understanding about how people made their living derived from answers to queries about "employment" contained in census questionnaires of 1950, 1971, and 1982.

Underlying such questions was the premise of certain labor market theories that workers were readily classifiable as either employed or unemployed, and that although not a perfect substitute for earnings data, the level of measured unemployment was, among other things, a useful approximation for the extent of poverty. That is, an approach to understanding that had shown itself useful in North America and Europe, indeed, an approach that arose directly from the circumstances of these continents, was presumed to be equally useful in Haiti. The presumption proved exaggerated, and the theory came later to be modified by the addition of such concepts as "underemployment" and "informal" activities.

But the difficulty remained that the only data available for the whole of the urban population were responses to the census questions, and, for elements of the political class unsophisticated in the ways of the data manufacturing process, they were often the statistical truths upon which to draw inferences. Optimists among them could therefore extract from the statistics a process of slow but steady improvement from 1950 to 1982 (table 2.1). Labor force, or what I prefer to call market participation, rates, declined slightly. According to the census, the drop resulted principally from an increase in primary and secondary school enrollment. A fall in participation and a rise in schooling rates, if the experiences of other countries served as guides, meant that average real income might have risen in the intervening decade. Such a rise, no matter how small, was good.

And the unemployment rate in 1982, unless it represented a statistical quirk associated with change in methods of classification, was far below the figure for 1971. A city with well over a third of its labor force out of work was hardly cause for satisfaction, but it was better than the situation in 1971 when half the workers could not find jobs.

More promising still was the noticeable change in the sectoral composition of employment among those who were indeed working. The share of self–employment, often an indicator of the extent of "traditional" economic activity in an economy, had fallen. At the same time, the rising proportion of manufacturing jobs seemed a positive sign of movement toward industrialization and "modernization," all the more so given the

TABLE 2.1
Employment and Unemployment in Port-au-Prince, 1950-82
(in %)

	1950	1971	1982
Market (labor force) participation rate[a]	n.a.	65	62
Unemployment rate[b]	n.a.	49	36
Share of employed in: self-employment	n.a.	35	31
wage employment	n.a.	65	69
Share of employed in: manufacturing	15	19	24
trade[c]	18	20	23
services[d]	47	46	33
other[e]	20	16	20
Share of self-employed in: manufacturing	n.a.	n.a.	27
trade	n.a.	n.a.	69
services	n.a.	n.a.	11
other	n.a.	n.a.	28
Number of individuals in labor force (thousands)	66.5	228.2	315.3

Sources: IHSI (1982, 1984), IHS (1975), and author's estimates from 1950 census.

[a] Proportion of the total population fourteen years or older at work or actively looking for work.

[b] Proportion of market participants actively looking for work.

[c] Wholesale and retail trade, restaurants and hotels. For 1950 the category also includes finance, insurance, and real estate.

[d] Public administration, social and personal services.

[e] Agriculture, quarrying, utilities, construction, public works, transportation, storage, communications, finance, insurance, real estate, and sectors not elsewhere classified.

small share of self–employment supposedly in the sector in 1982. Writ large, over a period of thirty years urban employment shifted from a service base largely dependent on public expenditure to a manufacturing base. Some observers went so far as to suggest that Haiti was perhaps becoming the Taiwan of the Caribbean (Preeg, 1984).

Unfortunately, without data on earnings there was really no basis for deciding whether changes in the characteristics of employment warranted positive interpretation. A simultaneous rise in school enrollment and a lowering in market participation rates was doubtless a good thing, but some of the increase in enrollment could have had more to do with earning immediate income than with spending it (see chapter 6). Perhaps participation rates fell because earnings fell, if not average earnings of all workers, then possibly those of a substantial segment of the working population.

There was also the matter of unemployment. If this category contained individuals who were actually jobless, the drop in the unemployment rate might represent an improvement. But if it contained workers who said they were looking for jobs even though they were already fully occupied in earning income, the drop meant nothing. Similarly, the proportional shift from self–employment to wage employment, or the shift from services to manufacturing and trade, also meant nothing in the absence of data to suggest that the changes were accompanied by movements from lower to higher earnings. In effect, census data contained very little information.

In an effort to produce some information that might shed more light on how workers made their living, and that might also suggest an appropriate method of interpreting census data, or indicate whether such data even warranted the time and effort required for interpretation, I undertook a household survey in early 1976. It covered eighty–eight households containing 464 people and 198 workers in a downtown neighborhood called St. Martin (see figure 2.1). Although too narrowly defined in space and too small for purposes of statistical generalization to the whole of the urban population, the neighborhood was typical of several in the downtown area that together housed 300,000 people, or about half the estimated urban population, and the heterogeneity of income in the neighborhood, from quite low to quite high, suggested that the data could at least provide a sense of economic circumstances across a broad spectrum of the city's populace.

I began the survey a year after first arriving in the city, and after having completed several hundred interviews to gather information about a variety of subjects, including housing rents, water consumption, characteristics of human waste disposal facilities, travel patterns, and other matters of interest to a United Nations Center for Housing, Building and Planning (UNCHBP)—now the United Nations Center for Human Settlements

FIGURE 2.1
Map of Central Port-au-Prince

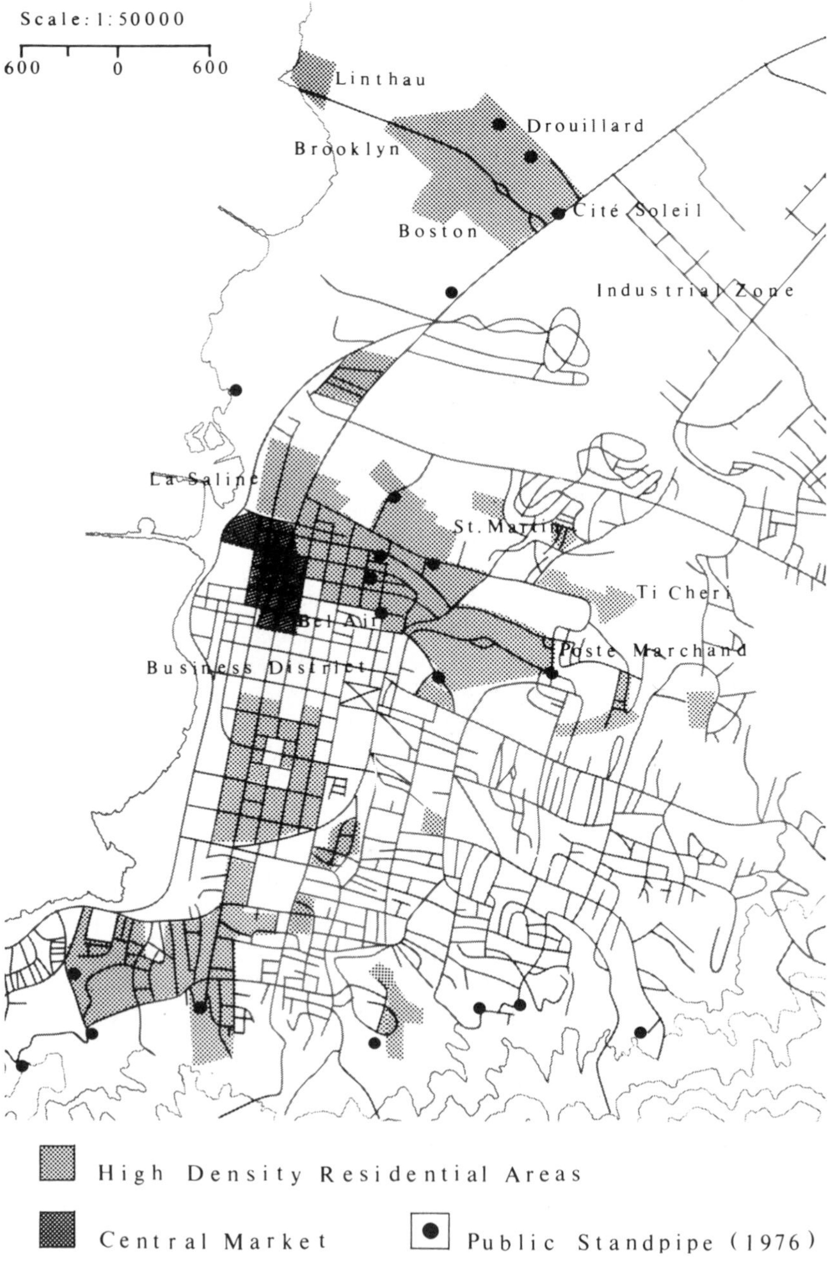

(UNCHS)—technical assistance project with which I was associated. That experience was important. Having visited and spent time in every neighborhood, I believed that I had developed a good sense of how St. Martin fit into the overall scheme of things. With an average family income of U.S.$42 per month, for example, the neighborhood was middle income by Port-au-Prince standards. No matter how destitute the poorest households in St. Martin might appear, by virtue of having the capacity to live in the neighborhood, they were considerably better off than the 80,000–100,000 people living on the periphery of the city or on the streets. Similarly, the wealthiest in St. Martin, though far from being the wealthiest in the city, seemed representative of the very basic middle class which I described in the previous chapter.

A more important aspect of the first year's experience was that it provided ample time to sort, select, and pretest concepts (as distinct from questionnaires) that might shape the data production effort. In the process, my early notions of conducting an employment and earnings survey, or an informal sector survey, fell by the wayside. The employment–unemployment distinction, even including an underemployment category, was at best ambiguous. Useful as they were for certain types of analysis, the categories made little sense when transformed into direct questions like: Did you work yesterday? or, How much did you earn yesterday? Similarly, an informal sector approach made little sense when the unit of analysis was not self-evident. Should the units be visually obvious "enterprises," or less obvious activities within homes? Should they be individuals or households?

In the event, I chose as a guiding concept the manufacturing process, and with this metaphor designed the questionnaire to provide data that could answer three basic questions: By what means do households and their members produce income? How much do they produce? Why are income results as they are? The resulting data, for lack of a better way to describe them, were "powerful." This is not to say that they were accurate. There is no ready way to assess accuracy without comparable data from other sources. Rather, they were powerful in their capacity to provide a basis for several conceptual ascriptions, including unemployment and informality, and for examining relationships that might otherwise pass by unnoticed, such as the process by which sending children to school served to increase income, and the process by which food consumption seemed to influence earnings, matters I will take up in later chapters.

But perhaps the most important effect of the first year's experience was evolution of the firm conviction that I had to conduct each interview myself. To be sure, there were excellent and reliable enumerators about who were quite able to conduct the "fieldwork." However, having not yet conducted the survey, I could not predict what the field would present in terms of types of worker activities, and even after extensive pretesting, remained uncertain about what questions would prove more fruitful than others. That is to say, I did not yet know what I was looking for. The enumerators could count, but I could not tell them what to count. To find out, I had to "be there."

Being there created two additional sources of power. The first, a technical matter, was knowing with precision the source of each recorded datum and therefore the range of meanings that could be imputed to it. The second, a conceptual matter of fundamental significance to me, was the capacity to view respondents and what they did as normal people conducting normal activities in what to them were normal conditions. There was nothing inherently special about them. And if there was nothing special about them, it was quite possible that abnormality, if there was a compelling need to ascribe it, might readily attach itself to people, activities, and conditions within the political class.

Employment

Economic circumstances in St. Martin seemed to demand that all or most of the able-bodied contribute productively to household welfare by participating in market activities as wage employees or as self-employed workers. Market participation rates, 88 percent for men fourteen years of age or older and 67 percent for women, were both higher than indicated by the census. A more significant difference was that unemployment seemed to be much lower. It was not as if workers in St. Martin lacked scope for working more hours per day or days per month. But because so many of them were self-employed, the practical meaning of the concept of unemployment became uncertain.

For example, if a self-employed worker earned nothing during a particular period, he or she was not necessarily unemployed. The worker could be fully preoccupied buying stocks, transforming raw materials, or marketing goods or services. Also, apparent idleness could sometimes mean that a worker was awaiting a custom production order, a request for consulting services, or a short-term job contract. A worker might have idle capacity from time to time, or go for lengthy periods without consummating a sale, but as is the case with farmers, the concept of unemployment could not easily apply to them while they were still "in business." The concept applied more readily to those who were no longer in business for themselves, or who did not have wage-paying jobs. But then there was the considerable difficulty of determining whether or not they were actually still in business.

If on the street, were they looking for a job, or were they simply marketing their goods and services?

Using "idleness" as a criterion, the data suggested a 30 percent one–day unemployment rate, a scale consistent with census data. About 56 percent of these apparently unemployed reported that they were not working because they did not have jobs, clients, or contracts in hand. On closer examination, only about one–third of this group seemed to be looking for wage–paying jobs. The rest were awaiting new orders, and dropping them from the unemployment category lowered the rate to 19 percent.

Over half of this remaining 19 percent, mostly women, reported not working because they were ill, breast–feeding newborns, or tending to the needs of sick children. All of them said that they had work that they would resume upon returning to health or after completing their nursing obligations. Their removal from the ranks of the unemployed lowered the rate to 9 percent. (Alternatively, dropping them from the market or labor force participation category yielded a rate of 10 percent.) The one–day unemployment rate was anywhere between 9 and 30 percent, depending on the criterion adopted for classification purposes.

But one day of idleness was not useful for estimating unemployment. After extending the period to cover the previous week, the initial estimate of 30 percent fell to 22 percent, and the adjusted estimate dropped from 9 to 6 percent. Over a four–week reference period, the respective rates were 20 and 4 percent.

Modification of the definition of unemployment to refer to the share of workers working less than full time yielded no better results. With twenty–two days per month as an arbitrary standard for full employment, data suggested that 26 percent of workers had been regularly unemployed during the previous month. This statistic might have had intelligible meaning for casual laborers, but did not provide much insight in cases in which the cyclical nature of a business interspersed idleness with periods of intense activity. Many of the self–employed in St. Martin worked only a few days each month, but their earnings during those days were often more than adequate to finance intermittent idleness.

None of this implied that the concept of unemployment was inapplicable. Although involving an ambiguous procedure, where there was a will to classify workers into one conceptual category or another, the data provided a way. The more important difficulty lay not in the concept, but in its implications. The problem of unemployment had meaning in the case of workers who could afford not to work for shorter or longer periods of time, and who could afford not to be particularly productive when they worked. St. Martin had enough of them so that, with proper enunciation of criteria, talk of unemployment remained intelligible. However, the concept held no obvious meaning for workers who by force of circumstance had to work all the time and who had to be productive all the time. Attaching the category of unemployment to such workers for lack of appropriate kinds of data to classify them otherwise, as the census seemed to do, could be misleading. It specified a problem that was perhaps not a major problem for most workers. A more pertinent issue was earnings.

Earnings

With the premise that all individuals were self–employed producers of services or goods, an assumption that circumvented several difficulties of conceptual application imposed by conventional labor market theories that made distinctions between wage employment and self–employment, workers could fall into three distinct categories allowing a convenient basis for exploring the issue of earnings.[1] The first category, containing 43 percent of the total, were people who combined time and skill to produce and sell a commodity called "labor" in the market.[2] They were "laborers."

The second category, with 26 percent of all workers, were "traders." They combined time and skill to produce labor, and then joined labor with working capital to buy goods in one location and sell them in another without changing the characteristics of the goods in the process. The remaining 31 percent of workers were "manufacturers." They differed from traders in only one respect. The goods underwent transformation before sale.[3] Conceptually, all these workers were "firms." Earnings, no matter whether payment took the form of regular or irregular wages, salaries, or transaction margins, constituted "sales" by each enterprise.[4]

Laborers

Laborers spread themselves across all principal sectors of the urban economy, and across thirty–six distinct occupations (table 2.2). Making allowance for differences in cultural meanings that, for example, might require reconstitution of herbal doctors as chiropractors, the list of occupations was much the same as one might find in any city.

Daily earnings ranged from a low of $0.15 to a high of $9.50, averaging $1.70, or substantially more than the minimum legal wage of $1.30 in effect in early 1976. Monthly earnings varied between $1.70 and $76.00, with the average of $25.40 coming out below the $28.60 that regular receipt of the minimum wage might have provided over twenty–two working days of a month. About 64 percent of workers received less than the equivalent of the monthly minimum wage.

Although useful for comparative purposes, the minimum wage was not a particularly meaningful standard of reference. A worker in St. Martin was minimally productive with respect to his or her household if he or she earned at least enough to cover the costs of food required to generate the earnings.[5] Assuming that a full and active day of work required roughly 1500 calories and 30 grams of protein, a matter explored in detail in chapter 3, the minimum cost of manufacturing a day of labor was $0.16, or $4.80 per month. Anyone earning less operated in deficit, and was either being subsidized by other household earners, or else was consuming less than 1500 calories and 30 grams of protein.

At around $0.10 per day, or the region of 800 to 900 calories, earnings would be so far below the amount required to produce it that survival and household welfare might be best served by having an individual not work.[6] Casually looking around for a job paying more than ten cents required less food energy output than actually earning it in a labor–intensive (i.e., energy– or calorie–) job. That is perhaps why there were no instances of people earning less than $0.10 a day, why any opportunity to earn $0.15 or more was attractive, and why unemployment, notwithstanding difficulties in defining it, was rare. In any event, using the monthly standard of $4.80, some 9 percent of laborers were operating in deficit at the time of the survey. They were not as productive as they or their households might have preferred, but as long as each day of work yielded at least $0.15, something was better than nothing.

A search for some nonconventional classification scheme that might explain differences in earnings between workers yielded little of interest. In one exercise I tried to reintroduce abstractions from labor market theory in order to compare the self–employed with wage employees. This exercise produced nothing consequential because one group could have significantly higher or lower earnings than the other depending on where I placed each worker. The classification process was not at all clear. A porter, for example, worked in a supermarket carrying packages from the checkout stand to automobiles outside. The store owner granted him the right to provide the service, but paid him nothing. He was nevertheless obliged to carry all packages, and since this was a normal store service, customers did not have to pay him either. Enough of them understood the system so that he earned a fair living. Similarly, gratuities were the exclusive source of income for the waitress, and sales commissions for the salesman of applicances. Were these self–employed or wage employees?

A second exercise involved a "modern–traditional" dichotomy. This approach also bore little explanatory fruit, for two reasons. First, the pattern of "traditional" employment practices in "modern" supermarkets, restaurants, and appliance stores extended into factories and the government as well. Machine operators working inside factories did fine, but the

TABLE 2.2
Occupations and Earnings of Laborers in St. Martin, 1976

Sector	Occupation	Number of Individuals[a]	Daily Earnings (U.S. $)	Days of Work per Month	Monthly Earnings (U.S. $)
Transp. & Util.:	Ship's captain	1	3.50	20	70.00
	Taxi drivers	2	3.10	22	56.00
	Drainage system cleaners	2	1.05	24	25.00
	Ship's crewman	1	1.00	20	20.00
	Subtotal (average)	6	(2.10)	(22)	(42.00)
Construction:	Carpenters	2	7.00	14	76.00
	Painters	3	2.50	15	43.00
	Masons	4	2.10	7	12.20
	Subtotal (average)	9	(3.30)	(11)	(36.45)
Trade:	Salesman	1	2.50	26	65.00
	Waitress	1	1.40	30	42.00
	Porter	1	1.00	26	26.00
	Lottery ticket vendors	2	1.40	15	21.00
	Subtotal (average)	5	(1.55)	(22)	(35.00)
Manufacturing:	Leather polisher (in factory)	1	2.00	22	44.00
	Machine operators (in factory)	4	1.65	25	40.30
	Baker	1	1.30	26	34.00
	Coffee bean washers (in factory)	3	1.10	24	26.60
	Knitter (on put out system)	1	0.90	22	20.00
	Embroiders (on put out system)	3	0.85	23	18.80
	Furniture makers	2	1.50	12	18.00
	Butcher	1	0.40	30	12.00
	Sculptor (on put out system)	1	0.50	11	5.50

	Bead collar makers (on put out system)	2	0.15	30	4.50
	Subtotal (average)	19	(1.10)	(23)	(24.15)
Services:	Fire fighter (gov't. worker)	1	2.30	26	60.00
	Dental technician	1	2.70	22	59.00
	Clerks (gov't. workers)	2	2.40	23	50.50
	Customs broker	1	3.30	15	48.00
	Priest	1	9.50	5	48.00
	Prostitute	1	3.00	15	45.00
	Shoe Repairer	1	1.20	27	32.00
	Musicians	2	3.50	12	31.00
	Gambler	1	1.10	26	29.00
	Electrical repair	1	2.50	12	29.00
	Building cleaners (gov't. workers)	6	0.60	24	14.80
	Herbal doctors	2	2.45	6	14.50
	Mechanic	2	3.10	5	11.00
	Domestic servants	11	0.30	20	5.50
	Launderer	1	0.30	10	3.00
	Day workers	4	1.00	2	1.70
	Subtotal (average)	38	(1.60)	(16)	(19.15)
	TOTAL (average)	77[b]	(1.70)	(18)	(25.25)

Source: Data from author's survey in St. Martin.

[a] In occupations containing more than one individual, earnings and days of work are averages for the group.

[b] Nine of the eighty-six laborers interviewed did not provide sufficient information for purposes of this table.

knitter, embroiderers, and bead collar assemblers who picked up materials from the factories and worked at home, therefore ineligible for coverage by minimum–wage legislation, earned less. The sculptor worked on the doorstep of a workshop with tools and materials provided by the firm. Being "outside," he qualified for $0.50 rather than the $1.30 that a shift of one meter would have required. A drainage system cleaner on the payroll of the Department of Public Works earned more than the minimum wage. Another on contract to the department earned much less. What was "modern" and what was "traditional"?

Second, certain traditional activities like prostitution, the priesthood, construction carpentry, and house painting paid more than modern activities like factory work. As far as laborers were concerned, the modern–traditional dichotomy did not help explain differences in earnings.

What seemed to explain differences better was what explained differences in most urban labor markets shaped by competition: skill. Defining skill as those attributes of a worker which are marketable (as distinct from skills associated with training or experience creating attributes for which there may be no demand), most workers in table 2.2 who earned substantially more than the minimum monthly wage sold skills that were in relatively short supply. Running a boat, driving a car, building or painting a house, reading and writing French and Creole to sell appliances or serve food, having enough primary schooling to apply for factory jobs, having a trade like baking, and all the various specialized bits of acquired knowledge essential to render the services from fire fighting to electrical repair were in short supply in Port–au–Prince.

But a better explanation was not a complete explanation. Often there was no particular reason why one worker should be "inside" and another "outside" a factory. Luck of birth or marriage into a "connected" family could move a person inside a factory, store, or government position. So could a bribe, and the Macoutes in St. Martin were often well connected in the job market. They, and others, sometimes earned sizable commissions from their sidelines as job placement agents. The drainage cleaner had paid $50 to get the Public Works contract, the waitress about $30, one machine operator $100, the knitter $40, and two building cleaners $20 each. There being no other employment agencies in the city serving populations like that, the service was well regarded. Not so the politics attached to it. A job given by a Macoute was a job that could be taken away. A worker with a good job, in order to retain the job, did not cause trouble. Nor did anyone in the process of saving up money to approach a Macoute for help in placement.

Workers without easily marketable attributes, their own connections, or good luck needed the Macoutes and other agents because the alternatives, independent trade and manufacturing, offered few prospects for substantially higher earnings.

Traders

Traders engaged in buying and selling almost as many different goods and combinations of goods as there were individuals to deal in them. This was a fiercely competitive occupation that demanded that each individual carve out a specific commodity and locational niche in the market, protect it, and ideally, use it as a basis for gradually expanding into larger scales of operation. Traders, therefore, did not often modify the composition of their commodity sets nor their places or routes of sale. Change involved considerable risk because an individual with experience in the marketing dynamics of one set of goods at one location might have to begin as a novice with respect to selling another set or the same set at another location. In this respect trade was a relatively rigid form of enterprise. All the traders in table 2.3 had not made any substantial changes to what they sold or where they sold during the previous year. This also meant that trade was highly sensitive to environmental factors like changes in the relative prices of goods and forced displacement from one location to another.

With traders filling every conceivable corner of a marketplace that had characteristics approaching perfect competition, entry into the occupation was quite difficult.[7] Although observers sometimes claimed that trade had the attribute of ease of entry, they rarely defined what they meant by ease or by entry (Lundahl, 1979: 158). Certainly there was little to stop an individual with funds from buying some goods and then setting up shop somewhere, but not everyone was in a position to accumulate savings of even one dollar for this kind of investment, let alone the larger amount that most required to generate reasonable earnings from it (table 2.4). A dollar in trade was a dollar not used to obtain other requirements like food, water, and shelter. Even with the possibility of making an initial investment, there was the matter of withstanding competition. Having set up a stock of goods, inexperience or other factors contributing to lack of marketing expertise could easily result in failure of the enterprise within a matter of days or weeks. Most of the domestic servants cited in table 2.2 had in fact tried and failed to make a go of trade during the previous two years. Entry into trade may have been easier than entry into certain other occupations, but it was not easy to remain there. In fact, were it not for the difficulty of entry and subsequent survival, trade could not yield profits.

The monthly profits or earnings of traders in St. Martin averaged $22.40, less than what the minimum wage might have paid over the course of a month. Three large-scale traders of poles, charcoal, and bananas

TABLE 2.3
Goods Sold and Earnings of Traders in St. Martin, 1976

	Number of Individuals[a]	Daily Earnings (U.S. $)	Monthly Earnings (U.S. $)[b]
Construction poles	1	5.80	151.00
Charcoal	1	2.80	74.00
Bananas	1	2.70	69.00
Grain	1	1.40	37.00
Underwear	1	1.40	37.00
Fish	2	1.30	34.00
Miscellaneous goods	1	1.00	30.00
Soap, face powder, linen	1	1.10	29.00
Grain	1	1.00	26.00
Tobacco	1	0.90	23.00
Bananas, potatoes, yams	1	0.90	23.00
Cooking oil	1	0.90	23.00
Detergent	1	0.80	21.00
Sugar cane, misc. goods	2	0.70	21.00
Sugar	1	0.70	18.00
Biscuits, prepared tea	1	0.60	17.00
Sugar, cooking oil	1	0.70	17.00
Grain	1	0.60	16.00
Cloth	1	0.60	16.00
Grain, charcoal	1	0.50	15.00
Miscellaneous goods	1	0.50	15.00
Handkerchiefs	2	0.50	14.00
Underwear	1	0.50	13.00
Cigarettes, candies	1	0.50	13.00
Dishes, glassware	1	0.40	10.00
Miscellaneous goods	1	0.40	10.00
Eggs	1	0.30	9.00
Sugar, biscuits, prepared coffee	1	0.30	9.00
Sugar, biscuits	1	0.30	8.00
Tablecloths	1	0.30	8.00
Soap, kitchen utensils	1	0.30	7.00
Sugar, butter, rum	1	0.30	6.00
Biscuits	1	0.20	6.00
Miscellaneous goods	2	0.20	6.00
Detergent	1	0.20	5.00
Underwear	1	0.20	4.00
Miscellaneous goods	1	0.10	3.00
TOTAL (average)	41[c]	(0.85)	(22.40)

Source: Data from author's survey in St. Martin.

[a] A number greater than one indicates two or more individuals working together and dividing earnings equally between them. Earnings figures in these cases are for each individual.

[b] Monthly and daily earnings do not correspond with each other exactly because of differences between individuals in numbers of days worked each month.

[c] Ten of the fifty-one traders interviewed did not provide sufficient information for purposes of this table.

TABLE 2.4
Distribution of Capital Among Traders and Manufacturers in St. Martin, 1976

Value of Capital[a] (U.S. $)	Traders (%)	Manufacturers (%)
(Number of individuals)	(45)	(58)
Less than 1.00	8	2
1.00– 6.00	27	29
6.01–10.00	21	17
10.01–20.00	19	18
20.01–30.00	8	7
30.01–40.00	9	11
40.01–50.00	4	3
50.01 or more	4	13
TOTAL	100	100

Source: Data from author's survey in St. Martin.
[a] Sum of fixed and working capital, including cash on hand, market value of stocks, raw materials and products in inventory, and replacement value of tools and peripherals (e.g., baskets and boxes).

pushed the average upwards considerably. Without them, it fell to $16.50, and the corresponding daily rate dropped from $0.85 to $0.60. Over three–quarters of traders earned less than the monthly minimum wage. Most, however, were able to earn enough to cover their caloric input costs of $4.80 per month. Only 5 percent seemed to be working at an individual deficit level.

Trade was not a bad way to make a living for those with the expertise required to generate profits, but it contained many occupational hazards. Besides relative price changes and dislocation that occurred from time to time, traders risked losing their capital through theft, rodents, flooding, fire, childbirth, and illness. Theft was usually a negligible factor in St. Martin, though pilfering was not uncommon in city markets and streets where traders had to keep a very watchful eye on their goods. But now and then one or more Macoutes might find themselves low on funds, and then, for payment, authorize a period of stealing in the neighborhood. The period was usually short because if the Macoutes in question did not appear to be doing something about the problem, their base of local support, such as it was, would quickly erode. Residents did not take long to call upon other Macoutes for help, or if this brought no solution, the police. In the few days of such burglary holidays, all houses with flimsy locks on windows and doors, or with low internal partitions allowing someone to climb from one dwelling into another within the same structure, were targets of opportunity.

The rodent problem was more permanent. Rats and mice could get through any crevice in a dwelling wall and thereafter consume or soil household goods or trade stocks. Rodent control programs were haphazard, and since cats were a delicacy, the neighborhood was sometimes invaded by rodents and considerable amounts of stock would disappear or lose its market value.

Seasonal flooding was more or less severe, depending on how much garbage had accumulated in drainage channels (see figure 5.7). If there was a lot, it created dams and the water would back up into houses bordering them, and at such moments a hard rain could bring torrents from upstream which, having no cleared channels to follow, flowed through the pedestrian pathways of the neighborhood, knocking down houses along the way. At least once a year substantial quantities of goods flowed into the sea, or became too damaged for sale.

Fire had not consumed stocks in St. Martin up to 1976, but fires in nearby areas destroyed several hundred homes between 1967 and 1976, and with them the stocks of several hundred traders (and manufacturers). The risk was therefore tangible.

The most common source of difficulty, however, was childbirth and illness. Most traders were women. A birth meant a brief period out of the market for nursing obligations, and illness of a trader, or that of a trader's immediate family, often had the same effect. If a household's resources were limited, the financing of inactivity, or medical bills, had to come out of accumulated working capital. The longer the period of inactivity, the lower the residual capital left to reenter trade. Women did not stay out of the market for very long after giving birth. The more serious issue was that even if a woman with an ailment wanted to resume trade after partially regaining health, her physical strength and mental alertness would not always be up to the level required to compete successfully. She might drop things, or make serious buying and selling errors.

The combined effect of these hazards was to keep the number of traders at work on any given day lower than it might have been otherwise, lowering competition and providing opportunity for profit and new entrants. At the time of my survey, 20 percent of traders in St. Martin were not working. Whether one might choose to call them unemployed or out of the labor market, the facts were that 30 percent of these women had lost their capital during the preceding six months through theft, flooding, bad transactions, and the need to pay medical bills; 30 percent were consuming some of their capital while attempting to recover from illness; and 40 percent were doing the same while breast–feeding or tending to the needs of sick children. A few might be able to resume trade where they had left off because husbands or other family members would recapitalize them for relatively less competitive areas of trade (e.g., fish, tobacco). Most would have to start all over again, and it would likely take them considerable time to reconstruct their former sales rates.

The basic obstacle faced by these women, or by any trader already in the market for that matter, was not usually capital. Credit was available (see chapter 7). It was also relatively inexpensive, costing 25 to 50 percent in monthly interest. A St. Martin trader worthy of the name produced a net earning of at least 5 percent of the value of her capital each day, and usually much more (figure 2.2).[8] Even if consumption needs extracted 60 to 80 percent of it, there would still be enough to repay interest and principal at the end of a month. The more pertinent obstacle for most reentrants who had been away from the market for a while, or for new entrants, was that they had lost their niches. Buyers established relationships with other sellers during their absence, and the location they vacated had another trader in it. Thus, a woman who previously used $10.00 in working capital to generate a turnover providing a daily earning of $0.70 could not expect the same turnover upon return. Even with $10.00 in hand she might turn over no more than one dollar to generate $0.10 to $0.30.

More generally, most women included in table 2.3 who earned less than $10.00 per month reported that they had resources available to expand their stocks slightly, but without a corresponding increase in turnover, they saw no reason to invest more. The buildup had to be gradual, with capital increasing more or less in step with their proficiency to increase the rate of sales. Few of the traders were able to absorb large infusions of capital because they were working at what one could call the limits of productive capacity shaped by immediate marketing skill.

Some workers, nevertheless, did seem on the verge of substantially increasing their scale of operation. A few were women who sold out their stock well before the end of the daily marketing period for their products and who believed that they could sell more in the remaining hours. They could not manage a larger stock by themselves, however, and were awaiting arrival of a family member to work with them before undertaking the expansion. The soup producer in Appendix A, though classified as a manufacturer, illustrates this kind of situation. Others, as implied earlier, were women who held comparative advantages in certain goods, like fish and tobacco, in which their direct connections to fishermen and tobacco growers in their extended families would help reestablish their market positions quickly. Still others were very talented traders who could, in fact, work productively with $5.00 or $10.00 immediately and who were already making $0.50 a day with $1.00 in capital. Their obstacle was (relative) poverty. They had nothing of sufficient market value to put up as collateral for credit.

FIGURE 2.2
Earnings-Capital Ratios for Trade and Manufacturing Activities in St. Martin, 1976

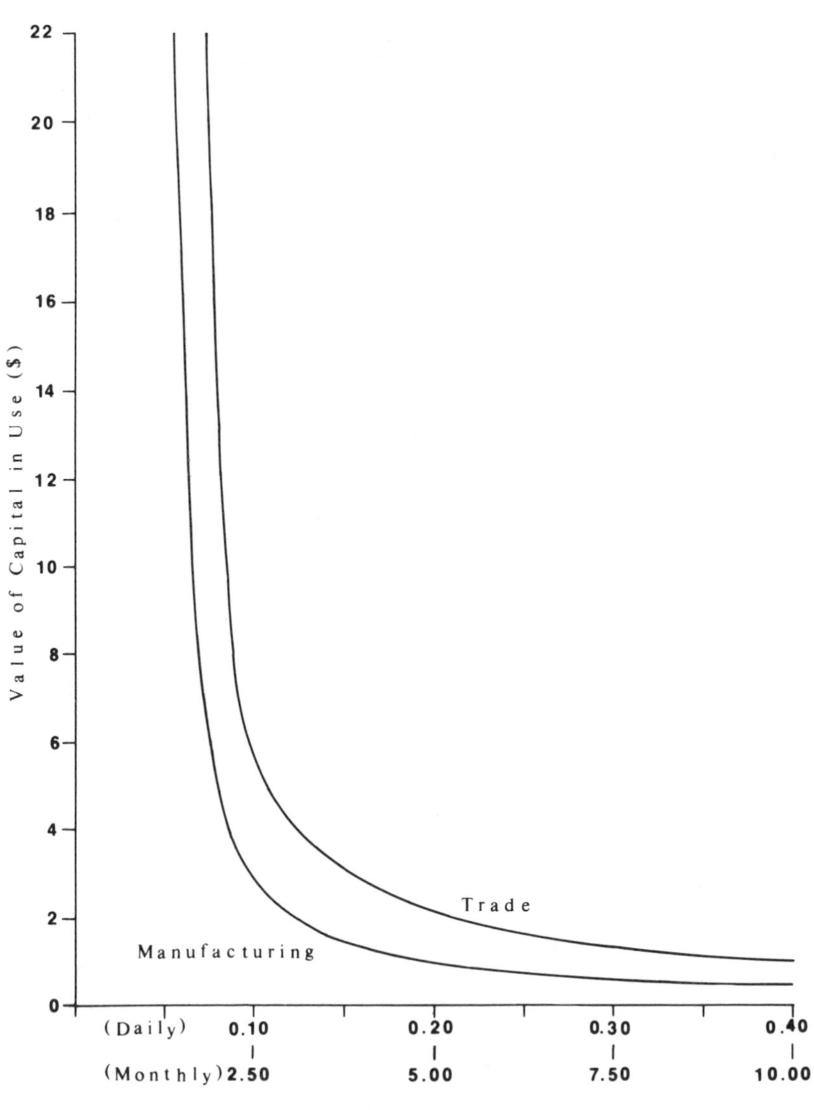

A secured loan of $10.00 costing 25 percent per month demanded $30.00 in collateral value. Without collateral, the loan might cost 50 percent, or repayment of $15.00 in principal and interest at the end of 30 days. Under these terms a trader had to set aside about $0.50 per day for eventual debt reimbursement. An exceptionally good trader might be able to extract a daily profit of $1.00 with $10.00 in stock, thus allowing $0.50 for basic consumption and $0.50 as the required amount for debt service (which the trader would set aside figuratively rather than literally because the opportunity cost of idle cash, as outlined in chapter 7, was high). Unfortunately, although most traders included in table 2.3 were very productive, few if any were sufficiently productive to borrow large amounts at 50 percent per month. Thus, as in most markets, talented people in trade, or wanting to enter trade, had first to demonstrate their talents by accumulating their own resources before seeking out loans. For women making $0.50 per day with $1.00 in capital, the process of accumulation could be short or long depending on the amount they could reinvest after meeting their own consumption needs and those of their dependents.

Overall, some 10 to 15 percent of the traders seemed to be candidates for capital additions, but well over half of them already had resources available for this purpose. Potential loan candidates represented less than 5 percent of all traders. For the rest, in the short run at least, skill and circumstance would dictate the course of business. For all, trade would remain a difficult enterprise to enter, and once entered, in which to survive.

Manufacturing

In manufacturing, consisting 60 percent of men and 40 percent of women, as for trade, there were as many different products and product combinations as there were individual producers (table 2.5). In fact, almost everything I have said with respect to traders seemed to apply as readily to manufacturers. The business was intensely competitive, demanding that each producer specialize and stay within a market niche for products. Skills and capital requirements were high (see table 2.4). Earnings were low, averaging $21.00 per month and $0.95 per day, resulting in over 80 percent of manufacturers earning less than the equivalent of a monthly minimum wage, and in 12 percent operating in deficit at a level below the $4.80 monthly calorie intake threshold. Risks attached to theft, rodents, flooding, fire, childbirth (for the women at least), and illness were also about the same as in trade, as were issues I have discussed with respect to capital and credit.[9] In fact, there seemed to be fewer candidates for capital additions among manufacturers than for traders. But there were some differences.

One difference was that capital was less of a barrier to entry, reentry, or

TABLE 2.5
Products Made and Earnings of Manufacturers in St. Martin, 1976

	Number of Individuals[a]	Daily Earnings (U.S. $)	Monthly Earnings (U.S. $)[b]
Coffins (wood)	1	3.80	100.00
Pants, shirts	1	5.00	78.00
Pants, vests	1	2.10	56.00
Purses (scrap leather)[c]	1	1.50	45.00
Decorations (wool)	1	1.40	42.00
Handbags (vinyl)	2	1.30	39.00
Shoes (wood)	1	1.30	39.00
Sculpture (wood)	1	2.50	37.00
Prepared soup (fish base)[c]	1	1.40	37.00
Baskets (banana leaf)[c]	1	1.40	33.00
Bead curtains[c]	2	1.50	33.00
Castings (lead)[c]	1	1.00	29.00
Sugar wrappers (paper)	1	1.10	28.00
Dresses	2	1.00	26.50
Handbags (coconut palm leaf, cardboard)	1	0.80	24.00
Prepared meat (raw and fried)	1	0.90	23.00
Buckets, stoves (scrap metal)	1	0.80	21.00
Shoes (wood)	1	0.70	21.00
Shirts	2	0.80	21.00
Handbag decorations (sisal)	2	3.50	18.00
Sculptures (wood)	1	0.70	18.00
Buckets (scrap metal)[c]	1	0.45	15.00
Handbags (sisal, palm bark)[c]	2	0.45	15.00
Prepared peanuts, coffee	1	0.50	15.00
Prepared meat and roots (fried)	1	0.60	15.00

Doormats (sisal)[c]	2	0.45	13.00
Shirts, vests	2	0.50	13.00
Prepared peanuts	1	0.50	13.00
Prepared meat and roots (fried)	2	0.40	11.00
Shirts, vests	1	0.50	11.00
Sugar wrappers (paper)	1	0.40	10.00
Bed frames (wood)	1	0.40	10.00
Furniture (wood)	2	0.60	9.00
Strainers (metal mesh)	2	0.30	9.00
Prepared peanuts[c]	1	0.30	8.00
Prepared soup (corn base)	1	0.25	7.00
Prepared bananas and roots (fried)	1	0.30	7.00
Sugar wrappers (paper)	1	0.40	6.00
Dresses	1	2.00	4.50
Carpets—oval (sisal)[c]	2	0.15	4.00
Spoons and forks (wood)	3	0.15	4.00
Paper bags (scrap cement bags)	1	0.10	3.00
TOTAL (average)	56[d]	(0.95)	(21.00)

Source: Data from author's survey in St. Martin.

[a] A number greater than one indicates two or more individuals working together and dividing earnings equally between them. Earnings figures in these cases are for each individual.

[b] See Note b, table 2.3.

[c] See Appendix A for a detailed description of this activity.

[d] Five of the sixty-one manufacturers interviewed did not provide sufficient information for purposes of this table.

expansion in manufacturing than in trade. Many producers worked on custom orders, and the down payments for such orders were usually adequate to cover initial production needs. At the same time, men could usually count on their wives or other women in the household to help them out financially. The willingness of women to invest in men's activities may have resulted in part from power relations within households, but there was evidence to suggest that earnings from investments of $15 or more in manufacturing were higher on average than similar amounts invested in trade.[10] On the margin, household incomes could rise appreciably by shifting some resources from trade to manufacturing, or more generally in the case of women who were laborers, from their own savings or consumption into manufacturing by someone else in the household.

The financial basis for shifting of resources was also apparent in the way men capitalized women. Few women in trade received support from their husbands, while most women in manufacturing got started that way. So, of the 13 percent of manufacturers who seemed idle, none were idle for lack of capital. Half were awaiting new orders. The other half were sick, expecting to resume activity within a few weeks.

Another difference was that although manufacturers did not like to change product lines, relative price changes for raw materials, and competition from imports, import–substituting factories as well as new entrants often forced many of them to do so. They were compelled by circumstance to periodically abandon their market niches, to search for new product lines, to find out how to produce such lines, to acquire the material wherewithal to begin production, and to reconstruct their positions in the marketplace. Like traders, they had to keep abreast of latest marketing information, but unlike traders, they also had to struggle to get useful information about sellable products that did not yet exist in the market, about manufacturing techniques for known or unknown products, about tools and raw materials, and about new clientele. To survive, a manufacturer needed to know as much about marketing as a trader, and more besides.

What seemed to make manufacturing particularly troublesome was difficulty in obtaining essential production information. Part of the difficulty was that some of this information was simply hard to come by in Haiti, some did not exist in Haiti, and some did not exist at all. A second part was that manufacturers could not tell in advance whether or not they would be able to find the data. The final part of the difficulty was that they had little time for industrial intelligence work. Time devoted to searching was time taken out of production and marketing. It cost earnings to get data, and the more elusive the data, the higher the potential opportunity cost. Most manufacturers did not spend a great deal of time on research and development.

Thus an important difference between traders and manufacturers in St. Martin was that almost all of the former were more or less secure in their niches. Some were moving ahead slightly, some declining, and all were exposed to risk. But short of some disaster, they could count on their earnings streams. Some of the manufacturers were in similar positions. At the same time there were many in declining industries who knew that their futures were not good unless they shifted out, but who did not have the means to do so. Others, often new entrants with new products and techniques, were expanding rapidly. A few of these last were candidates for capital additions. They had definite markets purchasing all they could produce, and knew exactly what tools and materials they needed to increase output while lowering production costs. The only ingredient missing was capital, and it seemed a question of only little time before such producers would make the required investment. For most, however, as several of the ten detailed case histories in Appendix A underscore, making a living in manufacturing was a sufficiently complicated challenge that additional capital respresented one of the least important factors to worry about. Expertise and luck appeared more crucial.

Productivity

A World Bank estimate of the distribution of labor earnings among employed urban workers in 1976, (i.e., excluding the officially unemployed who presumably comprised a substantial share of actually employed workers in St. Martin) indicated that 26 percent of them earned less than $20 per month, 12 percent between $20 and $40, and the remaining 62 percent more than $40 (World Bank, 1979: 161). The corresponding figures in St. Martin were 55, 30, and 15 percent (table 2.6). The two distributions were not comparable but they nevertheless agreed that a lot of workers obtained low earnings.

But in a zero to $40 range, the difference between making relatively more or relatively less was important. Some 72 percent of St. Martin workers earned less than the monthly minimum-wage equivalent, and perhaps 10 percent earned less than required to purchase an average of 1500 calories and 30 grams of protein each day of the month. In the greater scheme of things, the minimum-wage reference may have been less important to workers than the food intake line. The former was an arbitrary standard; the latter was closer to an absolute standard for estimating productivity.

TABLE 2.6
Distribution of Daily and Monthly Earnings of All Workers in St. Martin, 1976

Average Daily Earnings (U.S. $)	Share of Workers (%)	Average Monthly Earnings (U.S. $)	Share of Workers (%)
(Number of workers)	(174)		(174)
.10– .30	18	less than 6.00	13
.31– .50	16	6.01–11.00	17
.51– .70	12	11.01–16.00	18
.71– .90	9	16.01–20.00	7
.91–1.10	7	20.01–25.00	12
1.11–1.30	12	25.01–30.00	9
1.31–1.50	5	30.01–40.00	9
1.51 or more	21	40.01 or more	15
TOTAL	100	TOTAL	100

Source: Data from author's survey in St. Martin.

If the meaning of productivity is profitability, if the measure of profitability is the difference between an amount of earnings and the cost of producing it, and if in a calorie–intensive economy one assumes that the major factor of production on any given day is the recurrent cost of food, then most of the work done by people in St. Martin and in the city was profitable and productive.

In the case of traders and manufacturers who joined meager amounts of capital and considerable labor to yield net daily earnings of not less than 4 percent of the value of capital engaged (after deducting food costs), profitability seemed quite substantial.[11] Most of them were illiterate or marginally educated and inexperienced outside their particular domains of trade and manufacturing. As laborers, women in trade could not expect to fare much better than their counterparts in domestic service, and men not much better than day laborers without the luck of making a connection. Taking capital out of trade or manufacturing to buy a connection to put–out work or building cleaning, the kinds of jobs they could purchase with limited funds and little formal education, held promise only at considerable risk. Once invested in purchase of a job, capital was gone for a certain while, and so also the assurance of an earnings stream if the individual lost his or her job. For principal breadwinners with dependents to support, such risks were high. Making allowance for such risks, the profitability of trade or manufacturing seemed substantial relative to available alternatives.

Indeed, profitability or productivity in the market, here meaning not only in the particular work of the moment but also in the wider spectrum of things to be done to move from one kind of work to another, like investing in a connection or accommodating the political prerequisites of a Macoute, was essential to the production of survival. And profitability was hard in a place where the meaning of high market participation rates and low unemployment rates, or looked at another way, where the circumstances of a society cause it to produce an almost unlimited supply of people able to create their own jobs, was intense competition. Yet most workers succeeded, perhaps because the political economy of survival in the market demanded that they do so.

Almost all workers in the lowest earnings categories of table 2.6 were not survivors. Members of this 10 to 15 percent of the work force lived in households that had sufficient resources to sustain them, or received support from other households. They could afford to be nonproductive or, in the language of another theory for examining labor markets, to be "underemployed." [12] Conversely, workers with higher earnings, sometimes substantially higher than the minimum wage, were often desperately poor because they supported relatively large numbers of nonworking members. They could not afford to be less productive or underemployed. The prerequisites of survival may not have caused workers to be productive in a deterministic sense, but they certainly caused what seemed to be a constant search for ways and means to maintain profitability, or to increase it.

Income

Separate from its calculation of the distribution of earnings among employed workers, a distribution in which the 5 percent of workers with highest earnings received 14 percent of total labor income, the same pattern as in St. Martin, the World Bank also made an estimate of the distribution of total income (i.e., earnings plus revenues from all other sources) across the working population. The estimate suggested that only the 5 percent earning $250 per month or more received additional income, and that, as a result, these workers obtained 75 percent of total urban income (World Bank, 1976: 27). In order of priority, sources for this concentration of wealth were: 30 percent from commercial and financial intermediation; 30 percent from rents; 25 percent from manufacturing profits in large-scale industry; and 15 percent from construction, transportation, tourism, and the liberal professions (World Bank, 1978a: 62). Hidden away within this list was graft, what one might label as political intermediation or taxation. The list was an invention, but it served the purpose of drawing attention to the extraordinary concentration of material, human, and political capital in the hands of a very small number of people, and also of overriding a statement in an earlier Bank report to the effect that inequality in the distribution of income was much less glaring than in other countries (i.e., World Bank, 1976a).

Evidence from St. Martin tended to substantiate the Bank's claim that workers with high earnings also obtained substantial amounts of other income, but it also showed that the flow of different categories of nonlabor income was a complex process of receipt and disbursement that had a major impact on the standard of living of most households.

One important category of nonlabor income, rent, flowed to men in 15 percent of families. Two–thirds of these men were among the higher earners in the sample, receiving an average of $16 per month that added 20 percent to the income of their households. They were mostly Macoutes of varying degrees of importance, and since discussion of earnings from their various sidelines as job placement agents, protection racketeers, water monopolists (see chapter 4), or school admission brokers (see chapter 6) was constrained during my interviews, their earnings may have been higher than what they reported, perhaps close to or above the $250 per month figure guessed at by the Bank. They may have also understated their rental income.

The rest of the men with rental income had average or below–average earnings. Inheritances and other windfalls provided them with means to purchase and develop property, and rents accounted for a third of household income.

A second important category was private transfers. Women in 8 percent of households received an average of $18 per month from the fathers of their children. Slightly less than half of these women did not work, and the transfers constituted the whole of their income. For the others that did work, the payments represented 20 to 50 percent of income. Individuals in another 6 percent of households received money and/or gifts sent by relatives from elsewhere in the city, from the countryside, and from abroad. The value of these transfers was about $7 per recipient, and accounted for 10 to 20 percent of household income. Included among these were several students who lived with relatives in St. Martin and received food or money from parents residing elsewhere.[13]

The third category, less consequential at the time but nonetheless important to families benefiting from them, were public and charitable transfers. The most important of these flowed to 5 percent of families who had children enrolled in school under foster parent programs. The effect of such programs was to reduce the direct costs of school attendance through subsidies of about $2 per student per month (see chapter 6). In addition, the children received meals at school. The families in question were quite poor, and the effect of the meals alone was to raise income by a net value of 12 percent.

The result of these and other inbound flows, like pensions and interest on loans, was to create a distribution of gross income in which the top 10 percent of households with $95 or more per month received at least 25 percent of total income in St. Martin, while the bottom 10 percent with $14 or less received 2.5 percent of total income. Although not as extreme as the Bank's estimate for the city, the distribution did show a substantial concentration of wealth in the hands of a small proportion of families.

This wealth did not remain in households for very long, however. One-third of the workers transferred substantial amounts to other households. Some 15 percent of these workers were women sending money to children and other family members outside Port-au-Prince. The rest were men sending money to wives, ex-wives, and children, or more commonly, to secondary households.

Secondary households contained women, like the ones I mentioned above who received $18 per month, with whom the men had established permanent conjugal relationships, and their children. The possibility of polygamy being limited by the resources available to finance it, only men with substantial means maintained one or more extra households. Their general rule of thumb seemed to be that the first $20 of monthly income was for their primary households, and the balance, also in increments of $20, was for secondary or tertiary households.

Supporting more than one household was an old tradition in Haiti that had to do with social welfare within the extended family and with the economic basis of conjugal unions.[14] It also had a political dimension. Many of the men with extra households were Macoutes, and many of the women they supported served as informers, relaying information about various goings-on in their vicinity, and in particular about what other Macoutes might be saying or doing. Knowledge being a useful contributor to power, financing its production out of foregone personal consumption might have been a very productive investment of resources.

Whatever the full set of reasons, outbound transfers exceeded inbound flows and yielded three significant distributional properties. One, already mentioned, was that rent and inbound transfers provided substantial support to many individuals who were not working or who were not working productively. Generally speaking, were it not for such transfers, market participation rates might have been a bit higher and unemployment lower, and there might also have been slightly fewer self-standing households. That is, although transfers of up to $20 per household were substantial relative to what individuals could expect to receive in the market, they were not so high as to stop most recipients from working.

The second property, also noted, was the political economy of income redistribution. Whatever other reasons individuals might have had for accumulating and sharing wealth, political solvency demanded that the relatively powerful maintain or increase their part of it in order to finance all the investments and recurrent expenses required for reproduction of their current positions, or for production of political growth. Avarice may or may not have been the principal cause of Macoute voraciousness in such things as burglary, but their survival as Macoutes, and sometimes their lives, often depended on it. They, like the powerful in government, commerce, and manufacturing that the Bank alluded to, needed to be politically efficient and productive.

The third property was the outcome of the redistribution process in terms of resources available to meet household consumption needs. Earnings and other income of workers were supporting, in whole or in part, at least 30 percent more households than I covered in the survey. Some were in St. Martin, others elsewhere. The overall effect was to lower the standard of living of many higher–income families, and to lower average income in St. Martin from a pretransfer gross of $49 per household per month, to a net of $38.

The lowered income was nevertheless higher than the average of $35 for the city as a whole (table 2.7). Compared to the distribution calculated by the UNCHBP from rent data, the share of households in St. Martin with less than $20 per month was less, and the share with more than $40 was greater. Most St. Martin families were therefore relatively well–off.

Many, however, were absolutely miserable. As shown in the lower portion of table 2.7, after adjustment for household size, 75 percent did not have the means to spend more than $13.50 per "adult" (i.e., "persons" measured in adult–equivalent units) to meet all their consumption needs each month.[15] The figure of $13.50 was what the World Bank used as its reference line to estimate absolute poverty in 1976 (World Bank, 1978a: 63). Using the earnings data for employed workers, it came up with the suggestion that 40 percent of the city's population was "absolutely poor." Because this data excluded many workers in St. Martin, and the 80,000 to 100,000 people in lowest income categories, the 40 percent figure might have been an underestimate.

The Bank's standard of $13.50, like the minimum wage, was useful only as a relative reference. What one scholar calls an "ultra–poverty" in which individuals are unable to obtain 1500 calories per day without spending less than 75 percent of income for them, and who might therefore be driven to use every increase in income exclusively for food consumption, was perhaps a more salient standard for absolute misery (Lipton, 1983: 3). The standard implied an income of $6.40 per adult, and applying it to the lower portion of table 2.7, about 25 percent of families were "ultra–poor" in St. Martin. Noting that the share of all urban families with less than $20 per

TABLE 2.7
Distribution of Income in St. Martin and Port-au-Prince, 1976

Monthly Income (U.S. $)	St. Martin (%)	Port-au-Prince (%)
(Number of households)	(88)	
Per household[a]: less than 11.00	2	5
11.01– 20.00	20	34
20.01– 30.00	19	20
30.01– 40.00	20	10
40.01– 50.00	25	9
50.01– 60.00	13	5
60.01– 70.00	5	4
70.01– 80.00	2	3
80.01–100.00	4	3
100.01 or more	—	7
TOTAL	100	100
Average (in $)	38.00	35.00[b]
Per adult[c]: less than 5.00	12	
5.01– 7.00	20	
7.01– 9.00	14	
9.01–11.00	16	
11.01–13.00	11	
13.01–15.00	5	
15.01–17.00	9	
17.01–19.00	6	
19.01–21.00	5	
21.01 or more	2	
TOTAL	100	
Average (in $)	9.80	
—per household[d]	42.00	

Sources: Data from author's survey in St. Martin and Haiti (1975) for Port-au-Prince distribution.

[a] Net income (i.e., sum from all sources, less outbound transfers), not adjusted for household size or age composition.

[b] This average excludes the highest income class (i.e., with more than one hundred dollars).

[c] Net income divided by household size, measured in adult-equivalent units to adjust for age composition.

[d] Average income per adult multiplied by average age-adjusted household size of 4.3 adults.

household per month was almost twice as high as in St. Martin, 39 percent versus 22 percent, perhaps 50 percent of the city's families were "ultra-poor" in 1976. Survival may not have been a driving force for all people, but it may have been important for a great many.

And 1976 was supposedly a good year, what with upward trends in manufacturing exports and employment, foreign assistance, tourism, and remittances from abroad. Maybe income was higher than it had been before, maybe not. In either case, the trends had considerable distance yet to travel before creating an economic environment noticeably less desperate than the one present in 1976.

What happened to income over the next ten years is uncertain. In St. Martin, a survey of 300 families conducted by the Ministry of Social Affairs in 1982 suggested that notwithstanding what looked like a rise in the share of employment in factories and other establishments covered by the minimum wage relative to 1976, gross income had dropped by almost 15 percent in real terms over the six–year period (table 2.8). The share with $20 or less remained roughly constant, around 20 percent, but the proportion with incomes between $20 and $50 dropped substantially. The method of estimating income in 1982 was not the same as in 1976, and may have therefore yielded an underestimate, but the impression remained that the level and structure of real income was generally the same in both years.

For urban workers fortunate enough to have been covered by minimum–wage legislation in 1976, the next four years seemed to bring steady improvement. The wage rose to $2.20 in 1980. This represented an improvement in real terms. But by 1985, the $3.00 wage was identical to the real wage of 1970 (table 2.9). If the government's basis for calculating the consumer price index was a fair representation of the basket of goods and services purchased by minimum–wage earners, then their circumstances in

TABLE 2.8
Distribution of Gross Income in St. Martin, 1976 and 1982

Monthly Income Per Household[a] (1976 $)	SHARE OF HOUSEHOLDS IN	
	1976 (%)	1982 (%)
(Number of households)	(88)	(154)
less than 11.00	2	6
11.01–20.00	18	15
20.01–30.00	15	24
30.01–40.00	17	17
40.01–50.00	11	8
50.01 or more	37	30
TOTAL	s100	100
Average (in $)	49.00	42.00

Sources: Haiti (1982) for 1982 data, adjusted by author to 1976 dollar terms, and data from author's survey in St. Martin for 1976.

[a] Gross income, without adjustment for household size or age composition, is the sum of income from all sources before deducting outbound transfers. The distribution of gross income for 1976 is therefore not the same as the distribution of net income shown in table 2.7.

1986 were basically the same as in 1976 or 1970. And if the distribution of urban earnings and other income relative to the minimum wage had not changed appreciably over the period, then the characteristics of making a living in Port–au–Prince were also the same in 1986 as they were before.

More generally, technicians struggling with trying to sort through different economic trends in order to estimate the direction of per capita Gross Domestic Product (GDP) apparently came to the conclusion that for Haiti as a whole, real income may have peaked in 1980, reached a nadir in 1984, and then recovered in 1985 to a level 7 percent higher than in 1976. That was not much to show for a decade. Whether conditions in 1986 were or were not worse than in 1976, the poor and "ultra–poor" were still there in very large numbers.

Ideas and Actions

Most workers in St. Martin and Port–au–Prince earned their livelihoods from activities to which students of labor markets in developing countries, for purposes of simplified description or theoretical analysis, attach several adjectives. These include "subsistence," "informal," "marginal," "backward," "traditional," "artisanal," "petty," "penny," "unorganized," "unregulated," "irregular," "casual," "small–scale," "intermediate," and, a term with currency in Haiti, "scrounging."[16] These different classification labels, peculiar to developing countries but no doubt useful for various purposes, all refer to the same set of activities.

Stripped of such labels, provided with empirical substance, and viewed

TABLE 2.9
Indicators of Income Growth in Port-au-Prince, 1955-85

	GDP per Capita[a] (in 1976 $)	Consumer Price Index[b] (1948 = 100)	MINIMUM WAGE PER DAY	
			In current $	In 1955 $
1955	169	107.4	—	—
1960	171	102.8	—	—
1965	161	123.5	—	—
1970	158	134.4	0.70	0.52
1972	165	152.8	1.00	0.65
1976	187	268.4	1.30	0.48
1980	215	372.2	2.20	0.59
1984	195	511.4	2.65	0.52
1985	200	575.0	3.00	0.52

Sources: ADIH (1981), World Bank (1985), and author's estimates.
[a] For Haiti as a whole.
[b] For Port-au-Prince only.

through a perspective of applied microeconomic theory that does not allow wide deviation from a narrow lexicon of concepts, the activities present themselves as normal work carried out by normal people following normal principles of behavior in the competitive market. Many workers were desperately poor, but in Port-au-Prince as in other major cities of the developing world, poverty was also normal. The most destitute person in St. Martin, owning nothing but a cooking pot and a bucket, obviously afflicted with fever, and earning $0.30 per day to sustain herself and four children, told me that she considered herself fortunate not to be "miserable."

Ascription of normalcy to the activities, the workers, and *their* economy is important because it presents the possibility that conventional approaches to intervention can prove somewhat helpful in raising earnings. Port-au-Prince certainly did contain many workers who by one definition or another were unemployed, underemployed, or otherwise nonproductive at particular moments in time. However, as is the case in most societies where public and private income transfer mechanisms are severely limited, these categories were luxuries that most people could ill afford. Whether corporeal survival provided extra incentive was difficult to determine, but whatever the cause, the vast majority of workers seemed productive. Some were more successful than others, but they were all like "entrepreneurs" perpetually on the lookout for ways to increase efficiency and earnings under conditions of extremely intense competition for shares of a very small portion of total urban income.

The city may have had an unemployment or underemployment problem, but if so, it seemed of a type that extended well beyond the limits of the notion of job shortages in the "modern" sector—like the labels I noted above, a concept useful for several purposes but nevertheless one that ascribes a certain kind of abnormalcy to employment falling outside its purview. A job was a job no matter what it looked like. The only significant attribute was the earnings it provided. What mattered was not so much demand for "labor" (i.e., in its limited interpretation as an increase in the number of regular salaried positions), but rather general demand for all manner of goods and services produced by everyone in the economy. Where there was demand, people were quite capable of creating their own jobs to respond to it, and also of hiring others to help them.

In this context, expansion of the assembly export manufacturing industry was helpful. Supposing that by 1986 assembly work employed 30,000 people inside factories, the annual wage bill may have been of the order of $30 million. The jobs themselves represented about 7 percent of the labor force, but by pouring money into the city, they created a basis of demand for goods and services produced by other workers. If half the wage payments leaked out of the economy, enough remained to provide another

30,000 laborers, traders, and manufacturers with earnings equivalent to half the minimum wage. For similar reasons, expansion of public and private foreign assistance, tourism and travel, and worker export and remittance industries, notwithstanding reservations about dependency and related issues that one could raise about them, were all helpful while they were expanding.

Contrarily, government taxation, large-scale commerce, and many import-substitution industries were obstacles in desperate need of removal. Although they did sweep the countryside for resources and concentrate them in the city, this gain seemed to be offset by the loss of rural purchasing power for goods and services produced in the city, and by loss of resources for investment in agricultural growth. In any event, most of the resource extraction process transferred wealth within city limits. By shifting it into consumption by the few and investment abroad at a rate not compensated for by investment in export factories, the process drew out resources that might otherwise have served the dual purposes of expanding domestic demand and investment by ordinary people. And the worst part was that the extraction process took out of the economy of ordinary people what export factory wages, foreign assistance, travel, and remittances put in.

Efforts underway in 1986 to lower public and private taxation were therefore also helpful. There was a chance that even if total urban income remained constant, the share for which ordinary people could compete might expand appreciably. That kind of redistribution without growth, though not as helpful as it might be with growth, and impossible to discern in aggregate measures like the Gross Domestic Product, was important.

Growth and redistribution outcomes that did evolve through 1986 were in large measure outcomes of continuing struggle between competing factions and alliances within the political class. Although sometimes sustained on the margins by scholarly or other expert recommendations for "policy changes" that could induce more growth, equity, and other things of direct or indirect utility to abstractly defined consumers, producers, and sectors, the essence of the struggle, as I outlined in the preceding chapter, was individual and factional self-interest. Benefits acquired by ordinary people, at least until early 1986, were more in the nature of political side effects than deliberate creations on their behalf. This was to be expected in a country with a very narrow base of political representation.

Within the limits set by political and economic circumstances outside Haiti, the capacity of the factional struggle to yield further beneficial side effects would therefore depend, among other things, on the fortunes of any inter- or intrafactional battles that might occur, on the concepts through which different factions viewed ordinary workers, on the functions that concepts performed for the factions, and on the relationships, if any, between fortunes, concepts, and functions on the one hand, and tangible outcomes on the other. Unfortunately, the world of the political class did not present itself in a fashion readily susceptible to such a straightforward calculus. Insofar as it touched on matters to do with work and earnings, the world was largely unintelligible. It was a potpourri (in the English meaning of "mixture" and in the literal French meaning of "rotten pot") of ideas, actions, and inactions that were indecipherable.

But disaggregated into discrete units focusing on specific factional groupings within the foreign-assistance component of the class and their interests and activities with respect to particular themes, parts of the world could be made comprehensible. This partial understanding takes the form of five short stories that parallel the topical order by which I described St. Martin. The first concerns the political flow among multilateral agencies of employment concepts that led nowhere in particular. The second is a similar anecdote concerning ideas about traders that did produce something of value as a side effect. The third is a dismal history of the degeneration of practice among multilateral agency missionaries who directed passing attention to manufacturing activities other than larger-scale assembly export and import-substitution. The fourth recounts heroic attempts by PVOs and bilateral agencies to export products similar to those manufactured for export in St. Martin. The last story follows the appropriate technology movement as it searched for purpose in Haiti. Each story has something different to say. All of them conspire to portray a political class that was and remains largely removed from understanding the circumstances of ordinary workers. But while the overall picture the stories present is not one that should convey a sense of optimism that the class can yield useful outcomes for workers, there are faint glimmers of hope for possible progress in the future.

Employment Concepts

During the starting phase of the UNCHBP project one of our principal tasks was to produce background reports on the state of the urban and regional economy. These reports would help set the stage for our primary task, which was to prepare a plan for investment projects in several areas of physical works, principally low-income housing and environmental improvement. Already attuned to the professional and scholarly literature concerning the unemployment problem in developing countries, we accepted the employment and unemployment statistics provided by the 1971 census, and included them in a preliminary report (Haiti, 1974: 140). There was no question that the city had a massive unemployment problem requiring address. A year and several hundred visits with low-income families later, we found it more difficult to accept the thesis that the city contained enough households with enough resources to support unemployed members for extended periods of time. The 1971 unemployment rate was no longer acceptable.

We believed that actions to increase aggregate demand for labor were all to the good. However, with several million people residing within a day's journey from the city, any increase in demand had considerable likelihood of generating a matching supply, and therefore no appreciable change in earnings. In our opinion, what seemed in need of doing as a complement to such actions were efforts to lower the cost of living. Raising real income in this way might relieve pressure on ordinary households to put everyone to work, and thereby lower the rate of increase in the supply of workers. Also, to the extent that labor was already demanding itself to the maximum in self-employment, what most of us surmised the majority of the officially unemployed to be doing, lowering the cost of living might also make it possible for workers to shift resources from consumption to more productive investment, always a good idea in theory, and thereby help accelerate the rate of economic growth.[17]

This seemed an unusual way of looking at the workings of a labor market at the time, but the prime purpose of the exercise was not to explore the subject of employment. This was not our responsibility. In order to justify proposals for public investment in low-cost housing, expanded water supply, and other physical works in terms of their potential contributions to economic growth and poverty alleviation, our purpose principally was one of trying to convince other government and foreign-assistance officials and technicians of the utility of broadening conceptions about the causes of poverty to include not only unemployment, but also the cost of living. It was hard to rationalize what were being called "social overhead" investments in a place that desperately needed "productive" and growth-inducing investments. We had to make the investments synonymous.

No one argued with our emphasis on the high cost of consumption. The matter was obvious. No one agreed with the hypothesis that poverty was not a direct consequence of unemployment. Government statistics for 1971, backed in that year with assistance from the United Nations Development Program (UNDP), made the relationship as clear as the observation of misery on the streets. If the UNDP said unemployment was very serious, there was no reason to doubt the fact. Especially firm on the matter were UNDP statisticians still working on tabulation of the 1971 census. Equally certain were technicians of the International Labor Office (ILO) working on manpower planning and vocational training projects. We found little support for our notions within the rest of the United Nations family of organizations.

Convincing ourselves that we were right, and predisposed to think that all or most of the unemployed were working, we pursued our course by combining the self–employed and unemployed in census data into a single category called "undocumented" employment, and then claimed that 70 percent of urban employment fell into that category. As technical experts we also felt compelled to breathe life into the statistic, and therefore made up numbers for 1975 indicating that the structure of undocumented employment was 1 percent manufacturing, 21 percent trade, 40 percent domestic service, and 38 percent unspecified services (Haiti, 1975: 39). There being a fundamental contradiction in promulgation of specific numbers for something "undocumented," and some confusion associated with use of the adjective in other countries to describe illegal workers, we searched about for a better label, found one in an ILO publication (ILO, 1972), and then gave birth to the "informal" sector of Port–au–Prince. Shortly thereafter a short–term consultant from the ILO gave this invention quasi–official sanction by including our UNCHBP numbers in his report (ILO, 1976: 15). At the UNCHBP, however, the problem remained that the informal sector was without empirical form or substance. The invention was succeeding in beginning to move attention way from exclusive concern with unemployment, but other than supplying a label for ignorance, it accomplished little.

Some of us believed in 1975 that introducing the informal sector and then recommending that research be undertaken to find out something tangible about workers in the category was all that the technical assistance project could do, especially one concerned primarily with physical planning. Except in relation to some existing research about traders, discussed below, the project had no basis for making further recommendations. Others, I among them, argued that a technical assistance project with a budget of over $1 million would not be well regarded in the local development community if it did not present the appearance of knowledgeable expertise, and if it did not present the appearance of producing useful recommendations to deal with low earnings. Some scholars could perhaps get by with legitimate claims of ignorance, but not professional technical assistants. The purpose of assistance of the UNCHBP type was to deliver reports that looked useful. Recommending research was useful, but by itself was inadequate.

Proponents of usefulness won the argument, but ran into immediate difficulty. Documentation from other countries provided many interesting concepts, facts, and suggestions about "cottage" industry.[18] But about the informal sector there was little of empirical substance at the time to assist in describing what participants might have been doing to earn their livelihoods in the city, or about specific actions that might help them earn more.[19] In desperation, we borrowed ideas from an ILO report on Kenya in order to make recommendations for what we hoped would be corresponding types of activities in Port–au–Prince (i.e., ILO, 1972). For manufacturers, we suggested: easing access to credit; creation of mini–industrial parks; assistance in the creation of cooperatives; experimentation and demonstration of new, small–scale, appropriate technologies; promotion of subcontracting from large to small firms; and maximizing government procurement of supplies from small firms. For the rest, we recommended that social scientists do research on them. We did not take these ideas too seriously at the time, nor did most others in the development community. We did not take the ideas seriously because most of us understood that we did not know what we were talking about. Reasons that others did not take most of the ideas seriously may have been the same or different, but their methods of camouflage tended to be less constructive than ours.

The ILO expert who gave sanction to our creation of the informal sector, for example, stated that the sector did not contain "real" employment because productivity and earnings were too low. Research was required, but not typical employment surveys. The sector needed sociological inquiry to identify leaders and other dynamic elements that, presumably, could be encouraged to integrate more rapidly with the "formal" sector (ILO, 1976: 15, 42–43).

Soon afterward, World Bank analysts saved the sector from surreality, after concluding from my St. Martin data that habitual concepts of employment and unemployment did not apply easily to Haiti, by suggesting that it contained considerable "underemployment" and "disguised" unemployment (World Bank, 1979). And then in 1979, a UNDP/ILO employment survey of 6600 individuals, similar to that used for the census, yielded a proposition to the effect that in addition to a 37 percent "open" unemployment rate, there was a 26 percent underemployment rate that could be subdivided into a "theoretical employment" component (12 percent), and a "theoretical unemployment" component (14 percent) (ILO, 1979). Adding open and theoretical unemployment together gave an "equivalent" urban unemployment rate of 51 percent. Under this method, the 36 percent open unemployment rate for 1982 shown in table 2.1 was in fact an equivalent rate of 50 percent.

Using a similar approach in St. Martin in 1982, the Ministry of Social Affairs noted that market participation rates for men and women were respectively 57 percent and 34 percent, and reported an overall open unemployment rate of 22 percent, plus an underemployment rate of 30 percent (Haiti, 1982). In 1985, the World Bank simplified the discussion by returning to exclusive use of unemployment.[20]

The prefixes "un" and "under," and the adjectives "real," "disguised," "open," "theoretical," and "equivalent" were as useful for certain purposes in certain places as the various labels I mentioned earlier. But in Haiti they were used to define and redefine the unknown. They had no more operational meaning than what we at the UNCHBP had attached originally to the informal sector: *ignorance.* Perhaps like us, the struggle to survive as reputable experts in worthy organizations compelled professionals to make up numbers, to package them in congenial and marketable concepts, and then, after the compulsory caveat about lack of reliable information, to present them as if they were factual knowledge. This cultural practice was of itself neither good nor bad, but it contained a fundamental contradiction. If there was no information, how could all these technicians say anything of substance regarding productivity, unemployment, underemployment, or any of the other thematic variations?

The important aspect, however, was the manner in which these labels could direct thoughts about action. No useful purposes could be served, for example, by proposing research or other actions. Things that are not real require neither investigation nor intervention. Similarly, if people are assumed to be unemployed or underemployed, what purpose is served by knowing more about them? And by what logic is there a method of assisting such people except by finding them "real" productive jobs? In brief, among professionals engaged in talk about employment, concepts dominated caveats, and little more came to be known by 1986 about how people in the city earned their livelihoods, or about what they earned, than what I had learned in 1976.

If the concepts had any practical utility, then it took the form of providing support to factions that were struggling in the name of jobs, foreign exchange, and profits to increase investment in export (and import–substitution) industry. But to the extent that they may have served to forestall interest in learning more about ordinary workers and actual characteristics, they rendered a disservice. For on the margin of things, a little understanding of ordinary circumstances could sometimes yield a little improvement in certain of the circumstances, as happened in the case of attention to traders like the ones in St. Martin.

Traders

Between 1960 and 1971, several anthropologists and sociologists produced a series of monographs concerning the country's agricultural marketing system and the women who formed it (e.g., Comhaire–Sylvain and Comhaire–Sylvain, 1964; Mintz, 1960, 1961, 1964, 1971; Underwood, 1960). In general these studies presented the image of a highly complex network of relationships and flows that functioned efficiently and competitively to bring commodities destined for domestic consumption from producers to consumers. Except for the small scale of operation of most traders, which by itself meant little, the system functioned in much the same way as its wholesale and retail counterparts in competitive markets of other countries.

One scholar, however, interpreted the studies as suggesting that traders were minor monopolists who exploited farm producers at every turn (Johnson, 1970: 85–88). Another student of the subject proposed that such trade was a form of "scrounging" and hence not a "real" form of economic activity.[21] This accusation led to a counterargument to the effect that traders in the system were entrepreneurs with substantial talent (Mintz, 1964: 286). What prevented fuller development of the talent was absence of a stable or expanding rural economy. If there was something worth giving a special label, it was not the activity, but the environment in which an individual had to conduct it.

In any event, studies and the controversies surrounding them stimulated a UNDP consultant to recommend in 1967 that government establish a center for the study of marketing (Bartkowiak, 1967). The government did nothing with it, but in 1973 welcomed a proposal by the Interamerican Institute of Agricultural Sciences (IICA) to launch a new wave of investigations in Haiti as part of its hemispheric research program on the subject (Locher, 1974: 1).

The new monographs again described complex and apparently highly efficient marketing processes that, in combination with price analyses, provided substantial evidence of the operation of an intensively competitive market in agricultural trade (Murray and Alvarez, 1973; Johnson and LaGra, 1975; Locher, 1974). They also suggested that while a government might try to influence the system directly, through price control for example, traders were highly adept at circumventing such interference (Murray and Alvarez, 1973: 57–58).

More important were the effects some of the studies had on public action. A paper in 1974 pointed out what almost all earlier inquiries had lamented without effect: that taxes on traders in public marketplaces were oppressive and regressive. But this paper showed that the cost of collection exceeded revenues (Duplan and LaGra, 1974). Government was quick to repeal the tax (but running short of funds in 1982, it reinstated it).

The studies also influenced our work at the UNCHBP.[22] They guided us away from early ideas about clearing streets of traders in order to ease traffic flow, and toward such notions as wider street standards and expansion of marketplaces. Certain IICA calculations concerning the rate of commodity loss through dehydration, vermin, rodents, and flooding, and concerning health risks associated with contamination in the central market also led us to propose, and the World Bank to later finance, a $14 million rehabilitation project for the market.[23]

The overall importance of the studies, however, was their promotion of the notion that traders were real and normal, that relative to their investment of capital, labor, and the austere conditions of their economic environment, their services were productive, and that they largely fell outside the scope of direct intervention. Traders were expert at what they did, and because trade was a residentiary activity that expanded with growth in demand, increases in employment and earnings would result primarily from efforts to promote further aggregate growth of their share of the economy.

Here was a body of evidence that might have had some tempering influence on uninhibited ascription of surreality, underemployment, and related opinions, but this product of one small faction of the political class did not extend itself into other factions. There may have been several reasons, including lack of interest in the product of one set of disciplines by subscribers to another, or the imperfect nature of information flows. But much of it seemed related to faith, or what some scientists refer to less theologically as misplaced concreteness. Many proponents of the "modern," perhaps unacquainted with the narrow set of theoretical applications for which scholars originally invented the modern–traditional dichotomy, could not avoid ascribing traditionality to trade. And seeing reports of low earnings without corresponding data to reveal the costs of producing them, and hence the profitability of the activities, perhaps they could not help but interpret the research as confirmation rather than refutation of their premises.

Actual reasons were of little consequence. In the quiet struggle for dominance between holders of different opinions, assumptions, and theories within the class, credibility generally attached itself more readily to ideas in UNDP, ILO, and World Bank reports than to those in IICA reports or independent research monographs. But insofar as trade was concerned, political dominion was largely irrelevant because the activity could not be significantly affected by what the political class thought or did with respect to it. Dominion may have mattered more in "small" manufacturing.

Small Manufacturing

The idea that direct or indirect intervention on behalf of what, for purposes of simplicity, I call "small" manufacturing (i.e., other than assembly export and larger import–substitution firms) could induce positive effects on earnings and growth had an auspicious beginning. A UN technical assistance mission in 1949 included among its several recommendations for industrial expansion the "encouragement" of small-scale engineering, repair, and "handicraft" enterprises (UN, 1949). There was little data on the subject in 1949, and the mission's recommendation may have stemmed primarily from a need to say something about industrialization. That was an important part of development thought, and no report could go without a pertinent chapter. The missionaries could not have seen much upon which to build a discussion. Aside from a few agro-processing plants and household-level activities, the only tangible manifestations of industry were small engineering and repair workshops. Also, in 1949 Haiti was already making a mark in small manufacturing exports of the order of $1 million annually. These exports, which apparently looked like "crafts," accounted for 40 percent of Haiti's nonagricultural trade with the United States (Turnier, 1955: 347). There was little reason not to "promote" more of these exports.

The lexicon of development thought was also much simpler than it would later become. "Small," for example, was just an adjective, not an analytical concept. In those days, an expert had to take what he or she could get. All extant forms and scales of manufacturing, including what went on in households, were valid foundations upon which a process of industrial expansion could rest. And small was a precondition for anything becoming large.[24] Whatever their rationales may have been, the UN experts did not have reason to doubt the potential of the only things that Haiti seemed to offer. They did not, however, say exactly what they meant by "encouragement."

During the 1950s, progress in learning more about certain types of small manufacturing and in experimenting with methods to encourage them, fell primarily to anthropologists and sociologists with interests in obtaining a better understanding of how farm and other rural households earned their livelihoods, and of how the process might be improved. One of the more informative studies, carried out under auspices of UNESCO in the Marbial Valley between 1948 and 1953, reported that 75 percent of families supplemented their earnings with often substantial proceeds of small manufacturing activities (Métraux, 1951: Annex 5). The activities included carpentry, tanning, harness making, shoemaking, hat making, trunk making, basket weaving, rope production, embroidery, goldsmithing, brick making, furniture production, lime production, tailoring, and dressmaking. Some of these activities may have come from Africa, but most resembled the basic trades of seventeenth- and eighteenth-century France that would have been essential to efficient operation of a slave economy. These and other activities were old in Haiti, but many of them had new export markets.

After finding that most manufacturers had not learned their skills from parents, and unaware of Haiti's established apprenticeship system, UNESCO personnel concluded that such enterprise was relatively new to the valley. This was a useful conclusion because it coincided with UNESCO's interest in demonstrating the effect of various forms of formal training on rural income. Besides, education was the official service that UNESCO was supposed to render. Ascription of newness to existing and apparently informally acquired skills implied that more structured training in new products, techniques, marketing, and management would not only have an enthusiastic audience, but could also yield higher earnings for the producers. Accordingly, UNESCO set up a handicraft center to improve production of sisal, cotton, wood, leather, and ceramic products.

An assessment of this and other UNESCO efforts, and also of farmer credit and training schemes conducted elsewhere in the country with U.S. government assistance, concluded that education and credit could not, by themselves, yield significant results (Moral, 1961: 33–34). Contrary to the impression given by UNESCO, small manufacturing did not constitute embryonic elements of spreading industrialization that could be encouraged to develop more quickly. The enterprises were no different than they had been two centuries earlier and, together with trade and farming, constituted part of the previously mentioned system of scrounging for a living that had been brought about through policies of successive governments to shift wealth from rural to urban areas. Direct intervention at the microlevel would have no effect until the intervention took account of the economic realities facing rural people.

Whatever the merit of this assessment, it noted that such short–term effects as UNESCO may have engendered between 1948 and 1953 left nothing to show in Marbial by 1959. The process of encouragement proposed by the UN in 1949 was apparently somewhat more complex in practice than on paper. Unfortunately, from 1960 onward the notion of a scrounging activity, and its numerous variations like traditional or marginal would attach itself to almost anything that looked like "nonmodern" small manufacturing.

Research about small manufacturing and methods of its encouragement stopped, and would not resume until the 1970s when various themes prompted a new wave of inquiry. The subject nevertheless retained importance as a mechanism for improving the perceived quality of technical assistance reports.

In 1962 a joint mission of the Organization of American States (OAS), the Interamerican Development Bank (IDB) and the Economic Commission for Latin America (ECLA) estimated that 1.2 percent of the labor force was employed in manufacturing in 1960, and that 58 percent of this employment was in the "artisanal" sector (OAS, 1962). The total included

6100 manufacturing jobs in the city, which included 3100 artisans working in groups and 1000 working alone. These numbers were inventions.

Perhaps because this estimated proportion of manufacturing employment appeared low relative to other countries, or perhaps because it did not conform to activity apparent on the streets, an ECLA review in 1965 raised the share of manufacturing employment for 1960 from 1.2 to 5.3 percent of the total (ECLA, 1965). The method of this adjustment was a 630 percent increase in the estimate of artisanal employment, and an increase in the estimated share of such jobs from 58 to 83 percent of total manufacturing. These numbers were also inventions.

Nevertheless, these figures served as reference points for future reports. In 1972 an OAS mission used the ECLA figures to argue that the proportion of artisanal employment in total manufacturing had not decreased as much in Haiti as in other countries of the region. Industrial development in the country was therefore "stagnant" (OAS, 1972: 292).

As in the 1962 and 1965 reports, the OAS refrained from making recommendations directly pertinent to small manufacturing in 1972, a more or less logical result given its association between artisanal employment and stagnation. But had the OAS done so, the attitude of important elements of Haitian decision making with which it was allied would not have been particularly receptive. A ranking economist who would later become minister of finance opined in 1968 that except for a fractionof the bourgeoisie and middle class, the balance of Haitian society, which presumably included most small manufacturers, was as a result of inertia, ignorance, attitude, and the low value it placed on science, hostile to progress (Francisque, 1968: 91–92).

The basic effect of these antipathetic perspectives was to constrain positive interpretation by multilateral factions of the economic purpose of small manufacturing, and therefore the rate of production of "encouraging" recommendations of the UN type in 1949 and experiments like those of UNESCO. This was perhaps unfortunate because in 1970 small manufacturing (i.e., products made up of domestic raw materials shown in table 1.8) contributed almost 60 percent to net manufactured exports from Haiti.

Sometimes small manufacturing had a positive place. In 1969 a United Nations Industrial Development Organization (UNIDO) report included a proposal that the government envisage the creation of a public agency to assist small manufacturers in production and marketing (UNIDO, 1969: 83–86). The report suggested construction of a handicraft center near the port, where professional staff could help 150 craftsmen in cooperatively obtaining raw materials, in standardizing product quality for the tourist trade, and in assembling orders for export. The justification for this project was that such countries as Morocco provided this kind of public assistance and, more generally, that small manufacturing was an important component of "balanced" industrialization in developed countries, that developing countries did not appear to have a similar balance beween large and small, that Haiti was a developing country, and that small therefore warranted encouragement of some kind.

Besides its recourse to aesthetics (i.e., balance) as a rationale for action, a curious aspect of this effort, suffering as most reports by short-term consultants are wont to do, was its neglect of the experiences of the past and of ongoing encouragement efforts. The report mentioned nothing about UNESCO. It failed to note the existence of craft promotion divisions in the Ministries of Commerce and Industry, Social Affairs, Agriculture and Rural Development, and Education, or the failure of these divisions to accomplish much of anything except to sustain their professional staff. It did not point to some reasonably successful PVO marketing efforts, such as one run by a Baptist mission since 1943, a Mennonite Central Committee (MCC) project in the 1960s, or the very substantial 400 percent growth of small manufacturing exports from 1966 to 1969 that had already taken place without much in the way of direct public assistance.

Actually, the report was mostly about other kinds of manufacturing. Inclusion of small manufacturing, as in the case of the 1962, 1965, and 1972 exercises, may have had more to do with making a report about industrial development seem more comprehensive than it might have appeared otherwise.

But the UNIDO effort at least had something positive to say about small manufacturing. Subsequent analysts, more often than not attached to short-term World Bank missions, were much less constructive. In 1976, while their report indicated that 33 percent of exports were of small manufacturing origin, the mission's staff made no reference to it, noting only that there had been some growth in "non-productive marginal" activities (World Bank, 1976a). In 1978, when the share was 36 percent, they referred in passing to small-scale "cottage and quasi-artisanal" activities (World Bank, 1978a: 23). In 1979, although mentioning that the "craft-type workshops" were not really "industrial," mission staff noted that prospects for "craft" promotion were good (even though statistics in their report showed that prospects had been good for over a decade). They suggested that perhaps the government might be able to do something helpful in regard to training, raw material purchasing, credit, marketing, information, and maybe straightening out the "haphazard" way in which they believed PVOs were trying to promote crafts, a subject discussed below (World Bank, 1979: 27–29). My participation in that particular mission may have been instrumental in this somewhat constructive view.

The share was about 40 percent when a 1981 report and another in 1982 said nothing about the activities (World Bank, 1981a, 1982). IMF visitors, taking a good look at the statistics and noting that small manufacturing represented 41 percent of all manufactured exports in 1983, finally ventured to suggest they were important (IMF, 1983: 12–14). But upon return of Bank analysts in 1985 with a report proposing policy recommendations for long-term economic growth, the sector disappeared again (World Bank, 1985).

By and large, short-term experts visiting Haiti with stock or "boiler plate" methods of creating or disposing of information did not contribute a great deal to intelligible discussion about prospects for small manufacturing as methods to increase earnings and growth. Political process and outcomes in Haiti might not have been any different had they shared the UN perspective of 1949, but earlier attention might at least have stimulated more careful thought about the meaning of export statistics.

According to World Bank and other users of government statistics, the distinction between assembly manufacturing exports and production from domestic materials in table 1.8 was a distinction between "manufacturing" (i.e., modern-looking) and "small industry composed mostly of artisanal products" (World Bank, 1985: 138). The government's actual distinction was between goods that entered the United States under offshore assembly tariff provisions and goods that entered under the General System of Preferences (GSP) offered to products made up substantially of supposedly domestic raw materials. These products were manufactured by larger establishments covered by minimum-wage legislation, medium-sized operations containing 10 to 30 workers, some covered by legislation, others not, and St. Martin-type workers who sold their wares to tourists, tourist shops, other commercial exporters, and contractors in charge of put-out systems. Because export value-added in this sector was not much less than for assembly exports, and because a larger proportion of workers earned less than the minimum wage, it was quite possible that these exports generated direct earnings to more workers than did assembly exports from 1949 to 1986. They were not unimportant.

In 1970, and perhaps up to 1976, most goods entering the United States under the GSP may have been artisanal products made in small workshops or by independent craftspeople. But with growth of large- and medium-sized units, what looked artisanal was more and more the output of factory workers. Most items in categories of clothing, textile products, leather goods, wood products, brooms, brushes, and buttons shown in table 1.8 were no less "modern" in production than exports of assembled imports. Indeed, of the $45.4 million in exports of GSP goods in 1984, approximately $25 million emanated from such factories. And the rate of growth in these factory-made exports between 1976 and 1984 was greater than that of assembly exports.[25] The power of a label to obscure evidence was quite remarkable.

More explicitly perhaps than in the case of employment, the basic function of small manufacturing concepts and labels for most multilateral missionaries after 1960, and through the labels ordinary workers, was adornment of reports that had to look nice in Washington, New York, Geneva, and other headquarter cities. Other than serving basic expert survival needs, they had no purpose.

Because owners of large and some medium-sized firms were able to fight for and receive the same favorable set of fiscal benefits as owners of assembly and import-substitution factories, the assumptions, opinions, and theories of passing mission staffers about crafts were immaterial to outcomes for these owners. But the question left unanswered is whether more serious, responsible, and competent treatment of the subject might have generated some additional direct benefit to St. Martin-type manufacturers, even of the limited variety I mentioned in the section on traders. For while multilateral missionaries pursued their steady course of indirect disparagement and obfuscation, PVOs, especially from 1975 onward, picked up the theme abandoned by UNESCO two decades earlier. They launched themselves into craft export undertakings with considerable vigor. The idea of such efforts was congenial. Outcomes, however, were difficult to assess.

Exporting Crafts

PVO interest in exports seemed to flow out of the convergence of a number of different factors. Craft demand in Europe and North America was up, and exports almost tripled between 1973 and 1974, perhaps approaching $10 million in 1975. Also, introduction of the GSP by the European Economic Community (EEC) in 1971 and by the United States in 1974 made it much easier for exporters to have access to the markets and for tourists to carry goods home with them. The opportunity seemed to be there.

On the supply side, as I noted in chapter 1, 1975 witnessed a surge of new entrants to the PVO community, and also the diffusion of all manner of conceptual premises that could not help but steer interest toward assisting anything that looked small and productive. These themes included self-help, self-sufficiency, small is beautiful, development of cooperatives, community development, appropriate technology (more about which I will say below), women in development, income generation, labor-intensive employment creation, private enterprise promotion, and a number of others. Some of the concepts had been in currency for a long time in Haiti, but the number of actors carrying them mushroomed during the 1970s. At the same time, PVOs that had been in Haiti for a while and that were usually quite close to the urban and rural poor had tangible evidence that their previous and ongoing efforts in health, education, agriculture, and relief were not making headway against poverty. They needed to do more to raise income, and crafts seemed like the logical way to proceed.

The manner by which most PVOs proceeded was conditioned by a predisposition to view all domestic traders and exporters as exploiters who did not pay fair or just prices to producers. Some scholarly work touching upon Haiti, as I noted in the section on traders, supported this notion, but it found basic fuel in the massive differences between retail prices for crafts in local tourist shops or in retail outlets abroad, and prices paid to producers (see Appendix A, cases 3, 4, and 8). Distribution through "alternative" marketing channels was therefore an important component of PVO efforts.

The efforts showed mixed results. PVOs with extensive experience prior to 1975 seemed to do well. The MCC, for example, increased exports from $2000 in 1962 to $160,000 in 1980 (Beardsley, 1981: 38, 45, A–65). At the opposite extreme, newcomers sometimes did quite poorly. The experience of the Haitian–American Community Help Organization (HACHO) was typical. Launched in 1975 with technical assistance from the CARE foundation and financial support from USAID, HACHO created fifteen craft centers to house the activities of 300 producers. The project was an almost perfect duplication of the UNESCO experience at Marbial. A year later outside assessors suggested that the undertaking be scaled down because most of the products were no longer competitive in quality or in price (Brinkerhoff, Fotzo, and Ormond, 1983). The entry of China into the world market in 1976 was undermining craft sales of many countries, including Haiti. By 1982 HACHO had only five centers left. They were providing producers with $7 to $20 in monthly earnings, but HACHO was spending $5 for every $1 in producer earnings from cotton crafts.

At this time, devaluation of the Mexican peso put cotton products on the international market at one–third of HACHO's production cost. The outside evaluators implied that the project might have accomplished more if it had sought out new and more competitive product lines and if it had substituted a wage–labor orientation for the cooperative format adopted by HACHO.

Unfortunately, such retrospective suggestions oversimplified difficulties associated with the highly competitive handicraft business. Another project organized by COHAN, a PVO supported by the Netherlands government, did seek out competitive products and did use a wage–labor orientation, but nonetheless ran into its own problems (see Appendix B). Following the natural course of assistance logic, this gave rise to bilateral agency efforts to assist the assistance projects. The German government, working with the Haitian government's Office of Industrial Promotion, paid the way for several groups, including COHAN, to participate at craft trade fairs in Berlin and other cities in 1977. This proved quite successful in terms of increasing sales. Working more independently under the rubric of "private sector development" introduced in 1980, USAID tried to do the same thing with respect to a trade fair in Atlanta in 1984. It used about $65,000 to select ten of fifty producer groups, to train them in trade fair marketing and in production of marketable products, and to support them in Atlanta (Brinkerhoff, 1984). Total sales at the fair came to $48,000. In this instance, there were again all manner of retrospective explanations as to why some groups did better than others, or how USAID might have done things differently (see Appendix B). These explanations were as questionable as the ones concerning HACHO.

None of the various bits of information about different projects could answer the fundamental question: Were they making a difference? On the one hand, estimates concerning visible exports listed in table 1.8 gave no basis for deducing an answer. On the other, MCC exports and some evidence from COHAN implied that PVOs could have been responsible for significant export increases in certain years. There was no evident way to tell whether the PVO efforts, or those of the government, Germany, USAID, and other organizations were having any significant economic impact.

Multilateral mission staffers were certainly unimpressed, calling the PVO efforts haphazard for example. Bilateral evaluators invariably found something "not good enough" in most projects unfortunate enough to fall into their clutches. And a dispassionate observer might wonder at the logic guiding PVOs and bilaterals to promote self-help among people who were already helping themselves, self-sufficiency among those already self-sufficient, beauty among things already as small and beautiful as they were ever going to become, labor-intensity among activities that could not be more labor-intensive, or private enterprise among workers who were already entrepreneurs by necessity. Especially curious in this regard were efforts to introduce "appropriate technology" to small manufacturers who produced goods for the domestic market.

Appropriate Technology

Multilateral agencies were among the first, in fact, to make a foray into the subject of appropriate technology. It took the form of a 1975 visit by an engineer from India's Small Industries Services Institute. On behalf of UNIDO and UNDP, his assignment was to assess indigenous agricultural machinery and implements, and to design modifications that could improve productivity of their use (Kherdekar, 1976). His designs included such things as the addition of flanges to spades so that farmers could apply greater pressure with their bare feet while digging, shifting slightly modified yokes from one position to another on traction animals in order to maximize their pulling power for carts and plows, a more energy–efficient stove that could reduce charcoal requirements for cooking, and a simple instrument for quickly extracting corn kernels from cobs. In addition to the inherent promise that they seemed to offer for improving the technical efficiency of a variety of farm and home activities, the designs were extraordinary for their simplicity. Small manufacturers could make them with the tools, skills, and capital already in their possession, and would likely do so if a market were to develop for them.

Unfortunately, the engineer's recommendations, which included $1.4 million for a factory to produce new implements and fellowships to send Haitian technicians to India for training, were not interpreted by UN staff as having the same degree of appropriateness as his redesigned implements. However, after a period of submersion, some of the ideas resurfaced in 1983 with UNIDO funding of $80,000 for visits to Africa and subsequent return with prototype farming implements to be produced by a government–owned factory, and in 1984 with a joint UNIDO/UNDP proposal for $200,000 to assist the factory in mass–producing the prototypes (UNDP, 1984). In theory, these UN efforts might yield tangible results for farmers toward the late 1980s. The introduction of new products might also provide a basis for small manufacturers to assess their market potential and to decide whether to compete with the factory–made goods.

The American contribution to the appropriate technology theme began in 1978 when Washington–based USAID staff proposed a $1.7 million project to assist the government in developing low–cost rural technologies for food, fuel, power, and water systems, such as solar desalinization, pyrolysis, methane generation, food storage, and solar cooking equipment (USAID, 1978a). One of the difficulties with this proposal was that technologies that appeared low–cost and appropriate in the United States seemed more costly and less appropriate once they reached Haiti. The technologies were definitely not of a kind that small manufacturers could produce without considerable infusions of training and capital. Another difficulty was that although government could run a factory to produce simple tools, albeit with subsidies and management assistance, it had not yet demonstrated a capacity to successfully implement the type of extension work that introduction of these technologies would require. Still, in 1979 the government created the Office of National Technology in the Ministry of Planning, and USAID initiated a $600,000 appropriate technology assistance project to the office shortly thereafter (USAID, 1980: 48; USAID, 1984e). The project eventually focused much of its attention on looking for alternative energy resources such as rice-hull briquettes and windmills, and then ended in 1983 (USAID, 1984e: 32).

In the meantime, a group of USAID visitors, after noting in 1980 that the UNIDO/UNDP proposal of 1976 was still dormant and that the USAID appropriate technology project was heading in a direction unlikely to have a near-term impact on small manufacturing, suggested that predetermination of specific technologies by external experts was not an optimum way to proceed. Such experts were unlikely to know which technologies were more or less appropriate in terms of local demand for them, and were unlikely to have comprehensive knowledge of the wide variety of technologies available for a wide variety of purposes. The visitors then recommended establishment of an information transfer service that could respond to questions from business establishments and from PVOs working with small enterprises by searching about for appropriate answers, especially from such countries as India, the Philippines, Sri Lanka, and Pakistan where small manufacturing was more technologically advanced than in Haiti (USAID, 1982b: 162).

The visitors need not have troubled themselves with this proposal. Soon after they left, a PVO established an information clearinghouse with financial support from some other PVOs that had many questions in search of answers. These questions were sometimes pertinent to small manufacturing, more often not. The most popular technology was a method of oral rehydration (Pragma, 1984: 35). Along the same lines, the Haitian Association of Voluntary Agencies (HAVA), an organization linking about 100 PVOs, was in the process of setting up a technology microfiche data bank for its members in 1985. And in early 1986, a development project associated with the Mennonites had almost completed a similar data bank that it would use in conjunction with a small credit scheme (noted in chapter 7) to assist producers in finding the information they required to compete with imports and the products of import-substitution factories, and to develop new product lines. Time would tell whether this project was capable of making a difference. But after several years of wandering the wilderness of inappropriateness, appropriate technology seemed finally closer to organizing itself at a level and scale consistent with the characteristics of small manufacturing in Haiti.

Politics

The five accounts of a few components and historical episodes of the political class present a panorama of diverse interests and activities. Some of these interests and activities offer little basis for believing that the class can produce more in the way of benefits for ordinary workers. Others provide a small but important foundation for hope.

Cause for pessimism lies principally in the behavior of too many multilateral missionaries and agencies. Logical necessities of habit, professional standing, career security, organizational repute, and other similar factors would suggest that ignorance–camouflaging and other abuses of various conceptual categories about employment, informality, traditionality, artisanality, and so on are unlikely to subside. Data that might suggest that several of the categories may sometimes be analytically or operationally inappropriate or irrelevant, such as the features I described for St. Martin, cannot cause them to fade away. Data provide no information. The individual and organizational mind produces information from data by imputing order to them, and among the missionaires and agencies there is no obvious purpose to be served in altering current methods of imputation. There is, in fact, sound purpose in retaining them.

No matter how badly misused, the methods sustain claims to superior knowledge and expertise. And the risk–taking behavior required to run against the grain of expert tradition, no less for a foreign assistant or local technician than for a "peasant," is uncommon. Only the bold among career scholars, professionals, and consultants are capable of suggesting that ideas in World Bank or ILO reports, ideas reflecting considerable learning and research in reputable schools of economics, development studies, or other subjects, are being used for dubious purposes. Only the extraordinarily bold (or naive) are willing to undermine their rationales for being in or writing about Haiti, explicitly by claiming ignorance, or implicitly by leaving out of their reports sections pertaining to subjects about which they know very little. These are self–destructive courses of action, most especially in communities in which many members may treat the concepts as realities, and in which attacks on concepts and their applications may come to be viewed as affronts to reason. For the same purpose that few traders alter their stocks or places of sale, or that few manufacturers willingly change techniques and product lines, experts in particular niches do not readily abandon tried and tested approaches to doing things that bring valued cash and in–kind remuneration. The purpose is survival of the individual and the organization.

Pessimism, however, does not derive from the survival–oriented behavior patterns of experts and agencies in multilateral factions. Such behavior is normal. Indeed, any other type of behavior would deviate so much from the "norm" that one would be compelled to call it abnormal. The principal source of pessimism is the absence of countervailing political forces within this faction of the class to alter the calculus of survival, and through such alteration to bring about changes in habits of practice. Foreign assistance is beholden to little but itself in places like Haiti. Experts answer to other experts, and scholars to other scholars in a relatively isolated corner of the class. Haitians in positions of influence, if one is to judge by the attitude I noted earlier of a minister of finance toward ordinary people, are unlikely to challenge ideas in currency, let alone current practices on the subject.

In time the ideas will change. Applicability of the unemployment concept lost ground over the course of two decades to the concept of underemployment. The "informal" sector, similarly, gained dominance over "marginal" or "backward" activities. New ideas will eventually add themselves to the long list of extant adjectives and labels. The politics of ideas are not static, and perhaps one day the notion that workers and work can be viewed as basically the same everywhere will find a place in the conceptual sun. The calculus of expert and organizational survival will also change and may engender a process wherein standards of practice in the use of newer or older notions move toward an area where the welfare of these factions of the political class need not preempt production of beneficial side-effects for ordinary workers.

For an extended interim, however, use of labels describing the unknown will continue to distract this part of the class from learning more about the concrete circumstances of ordinary workers. Opportunities for uncovering small but important things, like the counterproductivity of market taxes, the utility of sanitation services on public health and trader income, the value-added of small manufacturing exports to the economy, and the function of housing as store, warehouse, factory, and office, will continue to be constrained.

However, there is cause for some optimism in the behavior of many PVOs and their bilateral agency allies. Necessities of habit, standing, security, and organizational repute operate within these factions no less than in others. Catchphrases like "self-help," "self-sufficiency," "appropriate technology," "private sector development," and so forth also serve to mask the unknown and to contribute to individual and agency solvency. But a fundamental difference between PVO-bilateral survival prerequisites and those of multilateral factions is the invocation of a call to direct action on behalf of ordinary workers.

The actions of a decade in matters of craft exports and appropriate technology, as for multilateral efforts like those of UNESCO that preceded them, produced ambiguous outcomes. From beginning to end, each project constituted an enterprise that challenged itself with inexperience and ignorance of the meaning of business. Whether the difficulty revolved around material supply, transformation technology, labor, management, capital, or marketing, every project duplicated the daily experiences of every laborer, trader, and manufacturer in St. Martin. By survival criteria in operation in St. Martin, most projects were nonsurvivors. But that was not important. What was important was the experience of the concreteness of the struggle to succeed in exporting or in finding a marketable technology in an intensely competitive domestic and international economic environment.

For individuals and agencies within the factions who could sense that what was happening to them was one of the very few tangible experiences that they shared with ordinary workers, the projects constituted a substantive step toward understanding by a few of the political class of something about the ordinary class. This small step was important because the essence of the macroeconomic problem for workers like those in St. Martin seemed to be stagnant demand in *their* section of the economy. For the better part of 500 years, tax machines left little to ordinary consumers for the purpose of buying, and to manufacturers for the purpose of investing, if they could justify investment in a stagnant market. And unable to battle, as could members of the political class, for a share of the fiscal benefits offered to larger establishments during rare periods of economic expansion, costs of acquiring materials and tools, after duties and commercial monopoly margins, were invariably high (Haggblade, Defay, and Pitman, 1979: 81–85).

If techniques of trade looked traditional, and if methods and products of manufacturers looked artisanal (either in the perjorative or in the positive–aesthetic sense), these superficial properties may have had less to do with the activities and, extending the reasoning of several commentators, more to do with a political economy that for all practical purposes guaranteed that little or no "modernization" could take place. In this respect, what ordinary workers desperately needed was reconstruction of the political economy to serve their interests. For that to happen in a state that excluded their direct participation, ordinary workers needed factions within the political class who, in the process of serving their own interests (including the interest of altruism), would press for changes that could spill over as benefits to ordinary workers. With PVOs and bilateral agencies engaged in activities fundamentally the same as those of manufacturers, there was some eventual chance of a beneficial side effect.

Although still far removed from an understanding of the circumstances of ordinary workers, the compulsions of PVO–bilateral agency factions to "do something" to help in the matter of earnings was a significant political event. For one decade at least, they wittingly or unwittingly provided a representation within the political class of what members believed were the interests of ordinary workers, and in the process did two useful things.

Within the political class as a whole, they constituted a countervailing force against the tendency of other factions to ignore, discount, or otherwise heap abuse upon ordinary workers. And they formed the embryo of what could eventually become a minor version of the perpetual nagging force that from 1949 to 1986 so ably served the interests of assembly and import substitution by introducing and lobbying for policy reforms. Nagging forces are crucial to change.

The amount of time it might take for the PVO–bilateral agency alliance to acquire better understanding of workers is uncertain. But so long as something of an implicit bridge of shared interests integrates parts of both classes with a common destiny, these is cause for hope.

Such a bridge, or some other version of it, is important for reasons that extend far beyond the limits of discussions about opinions, assumptions, theories, actions, and inactions pertinent to the matter of work in the marketplace. The fortunes of conceptual battle among multilateral factions in 1975 caused the demise of an important idea. It was the positing by some of my colleagues in the UNCHBP project of a tangible and important bidirectional relationship between earnings on the one hand, and the cost of living on the other. For my colleagues it was just a thought that seemed to have merits on its own terms while proving useful for arguing in favor of what our opponents called social overhead investment. But the thought rang true in the context of economies such as the one I explored in St. Martin.

If large segments of the ordinary population were so poor that their expenditure patterns left little over for purchases of other goods and services after food, water, and shelter, and if these costs were rising as quickly as their incomes, there was little scope for increase in domestic demand for the other goods and services. There was little scope for investment to provide more of these goods and services. There was no relenting in the pressure upon families to put almost everyone to work in the market. And if the cost of living was rising more quickly than income, then every ordinary laborer, trader, and manufacturer in this calorie–intensive economy, under pressure of rising costs, was becoming not only poorer, but also less efficient, less profitable, and less productive.

Indeed, for all practical purposes, and as I implied when introducing the 1500–calorie food standard as the reference for determining profitability and productivity of workers, the proper meaning of "making a living" was often very literally that of *manufacturing life.* In this respect, the evolution of the price of food, the principal factor of earnings production, seemed to be having a disastrous impact on productivity and earnings in 1976, and seemed to be getting worse through 1986. Whatever general incoherence the political class may have exhibited with respect to the matter of earnings, there was no such incoherence with respect to food. People were hungry. Many were slowly starving. And in the absence of a bridge of some kind to make the fact known in political terms, factions in direct control of events did little of substance to provide relief.

Notes

1. Schumpeter (1969: 19–23) suggested this premise under the concept of "self-direction."
2. Cairncross (1958) proposed the idea that all workers and households could be viewed as producers or firms.
3. The distinction between trade and manufacturing, as in all distinctions, is normative. Trade involves a certain degree of bulk-breaking, and thus incorporates some change to goods. A particularly troublesome group to categorize in St. Martin were sellers of prepared foods. Using U.S. classification schemes, they could be viewed as restaurants, in which case they were part of trade, or food-processing establishments, a part of manufacturing. However, since they did involve substantial transformation of raw materials, and since their value-added stemmed from both marketing and transformation, they looked more like manufacturers than like traders.
4. The method I used for producing earnings data combined the properties of an employment and income survey with that of a business survey. For "laborers" I inquired about the amount of money individuals had earned the previous day and the previous six working days, and the number of days during the previous week and month in which they had earned money. The survey took place during the slack part of the city's business cycle, and these data therefore depended on respondent recall to estimate the difference in the pattern of daily earnings and number of days of work between the slack season and peak season. Annual average monthly earnings were thus determined by combining daily earnings and days of earnings per month over both seasons. For traders and manufacturers, the process was similar, except that net earnings resulted from separate calculations of total daily and monthly sales, recurrent costs of production, and additions to or withdrawals from capital stocks. Appendix A provides a sense of the kinds of information that came out of the interview discussions.
5. This is an oversimplification. A worker was minimally productive if he or she earned enough to cover all factor costs besides food, including capital (e.g., fixed and working capital, housing) and a share of the paid or unpaid labor of others providing essential inputs like food preparation, shopping, etc. The calorie line may therefore overstate productivity, but it is closer to the region of where zero productivity might lie than the minimum wage.
6. The figure of $0.10 was therefore perhaps slightly lower than what some economists refer to as the nutrition efficiency wage (e.g., Binswanger and Rosenzweig, 1984: 4–10).
7. Locher's (1974) analysis of market women in Port-au-Prince suggested something very close to perfect competition.
8. The association between the earnings-capital ratio (i.e., daily net earnings divided by capital in use or, more simply, daily return) and working capital in a simple regression model was:

Rt = 4.1 + 33.4K
where: Rt = daily return in trade, expressed as a percentage of capital; and
K = the inverse of capital in use, expressed in dollars.

The squared correlation coefficient (r^2) of the expression was 0.48, and the beta coefficient was significant at the 1 percent level.

9. The association between the earnings–capital ratio, defined in note 8, and fixed plus working capital in a simple regression model was:

Rm = 5.4 + 13.6K
where: Rm = daily return in manufacturing, expressed as a percentage of capital; and
K = the inverse of capital in use, expressed in dollars.

The correlation coefficient (r^2) was 0.36, and the beta coefficient was significant at the 1 percent level.

10. The $15 incorporated into the expressions in notes 8 and 9, above, yield the same daily returns. Trade has higher returns below $15, and lower returns than manufacturing above this amount.
11. At a daily return of 4 percent a day for twenty–five working days, extrapolation yields a return of 100 percent per month and 1200 percent per year. Such calculations are not particularly meaningful because the rate of return is to the joint factors of production: time, skill, and capital. To calculate an average return to capital alone, one would necessarily have to estimate earnings of time and skill in closely allied alternative occupations (i.e., without capital) and to ascribe the differential to the addition of capital in a "with–without" comparison. A cursory examination of the occupations in table 2.2 that traders and manufacturers might be able to buy suggests that capital could add 20 to 25 percent to daily or monthly earnings, or perhaps a return of 1 percent per day and 25 percent per month.
12. Standing (1982: 38–50) provided an excellent review of various definitions of underemployment within the framework of measurements of labor underutilization, and their difficulties. In another framework, that of neoclassical economics, an underemployed person is often someone whose withdrawal from a market activity does not result in a lowering of output (Binswanger and Rosenzweig 1984: 5). Unfortunately, measuring this kind of underemployment in urban areas is extremely difficult.
13. I could not obtain useful data on these transfers. Ahlers (1978) indicated that net transfers to Port–au–Prince students from families residing in four towns ranged from $130 to $200 per year. He also noted that transfers from nonstudent migrants in Port–au–Prince to towns, $31 per year, exceeded transfers in the opposite direction, $12.
14. Lowenthal (1984) examined the sexual economics of households quite carefully.
15. Friedman (1952) and Keliman (1966) outlined the need for standardization of household size in order to compare households varying in both numbers of people and age composition of the people. For this purpose I assigned the following weights: five years of age or less = 0.5 adult equivalent units; six to

eleven years = 0.7 units; twelve to sixteen years = 0.9 units; and seventeen years or older = 1.0 unit.

16. "Scrounging" is the closest English approximation for the French term "grapillage" which Moral (1961: 335) introduced to describe methods used in small-scale activities in rural areas, and which developed considerable currency in the Francophone community.
17. As discussed in later chapters, consumption expenditures represented the cost of producing (or reproducing) only one factor of production: labor. If the cost of basic living was such that net earnings from self-employment had to be used only for consumption purchases, the possibility of savings for investment in other factors like fixed or working capital to permit changes in the proportions of factors used in production was lessened.
18. These works contained detailed operational descriptions of homework and other small-scale activities in Europe (ILO, 1948); Africa (ILO, 1962); the Middle East (ILO, 1952); China (SRI, 1958) and India (UN, 1955; India, 1956, 1958, 1960; Singh, 1961; Shetty, 1963). They also contained descriptions of how the activities fit into regional and national economies (Herman, 1956; BNB, 1958; Hoselitz, 1968), how they fit into the export sector (Smith, 1952; Willis, 1955; Ho and Huddle, 1973), and how policies and assistance programs might promote their expansion (Elkan, 1959; Ligget, 1959; Stepanek, 1960; Weddell, 1960; USAID, 1962; Schumacher, 1965). And one said almost everything there was to say from a technical perspective (Staley and Morse, 1965). The problem at the UNCHBP was that although staff could borrow many ideas from these various works, lack of knowledge concerning the extent and types of small manufacturing in the city did not permit matching specific ideas with specific facts.
19. Informal sector studies available at the time covered urban areas of Africa (Hart, 1970, 1973; Nihan, 1976; Norwood, 1975; Kennedy, 1976), Asia (Dasgupta, 1973; McGee, 1974; Marsden, 1975; Papanek, 1975) and Latin America (Diegues, 1976; DEWIT, 1976; World Bank, 1976b). Unfortunately, while often very interesting, these studies did not offer much in the way of operational utility for planning purposes. By definition, they imputed abstract labels to employment without sufficient facts to demonstrate that the labels were better than conventional ones, or that they had value beyond general description. More recently, after reviewing seventeen similar studies, Zaidi (1983: 143–49) came to a similar conclusion.
20. The World Bank (1985: 118) indicated that unemployment in the city was 26 percent in 1985. This figure seemed the result of a computational error.
21. Moral (1961: 335), see note 16, above.
22. Translating the studies into policy and design standards for the UNCHBP project was my task in 1974 and 1975.
23. The World Bank agreed to finance the rehabilitation project with $14 million in 1980, but by 1985 work on the market had yet to start. Either the government or the Bank's consultants had underestimated the number of families who lived in the path of the works, and funds to pay relocation damages were inadequate. The families were unwilling to move into relocation housing until this matter was settled. A fire in 1985 helped prod them, and by the end of the year the relocation process was beginning. Unfortunately, upon the fall of the regime in early 1986, the relocation units were all occupied by other families. Market improvement would therefore have to wait a while longer.

24. Staley and Morse (1965: 1–25) provided a good synopsis of dominant attitudes toward small manufacturing prior to the transformation of the adjective into a noun.
25. My estimate from disaggregated data on exports.

3

Food

The historical underpinning of the evolving food shortage, compounded in more recent times by importation policies that I will discuss later in this chapter, was stagnation in the growth of agricultural output. Many factors contributed to stagnation, but an important one was the lack of interest of the political class to matters pertaining to food production.

As long as Haiti produced food in quantities sufficient to maintain stability, its governments had few compelling political reasons to expend effort in raising output of crops destined primarily for domestic consumption. Effort was essential in the case of commodities with export and hence with revenue-generating potential, such as sugar, sisal, plantains, bananas, and cotton, and in cases in which large-scale farmers of the political class demanded such services as irrigation for these and other plantation-type outputs even if they were not destined for export. The demise of large landholdings and exports, the shift of the rural elite to towns and easier forms of livelihood, and the dominance in the countryside of small-scale producers whose primary desire was to have government leave them alone, gradually removed both the political and economic basis for productive public action in agriculture.[1]

Through replacement of export-oriented with domestic food production on current land, and through colonization of new lands, output managed to keep pace with population growth and demand. Governments did not discover new political reasons to intervene in the sector. Short-term inconveniences caused by drought or hurricanes, if they affected urban areas enough in terms of price increases or arrival of hungry (especially armed) migrants to warrant action, were disposed of by means of temporary food imports.

At some moment in history, data to indicate the period when this might have occurred are not available but 1920–1950 seems likely, farmers ran out of room for further crop substitution and for cultivating new land. With autonomous evolution of techniques to increase yields moving ahead more slowly than population growth, a process perhaps partially constrained by the ability of the country's best farmers to raise their earnings as temporary or permanent laborers in other countries, by Haiti's mountainous terrain demanding substantial technological change to offset effects of soil erosion, by low levels of income (made lower than necessary by public and private taxation) that often made risks of investment in technological experimentation life-threatening ventures, and by lack of significant government or foreign assistance interventions to lower the risks or to introduce new techniques, production did not keep up with demand.

Food shortages, accompanied by unrelenting increases in prices for basic commodities, presented themselves as new political justifications for some public action during the 1960s. With help and prodding from foreign assistants arriving in increasing numbers after 1967, government began to show interest in participating directly in the process of promoting increased agricultural production, especially rice, which tended to be a principal staple of higher-income groups. This effort was slow in producing results. Chronic shortages became more acute, and price increases for many basic commodities rose more steeply. Unfortunately, neither government nor its principal foreign assistants seemed to notice that the shortages were reaching crisis proportions among substantial segments of the population, or that they could engender serious economic and political consequences.

Inattention by political leaders may have stemmed from the traditional tendency of the indigenous component of the political class to ignore the circumstances of ordinary people, and perhaps also from lack of historical experience with sustained food shortages. Without prior experience, government officials may not have known what to look for, may not have been able to project political implications, and even if able to project them, may not have been able to identify appropriate remedies. Causes of inattention by Haitian technicians and foreign assistants involved in matters pertaining to food were more elusive. They did concern themselves with ordinary people, or so they said. They presumably knew what to look for and what to do. But somehow or other this concern and knowledge had difficulty transforming itself into actions commensurate with the scale of the growing crisis.

One hindrance may have been lack of appropriate data, an important factor when the essence of an issue is largely invisible except to trained observers. Certainly there was an abundance of numbers about malnutrition in children. But these malnutrition studies were not comparable and gave little indication of temporal trends. They nevertheless concluded that nutritional levels among children in the city were not good.[2] By their nature, and by the nature of the subject in general, the studies were unable by themselves to ascribe causes for the findings. In theory, malnutrition could result from inappropriate feeding habits, from illnesses and parasites, from the structure of relative food prices, or from a general shortage of food pushing all basic prices up relative to the income available to pay them. Nutrition studies could not determine causes accurately. However, they did lead to a significant number of programs touching on nutrition education, targeted mother and child nutrition therapy projects, school feeding programs, and other similar methods of linking food and people directly. The jump from research to action even without clear indication of cause was not entirely surprising. Malnutrition studies were of a clinical nature carried out by subscribers to professions that dealt with such issues clinically. The actions provided benefits to many, but if malnutrition found its causes primarily in matters not susceptible to clinical treatment, like widespread food shortages, the actions could have only limited effect.

Unfortunately, as a result of a lack of sustained interest in study of food consumption patterns, there was little to suggest the possibility of other causes. A small exploration of urban consumption and nutrition in 1956, more about which I will say later, and several others in scattered towns and villages before 1970, constituted the entire resource of factual knowledge about this subject. To be sure, there were valiant attempts to estimate national and urban patterns from estimates of agricultural production and food imports, but production figures had little basis in fact. They wandered about the statistical landscape at the discretion of those who prepared them and, consequently, consumption figures did the same.[3] In effect, substantive knowledge about urban food consumption and nutrition from 1970 to 1986 was considerably less than it had been in 1956.

Similar to the processes I outlined toward the end of the previous chapter, and both a consequence of and contributor to ignorance, another hindrance may have been risk avoidance associated with the politics of expert survival. Where the presence of numbers in reports was an indication of superior performance or where it seemed useful for other reasons, and where there were no numbers available, as in the case of our actions at the UNCHBP project with respect to the informal sector and employment statistics, compulsion to invent necessary figures often presented itself. With no contrary data available to raise questions about the inventions, this kind of action was virtually risk-free. Subsequent analysts needing numbers could report the original inventions and thereby avoid all risk, or they could engage some risk by adjusting the originals. Without empirical bases for the originals, adjustment was tantamount to reinvention. And if, as was almost always the case, later analysts had no new data upon which to rest arguments for new inventions, risk avoidance made it easier for them to report the originals. Beyond the problem of invention coming to be regarded as fact, this process lent itself to the creation of immutable inventive fact.

For example, in 1970 a group of health experts invented a national food consumption pattern that suggested an average intake of 1900 calories per adult per day.[4] Relative food prices changed considerably between 1970 and 1986, and there were indications that many households were unable to keep pace with price inflation during the period. Yet most documents prepared in the sixteen–year interval reported essentially the same pattern and nutritional intake as in 1970.[5] Even if the original estimate was accurate, changes in relative prices, and in other pertinent events like elimination of Haiti's pig population after 1980, should have provided a basis for adjusting the 1900 calorie number. Professional acceptance after 1970 of a permanent average of 1900 calories as fact when it was unlikely to have remained fact for 16 years may have camouflaged the growing shortage of food, may have masked the need for seeking more up–to–date consumption data, and may have engendered a certain degree of complacency with respect to food consumption and nutrition.

Nutritionists and others busy with weighing children were certainly not complacent, but as I noted above, they were not producing data (e.g., time–series malnutrition estimates) of the kinds that might raise concern across a wider spectrum of Haitians and expatriates engaged in setting agendas and priorities for government and foreign–assistance interventions. The estimate of 1900 calories was low relative to what passed for international standards of adequacy, and was also lower than measured or estimated averages in many other developing countries.[6] The number was therefore conceptually consistent with the general impression that most Haitians did not eat well and, making certain assumptions about the distribution of consumption about the average, with the sense that many Haitians ate very poorly.

But lost in diffusion of the permanent number was the fact that almost every empirical study of food consumption in rural areas between 1955 and 1965 reported average calorie intakes ranging from 1200 to 1700 calories per adult. Even making allowances for higher levels in urban areas, such facts as were available implied that the national average in 1970 might have been closer to 1500 calories than to 1900.

Thus a third hindrance to understanding and action, in some respects a variation of the second, may have been a reluctance on the part of reporters to accept facts that seemed to deviate too much from what potential readers among their colleagues might consider "believable" relative to facts or inventions from other countries, or relative to notional standards of what individuals required to live and work.[7] The 1200 to 1700 calorie range was perhaps socially unacceptable within foreign–assistance factions of the political class.

Because questions that might present themselves with respect to one number were sometimes different from questions that might arise with respect to another, social preference for an immutable invention rather than for available fact presented a difficulty that extended well beyond the narrow issue of statistical accuracy. At 1900 calories, questions pertaining to relationships between nutrition and health, and between nutrition and long–term consequences on the development of children, came to mind quickly. At 1500 calories, these questions remained, requiring adjustment only in terms of the size of the population of concern. But where most market activites were very labor–intensive, 1500 calories also introduced the question of whether nutritional intake was having a detrimental effect on things like labor productivity and earnings. And if changes in the price of food over time were serving to lower intake and therefore productivity and earnings, food shortages were (human) fuel shortages that might be having serious negative impacts on ordinary people, and more generally, on economic growth.

However, even if concerned members of the political class had accepted an average consumption of 1500 calories, most of them were unlikely to have posed questions about the potential causal relationship leading from food to income in microeconomic terms, or to economic growth in macroeconomic terms. These questions would not have easily presented themselves for two reasons that together may have constituted a fourth hindrance to understanding and action. First, notwithstanding a sizable literature about food, nutrition, health, and labor productivity in developing countries that provide ample bases for such questions, convention holds that food is a "final" consumption good, and that income is an independent determinant of this consumption. These premises flow from consumer theory that has shown itself very useful for certain explanatory purposes. Unfortunately, and in much the same manner as for concepts and categories attached to workers, the processes by which a theory comes to be viewed as "reality," rather than one of several available methods of interpretation, tends to hide certain facts that are inconsistent with the simplifying assumptions required for (any) theory, and to prevent exploration of relationships that are opposite to what the theory presumes. Consumer theory of the standard type does not permit food to have a causal influence on income, and those who treat it as a reality cannot look for such a relationship.

Second, even if not held captive by dominant convention, members of the political class did not fully grasp the process by which people produced earnings. Material of the kind I presented in chapter 2 was and remains relatively uncommon, and without a literature available from which to extract ideas, or a willingness to venture into neighborhoods in search of ideas, many of them would have found difficulty in describing the ways in which food might interact with the production of earnings and aggregate growth.

No less subject to this hindrance than most others of the class, I entered

St. Martin with the presumption that food belonged to the category of final consumption expenditure. But in my effort to understand how families produced income, how much they produced, and why they obtained what they did, I found myself incapable of ignoring the role that food might have in the process. For at prices prevailing in the retail market in 1976, the distribution of net income shown in table 2.7 did not permit most households to obtain 1900 calories after spending 50 percent of income for food, and almost a quarter of them, the "ultra-poor" that I mentioned earlier, would have had to spend over 75 percent to obtain 1500 calories.[8] Because the neighborhood seemed to have an income distribution similar to that for the city as a whole, these figures implied that many or most urban residents could not obtain 1900 calories. Whether this circumstance represented a general crisis in 1976 was difficult to say, but to me it seemed to have reached crisis proportions for a great many ordinary families.

It seemed to be a crisis because when viewed through the perspective of the manufacturing metaphor, food was the most important of several factor inputs that households used to produce nutrition, and nutrition was one of several inputs that they used to produce health, labor productivity, and ultimately the earnings required to obtain food and other more or less productive things. Rising food prices increased the cost of producing income, and because income did not seem to be rising at the same rate as costs, profitability and efficiency were falling in an environment in which there was relatively little room for declines that would not also threaten survival.

Food and Income

Relationships between food, income, and survival that underlay the crisis are quite complex. But above and beyond inherent complexity, the capacity of the political class to understand the relationships is constrained by uncertainties concerning the meaning and measurement of nutrition, uncertainties concerning the causes and consequences of inadequate nutrition, and uncertainties about how households in places like St. Martin might adapt themselves to the relationship. Difficulties associated with these uncertainties, however, are problems only for scientists and others of the political class who depend on thought for their understanding. Ordinary people are not inconvenienced by these things. Relationships for such people are simple and certain because they feel them.

The Meaning and Measurement of Nutrition

Although easy to understand conceptually, nutrition presents three practical difficulties that interfere with efforts to trace its direct relationships to income. First, nutrition eludes measurement by a single criterion. Economists and others often use the calorie as a basic indicator of quantity, relegating other attributes into the category of "quality" for purposes of theoretical simplification in applications of consumer theory, but the calorie measures only the heat-generating or energy content of the food.[9] It is not a synonym for nutrition. There is also protein mass, carbohydrate, fat, and fiber. Buried among these are various essential vitamins and inorganic substances like iron, calcium, and potassium, which also have useful attributes.

In addition to not having a single criterion by which to measure quantities of these and other components of nutrition simultaneously, a second difficulty is that the presence of some components influences intake requirements of others. Higher or lower quantities of fiber, for example, affect metabolic rates and hence calorie needs. Thus even a matrix of different nutrients may prove inadequate for measurement purposes. A diet high in calories and low in certain other components may have the same physiological properties as a diet lower in calories and higher in the other components, and may therefore make it difficult to infer whether one particular combination of components represents an inherently inferior or superior level of nutrition than another.

By extension, there is the question of whether physiological benefits of marginal increases in different components are the same at different levels of nutrition. When energy consumption is very low, for example, benefits from a further increase in calories may greatly exceed those derivable from other components. At high levels of calorie intake, the opposite relationship may hold. In this kind of circumstance a change in income leading to an increase in consumption of low-calorie foods, what some consumer theories would interpret as a marginal substitution of quality for quantity of nutrition, could in fact be little more than a change in raw material proportions allowing households to combine calories and other nutritional components more efficiently than before the change.

The third difficulty is that different people may have different requirements. Besides obvious variations associated with weight, health status, and other physiological properties, the types of work they do influences nutritional needs. Lower-income households in St. Martin tended to have larger proportions of workers in labor- (i.e., energy-) intensive activities than in capital-intensive ones like factory or office work, and hired fewer nonhousehold workers to assist in market or domestic activities. Higher- and lower-income households usually have different consumption patterns, but if the characteristics of their daily activities are also fundamentally different, differences in patterns may derive less from the income differential and more from nutritional combinations required to produce different kinds of work.

Table 3.1 indicates that energy expenditures can vary quite substantially from one activity to another. The difference in expenditures between manual workers engaged in moderate and light work is over 100 calories per hour, or perhaps 800 calories over the course of a working day. If moderate work generates lower income than light work, an emphasis on calories would be logical. Similarly, individuals required to pound their own grain, mix dense cereals, transport water, or wash clothes because they are unable to pay for milling services or for premilled grain, for lighter cereals like rice, or for transportation and laundry services of others, circumstances closely associated with low income, would also seem to have good reason to put an emphasis on calories.

Absence of a unique measure, interaction between different components, interpersonal variations in requirements, and other similar factors make the meaning of nutrition imprecise. Because of this imprecision there is no ready method of determining, within a range, whether some households are providing better nutrition than others, or whether they are producing it more efficiently than others. There may or may not be a significant difference between average intakes of 1500 and 1900 calories. In theory, either or both figures may be high or low relative to requirements, and neither one suggests anything about other nutrients. Compounding these definitional difficulties are uncertainties about the causes of malnutrition that I noted briefly at the outset of the chapter, and about its consequences.

Causes and Consequences of Malnutrition

Research concerning food consumption by gestating mothers and by young children provides evidence that malnutrition can increase the probability of lowered intelligence, smaller body weight, increased incidence of disease among the children throughout the course of the rest of their lives, and infant mortality (Belli, 1971: 2). Whatever the effects of early malnutrition might be on the future earning capacities of such children, the influence of disease on school attendance and of lowered intelligence on school performance may compound them (Selowsky and Taylor, 1973: 18–19). Where schooling is not available, the exacerbating influences work their effects through lowering of skill acquisition during formal or informal apprenticeship processes.

Parents unable to provide offspring with adequate nutritional endowments because of suboptimal feeding practices, financial circumstance, or other factors may therefore not only compromise the future income-gener-

TABLE 3.1
Food Energy Expenditures for Selected Household Activities

	Activity	Total Calories per Hour per Kg of Body Weight	Calories per Hour Net of Basic Functions[a]	Net Calories per Hour for a 52 Kg. Adult[b]
Basic functions:	Lying down, sitting, standing	1.4	—	—
Travel:	Slow walk	2.9	1.5	73
	Average walk	3.7	2.1	109
	Fast walk	4.2	2.8	146
Market production:	Office work	1.6	0.2	10
	Light manual work	2.9	1.5	78
	Moderate manual work	5.1	3.7	192
Nonmarket production:	Light domestic chores	2.7	1.3	68
	Moderate domestic chores	3.8	2.4	125
	Washing clothes	3.5	2.1	109
	Transporting water	4.3	2.9	150
	Mixing sorghum	4.0	2.6	135
	Pounding cereals	4.9	3.5	182

Source: Adapted from Mondot-Bernard (1981).
[a] Travel and production expenditures less 1.4 cal./kg/hr.
[b] Entries in second column times 52.

ating capacities of their children, and hence the level of support they might expect from them in their old age, but also expose themselves to higher probabilities of incurring health-related costs associated with childrens' illnesses over the shorter term.[10] In turn, as I discuss below, these costs often contribute to immediate declines in family income.

The causal properties associated with inadequate nutrition in this string of relationships is nevertheless limited by the independent influence of illness (Horton and King, 1981: 18). Disease lowers nutrient absorption and therefore raises intake requirements. This interaction makes difficult determination of whether subsequent effects result primarily from illness or primarily from malnutrition associated with it. More generally, although inadequate nutrition may expose individuals to higher risks of illness, certain diseases introduce themselves quite independently of nutrition and have the effect of exposing individuals to higher risks of malnutrition. Therefore, given a set of health risks associated with sanitation practices and public health conditions in a particular locality, the closer the level of nutrition is to the point where other factors become more significant, the lower the likelihood that illness will result from inadequate food consumption.

In this regard, an important question for parents is not whether nutrition is adequate relative to some general standard, but rather whether it is adequate enough in the immediate circumstances. The probability of a child becoming ill in the crowded and unsanitary conditions of St. Martin, which I describe in detail in chapter 5, was relatively high, and there was a point at which further nutritional intake would make little difference to the incidence of illness. Studies carried out between 1965 and 1975 in nutrition therapy centers in Haiti, for example, noted that the proportions of children with first- and third-degree deviations from normal weight standards declined by 23 percent when average consumption increased from 1365 calories and 32 grams of protein per adult to over 2252 calories and 64 grams.[11] But the proportion with second-degree deviations, resulting from a shift of children with third-degree deviations into this category, increased by 41 percent. The studies ascribed this outcome to high incidences of tuberculosis, pneumonia, and other infections that nutrition therapy could do little to prevent. Since children were likely to fall victim to certain illnesses anyway, parents in places like St. Martin seeking to provide offspring with health protection through nutrition might have found it efficient to provide consumption only up to a level where returns to further expenditure on prophylaxis were lower than returns to other allocations of that expenditure.[12]

One of the more important of these other allocations often stems from a requirement by households to maintain or increase nutrition among parents and other adults in order to maintain or increase market earnings and the efficiency of essential nonmarket production activities. Low levels of nutrition have a tendency to lower the productivity of labor in market and nonmarket activities directly by decreasing mental agility and physical strength and indirectly by increasing the incidence of illness that may exacerbate any lowering of mental and physical capacity as well as lead to withdrawal from market and nonmarket activities.

Relationships between nutrition and health in adults are subject to uncertainties similar to those for children. In addition, relationships between nutrition and labor productivity, and between health and productivity, although conceptually self-evident, have yet to establish as convincing a body of empirical support as have hypotheses concerning the effects of malnutrition and disease upon children. Many studies reported positive associations between indicators of labor output and calorie intake, relatively strong associations between output and intake of certain minerals and vitamins, and similar relationships between output and disease.[13] However, design and measurement issues, and interrelations among independent explanatory variables tended to weaken the findings; not to the extent of suggesting that causal relationships did not exist, but rather by limiting the independent causal influences of nutrition and health with respect to other factors affecting productivity.

But few studies examined populations comparable to the one in St. Martin. Most of them covered farmers and wage laborers who, with the exception of a group of U.S. volunteers in a starvation exercise, consumed an average of 2200 calories per day or more, and who often had relatively easy access to low- or no-cost medical services. Relationships that might obtain in a population largely dependent on urban self-employment earnings, consuming substantially less on average than 2200 calories, and without access to low-cost health services, may therefore still be open to relatively unconstrained conjecture.[14]

The Problem in St. Martin

In St. Martin, almost all households derived income primarily from individual market earnings, and most earnings were a direct function of the productivity of labor. Unemployed individuals had to be strong enough to look for work on a continuous basis, and many of the laborers needed to search for customers as part of their normal work routines. Similarly, traders and manufacturers required maximum strength and mental prowess in purchasing inputs, transporting or transforming them, and then marketing the goods; as did household members responsible for important nonmarket tasks such as meal preparation. In all these instances, significant declines in physiological and mental capacities resulting from inadequate nutrition, illness, or both could have serious repercussions on earnings and the efficiency of other household production activities.

Households with very limited resources therefore face unenviable resource allocation decisions. They can curtail adult consumption and increase that of children (and gestating mothers) in the hope of producing long-term income benefits and lower probabilities of health-related expenditures for the children in the short term. This approach runs the risk of lowering productivity and earnings, of lowering food consumption for everybody, and of increasing the probability of health-related expenditures for adults. Alternatively, they can feed children less, concentrate nutrition resources on adults, especially breadwinners, and hope that returns to this investment are large enough and arrive quickly enough to minimize the opportunity costs of not adopting the first strategy.

If resources are so low that households can finance only minimum consumption, well below 1500 calories per adult for example, then there may be no decision to make.[15] The second policy is almost mandatory, not only because adult earnings decline rapidly at sustained levels of intake substantially less than 1500 calories, but also because potential rates of return to small additions of calories up to and slightly beyond 1500 calories may often be quite high. An adult awarded an extra 200 to 300 calories by a family for a few days might not only generate enough to sustain himself or herself at the higher level, but can conceivably produce a surplus sufficient to repay the calorie loan and raise consumption of all members.[16]

As a practical matter, however, households operate within the flow of time and fortune. The choices they make are considerably more involved than allocating calories at arbitrary decision-making moments. The illness of a child, whatever its cause, might require payment for curative medical services. Funds to make such payments would have to come from savings or from borrowing. If from savings, disposal of cash or sale of a productive household good, usually at a fraction of original cost, might mean a long-term loss of wealth. If the cash or good must be drawn from income-producing activities, a health expenditure might mean long-term reduction in the rate of earnings until a family reconstitutes its base of productive market assets. Similarly, resort to credit would reduce net earnings until the household completes its debt service. In any one of these situations, lowered earnings might mean lower food consumption and possibly higher exposure to risk of additional illness.

Even if a household does not make curative medical payments, an ill child can often require the time-consuming attention of an adult, and concurrent loss of time at work. A "day off" in St. Martin usually meant a 15 percent reduction in weekly earnings, the need to use savings or credit to cover income deficits if nursing dragged on, and a sequence of events similar to those I outlined immediately above. If an adult became ill, time off from working or lowered productivity while working produced the same sequence. Among the women who were unemployed at the time I conducted the survey, 30 percent were ill, 12 percent were tending to health needs (rather than feeding needs) of newborns, and 5 percent were not working because they had used up their trade capital in paying medical bills.

The definitional, causal, and consequential imprecisions that afflict scientific practice do not present difficulties for ordinary people. From the perspective of those exposed to it, or threatened with exposure, illness is very precise, as are its causes and consequences. Relationships between illness and earnings in St. Martin were not ambiguous. They were absolutely real.

Inadequate nutrition might or might not have contributed to illness and to lowered productivity in St. Martin. Inappropriate feeding habits, financial circumstances, intrahousehold consumption strategies, and illness might or might not have contributed to inadequate nutrition.[17] However, it is certain that incomes were often insufficient to finance a food consumption pattern providing a satisfactory level of intake. And it was also certain that households, in much the same way as they generated earnings, went to great lengths to maximize the efficiency with which they produced each unit of nutrition.

Manufacturing Nutrition

The last study of expenditure, food consumption, and nutrition in Port–au–Prince took place in 1956 (Grant and Groom, 1958). It covered a sample of seventy households in La Saline, a neighborhood near St. Martin. Lower–income families in the neighborhood spent $0.05 per day per adult to provide each individual with an average intake of 980 calories and 25 grams of protein (table 3.2). They produced this result by concentrating expenditures on foods like cereals, roots, and beans that, at prevailing market prices, offered high energy–cost ratios (i.e., calories per penny). On average, the lower–income group consumed food combinations yielding 196 calories and 5 grams of protein per penny.

The very poorest families within this group, those spending perhaps $0.03 per day per adult, relied primarily on corn, sorghum, sweet potato, sugar, and some beans. These foods offered highest energy–cost ratios. A family spending close to the average of $0.05 relied more on mixtures of corn and rice, and of sweet potato and plantains. It also consumed more beans, sugar, and oil, and was able to add some meat and fish to the diet. At

TABLE 3.2
Food Consumption and Expenditure in La Saline, 1956

	LOWER-INCOME GROUP			MIDDLE-INCOME GROUP			HIGHER-INCOME GROUP		
	Daily Calories Per Adult	EXPENDITURE (¢)		Daily Calories Per Adult	EXPENDITURE (¢)		Daily Calories Per Adult	EXPENDITURE (¢)	
		1956	At 1976 Prices		1956	At 1976 Prices		1956	At 1976 Prices
Corn	145	0.31	1.14	73	0.15	0.57	36	0.08	0.28
Sorghum	27	0.06	0.20	—	—	—	—	—	—
Rice	144	0.97	2.13	322	2.18	4.79	480	3.24	7.13
Bread	34	0.31	0.43	104	0.96	1.32	137	1.27	1.75
Roots, tubers[a]	245	1.02	4.62	220	0.91	4.14	163	0.68	3.08
Beans	118	0.62	1.96	158	0.83	2.63	317	1.65	5.26
Sugar	56	0.20	0.65	93	0.33	1.09	159	0.57	1.88
Meat	6	0.14	0.39	48	1.07	3.00	101	2.20	6.24
Oil	80	0.59	1.20	203	1.52	3.07	389	2.90	5.88
Subtotal	855	4.22	12.72	1216	7.95	20.61	1778	12.59	31.50
Other[b]	125	0.78	2.28	114	5.05	13.09	527	14.41	36.05
TOTAL	980	5.00	15.00	1430	13.00	33.70	2305	27.00	67.55
Protein (grams)	(25)			(42)			(68)		

Sources: Grant and Groom (1958), Donas (1978), and author's estimates.

[a] Includes 40 percent sweet potato, 14 percent manioc, 10 percent yam, and 36 percent plantain.

[b] Includes milk, fruit, green vegetables, fish, etc.

expenditure levels higher than $0.05 the consumption pattern shifted towards exclusive reliance on rice, and to an even more diverse set of items. In general, the poorest of the lower–income group seemed to expend funds as if they were attempting to maximize energy, buying at a rate close to 350 calories per penny, while those with greater means and buying about 150 calories per penny seemed to temper the energy orientation with an effort to increase overall protein weights and specific nutrients.

The shifts in nutrition production orientations associated with increasing income continued through the whole sample. Middle–income households spent $0.13 per day to provide 1430 calories and 42 grams of protein to each adult. In principle, these families could have combined their purchases in the same way as lower–income households to produce over 2500 calories and 65 grams, but such a consumption pattern would have been inefficient. With their greater resources, the opportunity cost of producing more energy and protein weight, subject to the law of diminishing returns, may have been higher than the cost of producing other useful nutrients. Although their average purchasing pattern of 110 calories and 3.2 grams per penny, derived from a heavy emphasis on rice, bread, meat, oil, and other items like milk, fruit, and green vegetables, seemed less cost–effective in calorie and protein weight terms compared to the lower–income group, it was more efficient in producing energy, protein mass, calcium, and vitamins A, B, C, and D all at the same time.[18]

Similarly, higher–income families spent $0.27 per day at an average rate of 85 calories and 2.5 grams of protein per penny to provide each adult with 2305 calories and 68 grams of protein, achieving a level of energy and protein intake that the Food and Agriculture Organization (FAO) would later suggest was approximately adequate for Latin America.[19] As in the comparison between middle– and lower–income groups, although higher–income family expenditures were twice those of middle–income households, calorie and protein intakes were only 60 percent higher, again suggesting that higher income yielded an increase in the perceived rate of return to production of hard–to–obtain nutrients relative to production of energy, protein mass, and easier–to–obtain nutrients.

Although the study noted that 63, 54, and 37 percent of adults in the low–, middle–, and high–income groups respectively were more than 5 percent underweight in relation to their body frames, and that 20 percent in the last group were overweight, implying that nutritional estimates for each group were, if not precise, then at least in the correct order, the authors of the study found difficulty in drawing much in the way of conclusions beyond the observation that the majority of individuals may not have eaten well during the survey period. They could not understand how working adults could maintain intense levels of activity while consuming less than 1000 calories per day for extended periods, especially when nutritional standards at the time considered energy intakes of 3000 calories or more as minimally adequate.[20] They therefore qualified their findings by introducing the possibility of homeostatic regulation, a hypothesis still in search of verification three decades later, and the possibility of underreporting of consumption at home and away from home. They also suggested that income and food prices were subject to considerable variation, and that except for the indigent, average annual food consumption in La Saline was close to the weighted mean of the three groups, or 1350 calories and 38 grams of protein.

These caveats notwithstanding, the La Saline study was an important contribution to understanding about expenditure and consumption patterns in the city. Although relative changes in food prices during the next several decades would superannuate its specific findings, the work did suggest that patterns conformed to what some scholars refer to as axioms of food consumption.[21]

The data were consistent with Bennett's Law, which states that the proportion of calories derived from starchy staples like grains and roots tends to fall with rising income. They were also consistent with Houthakker's Law, positing an association between higher income and consumption of a broader variety of food items, yielding progressively lower overall average energy– (or protein–) cost ratios.[22]

The study provided no evidence with which to examine the applicability of Slutsky's Law, positing a negative own–price elasticity or downward sloping demand curve for almost all commodities; of Engel's Law stating that the proportion of household income devoted to food declines with increasing income except, perhaps, where income is close to zero (i.e., that the income elasticity of demand for food is usually less than one); and of Engel's Corollary to the effect that income elasticity for food is likely to be large among low–income households. Still, since the study did imply the applicability of two axioms to Port–au–Prince, and since the other three had yet to be weakened by contrary evidence from anywhere else in the world, there was little reason to suspect that they would not also hold for relationships in St. Martin.

But by their nature, the laws and the La Saline study revealed nothing about nutrition production. Between the act of buying food and the act of tangibly consuming (i.e., eating) it was an extraordinarily complex manufacturing process that seemed to demand as much skill and efficiency as the production of market earnings. Important factors in the process, as for any act of transformation, were the financial and technological attributes of the raw materials (i.e., food commodities), costs of securing skilled labor time for meal preparation, costs of making time available for meal consumption, and the cost of capital equipment required for production.

Raw Materials

In 1976 households would have had to spend three times more than in 1956 for a pattern of consumption identical to that for La Saline's lower-income group, and two and a half times more for patterns identical to those of middle- and higher-income groups (table 3.2). Average income in St. Martin was $9.80 per adult. If households spent half of it for food, or about $0.16 per adult per day, most households would have found difficulty in matching the intake pattern of La Saline's poorer families. Maintenance of something approaching adequate nutrition, or at least the calorie and protein mass components of it, required that families have different consumption patterns than their predecessors in La Saline.

In the two decades following 1956, sorghum gradually replaced corn as the most cost-effective food for producing calories, the gap in energy-cost ratios between these two cereals and rice had narrowed appreciably, the ratio for bread became higher than rice, and for beans higher than roots.[23] On the basis of these changes, outlined in table 3.3, a World Bank analyst proposed a 2160 calories per adult diet for 1976, emphasizing energy intake from corn, sorghum, beans, oil, and bread. Unfortunately, the daily cost of this diet, $0.34 per adult, greatly exceeded what most St. Martin families could pay.[24]

TABLE 3.3
Evolution of Food Energy–Cost Ratios in Port-au-Prince, 1956-84

	CALORIES PER $0.01					
	1956	**(Rank)**	**1976**	**(Rank)**	**1984**	**(Rank)**
Corn	468	(1)	128	(2)	51	(3)
Sorghum	450	(2)	141	(1)	56	(1)
Rice	148	(6)	67	(5)	46	(4)
Bread	110	(8)	79	(4)	53	(2)
Roots, tubers, etc.[a]	240	(4)	53	(8)	25	(7)
Beans	190	(5)	60	(7)	38	(6)
Sugar	280	(3)	84	(3)	40	(5)
Meat	44	(9)	16	(9)	8	(8)
Oil	136	(7)	66	(6)	n.a.	

Sources: Grant and Groom (1958), Donas (1978), World Bank (1984c), Borsdorf and Foster (1985), and author's estimates.
[a] See note a, table 3.2.

Households seeking to produce the proposed intake of 2160 calories (as well as adequate protein weight) could nevertheless have done so for about $0.16 per day by purchasing a combination of 90 percent corn or sorghum and 10 percent beans. But this pattern would not have proven entirely satisfactory because, though rich in calories and protein, the diet was poor in a large number of specific nutrients.[25] Constraining basic staple inputs to 1500 calories, at a cost of $0.11, would have permitted $0.05 for other foods and substantial increases in other nutrients (as well as a few more calories from the other foods). This kind of production pattern was perhaps not the most efficient method possible at an expenditure level of $0.16, but it seemed a more efficient method of improving overall nutrition than a pattern emphasizing only calories.

At the same time, while corn and sorghum seemed to be the most cost-effective inputs to calorie production, their preparation incurred higher human energy and time costs than such other staple items as rice or bread. Rice required about the same amounts of charcoal for heating and of time for general supervision of the cooking process as corn or sorghum. But, as suggested in table 3.1, sorghum, and corn to only a slightly lesser extent, required that an individual responsible for food preparation expend four calories per hour per kilogram of body weight in constantly stirring a pot of simmering cereal. Rice, by contrast, required about two calories directly.

Because it did not require constant attention, preparation of rice also allowed a cook to carry out other tasks at the same time, thus reducing overall time requirements for food preparation. A 50 kilogram adult spending an hour in cooking could therefore "save" 50 to 100 calories (and time) for use in other productive purposes. The calorie saving involved was small, perhaps 7 percent for a cook consuming 1500 calories and preparing one meal a day (or 14 percent for two meals), and 1.5 to 3 percent for a household consuming a total of 6450 calories. Households with very low income (in theory, ascribing a low value to time relative to families with higher income) and with a high elasticity of demand for calories might not have viewed the saving as sufficient to cause a shift from corn or sorghum to rice. But at higher levels of income, where elasticities were lower and where the value of time was relatively higher, a shift towards use of rice might have represented a more efficient use of all resources engaged in production.

Bread, in principle, seemed to offer much greater savings in energy and time requirements than rice. It was, however, technologically incompatible with other aspects of known methods of principal meal production. A meal of bread and beans, for example, had yet to develop widespread interest. Bread, biscuits, and other wheat products were therefore not appropriate substitutes for other cereals during principal meals, although they played important roles, as I discuss below, in producing nutrition at other times.

The assumption about probable shifts to rice at higher levels of income, in combination with the schedule of energy prices in table 3.3 and the laws I mentioned earlier, provided a basis for constructing a hypothetical model of what cereal consumption patterns might have looked like in St. Martin during 1976 (figure 3.1). This purely speculative exercise suggested that most families would have relied on corn as their principal staple.[26] At the lower–income end, about 24 percent of households would have used sorghum extensively, and at the upper–income end, perhaps 18 percent would rely mostly on rice.[27] Notwithstanding imposition of an absolute minimum–cost diet assumption at the low–income end, 20 percent of households could not have obtained 1500 calories, and 5 percent could not equal the 980 calorie average of La Saline's lower–income group in 1956. St. Martin households had resources and faced prices that permitted technical means to produce calorie intakes comparable to twenty years earlier, but at a higher opportunity cost of foregoing intake of other nutrients. In general, this seemed to mean that nutritional intakes by lower–income households were less adequate in 1976 than in 1956. Because La Saline was one of the poorest neighborhoods of the city, while St. Martin was middle income in the relative scheme of things, the model implied that large segments of the urban population would have found difficulty in feeding themselves adequately.

The model's predictive power was generally correct with respect to the dominance of corn in household diets and to the proportion of households consuming rice, but was well off the mark concerning sorghum (table 3.4). Seventeen percent of families reported rice as their most common staple, but only one family used sorghum extensively. The overestimation of sorghum resulted from my use of prevailing retail prices for cereals at that time rather than actual prices paid by households. A particular grade of corn was available at a price almost identical to sorghum, and since corn offered a small preparation advantage over sorghum, families had no real incentive to produce calories with sorghum.

Unfortunately, even though some price adjustments might have increased the general accuracy of the model, the data in table 3.4 make clear that its assumption of a neat and direct relationship between income, expenditure, and cereal use was, at best, an oversimplification. Differences between income means were statistically weak. Had the model's assumptions been accurate, the average income of families purchasing inferior grade corn should have been lower, and the income of those using superior corn or rice, higher. The proximity of the means to each other meant that

FIGURE 3.1
Hypothetical Model of Cereal Consumption in St. Martin, 1976

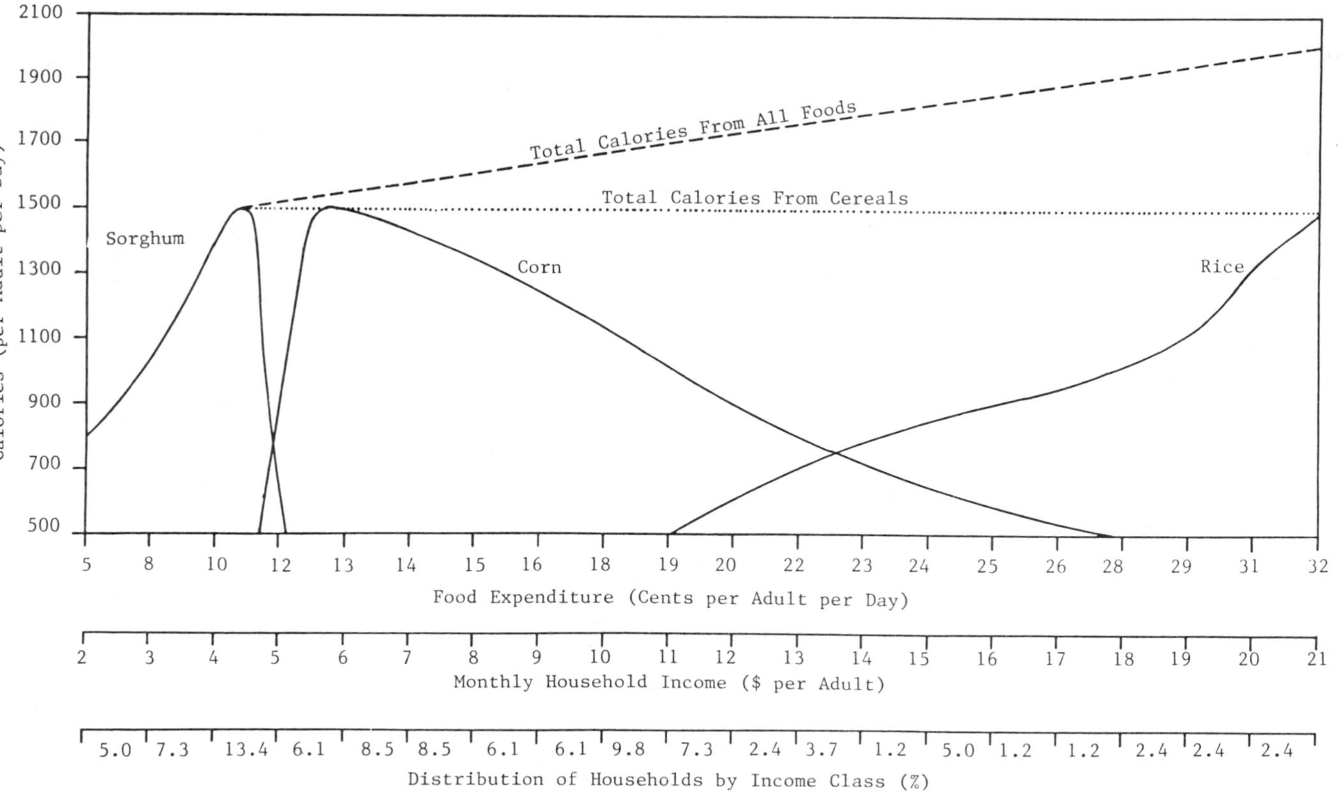

TABLE 3.4
Distribution of Principal Cereals Consumed in St. Martin, 1976

			Households (%)	Price Paid per Kg (U.S.$)	Monthly Income Per Adult (U.S. $)
(Number of households)			(87)[a]		
Rice			17	0.59**	11.70**
Corn:	Whole		15	0.33	10.40
	Milled:	Superior grade	30	0.35**	10.50**
		Intermediate grade	22	0.29**	9.50**
		Inferior grade	16	0.24**	7.40**

Source: Data from author's survey in St. Martin.
[a] One household used sorghum.
** Differences between means are significant at the 5% level.

some lower–income families purchased higher–priced cereals, and that some with higher income used lower–priced cereals.

Production Time

A partial explanation for the observation above, at least with respect to the various grades of corn, was that methods by which households produced income, as distinct from the amount of income, influenced the relative proportions of time and money that they could use for efficient meal production. Because each grade of corn required different time and money inputs, households may have made their selections on the basis of whether a grade made efficient use of available resources.

Superior corn had a finer grind than other types, and was free of nonedible material. It cooked quickly, required less stirring, and used less charcoal in heating, but these were minor advantages. The major advantage was that it did not require extensive time for cleaning. Preparation of a meal for a typical family required about one hour with this grade.

Whole corn presented a household with the advantage of maximum control over the grinding process, in terms of coarseness of the grind and minimization of nonedible material. Families could grind the corn by hand, but all of them paid for mechanical services at various establishments in the central market. It was the most expensive grade in terms of total money cost and the least expensive in terms of preliminary time costs of cleaning.[28]

Intermediate and inferior corn were both coarsely ground relative to the superior grade. The basic difference between them was the amount of time required for cleaning. Meal preparation with the former took about two hours, and with the latter almost four hours, or more in both cases if families pounded the cereals by hand to reduce coarseness.[29]

Therefore, if a family was in a position to substitute time for money in production, it could increase corn consumption and hence calories by potentially substantial amounts. Being in such a position, however, implied that shifting time into production incurred a low opportunity cost. In principle, children or adolescents not otherwise preoccupied constituted a potentially productive time resource for grinding, cleaning, or stirring, but their limited experience imposed considerable risks of wasting grain, nutrients, and human energy.[30] A family's most skilled and energy-efficient source of preparation labor was usually its adult women.

Approximately 60 percent of families had such women available in the home during the day, either exclusively occupied in household management tasks or else engaged in trade or participating in manufacturing activites at home. In these cases, the opportunity cost of spending more time preparing food, in terms of foregone earnings, was usually (but not always) relatively low throughout the day. The remaining households did not have food preparers at home during the day because the women worked or searched for it outside St. Martin. The opportunity cost of starting market activities late, taking a midday break, or stopping early in order to add one or two hours to food preparation time was high. A one or two hour time shift in a ten-hour working day was a 10 to 20 percent reduction in market time that, in trade, often implied a similar reduction in earnings. Additional hours were possible only in the evenings, but by then women ending a long day of work had drawn their stocks of caloric energy down to a low level. The prospect of adding one or two hours to cooking, and expending yet another 50 to 150 extra calories in the process before being able to replenish the stocks, especially when demand for eating by other family members was also high, would not have appeared as the most efficient method of producing a meal. At such times, families had considerable incentive to use more costly grades and to save on preparation time, for much the same reasons as their counterparts in wealthier countries paid premiums for frozen meals.

Average income of households with nonworking adult women, or with women working at home, was not significantly different than the average for families with women working outside St. Martin. What seemed to be happening was that at every income level, except the highest, at which rice was the dominant staple, households with women at home generally opted for lower grades of corn than others. The weak association between income classes and prices in table 3.4 may therefore have resulted, at least in part, from the tendency for commuting women to substitute money for time in meal preparation.

Although meal preparation characteristics seemed to have some influence on selection of raw materials, production costs associated with shopping did not. Households, or more precisely, the adult women with skill in bargaining, could buy grain from mobile vendors wandering through the neighborhood, at the local St. Martin market, or in the city's central market. Vendors were the quickest, but also the most expensive sources. No one in the sample regularly bought grain from them, and there were few in the area. The St. Martin market was closer to homes than the central market, but since a large proportion of household buyers worked elsewhere, mostly near the central market, it was often further away from buyers during the day. About 60 percent of families purchased in the neighborhood market, and the rest in the central market. This distribution corresponded almost exactly to distribution of at–home/not–at–home women I noted earlier, with households in the first category using the local market, and those in the second using the other.

In principle, the downtown market should have offered lower prices than the local market, but data revealed no significant price differentials between markets for any of the grains in table 3.4. One reason for the coincidence of prices was that some grain reached the St. Martin market directly from rural areas (Duplan and LaGra, 1975: 82). A more important reason, mentioned in chapter 2, was that agricultural product marketing in the city functioned at a level close to perfect competition, and yielded almost identical prices for identical cereals in all urban markets (Locher, 1974: 17). Bargaining skill could alter the price paid for specific cereals somewhat, but other characteristics of shopping could not influence choice among cereals.

Consumption Time

Another complicating aspect, on the consumption side, was that the high level of labor market participation in St. Martin often made it difficult for all household members to eat shared meals except early in the morning or in the evening. For the better part of each working day, almost all households would have at least one member away at work, looking for work, or at school. Cooking for different members at different times of the day was an inefficient use of time and, perhaps more important, wasted charcoal and water. Charcoal added about 15 percent to the cost of cooking a large pot of ground corn. Although charcoal requirements for each of two smaller pots would be slightly less than for a large one, total requirements for two small pots were about 60 to 80 percent higher. Cooking twice increased the share of charcoal in total cooking costs to about 25 percent, and therefore implied a significant opportunity cost in terms of money available to purchase grain. Corresponding water costs were 3 to 5 percent for one large pot, and 5 to 8 percent for two small pots.

After breakfast, usually consisting of coffee and a biscuit or piece of bread, individuals preferred to take their principal meal at midday. However, only half of the households were able to provide all or most members with this meal.[31] The other half waited until evening, and their members, especially those at work in energy-intensive activities, usually needed to replenish some of their calorie and protein stocks by midday.

The least expensive method of doing this, in theory, was to purchase a bowl of corn or sorghum mixed with beans from a street vendor. Depending on the seller's margin, the cost of this method was 15 to 25 percent higher than home consumption of the same quantity.[32] An obstacle to adoption of this method was that sellers rarely sold this kind of food in quantities priced less than $0.04 per bowl or, in nutritional terms, in lots of less than about 400 calories.[33] For an individual unable or unwilling to spend that much, to consume as much energy, or to lose the cost advantage of eating at home later on, the least expensive alternative for calories was sugar, and for calories and protein at the same time, bread.

A penny's worth of bread yielded about 80 calories, and 120 calories with another penny added for a teaspoon of butter, margarine, peanut butter, or jam. Bread yielded only 60 percent of the calories per unit of expenditure possible with corn or sorghum, but the spatial organization of household activities often made it an effective method of keeping daytime outlays down, thereby conserving more of the efficiency associated with shared meals at home. Bread was therefore an important food to many low-income individuals and households wishing to save money for more productive use later, to avoid incurring the opportunity cost of not eating, and to prevent loss of earnings associated with a trip home during working hours. It was also an important item for those higher-income families in which the opportunity cost of using even one hour for food preparation was high. Not surprisingly, every household reported daily use of some bread or biscuits and, among highest-income families, occasional substitution of bread for rice in principal meals. Given its apparent useful properties, the one relative bright spot in the evolution of food prices between 1956 and 1976 was that the price of bread had risen much less than other items (table 3.3).[34]

Capital Equipment

The foregoing discussion contains the implicit assumption that households, in whole or in part, could take advantage of the production advantages associated with shared meals prepared at home. At any one time, however, there were several thousand households, containing perhaps

5 percent of the urban population, who lived on the streets and could not benefit from this advantage because they were unable or unwilling to invest \$3 to \$5 for a cooking pot.[35]

In this circumstance, if households could not earn the minimum of \$0.04 per day per adult, their best marketplace approach to producing some calories and protein was, as outlined earlier, eating bread. They could nibble on it as the day progressed and as they managed to earn and spend one penny at a time. But this provided less than 300 daily calories and after a while, households would be compelled to ask, or beg for, or borrow food. Such desperation measures usually permitted households to make up severe nutritional shortfalls for brief periods of time.

Households able to defer immediate consumption for a few hours or a day until able to accumulate \$0.04 for eventual investment in a bowl of prepared corn or sorghum and beans could increase nutritional intake to about 380 calories, 20 percent more than possible through use of the bread technology.[36] A family with a pot spending the same amount could increase intake another 26 percent, to 480 calories per day per adult. These 100 additional calories provided an average-size household with an annual "saving" of \$13, and a financial return to the \$3 to \$5 investment of 160 to 330 percent per year.

This substantial gain in efficiency went a long way toward explaining why every household in St. Martin had a pot, and why, together with a bucket for storing water, it was sometimes the only visible asset in homes of lowest-income families. However, although a pot could improve the efficiency of production, saving for its eventual purchase by very low income families incurred high opportunity costs of decreased food consumption in the short term. Three dollars equaled 29,000 calories of prepared cereal, and a family willing to curtail daily consumption by 100 calories per adult, or 430 calories in total, would nevertheless require at least two months of saving to finance the investment. It would have to hope that over the two months, lowered consumption would not have an adverse affect on health and labor productivity.

A pot was a very productive investment, but a hard one for very poor people to finance. The difficulty for low-income families in St. Martin was that although they had pots, this equipment was sometimes the only disposable asset left that they could exchange for cash to meet an unforeseen eventuality. If required to sell it, production efficiency would drop and it would take a long time to save for another.

Policy

The process of producing nutrition in St. Martin seemed to enjoin families to behave as if they understood the nutritional, technological, and economic properties of different food items, to combine foods in manners appropriate to available resources of money and skilled meal preparation time, and to adapt production and consumption to such things as the spatial organization of household activities and the availability of equipment. Simply put, it was a process of manufacturing no different in substance the various types of manufacturing that I described in chapters 1 and 2, and in Appendix A.

Production of nutrition used up much less time in general than production of income, perhaps four of the forty waking hours per day available to a pair of adults and an adolescent in the typical household, but it consumed more than half of available financial resources. Consumption of 10 percent of time and 50 percent or more of income for nutrition may not have been the most efficient use of resources relative to other productive possibilities. An admittedly heroic set of assumptions indicated that families with average incomes of $9.80 per adult per month, even after making some allowances for the cost of charcoal, water, and meals taken away from home, could have used available technologies to produce nutritional intakes in the range of 1600 to 1800 calories per adult per day. This range was lower than notional standards of what adequate nutrition should be. But whether such an intake range was adequate relative to energy expenditure levels in market and nonmarket activities; to the health status of individuals; to the public health environment of St. Martin; to the developmental needs of children; or to protein, vitamin, mineral, and other nutritional components, was difficult to assess. There was little certainty that health risks, labor productivity declines, and other costs associated with marginal shifts of resources out of nutrition manufacturing would have been higher than the benefits of using the resources for other things, or that the benefits of more nutrition production would have outweighed the costs.

This uncertainty applied only to average income and to the average intake range. Over 60 percent of the households had incomes below the average, and for the lowest 15 to 20 percent who might have been spending 70 to 80 percent of income for food, no available technology could have enabled them to produce even 1500 calories, let alone adequate quantities of other nutritional elements. In these cases, there was more assurance that an improvement in nutrition could make a substantial difference to income, and that the evolution of the structure of food prices from 1956 to 1976 had placed a significant constraint upon prospects for the economic development of a large segment of the Port-au-Prince population. This seemed more certain not only because of general health and labor productivity factors, but also because the rise in prices relative to income limited the extent to which families could save and invest in efficiency-enhancing capital equipment like pots, and in income production activities like trade, manufacturing, and a number of the service activities I described in chapter 2.

And there was a kind of absolute assurance that for lower–income families of the ordinary class, nutritional intake had a great distance yet to travel before the act of manufacturing a meal could be construed as anything other than a vital act of productive consumption. There was nothing final about it. Nonproductive final consumption in Port–au–Prince was what government did in collecting and distributing taxes, what friends of government did in investing in import–substitution industry and large–scale commerce, and what many foreign technical assistants did in exchange for salaries paid out of foreign–aid allotments. What looked productive was nonproductive, and what looked nonproductive was in fact very productive.

At the level of the household, production of income and the possibility of income growth depended heavily on the nutrition manufacturing sector. At the level of the city, where perhaps half the population had incomes equal to or lower than the St. Martin average in 1976, economic growth depended to an important extent on the level of effort made by the political class to promote this sector of urban manufacturing.

As for any type of manufacturing, promotion, in theory, meant stimulation of demand, technical assistance to improve management, introduction of more efficient capital equipment, credit, or assistance in procurement of raw material supply. Demand, obviously, was not a constraint. The need for management assistance was not evident, and, in any event, there was already a good deal available through nutrition education programs. The appropriate technology movement had introduced an interesting design for a charcoal–conserving heater, but the evolution of the movement, as I noted in chapter 2, had some wandering still to do before approaching appropriateness to concrete circumstances. Credit was not an issue, in part because there was nothing on the market to finance with it except pots, and because credit to purchase pots was readily available, as I note in chapter 7. What remained was procurement of raw material.

An important item in this regard was charcoal. The price had risen by over 500 percent since 1956, a much higher rate than for corn or sorghum (IHS, 1974: 80). By 1976 this source of energy was adding 10 to 15 percent to the cost of preparing a cereal–based meal. A reduction in the price, or a slowdown in its rate of increase, might therefore be of considerable help. But this possibility was remote. Haiti was heavily deforested, and the rapid increase in price reflected a growing scarcity of wood for making charcoal. Numerous attempts at reforestation had been tried but had failed to stabilize or increase renewable supplies of trees, and even if a project did prove successful, as one seemed to do in the 1980s, it would take at least five, and more likely ten to fifteen years for enough trees to grow to commercial maturity to have a discernable impact on price. The notion of importing wood or charcoal to serve productive purposes similar to that of petroleum for electrification of industry was not widespread before or after 1976.

A more important raw material was food, and since the political class was doing little of significance to promote domestic production in 1976, the basic instrument of policy through which procurement difficulties could be eased was importation.

Food Import Politics of Government

Importation contained several potential disadvantages, including lowering of producer price incentives and of foreign exchange useful for import of other items. But governments focused on matters crucial to immediate political solvency were inclined, as in the case of coffee taxation, to discount such disadvantages relative to the method's immediate benefits. If domestic prices were significantly higher than border prices of identical or substitute commodity imports, advantages included presentation of the appearance of action on behalf of consumer welfare, additional fiscal revenues from import duties, and allocation of monopoly rents to friends of government through import and distribution licenses.

The cornerstone of government intervention in food supply, the political advantages of which in terms of fiscal and nonfiscal taxation and private distribution monopolies I described in chapter 1, was importation of wheat for the purpose of flour production. Flour sales, measured in equivalent tonnage of wheat imports, increased at an annual average rate of 4 percent from 1960 to 1971, significantly less than the 5.6 percent rate of the city's population during the period.[37] These imports seemed to address demand mostly by the city's higher-income groups for bread and other wheat products.[38] Sales growth increased substantially after 1971, and averaged about 12 percent per year through 1982. This surge may have been caused in part by rapid income growth associated with expansion of foreign assistance, industry, and other stimulants to the urban economy, and the changes in consumption patterns associated with the growth. Another factor seemed to be significant change in relative prices between traditional cereals, like corn and rice, and bread.

Although charging considerably more than border prices for flour, as I noted in chapter 1, government kept the rate of increase of wholesale prices (i.e., from the mill) lower than the rise in farmgate prices for other cereals, and therefore kept retail price increases for bread and other flour goods below those for rice and corn. While the estimated price for bread increased by a factor of 2.5 between 1970 and 1985, the factors for rice and corn were respectively 3.6 and 7.0 (table 3.5).[39] Bread still remained less cost–effective than corn in terms of providing overall nutritional benefits, even after adding the cost of cooking to the latter, but by 1985 it no longer had the same clear disadvantage as it did in 1976 in terms of energy costs. Families seeking to maximize calorie inputs could do as well or better with bread than with corn or rice, as shown earlier in table 3.3. Growth in flour sales therefore also derived from low–income households that had the wherewithal and the time to produce energy with corn or rice but that could see little advantage in doing so when bread performed the service as effectively. Government and its close allies could not claim a large share of monopoly rents from low–income households in 1970 or 1976, but were able to do so without too much difficulty in 1985.

Evidence to sustain the hypothesis that after 1976 bread was increasingly becoming a substitute for corn, and that changes in the relative prices between the commodities had a bearing on flour sales, was reasonably strong. Every year that the price of corn (and rice in parallel) increased, as in 1977, 1979–81, and 1983, flour sales jumped significantly. And in the years that it decreased, such as 1978 and 1982, sales dropped back to almost their previous levels. More generally, for the whole price series from 1966 to 1983, multiple regression analysis showed a convincing correlation between flour sales and the relative prices of corn and flour after controlling for income (World Bank, 1984a: 18).

None of this, including wholesale flour prices from the mill substantially higher than landed costs for imported flour, would have mattered very much if household incomes kept up with rising food costs. But, as suggested earlier, the possibility that many or most urban households would have been able to keep abreast of inflation, as measured by the overall consumer price index or by the slightly higher food component of the overall index, seemed remote. Even more remote was the possibility that they would have been able to keep up with a rate of inflation measured by an index that more closely reflected their expenditure and consumption patterns.

The official index was built on data and assumptions about middle–class consumption patterns in 1976. Weights attached to water expenditures, 1.2 percent, housing rents, 3.7 percent, and school fees, 4.8 percent, were, as will be evident in following chapters, inconsistent with the kinds of weights necessary to produce an index for the majority of urban residents (IHSI, 1983: 14–16). As regards food, the overall weight of 64.5 percent appeared more realistic. However, the composition of the food component, principally beans (11.1 percent), rice (11.0 percent), bread (4.8 percent), meat (4.6 percent), plantains (4.3 percent), and corn (3.1 percent), seemed at odds with circumstances like those in St. Martin.

TABLE 3.5
Evolution of Relative Cereal Prices in Port-au-Prince, 1970-85
(1970 = 100)

	CORN			RICE		BREAD AND WHEAT FLOUR		
	Border Price (whole)	Retail Price (milled)	Imports[a] (tons)	Retail Price	Imports (tons)	Bread Price (retail)	Flour Price (wholesale)	Flour Sales[b] (tons)
1970	100	100	11	100	19	100	100	28,000
1971	100	115	12	110	74	101	100	42,000
1972	96	124	8	124	276	102	100	48,000
1973	168	228	576	145	4,931	107	100	69,000
1974	227	242	19	170	39	136	130	89,000
1975	205	331	3,970	236	5,995	160	150	97,000
1976	193	255	94	235	21,885	163	150	97,000
1977	164	316	433	232	1,600	165	150	144,000
1978	173	269	123	217	555	165	150	91,000
1979	199	353	196	271	141	169	150	103,000
1980	216	460	1,191	317	670	177	150	139,000
1981	268	492	464	357	2,209	214	188	150,000
1982	220	421	298	284	1,830	218	188	123,000
1983	274	573	n.a.	332	n.a.	224	188	157,000
1984	236	565	n.a.	341	n.a.	234	193	n.a.
1985	200	700	n.a.	358	n.a.	245	193	n.a.
1986	165	620	n.a.	345	n.a.	n.a.	150	n.a.

Sources: Economist (1982), USAID (1984g), World Bank (1984c), Borsdorf and Foster (1985), FAO statistics for various years, and author's estimates.

[a] Excludes imports supplied by the United States under the P.L. 480, Title II program.

[b] Measured in equivalent tons of wheat.

The food component was therefore largely a rice, beans, and bread index that allowed government to keep in touch with the economic circumstances of a large segment of its constituency and to manipulate the cost of living in favor of the class. Maintaining a low relative price for flour was useful in this regard, but equally or more important was control of the price of rice. To this end, government imported 40,000 tons between 1970 and 1982, with most of it coming in 1973, 1975, 1976, 1981, and 1982 to respond to and/or to prevent sharp rises in the price. Combined with efforts to promote increased domestic production, the result was a pattern of rising prices that, though higher than for bread, was approximately half the rate of increase for corn.

Government also imported corn, 7400 tons between 1970 and 1982, but because this was the staple of ordinary people having little political consequence, such actions took place only during political emergencies. The importation of almost 4000 tons in 1975 to respond to a drought in the northwest part of the country came after months of pressure by foreign governments and PVOs operating in the affected region, and after some 40,000 people reportedly died of illnesses associated with extreme malnutrition.[40] The importation of 1200 tons in 1980, after the price jumped by 30 percent, had similar characteristics. Unrest in two major towns in 1983, catalyzed by a 36 percent increase and record levels in the price of corn, yielded another surge of imports notwithstanding IMF protests about the government's deviation from fiscal austerity.[41] At that moment, corn was politically more important than the IMF. Prices seemed to reach a new high in 1985, perhaps contributing to the Duvalier ouster, and though dropping, remained quite high through 1986, perhaps also contributing to ongoing dissatisfaction with the new government.

The economic problem faced by households in 1986 was that the market price for corn was 145 percent higher than in 1976 while the world price was 15 percent lower. In 1982, if they had not already shifted to rice and bread, households were paying 67 percent more for corn than imports would have cost at the retail level.[42] In 1986 the differential exceeded 100 percent. Ordinary households were much poorer than they would have been if government had cared to address their interests in the same way it did middle-class interests. Unfortunately, they were to remain artificially poor a while longer. The new government's principal foreign allies needed more time to work through their conflicting opinions about the form that food import policy ought to take.

Food Import Politics of Foreign Assistance

First among these allies on matters of food was USAID, the major initiator of nutrition studies, the major provider of emergency food relief and foodstuffs for nutrition projects (e.g., school feeding, maternal and child health, and other components of the Title II program not reflected in table 3.5), the major source of concessional financing for government wheat (the Title I program) and other grain imports, and, in 1986, the major sponsor of large-scale food grants to subsidize the new government (the Title III program).[43] For Title II, which provided 30,000 tons annually from 1983 to 1985, agency decisions were dominated by nutritional concerns, and the average annual composition of commodities between 1983 and 1985 was vegetable oil (1900 tons), dried milk (3850 tons), bulgar wheat (14,000 tons), and corn meal (10,000 tons). The program was large, and plans for 1986 called for food to be provided to over 700,000 people, or about 13 percent of the national population.[44] The program may have prevented the prices of corn and rice from rising faster than they did.

Title I programs were wheat and cooking oil strategies, and from 1978 to 1983, USAID provided concessional financing for an annual average of about 40,000 tons of the wheat imports shown in table 3.5, thus helping government draw a larger monopoly margin from flour sales. Planning for a Title III program in 1984, a process that began in 1979 but that did not begin to move beyond planning until 1986, called for wheat grants averaging 140,000 tons a year from 1985 to 1989, and for flour sales at the end of the period to be 80 percent higher than in 1983 (USAID, 1984g: 68). USAID was an active party to the process of shifting demand towards bread.

The agency's role in the process was not without controversy among its staff and consultants in Port-au-Prince.[45] Proponents of wheat argued that it was a nutritious foodstuff; its preparation for consumption was easy and saved charcoal and time; all income classes consumed it; after 1980 it was a more economical source of nutrition; a simple regression analysis showed no statistical association between flour sales and corn or rice prices and therefore wheat was not a substitute for the other cereals; corn or rice imports would lower prices and act as disincentives to domestic production and put downward pressure on farmer income; and while facilities were already available to manage bulk import, storage, and distribution of wheat, such facilities were absent for corn and rice, thus requiring major capital investment.

Opposing arguments, to some extent supported by World Bank mission staff in 1984, included opinions to the effect that corn was inherently more nutritious than wheat; that extra preparation costs were small compared to nutritional benefits; that it was essentially a middle-class staple; that it was more economical only in terms of calories and only because of the historical bias in import and production strategy; that a multiple regression equation, as I noted earlier, showed that wheat was indeed a substitute for corn under changing relative prices; that lowered prices would act as disincentives primarily for a minority of farmers who derived significant shares of cash income from sale of corn; that since most small farmers were net buyers of grain and consumed most of the corn they produced, lower prices could as readily imply an increase in real income as they could a decrease; and that investment in bulk handling facilities was small relative to the potential gain of 15 to 25 percent in real income and nutritional intakes that most of the urban and rural population could obtain through significant lowering of the relative price of corn.[46]

As far as I could determine, USAID had no compelling political reasons to prefer a wheat strategy. Title I allowed importation of any basic U.S. commodity. The government could have continued to extract monopoly margins by providing the mill or another public agency with exclusive rights to import other USAID–financed commodities. Similarly, there was nothing to inhibit the allocation of domestic distribution rights to friends of government. The differential between border and domestic prices for corn, especially after installation of bulk handling facilities, was large enough to satisfy the needs of all parties while still allowing the market price of corn to drop appreciably.

In this instance, policy seemed to flow out of a process wherein proponents and opponents of wheat simply "believed" that they were right, and as fortune would have it, democratic practice among the handful of individuals within the agency who could influence policy outcomes invariably worked in favor of the proponents. USAID therefore maintained a steady course of wheat imports, adopting it as the pivotal component of the $55 million government budget rescue operation in 1986. Proponents and opponents nevertheless agreed on several things, including the need for more significant effort to raise corn and other domestic grain production, the need for a feasibility analysis of grain bulk handling facilities, and the need for a national income and food consumption survey that could eventually provide empirical substance to at least a few of the assumptions and opinions put forward in the arguments about the relative superiority or inferiority of wheat relative to other cereals (USAID, 1984g: 116–17).

Research Politics

After years of talk among foreign–assistance agencies about the potential utility of having a national food consumption survey, USAID initiated the process of working towards one in early 1985 by requesting that I and an economist from the International Food Policy Research Institute (IFPRI) design a project for this purpose (Fass and Alderman, 1985). At this time, USAID was already financing an agricultural production survey, and had arranged for the U.S. Census Bureau to assist Haiti's census office, IHSI, in preparing and carrying out another type of production survey as well as an expenditure survey designed to develop new weights for the consumer price index. Noting that funds available for the food consumption study were inadequate for USAID's stated purposes in having it, we proposed, and the agency agreed, to join the fieldwork to the Census Bureau–IHSI project.

The idea, elegant on paper, ran into difficulty almost immediately. There were arguments among local and expatriate statisticians concerning the relative merits of using different types of sampling frames (e.g., list or area frames). There were more arguments between statisticians and economists concerning the relative merits of different sampling methods in deriving price index weights, in econometric analysis and estimation of consumption and nutrition patterns. More compelling were differences of opinion between USAID and IHSI regarding respective use of U.S. and Haitian government funds. And because the nature of the study we proposed was relatively "basic," meaning that findings would produce data useful for Haiti but not useful to the cause of advancing the "state of knowledge" in disciplines concerned with food consumption and nutrition (because several such studies had been conducted in other countries), USAID encountered difficulty in finding a competent research institution willing to implement the work.

With the politics of research serving to slow the pace of progress, and with growing unrest toward the end of 1985 making fieldwork impossible, the survey project foundered. USAID came close to abandoning the effort. The agency did not give it up, but in the aftermath of the Duvalier departure and ongoing unrest gave the project low priority among things warranting attention.

Although most parties to the arguments about survey techniques and use of funds remained at their posts, meaning that the difficulties of 1985 did not leave with the old regime, enough progress had been made to provide hope that the survey would regain its earlier momentum later in 1986. If it did, field work for Haiti's first national consumption study might have a fair chance of completion by the end of 1987 or early 1988, might produce helpful analyses toward the end of 1988 or early 1989, and might perhaps allow a more substantive reconsideration of the wheat–corn controversy and some change in government and foreign-assistance import orientations around 1990; if the IMF did not protest too much about fiscal austerity or balance of payments issues at that time.

The delay between the beginning of survey work and the completion of analyses required to inform policy was normal. The difficulties that USAID encountered in moving the project along were normal. The lapse of almost twenty years from the end of the last consumption study to the projected date of completion of the current one, if one rejects the hypothesis that numerical invention and other consequences of the politics of expert survival that may have masked the need for research constituted deviant forms of behavior, was normal. And if one accepts the hypothesis that claims to superior knowledge underlying the presumption of expertise are sometimes inherently dictatorial, then it is perfectly normal in a country offering no means for ordinary people to challenge such claims for members of the foreign–assistance component of the political class to never propose the one type of survey that Haiti seemed to desperately need. That type of survey, the most common variety in societies in which participatory politics places a premium on consumer sovereignty and in which, as a consequence, expertise is defined more often as a capacity to listen carefully rather than as a capacity to dictate, was an opinion or market research study to find out what foods the bulk of the population might have wanted imported on their behalf.

Given the opportunity to answer a question such as, "If it were possible to lower the price of either sorghum, or corn, or rice, or bread, which would you prefer most?" ordinary people with expertise drawn from concrete circumstance would have no difficulty providing an answer. Majority opinion in St. Martin during 1976 was for corn. Majority opinion when I asked the same question in the downtown market and in very poor neighborhoods in 1986 was also for corn.

It being abnormal for governments to concern themselves with opinions of the ordinary class, one could not have expected political leaders to press the idea of such a survey among foreign–assistance factions. And given the quasi–total absence in the literature about food, nutrition, health, and labor productivity in developing countries of anything that could direct expert attention to the political presumptions of their trades (in nondemocratic societies or in general), one could not have expected the culture of foreign–assistance (or Haitian) expertise to give rise to the idea within the factions either. What was important about the politics of research, and through research about the general politics of food import policy, was not so much a lack of answers to questions typically posed by members of the political class, but rather an incapacity on their part to conceive of salient questions. On this matter there was no nagging force apparent to struggle against the current of prevailing thought. The normal imperialism of expertise was total.

Food Import Politics of Freedom

Nevertheless, 1986 presented the possibility that reconsideration of policy might not have to wait until 1990, and that it might not have to depend entirely on the outcome of arguments among technicians and technical agencies of the political class. Haitians and foreigners sensitive to politics might come to earlier conclusions concerning relationships between urban unrest and cereals significant to ordinary people, and listening to the outcries for lower food prices, might notice the subtle distinctions made by different protesting groups with respect to different commodities. Politicians seeking support for the elections, if the provisional government failed to act, might conceiveably put corn on their agenda if they believed that ordinary people mattered to their ambitions.

These "mights" and "maybes" offered more hope after 1986 than before, but no assurances of explicit change in policy. Fortunately, by late 1986 the matter of food was not entirely subject to formal policy. With the disbanding of the Macoutes, with redirection of the police and army to fill the political security vacuum resulting from the disbanding, and with the collapse of effective centralized control of the whole country, coastal ports and the border with the Dominican Republic lay open for expansion of contraband trade. Principal among the commodities that flowed into the country was rice, but with high differentials in prices for corn and flour between Haiti and neighboring countries, there was also a growing movement in these commodities.

How long the government would permit this form of free trade to continue was uncertain. But for the moment, families like those in St. Martin who until 1986 were no better, and perhaps worse off, than in 1976, were being afforded a rare period of grace in which their efforts to eat; to maintain health, efficiency, and productivity; and ultimately to survive, were becoming slightly easier. In the aggregate, and much in the way that theories of trade and comparative advantage would usually suggest, free trade was proving a boon to the urban (and perhaps national) nutrition manufacturing sector.

There was, however, a commodity even more vital to income, survival, and economic growth than food, the supply and price of which could not be altered except through direct public intervention. The commodity was water, and circumstances for urban families with respect to this commodity in 1986 did not appear to have improved since 1976. If anything, they seemed to have deteriorated.

Notes

1. Basic references to the history and characteristics of Haiti's rural economy include Moral (1961), Herskovits (1971), Zuvekas (1978) and Lundahl (1979, 1983).
2. A 1975 survey of 1100 urban children reported a Gomez scale proportional

distribution of 15 percent normal, 21 percent first degree, 40 percent second degree and 24 percent third degree (World Bank, 1978b: 30). The same year, a study in Brooklyn, one of the poorest parts of the city, reported corresponding proportions as 14, 14, 47, and 25 percent (Haiti, 1980). Three years later, a broader sample of 890 children in the city showed a distribution of 41, 44, 13, and 2 percent (USAID, 1978b: 28).

3. HEW (1975: 67–68, 70), King (1978), and King et al. (1968: 115) provide comprehensive summaries of food consumption and nutritional intake estimates produced since 1951. The variation in figures is large. Per adult cereal consumption ranges from 165 grams to 305 grams per day. Within cereals, estimates for items like corn and sorghum spread from 58 to 155 grams, and from 27 to 130 grams respectively. Corresponding ranges for nutrition intakes situate themselves anywhere between 1180 and 2630 calories, and from 28 to 60 grams of protein per adult.
4. Beghin, Fougère, and King (1970). The actual estimate was about 1760 calories per capita. Per capita figures are lower than per adult figures because two young children generally have food intake requirements equal to that of one adult. Preliminary data from the 1981 census (IHSI 1982: 32), suggested that per capita figures required a 7.5 percent upward adjustment to equal per adult ones, and that the 1970 estimate was therefore about 1900 calories per adult. Unless otherwise indicated, all references are in per adult terms.
5. King (1978), USAID (1982b), and Haiti (1984), for example, all used the 1970 estimate without modification.
6. FAO/WHO standards for Latin America, reported in HEW (1975: 68), suggested that "normal" intake should be around 2400 calories and 60 to 65 grams of protein per adult (i.e., 2200 calories and 55 to 60 grams per capita). With regard to estimated averages, Berg (1981: 64–66) reported a 2000 to 3100 calorie per adult range for forty developing countries during 1960–70.
7. Trairatvorakul (1984: 47, 49), for example, suggested that intake observations of less than 1000 calories per capita (and more than 4000) in Thailand were unacceptable, and that such figures "must" have resulted from under– or over–estimation. Selection of the two figures was, according to the author, "arbitrary."
8. As I noted in chapter 2, Lipton (1983) defined the "ultra–poor" as that segment of a population unable to produce about 1500 calories after spending 75 percent or more of income for food. The average range reported for Port–au–Prince in 1970 was 43 to 52 percent (IHS 1975: 46). This range was similar to Hong Kong's 42 to 47 percent (Grootaert and Cheung, 1984: 17), but lower than reported urban ranges for Egypt, 56 to 63 percent (Alderman and Von Braun, 1984: 24), and Thailand, 56 to 61 percent (Trairatvorakul, 1984: 54). The Port–au–Prince estimate seemed low.
9. Timmer, Falcon, and Pearson (1983: 19–76) provided an excellent overview of economic analysis of food and nutrition consumption. Although they use calories as the measure of nutrition for discussion purposes, they note that more attention needs to be put on analysis of other nutrients, pointing to the work of Pitt (1983) as an example of a desirable research direction.
10. Lundahl (1979: 409–51) devoted a chapter to the subject of malnutrition and disease, and their combined effects on labor productivity in Haiti.
11. King et al. (1978). Figures adjusted from per capita to per adult basis.
12. Analysis of nutrition of children through the perspective of economic theory is

part of a broader subject of inquiry concerning intrahousehold allocation of resources. In recent years, the subject has received increasing attention from economists, and has resulted in an increase in the number of hypotheses presented to explain why food consumption within households varies between members. Rogers (1983: 18–20) summarized several of these inquiries and concluded that evidence to support any of the hypotheses is not yet clear enough to provide convincing explanations.

13. Horton and King (1981: 18–25) reviewed sixteen studies on the effects of nutrition on productivity, and nine on the effects on health, and concluded that evidence of causal relationships were weak. Although the reviewers' criteria for questioning the findings of many of the studies seemed analytically sound, the importance they attached to some of the criteria were open to discussion. Oshima (1967), after reviewing many of the same studies, seemed to feel that at very low nutrition levels, substantially less than 1500 calories, the studies provided strong evidence that effects on labor productivity were significant.
14. Pitt and Rosensweig (1984), for example, could not find a clear relationship between food consumption and farm profits in Indonesia because, among other things, indisposed farmers could substitute hired labor for their own without reducing the productivity of land. In St. Martin there were few opportunities to substitute labor without witnessing a simultaneous decline in the productivity of other factors of production. That is, farm profits were more dependent on capital inputs than were market activities in St. Martin. Similarly, Baldwin and Weisbrod (1974) found some evidence of a relationship between schistosomiasis and piecework earnings of plantation workers in St. Lucia, and between illness and weekly days of work. Leaving aside some problems in this study, which Horton and King (1981: 22) suggested undermines the conclusiveness of findings, the St. Lucia workers were not comparable to St. Martin workers. The former had jobs within which they could vary their levels of effort and days of work within a range. They did not have to seek out clients every day. They did not have working capital at risk for things like medical expenses. They did have employer–provided medical services that kept them, if not absolutely healthy, then relatively healthier than St. Martin workers most of the time.
15. Oshima (1967) suggested the 1500 calories benchmark figure for Asia. It may not be appropriate for Haiti.
16. Shoup (1965) provided a useful elaboration of this hypothesis.
17. Wiese (1976), King et al. (1978), and others argued that inappropriate individual and cultural eating practices in Haiti may play important roles in maintaining lower nutrition levels than otherwise possible with available resources. The argument served as the basis for several nutrition education programs in Haiti. The cost of these programs, including some nutrition therapy, curative medical, and agricultural extension services, was $10 per child in 1975 (King et al., 1978: 87). The investment apparently provided lifetime protection from fatal malnutrition for each child. Alvarez and Murray (1981) argued that most Haitians have very appropriate eating practices, in which case the benefits from the $10 investment may have stemmed more from the food and less from education.
18. The middle–income group expended 160 percent more on food than the lower–income group, but consumed only 46 percent more calories and 68 percent more protein. However, although this implied a cross–sectional income elasticity of demand for calories and protein substantially less than one, increases in consumption of animal protein and fat, linoleic acid and cholesterol in

general, and such things as calcium, and vitamins A, B, C, and D were all in excess of 160 percent, implying the possibility of an elasticity of demand for these nutrients closer to and possibly higher than one. Households could have increased consumption of some of these nutrients by increasing rather than diversifying their food intakes, but such a procedure would have proven technically and economically inefficient. According to data in Sirinit et al. (1965: 422), consumption of 400 daily grams of a blend of 70 percent corn and 30 percent beans could provide about 1500 calories and 50 grams of protein for about $0.04 at 1956 prices, but only 10 percent of daily calcium requirements. In theory, an individual seeking to meet calcium requirements without a change in consumption patterns would have had to spend $0.40 per day and consume 15,000 calories and 50 grams of protein. Adding a penny for milk, which offered much more calcium per calorie or per unit of protein than corn or beans, was a much sounder approach both physiologically and economically.

19. The FAO figures, reported in HEW (1975: 68), were 2200 calories and 55 to 60 grams of protein per day per adult.
20. Sirinit et al. (1965), for example, seemed to assume an adequate diet to consist of 4000 calories and 60 grams of protein per day per adult.
21. Timmer, Falcon, and Pearson (1983), Alderman (1984), and Waterfield (1985) provided excellent summaries of the laws and of many of the studies underwriting them.
22. Students of the subject do not usually express Houthakker's Law in this manner. Timmer, Falcon, and Pearson (1983: 58) and Alderman (1984: 48), for example, express it in terms of a positive association between higher income and higher food "quality."
23. Table 3.3 presents cost–effectiveness only in terms of calories. In terms of grams of protein per penny, the 1976 figures were: corn, 3.4 grams; sorghum, 4.2 grams; rice, 1.5 grams; bread, 2.4 grams; roots and tubers, 0.6 grams; beans, 3.7 grams, and meat, 1.2 grams. Sugar and oil had negligible protein value. Since sorghum protein, according to Sirinit et al.(1965), did not have good protein content characteristics in Haiti, beans were the most cost–effective source of this nutritional component. Water and charcoal for cooking altered individual energy–cost ratios, but did not change the relative ranking of the various foods in 1976.
24. The analyst's figures were 2010 calories and $0.32 per day per capita (World Bank, 1978b: 28), or about 2160 calories and $0.34 per adult. The analyst based the diet on the following distribution of calories from different foods: 39 percent cereals, 9 percent bread, 6 percent roots, 18 percent beans, and the balance from other items. This was probably a good diet, but families could have obtained a more or less equivalent result by stressing corn, beans, and certain other items with high energy–cost ratios.
25. Feeding experiments with laboratory animals suggested that weight gains and protein efficiency ratios increased significantly with the addition of a 10 percent mixture of Haitian beans to sorghum or corn (Sirinit et al., 1965). Although this combination could provide ample calories and protein, it was sorely deficient in other nutrients even at an intake level of 4000 calories per adult. The researchers recommended that such cereal–bean mixtures represent no more than 75 percent of total calorie intake.
26. The first of five basic assumptions was that households paid average 1976 market prices for sorghum, corn, and rice, or $0.24, $0.28 and $0.53 per

kilogram respectively, and that the energy–cost ratio of all other foods was an average of 50 calories per penny. Second, lowest-income families would spend up to 85 percent of income for food, and this proportion would drop to a minimum of 46 percent for highest-income families. Third, all families would seek to produce a minimum of 1500 calories per adult from cereals. A fourth assumption was that the highest-income family would seek a 2000 calorie intake from all foods, and that targets for families with lower income were represented by a line drawn between 2000 calories and the point at which expenditure permitted the first family to obtain 1500 calories from cereals. Fifth, families would attempt to maximize consumption of energy-efficient cereals within the 1500 calorie ceiling, that is, they would begin to shift from sorghum to corn and from corn to rice as soon as their resources permitted them to obtain 1500 calories with either sorghum or corn.

27. Reading from left to right, figure 3.1 indicates that families would have had to spend about $0.10 per adult for food in order to reach 1500 calories with sorghum. From this point to about $0.12 they could maintain the 1500 calorie level by mixing corn and sorghum, and also have a bit left over to increase total calories above the 1500 level with other foods. Similarly, families spending between $0.12 and about $0.22 could mix corn and rice and get 1500 calories, but corn would remain dominant within this expenditure range. Rice would begin to dominate when expenditure exceeded $0.22, and would virtually eliminate the need for corn at an expenditure level of $0.32 per adult.
28. The typical practice among households purchasing whole corn was to have a week's supply ground immediately after purchase. Once transported home it could be prepared each day with only a cursory glance to make sure that insects, mice, or other vermin had not invaded the stock.
29. The overall average, which I estimated from direct observation, was about two hours. The time was comparable to the figure of 3.1 hours per day reported for the Philippines by Evenson, Popkin, and Quizon (1980: 301), and to the 3.3 hours reported by Reid (1934: 82) for the United States in 1930. The St. Martin figure was for one meal while the others were total daily averages for food preparation. In St. Martin, households prepared an average of 1.5 meals at home per day.
30. With respect to energy, table 3.1 suggests that stirring and pounding cereals respectively demanded marginal energy outputs of 135 and 180 calories per hour for an adult, and 70 to 90 calories for a young adolescent weighing around 26 kilograms. Assuming an intake level of 1600 calories for the adult and 1000 calories for the adolescent, the marginal decrease in calorie stocks (or required increase) is roughly the same, about 9 percent. The question of importance here is the impact that a 9 percent decrease might have at an intake level of 1600 calories as compared to 1000 calories. Somewhere along the line, a family would find it more efficient to use adult rather than nonadult calories. Young children consuming 600 to 800 calories would certainly not represent ideal sources of food preparation energy. With respect to skill, relatively inexperienced children and adolescents tend to waste more grain during milling, cleaning, or mixing than experienced individuals, or may do such a poor job that an adult has to do it over again. What often happens in families is that younger people (girls) receive small portions to mill or clean until they are able to carry out preliminary milling and cleaning without supervision. An adult then does the work again, but spends less time because of the preliminary work.

On the matter of cooking, Evenson, Popkin, and Quizon (1980: 307) reported a statistically significant positive association between the time spent by mothers on food preparation and nutritional values consumed by families. The analysis does not make clear whether the additional time means slower and more careful preparation of identical food combinations, preparation of different types of meals requiring different preparation times, or different shares of mothers' time as a proportion of total family food preparation time (i.e., different combinations of skill levels invested in preparation). Whatever the meaning of the data may be, they imply that cooking skill is a determinant of nutrition that is to some extent independent of the particular foods being cooked.

31. Grant and Groom (1958) reported that most La Saline families took their principal meals at midday. Their sample, however, covered a population in which the majority of working adults held salaried jobs providing two-hour lunch breaks. Midday was still the preferred time for taking a principal meal in 1976, but the nature of St. Martin household activities, especially work activities, obliged many families to postpone it for several hours.
32. The 15 to 25 percent difference did not represent a vendor's net margin. In addition to costs of food, charcoal, and water for cooking, production often incurred additional costs such as porter transportation services, additional water to clean bowls supplied by vendors to customers, labor services of bowl cleaners, and periodic replacement of bowls no longer usable.
33. The vendors did not refuse to sell in smaller lots. They would sell lots as small as $0.02 if a customer provided his or her own small bowl, but customers did not usually carry bowls with them while working. The vendors supplied bowls in two sizes with corresponding set prices of $0.04 and $0.08.
34. Gray (1982: 85), Pinstrup-Anderson, de Londono, and Hoover (1976: 137), and others reported relatively higher income-elasticity coefficients for bread across a broad range of low-income classes in urban areas. The importance of bread in St. Martin was not unusual.
35. See chapter 5 for discussion of the general characteristics of households living on the streets.
36. That is, $0.04 could obtain either 316 calories of bread or, after deducting a vendor's margin, about 380 calories of cereal and beans.
37. Flour sales calculated from data in USAID (1984g: 65).
38. Assumed from the 1956 structure of consumption and expenditure for bread and related products in La Saline, as shown in table 3.2.
39. Systematic price data for comparable types of bread are not readily available. I estimated the evolution of its price from my own small surveys for the least expensive type of small roll in 1976 and 1985, and from a 1978 survey by Donas (1978). After controlling for the wholesale price of flour, price increases associated with rising costs of processing and marketing from 1976 to 1978, and from 1978 to 1985, were almost identical to the evolution of the overall consumer price index over the period. Using the index, and making an adjustment for the rise in energy costs in 1974 and 1975, I projected the price of bread back to 1970 and then standardized the series at the estimated 1970 price for comparison with other cereals.
40. Rumors about the number of deaths varied from 20,000 to 60,000 at the time, without making clear if the number was only for the affected region, which had a population of about 400,000, or if it included premature deaths elsewhere in the country resulting from the jump in price.

41. The price of rice reached its historical high in 1981, contributing to some unrest that ebbed soon after the arrival of imports from the United States. Corn also reached a high in 1981 but price increases for both commodities relative to 1980 were relatively low. The 36 percent corn increase of 1983 had no parallel since the drought of 1975, and the violent uprising that accompanied shortages in Gonaives and Cap Haitien, not matched by similar protest when rice increased in 1981, suggested that corn had replaced rice as the dominant political commodity of the 1980s.
42. The World Bank (1984a: 61) calculated a wholesale differential of 25 percent on the assumption that producer prices were 60 percent of retail prices. This may have been a fair estimate for wholesale prices. The retail differential, not only assuming that producer prices were 60 percent of retail prices but also that border prices were 80 percent of retail prices in the city, came to 67 percent.
43. Because formal signing of a Title III agreement by the U.S. and Haitian governments was still some months away, USAID organized an ad hoc arrangement to secure funds primarily through what it called an "Emergency Monetized Title II" program that functioned during the interim period the same way as Title III would do later.
44. Data obtained from USAID in December 1985.
45. My information about the composition of arguments for and against wheat stem from discussions I had with USAID staff and consultants in 1983, 1984, 1985, and 1986, and from agency documents such as USAID (1984g).
46. The World Bank mission's consultant on wheat recommended raising the price of flour to discourage further increases in flour consumption (World Bank, 1984b: 35), and reversing the pattern of relative price trends to encourage more consumption of corn (World Bank, 1984a: 18). Until one of its former employees became minister of finance in 1986, Bank recommendations, especially those emanating from short-term visits, carried little weight in policy arguments. USAID, because it financed food imports while the Bank did not, had more influence. In any event, the Bank's audience on the question of wheat imports was only nominally the government. The prime target for the mission's questions about the policy was USAID.

4

Water

Supply of sufficient quantities of potable water having adequate quality attributes, the bane of urban administrators in developing and developed countries alike, was a recurrent source of aggravation to residents and governments of Port-au-Prince. Major investments in sources of supply and distribution systems, followed by inadequate maintenance and population growth, periodically conspired to lower consumption quantity and quality, to produce protests by irate citizens, and to push governments into taking remedial action. Whether the result of lack of maintenance or poor initial design, such action included not only investments in additional supply and distribution mechanisms but also reconstruction of projects completed many years earlier.

In 1841 newspapers complained bitterly about the feeble quantity and unacceptable quality of water flowing out of public standpipes, the only method of distribution at the time, and government responded two years later with a major project to repair old standpipes and add new ones (Corvington, 1974: 60, 88). Severe shortages recurred in 1860, and in 1862 government reacted with investment in new source supplies from springs, with additions to distribution lines and the number of standpipes, and with reconstruction of old lines and fountains (Corvington, 1974: 137–39). Following disastrous fires in 1885 and 1866, during which water to fight them failed to flow from nearby standpipes, government initiated a long-term improvement program (1866–78). Among other things, the program introduced the novelty of piped water service directly into private homes. The effort was apparently very successful. It caused the water portering business, wherein women with buckets would for a price transport water from the standpipes to consumers at home, to disappear for a time (Corvington, 1974: 191). Problems resurfaced and were again treated in 1897 and in 1913 (Corvington, 1977: 70, 241). Relative to the technologies available at the time and to the size of the population, about 65,000, the city had a respectable water supply system in 1916. Sources provided 17 million liters per day (mld), or a gross flow of 260 liters per capita per day (lcd), which was substantial. Some 3500 families, or a third of the population, were connected directly to the distribution system and received piped water at home. The remaining 6500 families relied on sixteen standpipes (Corvington, 1984: 157). At a ratio of 400 families per standpipe, this form of distribution could have stood expansion, but it was adequate, as were the sixty-six fire hydrants serving the city's 300 hectares, if water flowed to them.

The pattern of ad hoc response to recurrent water crises continued through the 1950s. During the 1960s the municipal water company, CAMEP, assumed for lack of data that the population was not much larger than it had been at the time of the 1950 census, about 150,000, and believed that the main issue with respect to water was quality assurance, and to a lesser extent, increased supply and forward planning. To assist in these matters the Pan American Health Organization (PAHO) provided CAMEP with cooperative assistance services of a sanitary engineer, and the IDB lent it $2.4 million in 1964 to improve supply (Moore, 1972: 103).

In 1971, when the census indicated a population of about 500,000, the combination of inadequate maintenance and increasing demand was again causing water shortages and quality deterioration. Dissatisfied higher-income consumers who received sporadic service to their home connections, or who bought water from vendors exerted pressure on CAMEP to improve the system, to provide more home connections, and to extend distribution to the periphery of the city where a growing number of them now lived.[1] Unwilling to wait for CAMEP action, many of these residents established clandestine private connections wherever nearby trunk lines permitted them to do so, and thereby contributed to further system deterioration. The government requested and received technical assistance from the IDB in 1970 to prepare a second stage of what was supposed to become a long-term capital improvement program, and a $7.7 million loan to finance its construction.[2]

Toward the end of 1975, a year prior to completion of the second stage, the city's water supply system still did not function well. Continuing inadequacy in the treatment of alkaline source supplies produced excessive buildup of calcium deposits in trunk lines and a need for frequent pipe replacement. Location of some sources below residential areas, holes in pipes lying on street surfaces, intermittent pressure, and recurrent flooding yielded chronic contamination. Waste by connected households, who had no valves or meters, and leaks throughout the system caused loss of a substantial amount of the total supply before water actually reached consumers. Exacerbating CAMEP's weak maintenance capacities were a low, flat-rate tariff structure and a political inability to control or charge for illegal connections that resulted in it operating in financial deficit every year.

Still, CAMEP officials believed that by 1975 they had managed to develop a reasonably good system for getting water to consumers. Apparently uninterested in using census data, they assumed that system flows of 65 mld provided a total of 400,000 consumers with 41.5 mld, the difference of 22.5 mld consisting of normal system losses and nonresidential consumption (table 4.1). Some 200,000 people supposedly received water from private home connections, thereby consuming an average of 175 lcd, and the other 200,000 received a lower but still adequate 32.5 lcd from forty standpipes scattered across the city. According to this description, the system was in some respects better and in other respects worse than in 1916. Half the population receiving water from private connections was a definite improvement. Gross source flows of 160 lcd, a 38 percent drop relative to 1916, and a ratio of 940 families per standpipe, an increase of 135 percent, were definitely not improvements. But if consumption levels were what CAMEP presumed they were, the system was adequate. Unfortunately, CAMEP's assumptions were incorrect.

The Water Industry

In 1974 the UNCHBP project did not examine water supply closely because we assumed that consultants retained by the IDB in 1971 had carried out all basic analyses and that necessary improvements would be forthcoming upon completion of the second stage of the construction program. That stage envisaged an increase in source supplies to 78 mld, and the addition of 1500 private connections and ten standpipes on the urban periphery (Fass, 1978: 171). But after noting that the IDB consultants and CAMEP had used population estimates inconsistent with the census and maps of population distribution and density that did not correspond to recent aerial photographs, we spent several months of 1975 conducting surveys of 2600 consumers and vendors and retained our own consulting engineers to look at the operating features of the distribution system.

In addition to indicating that the consuming population was 640,000 people, the result of this effort was a description of water supply that differed fundamentally from the one proposed by CAMEP. With respect to engineering, our staff and consultants reported that system losses were higher, about 30.5 mld. Together with lower nonresidential consumption of 1.8 mld, this meant that 31.7 mld, or 24 percent less water than proposed by CAMEP, was available for a residential population 60 percent higher than the company's estimate. Moreover, although the system supplied direct service through 30,000 legal and illegal connections to 150,000 people,

TABLE 4.1
Competing Descriptions of the Water Supply System in Port-au-Prince, 1976

	FLOWS OF WATER AND PAYMENTS	
	According to CAMEP	According to UNCHBP
Net Water Flows (mld)[a]		
Daily outflow from all sources	64.0	64.0
System losses from leaks and wastage	18.0	30.5
Industrial, commercial, institutional use	4.5	1.8
Net flow available for household use	41.5	31.7
Household consumption obtained by means of		
—broken pipes	—	0.7
—public standpipes (free)	6.5	0.8
—public standpipes (purchased)	—	0.2
—directly from legal or illegal connections	35.0	23.4
—from connected households (free)	—	3.0
—from connected households (purchased)	—	3.1
—trucked from fire hydrants (purchased)	—	0.5
TOTAL	41.5	31.7
Net Financial Flows (thousands of dollars)		
From consumers to truckers	—	980
From consumers to porters	—	930
From consumers and porters to connected households	—	1,220
From legal subscribers to CAMEP	650	650
TOTAL	650	3,780
Number of consumers (population)	400,000	640,000

Sources: Haiti (1976a) and Fass (1982).
[a] Millions of liters per day.

standpipes provided water to very few. Several of CAMEP's standpipes existed only on paper, and after allowance for waste, short periods of operation, low pressure, and their locations with respect to residential areas, the twenty–seven in operation provided no more than 0.8 mld to 55,000 consumers (see figure 2.1). The other 435,000 people relied on indirect sources of supply.

One of these sources was broken pipes. Wear and tear accounted for some breaks, but individuals often dug into streets or found surface pipes into which to knock holes. The pipes usually connected higher–income subscribers with trunk lines, and when water pressure dropped as a result of too many breaks, they called upon CAMEP, the police, or a neighborhood

Macoute for remedial action. Since penalties for vandalizing public property were severe, the practice was not widespread; at any one time it provided about 40,000 people with 0.7 mld.

More common was the sharing of water between households with connections and those without, especially where high– and low–income families were neighbors. Some 95,000 consumers received 3.0 mld this way. The price of water being quite low for connected households, the cost of sharing was negligible compared to the benefits of offering kindness, of maintaining good neighborly relations, and of lowering the incentive for unconnected households to break pipes.

The remaining 300,000 consumers, most of whom had low incomes and lived near the center of the city where there were relatively few connected households, purchased water from one of three types of private vendors. The first were tanker–truck operators who drew water from the city's 100 fire hydrants and then transported it to nonresidential consumers and to 1200 high–income homes without piped service. Depending on availability and transport distance, the unit price of water ranged from $0.30 to $0.60 per hundred liters. Average consumption by regular residential customers was 100 lcd, and families paid $68 per month for this service. Excluding nonresidential sales and irregular service to connected residences with reservoirs whenever piped supply broke down, the operators' gross income was $2700 per day and $980,000 per year. Each of the twenty–five trucks in operation produced annual gross flows of $39,000, or $25,000 after deducting costs of fuel, labor, repairs, depreciation, and various payments to prevent interference with their taking of water and to prevent potential competitors from importing or receiving licenses for additional trucks. These last expenditures were important because the import cost for a used truck was $10,000. At that price the net return on investment was 150 percent in the first year, or 200 percent discounted over five years.[3] Expenditures to protect market share provided handsome dividends, as did occasional vandalism of pipes in order to stimulate a brief surge of demand until CAMEP found and repaired the breaks.

In the second group of vendors were about two thousand connected households in central areas of the city who sold water by the 18–liter bucketful. Prices varied by season, by day, and by neighborhood. The minimum price in 1976, in effect during the rainy season if water flowed through city pipes in quantity, was $0.02 per bucket, or a unit price of $0.11 per hundred liters. In the dry season, the price rose to $0.10 per bucket ($0.55 per hundred liters), and during droughts could reach $0.18 to $0.36 per bucket ($1.00 to $2.00 per hundred liters) for several months at a time. At such times the unit price was 100 times more than in the United States or Europe.

Annual gross revenues of the 2000 vendors amounted to $1.87 million (or a net of $1.22 million after payment of user fees to CAMEP) with individual gross earnings ranging from $500 to $1500. In this instance, if the connection was legal, the aboveboard investment was $100 for a reservoir, $25 for a connection fee, and $20 in annual use fees. In theory, first-year returns on the $125 outlay could be between 280 and 1100 percent depending on sales. In practice it was lower because the absence of major financial obstacles to entry and intense competition between existing vendors required that they incur high overhead costs. Unless a vendor was a Macoute of importance, which happened often enough, essential business costs included payments to CAMEP crews or independent contractors to install clandestine connections or to cut off those of others; payments to CAMEP valve operators to shut down service to certain areas, thereby creating scarcities to drive prices up and shift demand from one group of sellers to another; and payments to Macoutes for general protection and for permitting destruction of standpipes, especially when water was so exceptionally scarce that small increases in sales quantities could yield very substantial profits. These various payments, to individuals who understood the value of their services, were not inconsequential.

Attaching themselves to this group from time to time were gangs of low-level Macoutes, or hirelings of higher-ranking officers who needed money in a hurry. They commandeered standpipes serving densely populated neighborhoods under the pretext of restoring order to the general chaos that occurred when water flowed through taps (figure 4.1). Naturally, they charged users for the crowd-control service they provided. Unless a neighborhood chief was behind the action, the practice was short-lived because any large group of users was likely to contain individuals with connections to rival groups of Macoutes who would usually intervene on behalf of "their" constituents. If a neighborhood chief was the source of the problem, relief would take longer, but eventually the policy (army) would appear on behalf of the populace. Facing superior arms, the Macoutes usually withdrew. Commandeering a productive standpipe for even a few days was profitable because daily service charges could average $80 to $120.

The third group of sellers, constituting the city's traditional method of supply, were women who bought water from the second group and then carried it to consumers in surrounding areas (figure 4.2). Numbering about 14,000 when shortages were severe and demand for delivery high, their usual margins were $0.01 to $0.02 per bucket ($0.06 to $0.11 per hundred liters) depending on distance traveled, and doubled in periods of extreme scarcity. With an average daily rate of sales of ten buckets under normal conditions, their net earnings might be $0.15. During shortages they made $0.30 from twenty sales, and with a margin of $0.04 per bucket during droughts, perhaps $0.80 per day. On average these porters earned approx-

FIGURE 4.1
Water Pirates and Queues in St. Martin

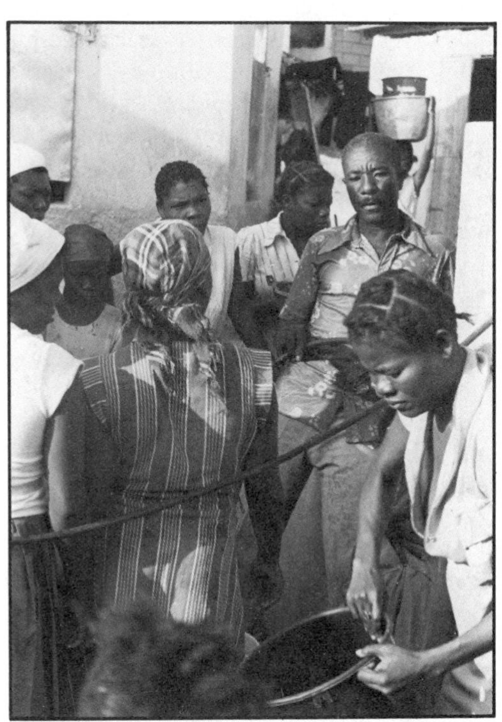

imately $930,000, or $5.50 per month each. This low rate of earnings, $0.18 per day, resulted from intense competition in an occupation having relative (but not absolute) ease of entry, no methods of protecting market share, and no available technology to increase sales quantities beyond the rate of one bucket at a time.[4] The occupation nevertheless yielded a small profit of 8 percent per day (i.e., a profit of $0.015 after deducting $0.16 in food costs and $0.005 for depreciation over three years of the $5.00 investment in a bucket), in part because the price of buckets did serve as something of a barrier to entry—a subject I explore further below.

According to us at the UNCHBP, water distribution was not a public service in the narrow sense of the phrase, but rather a sizable private industry producing $3.78 million in value-added. About 26 percent of this value accrued to twenty-five truckers, 32 percent to 2000 connected households, 25 percent to 14,000 porters, and 17 percent to CAMEP. This kind of industry was not uncommon in cities of developing countries where water systems fell short in supplying demand. The more unusual aspect with respect to other cities, but quite normal in Port-au-Prince, was the way in which a relatively few suppliers with privileged access to advanced technology like trucks, reservoirs, and pipes amassed revenues from the many without such access, and then like the relatively wealthy in St. Martin, expended a sizable share of the revenues to protect privileges.

One important outcome of this process was an annual transfer of $1.22 million from 295,000 low-income people in 56,000 households, or $22.00 per household per year, to higher-income households of the political class supplying various goods and services to the industry.[5]

A second outcome was highly uneven distribution of water consumption (table 4.2). High-income families with piped service to their homes or able to pay for truck deliveries consumed 156 and 100 lcd respectively. The 180,000 people who managed to get water at no charge consumed between 15 and 32 lcd, depending on source. And the 295,000 people that regularly purchased from porters, connected families, or standpipe pirates, and who paid what may have been the highest urban water prices in the world, obtained 11 lcd. In the aggregate, 24 percent of the population used 76 percent of water supply, while 46 percent consumed 10 percent.

Residents of St. Martin were part of the 46 percent. There, consumption ranged from 4.5 to 36 liters per adult per day (lad), and averaged 12 lad.[6] This was more than the 7 to 10 lad in lowest-income areas of the city, less than for most low-income groups in other developing cities, lower than the 24 to 44 lad that some researchers claimed could provide all essential health benefits, and lower than the 20 liters used up in a simple flush of a North American or European toilet.[7]

To purchase such amounts, St. Martin households spent from 5 to 50

FIGURE 4.2
Water Porters in St. Martin and Brooklyn

St. Martin

Brooklyn

TABLE 4.2
Structure of Water Consumption in Port-au-Prince, 1976

	CONSUMERS		DAILY CONSUMPTION		
Source of Supply	**Number**	**% of Total**	**per Capita (liters)**	**Total (mld)[a]**	**% of Total**
Private connection (legal and illegal)	150,000	23	156	23.4	74
From another's connection (free)	95,000	15	32	3.0	9
Standpipes (free)	55,000	9	15	0.8	3
From leaks and breaks	40,000	6	18	0.7	2
Purchase from porters and connected households	295,000	46	11	3.3	2
Tanker truck delivery	5,000	1	100	0.5	2
TOTAL (average)	640,000	100	(49)	31.7	100

Sources: Haiti (1976a) and Fass (1982).
[a] Millions of liters per day.

percent of cash available on any given day, depending on price and quantity, and over the course of a month paid 13.5 percent of income for water. Two-thirds of them paid more than the average, and this while water was relatively plentiful. The poorest in Port-au-Prince sometimes paid up to 20 percent of income, but the share was generally higher than for low-income groups elsewhere. In Addis Ababa and Manila, for example, such groups respectively spent 8.7 and 9.3 percent (Linn, 1983: 159).

Among households like those in St. Martin in which expenditure was high and corresponding consumption low, a third outcome of the industrialization of supply was the transformation of what should have been final consumption of a simple commodity into a major household production activity that in many instances was more preoccupying than the manufacturing of nutrition.

Producing Water

Families paid as much as they did for meager quantities because water was vitally important to them. The basis of its importance may have had a cultural component.[8] Ultimately, however, the importance stemmed from water's service as a fundamental physiological factor of household production.[9] Toward the lower end of a 4.5 to 36 lad consumption range, having one or two more liters could make a noticeable difference to health and productivity, in much the same way as a few more calories or grams of protein do. Indeed, at the lower end, gains from an increase in quantity usually outstripped those from improved quality (USAID, 1981). After controlling for socioeconomic status and location, a 1977 study of 800 city families reported that where consumption was less than 22 lad, children had higher rates of diarrhea, scabies, conjunctivitis, febrile illness, and malnutrition than comparable children in families consuming more water (Thacker, Music, and Pollard, 1980: 43). More generally, it found that 52 percent of children in low-consumption families had been ill at least once during the survey week, while the proportion in high-consumption families was 33 percent. Another study reported that 46 percent of all urban children were likely to be ill within a reference week (USAID, 1978b: 50). In combination, the two reports implied that water quantity might have been an important independent variable in the frequency and incidence of illness, and through illness, perhaps also in the prevalence of child malnutrition. Presumably, quantity could affect the well-being and output of adults as well, and together with the complicating impact of illness among children, water could have been a significant bearing on earnings and household income.

Unlike food, which individuals might be able to go without for a while if circumstances demanded, risks associated with dehydration in tropical climates made daily consumption of water almost mandatory. There was a point at which individuals would forego everything for some water. In St. Martin, the coefficient for the income elasticity of demand was 0.26.[10] The simple regression equation's intercept, that is, the projected quantity of water consumed when income approached zero, was about 4 lad. Simplistic as the estimate was, consumption of 4 lad was close to what different sources indicated was the minimum range required for physiological equilibrium.[11] More pertinent was the question implicit in the equation: How did people obtain 4 lad if their incomes were close to zero? Street people provided some answers to this question.

Street Techniques

For the poor, water had three purposes, drinking, cooking, and washing, that transformed it into three distinct commodities. Questions about how much to obtain and how much to expend, therefore, had to do not only with choices between water and other items, but also with choices between drinking, cooking, and washing, and with choices between any one of these uses and other things.

Drinking, for the poorest people on the street, was primordial. With no assets but the clothes they were wearing, the poorest could wait to earn a penny and then pay for two large glasses, a price equivalent to $1.00 per one hundred liters. For more pennies they might choose bottled drinks, sugared ice, fruit, or soup. Or they could spend time trying to get water without spending cash. This meant stopping whatever it it was that they were doing to beg someone to give them some, to find or make a break in a pipe, to travel a distance to a standpipe in the hope that it was working, free of pirates, and that the struggle to get through the crowd to the taps would not prove too exhausting or time-consuming.[12]

Spending money meant not having the penny for, say, a piece of bread. Spending time meant a break from work or the search for it, and the risk of missing the opportunity to earn another penny. Time expenditures incurred other costs as well. The method of begging, if the individual did not look destitute or lacked skill in presenting the appearance of it, risked insult. Breaking or using already broken pipes, as mentioned earlier, risked arrest and beatings. Accessing standpipes could result in injury from the perennial fights that occurred there, especially in the dry season. Sometime during this process, the quantity of body fluid (and nutrition) used up in searching for water could exceed the quantity gained when a person found it. But whether payment was with money or time, it was useful practice to conserve as much body fluid as feasible by limiting physical exertion to the minimum required by the immediate circumstance, such as keeping a job.[13]

Individuals in this condition did not buy water for cooking or washing. Even if they had the money, they did not have, by definition, a pot or other impermeable container that could allow them to produce these services for themselves. They bought prepared food. For washing they might set aside an evening or a Sunday to walk to ravines and rivers on the periphery of the city. Between such trips, they used runoff in storm drains or in gutters from broken water mains to wash dust off their arms and legs. Production of water consumption by such people was hard and extremely inefficient in terms of money, time, and energy use. A technological breakthrough was essential, and the technology in question was the bucket.

Bucket Economics

The elite of the street, those who had saved or borrowed $3 to $5 to invest in a cooking pot, operated more efficiently. Because the penny was the smallest unit of currency, they could fill the pot with 4 to 6 liters of water for the same price that others paid for one liter when buying by the glassful. Because the time cost of searching was also the same, a pot lowered both money and time expenditures per unit of drinking water. Even if work demanded that they buy glassfuls (and prepared food) during the day, they could drink more for less before and after work. The pot also permitted some cleaning of utensils, but street people with pots did most of their washing in the same manner as those without them.

A pot was something of an intermediate technology, however. Heavy, ill-shaped to the purpose of transporting water, and with limited volume, it would do in the absence of an alternative. A lightweight bucket with an 18-liter capacity was far superior. This $5 item presented wonderful possibilities for raising consumption and lowering expenditure. A family of 4.3 persons without a pot or bucket, and paying one penny per liter, would have had to spend $0.52 per day to produce consumption of 12 lad. Paying a penny to fill a 6-liter pot reduced the outlay to $0.09. But paying $0.02 for a bucketful took expenditure down to $0.06. And because time used up in searching for water rather than paying for it with cash could yield a bucketful rather than a cupful, time savings were also significant. Moreover, in conjunction with a pot, a bucket permitted households to drink and cook at the same time, cook and wash, or, with the addition of a second bucket, do all three. Buying water for washing was nevertheless rare among these street people. Drinking and cooking were all that water seemed worth paying for.

Buckets also had income-producing potential. Boys could increase their contribution to family income by using idle capacity of empty buckets during the day or night to sell carwashing services. The market for this service was competitive and earnings were low, but because the value of even a small amount of earnings was high for low-income households, because buckets were not available to everyone, and because many households kept their buckets in continuous use storing water, the earnings were significant enough to the households receiving them that sale of the service was usually worthwhile.

Bucket rental services, though not widespread, did exist in certain areas of the city. For $0.02 per day families with idle equipment would rent them to trustworthy boys, or to women wishing to become water porters. The rental charge lowered porter earnings from the $0.18 possible with use of an owned bucket to $0.16, but $0.16 was still important to people who would earn even less if they did not rent one.

The challenge of financing purchase of a bucket was formidable. For a household without a pot, the bucket offered a production cost saving of $0.46 per day for a 12 lad output. In theory, the $5 investment would pay for itself in eight days, and over the subsequent month could yield a cost reduction of almost $14. The problem lay in finding the $5. In trade, such an amount could produce an earning of $0.50 per day. Taking funds out of trade or manufacturing, therefore causing not only a substantial loss of income for eight days but also the potential loss of a market niche, was impractical. Borrowing was perhaps better, but a low-cost commercial loan with an interest rate of 25 percent per month required $15 in collateral, which street people did not have, or friends with $5 to lend at the same or a higher rate without collateral, which most street people were also unlikely to have (see chapter 7). For them, $5 was a very large amount, and without ready access to credit the only means to acquire funds for this major investment was through slow accumulation of savings. A set-aside of 10 percent of daily earnings of $0.50 for this purpose, for example, could yield a bucket in three or four months' time.

A bucket could do a lot, and most families did save for its purchase. Every household in St. Martin had at least one, and in five cases one bucket and one pot were the only objects of value they had. Except for these five cases perhaps, the circumstances of St. Martin residents were not as severe as for street people or for other very poor households. The ways most of them went about the business of obtaining water were nevertheless similar in terms of decisionmaking about efficient resource use.

Efficiency

The price of water in 1976 varied between $0.02 and $0.10, and averaged $0.04 per bucket in St. Martin. In principle, families could send adolescents to fetch water from distant standpipes at certain times of the day. The nearest one offering more or less regular service was 800 meters away and required an hour and a half to two-hour trip, depending on how long it took to reach the tap once an individual joined the crowd surrounding it. Such a procedure was not particularly efficient. If a household valued the time of an adolescent at 1.3 cents per hour (i.e., $0.10 per eight-hour day), the cost of one trip to carry one bucket, including the extra calories used up in the process, was about $0.03. For an adult the cost would have been higher. In either instance, families must have decided that these and other associated costs were high because none of them used standpipes.

The remaining choices were between spending a half-hour to forty-five minutes (per bucket), therefore obtaining a 25 to 35 percent price reduction, by walking to and purchasing water from connected households on the periphery of the neighborhood or buying at the higher price from one of the 1200 porters who constantly meandered through the area in search of customers.

About 37 percent of the families with average monthly incomes of $8 per adult per month substituted time for money and bought from connected households. The rest, with incomes of $11, used porters. The difference in incomes was significant, but many families alternated between the two methods in response to price changes.[14]

In terms of use, lowest-income families restricted purchases to drinking and cooking, reserving Sundays for washing trips to ravines and rivers in the same way as street people did. Higher-income families bought water for washing, usually doing it twice a week at home. But they seemed to wash only if they had adult or adolescent women not otherwise engaged in more productive activities. Washing had to take place in the morning in order to allow for drying in the afternoon. For working women, the opportunity cost of wasting a day in washing was high. A laundress cost $0.15 per day if the household provided water or $0.30 if she had to purchase it or travel to a ravine. Families with working women earning more than the cost of a laundress usually retained their services.

In these variations on a theme about water, families in St. Martin, together with those in the street, seemed to go to extraordinary lengths to assure efficient use of resources in the procurement of supply and in the production of water's various vital services. Where expenditure of 13.5 percent of income could yield no more than an average of 12 lad, households had little choice but to be efficient in combining money, time, and nutrition in an activity absolutely fundamental to health, productivity, income, and, ultimately, to survival. Under such conditions, expenditures for water and buckets, like expenditures for food and pots, looked much less like final consumption than productive consumption. In a great many instances, perhaps in most instances, investment in water was an act of production that generated higher returns than possible from any other activity.

Improvement Efforts

The water industry of Port–au–Prince and the characteristics of consumption attached to it were not unique. In certain parts of Jakarta, a connected supplier could earn over $5000 per year from sales to porters in 1976, and porters made $1.20 per day transporting ninety–six buckets with the help of carts. Some 5 to 10 percent of consumers in areas not subject to competition between suppliers used 10 to 20 percent of income to consume 13 lad after paying $0.02 to $0.03 per bucket (Berry and Sierra, 1978: 66, 74–75). What made Port–au–Prince unusual was scale. Over half the city's residents faced the same predicament as the very poorest of Jakarta.

There might have been a few cogent arguments to justify maintenance of high food prices, but to us at the UNCHBP no such arguments presented themselves for water. The purposes of urban economic development could not be served when the price of water rendered savings accumulation and productive investment in more enduring things difficult or impossible for half the populace. Nor were they served when average intake levels of 12 lad contributed to higher frequencies of illness, of resource diversion to curative medical care, and of downward pressure on income. And there could be no financial argument because the effort required to double or triple consumption, to reduce expenditure shares by half, and to thereby raise real income by perhaps 5 to 10 percent, was small.

There was, in principle, the possibility of reintroducing the "centime" or one–fifth of a penny, into the currency system. The combination of having the penny as the smallest unit of currency and the bucketful as the largest quantity available for purchase by most people made it difficult for the price of water to fall below $0.01 per 18 liters. The centime created the technical possibility for lower unit prices, both for bucketfuls and for cupfuls. Another possibility was development of intermediate transport technologies to fill the space between the bucket and the truck, as carts did in Jakarta.

But the most practical, immediate possibility presenting itself to us was to reduce price by increasing competition among suppliers. That meant increasing the number of connected households and building (and protecting) a few more functioning standpipes in densely populated areas of the city. Keeping prices close to $0.01 and $0.02 per bucket rather than the $0.04 average in places like St. Martin was likely to constitute a major improvement. In 1975 this required convincing CAMEP and the IDB to immediately modify the design for the second stage of their construction program by shifting some connections and standpipes away from the periphery and toward the center of the city, or if impractical, then at least adding more standpipes in the center. For the longer term, increasing competition required more attention to improving CAMEP's capacities in planning, technical maintenance, financial management, and personnel administration. We also reasoned that if several years of IDB and PAHO assistance to CAMEP had failed to note the existence of a sizable water industry and had failed to estimate actual consumption levels, then the two foreign agencies could also benefit from institutional strengthening. But protocols of conduct among such agencies made it difficult for us to make such an opinion explicit. It was easier to criticize CAMEP than the IDB or PAHO.

In any event, we launched ourselves into informal discussions about water supply with our counterparts in other agencies toward the end of 1975. With some change in participants, the discussions would continue in haphazard fashion for the next several years.

In initial exchanges, CAMEP's administrative staff disassociated itself from any responsibility for the second-stage improvement program. They felt that the agency was responsible only for administration of the water system and that this did not include planning for new works. They had cooperated with IDB consultants because the Ministry of Finance had requested that they do so. The consultants, not CAMEP, were responsible for the plan. The agency would accept any changes in the program if the IDB and the Finance Ministry agreed to them first.

Irregularities in day-to-day operations were of more direct concern to some of CAMEP's upper-level staff, but they argued that little could be done to correct matters. Low salaries encouraged both managerial and technical personnel to accept payments for special services. Some admitted to such practices themselves. Moreover, many of the agency's personnel were political appointees (including the staff we spoke with, as with most senior staff in government), and hence were protected from any possible administrative sanctions. All our respondents said that they deemed reform of CAMEP essential but noted that pressure for such reform had to originate outside the agency, from higher up in the decision-making apparatus of government.

In other discussions, representatives of the IDB offered no objections to making adjustments to the second stage because the additional financial burden of providing the thirty to forty standpipes in downtown areas we suggested would be less than 1 percent of the total cost of the program. However, IDB staff felt that approval had first to be obtained from the PAHO sanitary engineer because that organization was responsible for monitoring water quality.

IDB officials were much more concerned with our overall description of the water supply system. If that description was correct, it called into question several hundreds of thousands of dollars of technical assistance effort that had already been spent, and several millions for capital investment in the process of being spent.[15] The representatives suggested that we hold discussions with the firm in charge of construction in order that they evaluate the accuracy of our analysis. Afterward, if necessary, the IDB would see what changes could be made at the last minute.

In the end, the construction firm completed the second-stage program without changes in the original plan. The PAHO engineer objected to the construction of any additional standpipes because they did not conform to international health standards. The engineer considered such methods a necessary short-term evil that had to be minimized, and ten new standpipes seemed more than enough. He made this decision even though he agreed with us that high water prices that resulted in use of street runoff or reduced food consumption led to serious health hazards as well, and that piped water in central areas was already sufficiently polluted for additional contamination at standpipes to be insignificant. Standpipes were simply not acceptable to PAHO, whatever the consequences.

Engineers of the construction firm agreed with our analysis, and indicated that early in their work they had suspected that the program was inappropriate. They would not, however, openly endorse the analysis. They could not do so because it would have meant criticizing the technical review capacities of their clients, the IDB and CAMEP, and the analysis and design capabilities of their colleagues who had prepared the second-stage program years before. Moreover, an open endorsement would halt construction and generate renewed political pressure on CAMEP from high-income families who had been counting on the project to provide them with new connections and improved service. A stoppage would also increase project costs, and the firm had no assurance that it could recover them. The firm's personnel did agree, however, that a major ungrading of CAMEP's capabilities was essential, and began to promote the idea with the IDB.

With the ending of the UNCHBP project in 1976, its expatriate staff left the country or took other jobs in Haiti, and local staff seconded to it from the National Planning Council and the Ministry of Public Works retrieved their old positions. Because many of the reports prepared by the project contained implicit criticisms of public and foreign-assistance agencies, often couched in less than the most tactful diplomatic language, the government and UNCHBP headquarters in New York did not approve them.[16] Circulation of several volumes of the project's final report, including one containing the analysis of the water system, received extremely limited circulation. That same year, employees of the IDB and the construction firm that had joined discussions with us also left Haiti.

But the process continued. In 1977, pursuing recommendations made by the construction firm, the IDB provided CAMEP with a special PAHO consultant to assist in upgrading its technical and management capacities. Many of the agency's staff considered his presence at CAMEP an imposition. He received little cooperation within CAMEP and little support from outside the organization. The consultant faced a task of monumental proportions because he was confronting over 300 mostly inept employees with considerable political influence, and challenging the ability of a few thousand powerful families to make a lot of money in the water market.[17]

At the same time, the IDB retained a new consulting firm to design the third stage of the capital improvement program. The firm's mandate was to design an extension of the system into high-income peripheral areas. Nothing in the contract required consideration of overall supply or of actual consumption in central areas. The firm proposed a \$27.5 million project that included 5000 new private connections and another ten standpipes in the suburbs (IDB, 1977). The government was counting on this proposal to respond to the pressures of influential groups not served by the first two phases. By the end of the year, the IDB had begun to process the government's new loan application.

A World Bank mission on which I served arrived in Haiti at the end of 1977 to explore possibilities for financing urban projects. Necessary data for this purpose were not readily available in Port-au-Prince, and members of the mission therefore drew upon several sections of the UNCHBP project reports that I found for them after return to Washington. They paid considerable attention to water supply, and accepted the UNCHBP's earlier analysis as essentially valid.

Permanent World Bank staff of the mission thereafter initiated discussions in Washington with their counterparts at the IDB, aimed at avoiding a potential embarrassment. The issue was that the World Bank would soon make its findings known in a report, the report would circulate among foreign-assistance agencies, and would suggest that the loan being processed by the IDB for the third stage was not warranted.[18] By mid-1979, the IDB had shelved the loan request. To allow time for progress in bringing about administrative, financial, and technical improvement at CAMEP, the IDB extended the PAHO special consultant's contract to 1983 and decided not to grant a major water supply loan before that time (IDB, personal communication, October 1982).

This postponement was designed to provide the special consultant with some leverage at CAMEP, and through CAMEP to higher levels of public decisionmaking. The combined effect of the IDB action and pressure from higher–income families on the periphery for improved service was supposed to have convinced government to permit basic changes such as installation of water meters, higher user charges to connected families, penalties for taking bribes and for illegal connections, introduction of charges to truckers, licensing and inspection of truckers, and issuance of sales permits with corresponding higher fees to households selling water in low–income areas. Once CAMEP regained control of the system and increased its revenues, construction of standpipes could begin on a large scale.

Missing from this calculus was the influence upon decisionmaking of the truckers and connected households who benefited from the status quo, and who financed the production of benefits by sharing them with public officials. Government required a solution other than the one being pressed by the IDB. It explored alternative sources of financing, and in 1980 an assistance fund in the Middle East showed some interest. Little came of it, however.

But in small, halting steps, movement did occur. In 1980 and 1981, CAMEP operated with losses of $160,000 on revenues of $1.5 million per year. In 1982, after receiving a small loan of $2.8 million from a source I could not identify, it made a profit of $260,000 on $2.2 million in revenues. By 1984 profits were up to $280,000 on sales of $2.7 million (see table 1.1) (World Bank, 1985: 165–66). And there were gradual additions to the number of standpipes, although the flow of water through them was often negligible. In St. Martin, for example, CAMEP built four standpipes within the neighborhood, and thirteen adjacent to it (UNCDF, 1984: 74). However, with service limited to six hours per week, the effect on prices and consumption was minimal. Indeed, in 1983 average prices for water in St. Martin varied between $0.08 and $0.10 per bucket, an increase of 125 percent relative to 1976, and substantially higher than the 73 percent increase in the consumer price index during the period. CAMEP may have been improving its performance in terms of claiming a larger share of the industry's value–added, but because connected households were passing on higher costs associated with CAMEP claims to consumers, the effect was often to make things worse. In the absence of ways of controlling employees or increasing the number of connected households in central areas that would withstand the quiet competitive war that raged there every day, CAMEP and its expatriate advisers did not, and perhaps could not raise supply relative to demand. In 1985, the new average price in St. Martin seemed to be $0.12 to $0.14 per bucket.[19] This increase of 225 percent over 1976, more than double the 105 percent increase in the consumer price index, and set in a context where real income was unlikely to have increased by much over the decade, did not suggest that the political economy of water was any different in 1986 than it had been a decade earlier.

The departure of the Duvaliers and the conversion of Macoutes into less visible men and women of importance in 1986 presented the possibility of at least a few changes. With use of guns no longer requiring toleration, standpipe pirateering was unlikely to occur as often. Competition among connected suppliers for market share might come to rest more on the use of money, and less on brute force, for advantage. Both changes might make it easier for a few new investors to enter the sector and thereby put downward pressure on prices, if CAMEP had enough water to direct to them. And on this matter the appearance of a free press and a partial broadening of the political constituency held out a little bit of promise. Complaints about water and demands for such things as public and private tanker trucks to serve low-income areas were not long in presenting themselves (Jacques, 1986: 6, 37). And because the French government was providing CAMEP with assistance in developing a master plan for water supply, the first in seventy years, there was some basis for believing that the third stage might yield improvements that the first and second stages could not.[20] But consumers would have to wait. Even if construction began immediately, significant effects could not begin to become apparent before 1990.

Although circumstances in 1986 offered a small prospect that members of the ordinary class in areas like St. Martin might eventually be relieved of part of the oppressive burden imposed by a "public" service that had turned into a mechanism for private taxation, there was little of political substance to assure it. The Duvaliers, a few Macoutes, and others were gone from the immediate scene, but the machinery and most of its beneficiaries were still in place. They had everything to lose and nothing to gain from change. Higher-income families still demanded that water move in their direction. CAMEP, though financially more secure, was still a CAMEP full of old and new appointees and their political alliances and allegiances. A new government resting on precarious political foundations, or any future government that depended for an important part of its solvency upon these various factions, was unlikely to step on its own toes by pressing the issue of water for ordinary people too aggressively, even if it were to arrive at the conclusion that there was such an issue.

In this context, the foreign-assistance factions that after a period of over a decade had finally come to what looked like a shared opinion that water supply constituted a problem worthy of some attention, were not likely to press the matter with vigor. Besides an interest in maintaining governmental stability in order to render the task of assistance more convenient, the politics of survival of technical experts, administrators, contractors, and organizations did not lend themselves to cultivation of strong and concerted political action, at least not on behalf of ordinary people or on the basis of UNCHBP data, still the only sources of factual information about water consumption and distribution, more than ten years old. Progress, if any, had every likelihood of being slow.

If accurate, this prospect was unfortunate. Besides alteration of food policy, interventions to reduce the price of water were one of the very few available means of raising real income of ordinary people relatively quickly, of lowering the rate of artificial (i.e., politically induced) poverty of a large share of the urban population by a substantial 5 to 10 percent, of allowing ordinary people more scope for purchasing and investing in other things, and of thereby giving a small boost to the segment of the economy in which ordinary people extracted their livelihoods.

None of this, or the discussions of behavior with respect to matters of employment and food, necessarily implied that the complex machinations of the political class were systematically incapable of yielding a functional consensus to act on behalf of ordinary people. There were issues around which survival needs and other characteristics of enough factions could combine to yield actions that seemed as if they might benefit some segments of the ordinary class. One of these issues was shelter. The difficulty was that in a political economy that often converted food and water from final into productive acts of consumption, matters of shelter were relatively unimportant to many members of the ordinary class.

Notes

1. After 1971 these consumers comprised increasing numbers of foreign households attached to bilateral, multilateral, and private voluntary organizations. They put pressure on CAMEP directly as consumers, or indirectly through their landlords and representatives of their organizations.
2. Communication from the IDB in December 1981 indicated that the original loan agreement was for $5.1 million and then rose to $7.7 million in 1984.
3. The 200 percent figure is the internal rate of return on investment discounted at 12 percent per year. The 12 percent discount rate, a figure used as convention for project analysis in developing countries, was low for Haiti, as I argue in chapter 7. With a higher discount rate, the rate of return would have been lower.
4. Portering was the occupation of the very poor and usually served as a means of livelihood for women who had not yet accumulated enough funds to enter other forms of trade, or who had tried and failed in other enterprises. Selling water took more strength than skill, but some skill, for example, mastering the daily cycle of water demand in different areas, was essential if a porter wanted to maximize the number of daily transactions.
5. How much of this $1.22 million represented a tax due to monopoly rents was hard to determine. If competition among these suppliers had been as free as that among porters, the price of water should have remained steady at the

technological limit of $0.01 per bucket. At that price the transfer of resources for the same level of consumption would have been about $660,000 per year, assuming no competition from standpipes.

6. In St. Martin, 12 lad was equivalent to 9.7 lcd. Average consumption was therefore slightly less than the 11 lcd average for the 295,000 people in the city using similar methods of supply.
7. Boulos (1978) claimed a daily consumption level of 25 liters per household in Boston, a very poor neighborhood of the city. Because average household size was smaller in Boston, the level of consumption was equivalent to 7 to 10 lad. Saunders and Warford (1976: 124) reported minimum consumption levels equivalent to 30 lad in other cities. Kalbermatten, De Anne, and Gunnerson (1982) suggested the equivalent of a 24 to 44 lad range as satisfactory to meet all health benefits.
8. Alvarez and Murray (1981: 158) reported that Haitians often view water as nourishing, in the sense that it assists in extracting value from food in the digestion process. Habit demands a glass of water after a meal.
9. Water, as I indicate in Appendix A, was also a raw material input to certain trade and manufacturing activities. It rarely represented more than 5 percent of total input costs and therefore contributed less to household income on the market side than it did through its contribution to health and labor productivity.
10. The (cross-sectional) income elasticity of demand for water was estimated by regressing the logarithm of monthly household water purchases, measured in buckets (the dependent variable), on the logarithm of net household monthly income (the independent variable) for a subsample of households which paid $0.04 per bucket. The results were:

    monthly income: 0.26 (t value = 3.6, significant at the 1 percent level)
    constant: 1.5
    r^2: 0.35
    f value: 12.65 (significant at the 1 percent level)

11. The World Bank (1980b: 8) referred to a figure of 1.2 to 2.4 lad. Others, such as Tilman (1981: 23), proposed 7 lad. Whether these figures are for drinking only, or for drinking and cooking, is unclear.
12. Of the twenty-seven standpipes in operation in 1976, thirteen operated twenty to twenty-four hours per day, two from twelve to nineteen hours, nine from four to eleven hours, and the rest for less than three hours (Haiti 1976a: 14). None of the standpipes were in the downtown area where street people spent most of their time.
13. This tendency applied equally to undernourished individuals. Oshima (1967) noted that much of what appeared to outsiders as laziness, indolence, or, less pejoratively, as painfully slow work habits, could result from attempts to conserve water and energy outflows.
14. The difference in the means of monthly income between households that bought water from connected families and those that purchased from porters was significant at the 5 percent level.
15. What concerned the IDB about our UNCHBP analysis was that population growth estimates suggested that the 20 percent increase in source flows anticipated at the end of the second stage would not be sufficient to satisfy demand in

three or four years time, the proposed connections and standpipes on the periphery would have little or no supply impact on the private market concentrated in the middle of the city, and the whole of the noneffect would nevertheless require CAMEP to pay between $300,000 and $350,000 per year in debt service. Moreover, if CAMEP remained unable to improve its revenue–generating capabilities, it would continue to require subsidies.

16. The reports were a severe indictment of Haiti's institutional capabilities, of its implicit policy with respect to the social distribution of the financing and of the benefits of public action, and of the activities of many international assistance organizations. Few would have been pleased if the reports had reached a wide audience.
17. The shorter–term objectives of the consultant were to undertake a complete survey of water users, to prepare up–to–date plans of the city and the pipes underneath its streets, to install and test water meters, to develop a centralized valve control system that could eliminate independent practices of operators, and to train personnel in the basics of system maintenance. Longer–term objectives included management and personnel upgrading, reform of the tariff structure to make CAMEP financially self–sustaining, construction of 500 standpipes over a ten–year period once CAMEP had been sufficiently upgraded to maintain such sources, and control of third–party sales by means of licensing and inspection of tanker operators and issuance of temporary permits for such sales by connected families in low–income areas.
18. As is natural among banks, the discussion turned on financial matters. The World Bank estimated that if the IDB were to finance a third phase, CAMEP's book expenditures would rise from a 1978 figure of $2.5 million to $5 million in 1982, while annual revenues still hovered around $700,000. The World Bank's final report (1979), which covered these and other matters, was as controversial as those of the UNCHBP. Prepared in draft form in early 1978, it did not receive Haitian government approval until, after considerable rewriting, it was allowed to circulate in the spring and summer of 1979.
19. At that moment Haiti was facing a fuel shortage, and CAMEP may have been curtailing its pumping of water from wells, thus lowering supply by a small amount. In such an event, prices of $0.12 to $0.14 may have exaggerated the normal average for that time of year.
20. The French government's bilateral assistance agency, FAC, initiated the $300,000 master planning project in 1984.

5

Shelter

Members of the political class who subscribed to bourgeois principles of urban aesthetics had much to lament in history's unkind treatment of Port–au–Prince. Situated pleasingly at the base of a mountain bordering a bay, a setting vaguely reminiscent of Naples, the course of events never permitted visual aspects of the built–up portions of the site to match its natural attractiveness. Viewed as a whole, the city was at best mediocre. Viewed in parts, some of it was pleasant enough. Most parts were unattractive, for good reason. Two hurricanes and two earthquakes flattened three–quarters of the city in 1751. Bombardment and pillaging between 1794 and 1798, and again in 1807, 1812, and 1869, destroyed major portions of the built–up area. Fire did the same in 1820, 1822, 1866, 1875, 1883, and 1894, fourteen other times during the nineteenth century, and several times more in the twentieth (Godard, 1983: 61–65).

Until about 1945, Port–au–Prince had a functioning cadastre and a town layout plan that allowed orderly reconstruction after each disaster and a method of guiding urban expansion (Haiti, 1974: 119). Visitors and local commentators rarely found the city pleasing to look at, but the unpleasantness was more or less well organized within the town plan. But as in most cities faced with sudden and sustained rates of population growth, the cadastre, the plan, and other mechanisms of land management broke down. Population growth after 1945 spread itself in uncontrolled fashion across various scattered parcels surrounding the the city's core. Higher–income families able to pay for public and private transportation moved along major thoroughfares to the east and west, finding accommodation at higher elevations or on shaded parcels offering more comfortable environments than the central area of the city. Lower–income families, for the most part tied to the central market and the downtown area for their livelihoods and unable to pay for public transportation, either filled the already built–up areas, like Bel Air, left behind by the higher income groups or settled on vacant parcels such as Poste Marchand, La Saline, and

Ti Cheri made available to them in and around the downtown (see figure 2.1).

For higher–income families able to purchase relatively large parcels of land or to lease them for purposes of constructing sizable homes, conversion of vacant or agricultural tracts into residential use proceeded in traditional fashion. Rising demand stimulated higher prices, and supply responded accordingly. For lower–income families able to purchase or lease only small parcels, the supply response was slower, thereby stimulating intense competitive bidding between households for scarce residential space, and the spread of ugliness.

Characteristics of Shelter

The upward pressure on land prices and rents on the one hand, and income levels that after expenditures for food and water did not permit households latitude for spending large shares of it for housing on the other, caused most of the population growth from 150,000 in 1950 to 640,000 in 1976 to concentrate in a very few areas. Over half the population lived in one–story homes at gross residential densities of more than 600 persons per hectare in 1976 (figure 5.1). A third lived at densities of more than 1000 persons per hectare, with each individual having less than 10 square meters of gross residential space (World Bank, 1979: 36). For ordinary people, dwellings were small (see figure 5.2).

They were also built with the least costly materials available on the market. Among the 69 percent of households with income below $40 per month in 1976, 20 percent lived in wattle (i.e., mud and straw) homes with thatched roofs typical of rural areas, 40 percent had dwellings of scrap materials like broken crate boards or flattened cans and cardboard, with either thatched or corrugated metal roofs, and toward the upper end of the income scale, 32 percent had wood plank or cinder block walls with metal roofs (figure 5.3). The remaining 8 percent lived on the streets and used downtown arcades and market buildings as protection from the elements (Fass, 1978: 167). This street population included many individuals obliged to sleep on their doorsteps in relays because homes were too small to accommodate all family members at once.[1] Ugliness was probably no different in 1976 than before 1945, but it had lost its earlier attribute of neat organization.

Depending on location, unit size, and type of rental contract (i.e., prepayment for a week, a month, or six months), the 80 percent of this population occupying rental housing paid between $2.50 and $7.50 per month, or 10 to 30 percent of income, for what were often no more than small tents made of scrap. The characteristics of housing for ordinary people were not

FIGURE 5.1
Aerial Views of High-Density Neighborhoods in Port-au-Prince

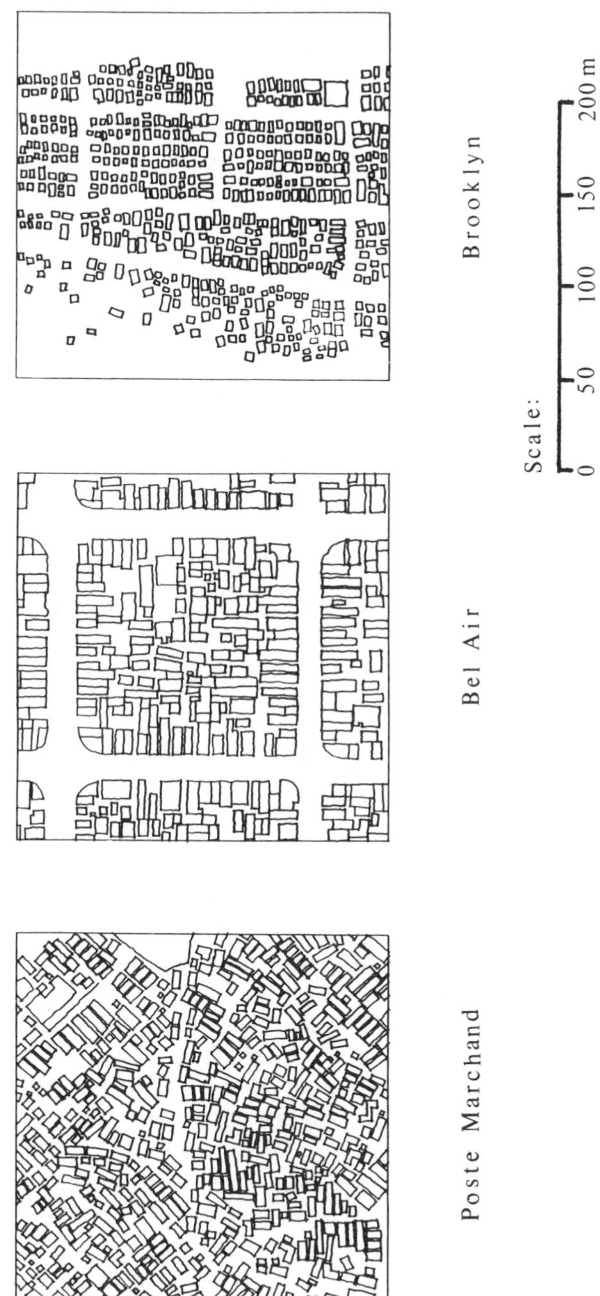

FIGURE 5.2
Floor Plans, Sections, and Occupants of Small Low-Income Dwellings in Brooklyn and Ti Cheri

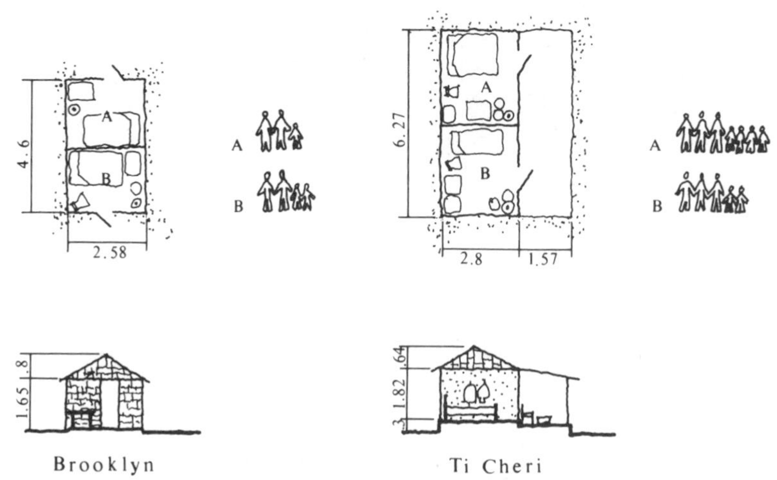

good in 1976, but they did no more than reflect in physical terms what food consumption of 1500 calories and water intakes of 12 lad meant in physiological terms.

St. Martin, with 20,000 people living on 13 hectares at a density of 1540 inhabitants per hectare, was typical of several vacant areas that filled up as population growth spilled over city limits after 1945. In 1976 the average dwelling was 6.4 square meters in size and offered 1.7 meters of net habitable space per adult. For the 74 percent of families who rented their dwellings, the respective figures were 5.1 and 1.2 square meters, and they paid an average of 17 percent of monthly income for this small space.

Such characteristics were not uncommon in other cities. Dwelling size in low–income areas of Kingston, Panama, Bombay, Nairobi, Calcutta, and Hong Kong ranged from 0.6 to 2.7 square meters per adult.[2] Expenditure shares in Bogota and Nairobi were also similar (Grimes, 1976: 67). The only feature different in Port–au–Prince, as for water, was scale. Statistics for other cities were about the very poorest inhabitants. By Port–au–Prince standards, St. Martin was a middle–income neighborhood, and in the relative scheme of things had reasonably good housing characteristics.

FIGURE 5.3
Floor Plans, Sections, and Occupants of Large Low-Income Dwellings in Poste Marchand and Bel Air

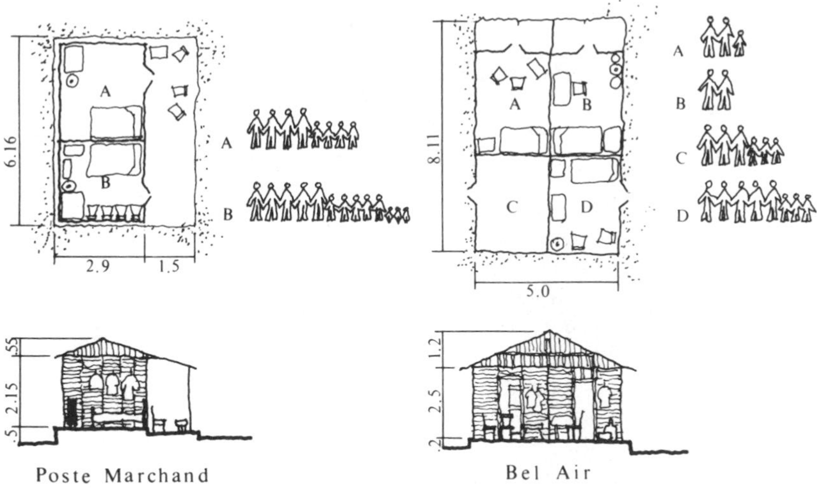

The environment surrounding the houses left much to be desired. High density of wooden structures, lack of water service, and the absence of roads leading to the interior of the neighborhood made it a tinderbox (figures 5.4, 5.5, and 5.6). There was no easy way to halt the spread of flames. The widest space that could serve as a firebreak was a major storm-water drainage channel, the Rockefeller Canal, that passed through the center of St. Martin (figure 5.7). Without garbage collection service, residents used the canal as a dump, which then doubled as a feeding area for pigs and goats. Each rainy season debris from upstream accumulated with the garbage to form dams, flooding major portions of the area behind them and then causing a downstream surge to knock down homes when particularly heavy rains broke through the barriers. These were the periods when many traders and manufacturers lost much of their stocks and tools. And stagnant ponds behind dams were ideal breeding grounds for vectors of disease that, in an area as dense as St. Martin, had little difficulty in spreading from house to house.

These environmental conditions were better than some places and worse than others in the city. They were better than in La Saline or similar areas immediately adjacent to the central market, where years of garbage ac-

FIGURE 5.4
Aerial View of St. Martin, 1976

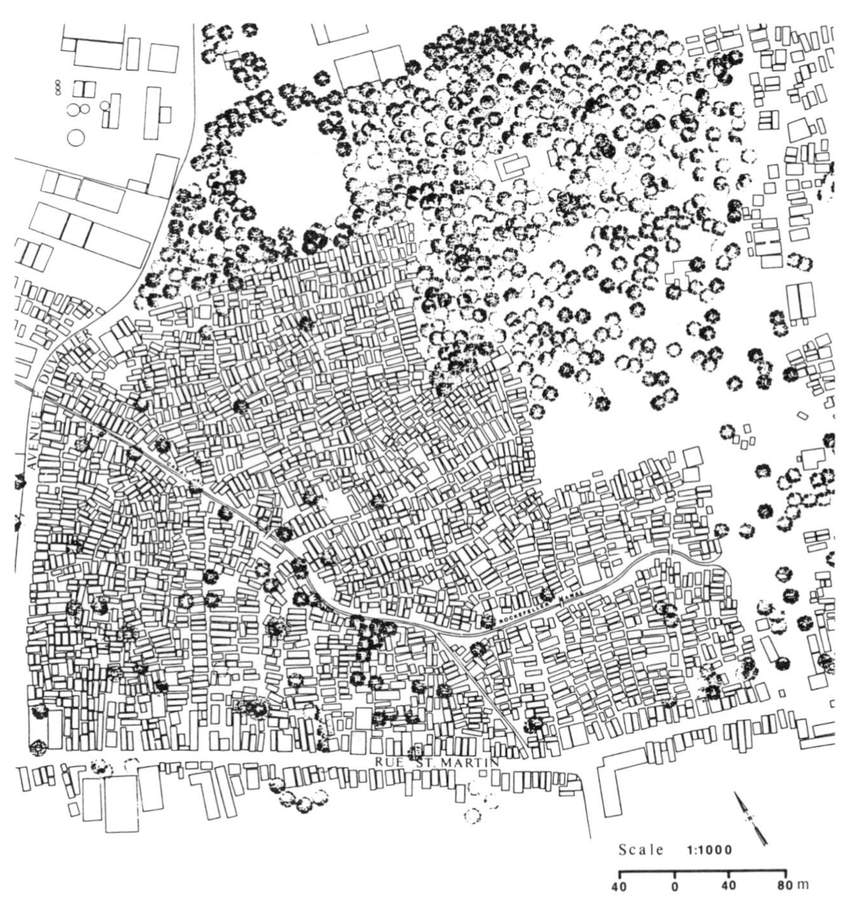

cumulation made hills of waste, where water was hard to find, and where several drainage channels converged to create wide areas of periodic flooding. Housing costs were lower than in St. Martin, but health risks were higher. Conditions were also better than in such newly urbanizing low-income areas to the north of the market as Brooklyn. The areas were swamps that remained completely flooded for weeks at a time during the rainy season and, because of a high water table, did not permit construction of pit latrines in the ground or torrents to sweep away garbage. In

FIGURE 5.5
Aerial View of Central Port-au-Prince, 1980
(St. Martin in foreground, President's Palace in background)

---

addition, however suspect the quality of water might be in St. Martin, it was more suspect in places like Brooklyn, where its price was twice as high. Housing costs in Brooklyn were half those in St. Martin, but commuting (i.e., walking), water costs, and health risks lowered the attractiveness of the price advantage. Brooklyn, and to a lesser extent La Saline, were for the city's poorest who nevertheless had enough income to want to pay for housing.

FIGURE 5.6
Principal Thoroughfares in St. Martin, 1976

FIGURE 5.7
The Rockefeller Canal, 1976 and 1986

1976

1986

Better areas were to the south, east, and west of downtown. Water was generally less expensive, neighborhoods less dense, and housing costs often lower than in St. Martin. But all of these areas, like Brooklyn, were further away from downtown. The problem with being further away was that it incurred higher money and/or time costs of commuting. For households heavily engaged in trade, manufacturing, or other activities in which the downtown area, on one side, was the principal zone for purchasing and marketing, and houses, on the other side, were not only residences but also warehouses, factories, and offices, a location close to downtown increased efficiency in the use of time, money, and, to the degree that traders and manufacturers transported heavy loads back and forth between home and downtown every day, water, calories, and other nutritional elements.

In this context, poor environmental conditions in St. Martin, La Saline, Ti Cheri, Poste Marchand, and similar areas were in certain perverse ways advantageous from the perspective of income production efficiency. Households with incomes higher than those found in St. Martin, but with equal interest in locating in or around the downtown area, filled every available space in built-up neighborhoods like Bel Air that did have basic infrastructure services in 1976. Inadequate services and relatively unhealthy conditions in areas like St. Martin served to dissuade many of them from showing interest in moving there, and by the same token dissuaded property owners from investing in the kinds of dwellings that might appeal to them.

Unfortunately, although environmental inadequacy had a restraining effect on demand by higher-income households, locational advantages were sufficiently high that the prophylactic effect was imperfect. From 1972 to 1976, rents in St. Martin increased at an average annual rate of 21 percent, or about 6 percent in real terms, suggesting that competition for space was already intense.[3] And just as they faced prices for food or water high relative to their income, households paying the premium for central location did not have very much left over to pay for more than small and flimsy shelters.

The fact that they bothered to pay for such shelter, or more tangibly, that renters in St. Martin were willing to pay an average of 17 percent of income for it, was in certain respects surprising. Expending such a large share of income involved a high opportunity cost in foregone food and water intake, and in possibilities for increasing market capital. In principle, households could retain locational advantages by living under arcades and thereby have significantly more resources for other things. Yet they were willing to give up a great deal for rudimentary housing. To justify such sacrifice, small and flimsy shelters had to be important to them.

Economics of Housing

Relative to subjects like food and water, research on the relationship between housing, defined here to exclude everything but the dwelling unit or structure, and efficiency is scarce. But one endeavor, the International Housing Productivity Study, provides some evidence of a relationship. In Korea, one of seven countries covered in the study, evidence showed that a doubling of house size, improvements in physical characteristics that afforded better protection from the elements, and reductions in overall density that limited the spread of communicable illness not only reduced the frequency of medical care services, but also increased the hourly output of workers (Burns and Grebler, 1977: 170–92).

Reasons for the increase in worker output were not entirely clear, but the associations between size, quality, density, and medical care indicated that housing, like food and water, offered certain efficiency-enhancing benefits through the medium of health. A household could better protect its members from illness by obtaining a dwelling and then, up to the point of diminishing returns, could provide further prophylaxis by obtaining a larger unit and a more impermeable unit and by moving to an area having lower residential density. At a certain level of food and water intake, if greater health benefits were possible from expenditure for improved housing than from further food and water intakes, then spending 10 to 30 percent of income to obtain this useful input was perhaps worthwhile.

Health may have been an important factor in prompting most low-income households to acquire housing, but it did not seem by itself an entirely satisfactory reason for people with very low incomes. Some families in St. Martin provided members with much less than 1500 calories and 12 liters of water, skimping on these items in order to pay for housing. The health benefits they were able to derive from shelter seemed to be considerably less than would have been possible from more food or water. In theory, they must have perceived other advantages.

The housing literature sometimes mentioned in passing that dwellings sheltered nonmarket production activities and market activities like service, trade, and manufacturing, but provided no exploration of possible relationships between shelter expenditures and the efficiency of such production.[4] The absence of an exploration was unfortunate because scholarly arguments about whether housing could or could not contribute productively to economic growth, or whether as a "basic need" it should or should not have priority over productive, growth-enhancing investment, based themselves on the conceptual opinion that dwellings were dormitories serving no other essential purpose than housing people.[5] Like food and water, housing appeared to be more like a form of final consumption than a form of productive consumption. The notion that houses were also stores, warehouses, offices, and factories did not enter the arguments. But if houses contained a major share of a city's commercial and industrial plant, then issues of housing policy were issues of commercial and industrial policy.

In Port-au-Prince dwellings often seemed to be vital factors of income production as well as protectors of health. This function of housing was apparent in the characteristics and circumstances of the city's street population, and of residents of St. Martin.

Households on Streets

Depending on whether a principal market day was at hand, and excluding individuals sleeping on doorsteps because their dwellings were too small to accommodate all family members, the city's nonhoused population in 1976 varied between 30,000 and 33,000 over the course of a week.[6] This population contained three distinct groups. The first, with 3,000 people, were rural–urban commuters who came into town for peak market days, slept outside for two nights, and then returned home. The group contained 2,000 market women traveling into town with agricultural commodities. The rest were mostly market women coming with cash that they used to buy and then resell various items after they arrived, and porters working the inbound trucks or seeking day jobs in the markets.[7]

Among the traders with commodities, those with stocks valued at over $100.00 paid storage fees to house their goods in warehouses in and around city markets. Rates varied with location and with the type and bulk of the goods, but seemed to average $0.20 per night per $20.00 of stock, or 1 percent of wholesale value. For an additional $0.50 per night a woman could sleep inside the warehouses, but most of them apparently opted to save something in trade transaction costs by sleeping outside. This saving was not inconsequential. One hundred dollars in stock yielded an average gross margin of around $15.00. This margin had to finance the return trip ($0.50), two days and nights of food and water ($0.50), and the storage fee ($1.50).[8] Another dollar to house themselves, reducing the remaining $12.50 by 8 percent, was perhaps not the best use of money. Paying a storage fee of $1.50 to protect the goods from spoilage, or more important, from pilferage and rodent attack, was better. Besides protecting commodities, paying the fee allowed a trader to sleep without worry and without having to awaken at the slightest suspect sound. This was important because success in fiercely competitive trade demanded a high level of mental alertness during the day.

Women with stocks valued at around $50.00, anticipating a margin of

$7.50, rarely paid the storage fee. Return transportation and meals would bring the margin down to $6.50, and spending $0.75 or 12 percent of it for storing goods, not to mention 17 percent of the remainder to store themselves, was inefficient. Besides, a smaller volume of stock was easier to manage overnight. The risk of loss to pilferage or rodents was less. Not surprisingly, traders with stocks valued at between $50.00 and $100.00 often paid the fee the first night and slept outside with the goods the second.

Market women and porters traveling without goods slept outside for what looked like similar reasons. The upper limit of what they could expect to earn from two days and nights of work was $2.00. Even supposing that they could save by spending half of what the others did for food, they would have only $1.25 left to take home. Spending 80 percent of it for housing contradicted the purpose of coming to town in the first place.

Commuters constituted less than 0.5 percent of the urban population and only about 10 percent of the nonhoused population. What made them interesting was the way in which they seemed to make a clear distinction between housing themselves and housing goods, or if they did not have goods, the way in which they discounted personal housing against the benefit of saving earnings for subsequent use in other things upon their return. Potential health benefits did not seem to concern them.

The second group, with a population of 18,000, contained the city's very poorest people. A group with fluid membership of individuals and families reduced to their state by financial disasters of various kinds, they had nothing but the clothes they wore. Able to obtain only irregular earnings from casual labor permitting irregular expenditures of $0.10 to $0.30 every few days, they had no money for housing payments. Any savings they might be able to accumulate were destined for food, pots, buckets, tools, trade stocks, and a range of other items eminently more productive in providing health or other things than a dwelling. In fact, most adult women in the group indicated that their first order of business was to accumulate enough money to enter trade.

The third group, with 12,000 people, had possessions. These included one or a combination of the following items: extra clothing, a cooking pot, a water bucket, grain for consumption and/or trade, dry goods for sale, tools, raw materials, finished products, fuelwood, and so on. Some in this group had moved into the street when financial misfortune caused them to dispense with housing. Some were upwardly mobile, passing into the group from the previous one and accumulating things as they went along. Still others decided to save on current housing expenditures temporarily while they built up savings to prepay six months of rent and thereby obtain a 50 percent reduction in monthly housing costs. Having goods to protect and manage, almost all of them were making expenditures for such quasi-housing items as boxes, baskets, and bags that kept the rain and dust out and that made travel about town somewhat easier. At the limit, a few assembled enough cardboard to cover some or all family members as well as goods. They established a first approximation of housing for themselves, in this case a portable variety.

This portable cardboard might protect people and goods, but the continuing need to keep weight and volume of possessions to manageable proportions meant that food, water, and other production costs were high. An individual or family could not easily purchase a week's supply of grain, beans, or charcoal; a similar supply of trade goods or raw materials; and maintain an inventory of finished products all at the same time. Nor could they safely store away a bucket of water for later use. Each set of purchases had to be in small and manageable proportions, thus incurring higher unit expenditures for each item.

A dwelling therefore seemed to serve the same productive purpose as a pot for cooking or a bucket for storing water. At some point families reached the limits of productive capacity possible with an extremely labor-intensive household production technology, and would begin to obtain negative returns to further additions of capital, labor, or other inputs unless they changed the technology by obtaining a larger container planted firmly and securely on the ground. A dwelling could reduce risks of child and adult illness relative to living on the streets, but for many people this advantage seemed of secondary concern relative to operational efficiency and protection of productive assets.

Renters

Although a dwelling might raise efficiency and reduce risk relative to the street technology, the degree of improvement, as for food or water, was a function of the unit's size and other physical attributes. If too small to accommodate all family members and all possessions at once, a larger dwelling might provide further improvements. Similarly, houses with holes in roofs and walls, or without secure methods of locking window openings and doorways, attributes that ordinary people in Port-au-Prince perceived as principal indicators of housing quality, yielded less improvement than more airtight and burglarproof units (figure 5.8). But just as there were gains to be had with greater size or superior quality, there was a point at which further expenditures for larger or better housing yielded diminishing productive returns. Beyond that point, housing provided more in the way of intangible benefits than efficiency gains. Renters in St. Martin, 74 percent of its households, did not seem particularly interested in intangibles.

FIGURE 5.8
Dwellings of Average and Below-Average Quality in St. Martin

Average Quality

Below–Average Quality

Those with incomes below the neighborhood average of $9.80 per month per adult, a group that for simplicity I will call the lower-income population, obtained an average of only 1.3 square meters per adult, just enough to allow family members to sleep horizontally inside the dwelling (table 5.1). Most of this group occupied units that were, like the units shown in figure 5.8, of average or below-average quality in the relative scheme of housing types available in the neighborhood.[9] The average share of income that they expended for rent, 20 percent, was not excessive in comparison to what families with similar incomes paid in other developing countries, but the opportunity cost of having only $5.40 per adult left over after rent, considering that around half the families had less than the average, could be very high when minimum diets cost $4.80 per month per adult. For these families, use of 20 percent of income for minimal shelter suggested that they perceived substantial benefits to be had from housing relative to living on the streets.

Higher-income families (i.e., those earning more than $9.80), with an average income 133 percent greater than lower-income households, spent 65 percent more for housing (per adult). They obtained a 54 percent increase in habitable space and dwellings that, in general, were of higher quality (like the average unit shown in figure 5.8, and the above-average units in the background of the upper portion of figure 4.2). Notwithstanding their better housing, these families seemed to behave as if they believed that there were more important uses for available resources than improved shelter. The 54 percent increase in space seemed to be substantial, but it was relative to such a low base that the result, 2.0 square meters per adult, represented a very marginal expansion in absolute terms. And the difference in the dwelling quality score, 1.7 versus. 2.3, meant that the majority of both lower- and higher-income families lived in average units of the type shown in figure 4.2. Higher-income households may have obtained better housing, but they nevertheless seemed to be constraining their demand for space and quality. They kept expenditure to 13.2 percent of income and, correspondingly, allowed themselves proportionately more scope to use resources for other consumption or production purposes.

These data implied that demand for space and quality were unlikely to change by very much. The distance from an income of $6.60 per month to $15.40 was great. At a 6 percent annual rate of real income growth, lower-income families would take fifteen years to reach the standard of their higher-income counterparts. The effect of an increase in earnings or a decrease in the relative price of housing seemed unlikely to make an appreciable short-term difference in the way most people housed themselves. Proportional changes, like the 54 percent increase in space, might be large and might be important to the households benefiting from them, but abso-

TABLE 5.1
Rental Housing and Household Characteristics in St. Martin, 1976

	Lower-Income Households[a]	Higher-Income Households[b]	Difference of Higher Relative to Lower Income Households (%)
(Number of households)	(39)	(27)	—
Housing characteristics			
Quality score[c]	1.7	2.3 ***	—
Total habitable area (sq. meters)	4.7	5.5 **	+ 17
Habitable area per adult	1.3	2.0 ***	+ 54
Total monthly rent	$4.50	$ 5.40 **	+ 20
Monthly rent per adult	$1.20	$ 2.00 ***	+ 65
Household characteristics			
Number of adults	4.4	3.1 **	− 30
Monthly income per adult	$6.60	$15.40 ***	+ 133
Rent as % of income per adult	20.0%	13.2%***	− 34
Disposable income per adult after rent	$5.40	$13.60 ***	+ 152

Source: Fass (1987).

[a] Households with income below the sample average of $9.80 per adult per month.

[b] Households with income above the sample average of $9.80 per adult per month.

[c] This is a subjective rating that the author gave to each dwelling based on its closeness to the characteristics of "average-looking" dwellings in the survey area. Below-average units received a score of 1, average units a 2, and above-average units a 3.

** Difference between means is significant at the 5% level.

*** Difference between means is significant at the 1% lelvel.

lute changes in space, from 1.3 to 2.0 square meters, and changes in quality remained small in absolute terms. Such changes were certainly not of a type that most members of the political class who concerned themselves with housing would construe as "improvements." Therefore, what was unusual in the data was what appeared to be a high discount rate that St. Martin renters, once housed in a basic fashion, attached to the value of further improvements to their shelter.

Since the discount rate applied to any one item was meaningful only in terms of its relationship to other items, the obvious question posed by the data was: relative to what? More food was certainly a possibility, as was water, but with an average disposable income of $13.60 per adult after rent, the elasticity of demand for food would have had to be extraordinarily high to warrant the maintenance of such minimal housing standards by higher–income renters. The "what" had to include other things besides food or water, and one important thing seemed to be the need to reserve funds for production of earnings.

This possibility suggested itself in the types of rental contract selected by lower–income households, shown in the first three columns of table 5.2. All families had to opt for one of three available time packages. They could pay in advance for a week, a month, or six months, and as with all things in the market, the smaller the time package, the higher the unit price. Payment by the week cost 10 to 20 percent more in monthly rent per square meter than payment for a month, and payment for a month cost twice as much as for six months. But offsetting the higher unit costs was the advantage of lower cash outlays. A week of housing required prepayment of $1.55 on average. A month cost $5.30, and six months $18.90.

If housing had represented a final consumption good for these lower–income households, the notion of an opportunity cost of foregone final consumption would have suggested outcomes in which weekly housing was occupied by the poorest families and monthly and six–month units by families with respectively greater means. Data in the first three columns of table 5.2 indicate a contrary outcome. Average income of weekly renters was $7.90 per adult per month, of monthly renters, $6.90, and of six–month renters, $5.80. Moreover, weekly renters spent the highest share of income, 24 percent, to obtain housing that generally offered less space (per adult) and lower quality than among monthly renters. Relationships between monthly and six–month renters were similar.

This contrary finding seemed related to the fact that the vast majority of lower–income renters derived most of their earnings from use of capital in trade and manufacturing. To whatever extent they may have decided between consumption of housing and consumption of other things, they also had to decide between the most productive tangible uses of available re-

TABLE 5.2
Rental Housing and Household Characteristics in St. Martin, by Rental Contract, 1976

	LOWER-INCOME HOUSEHOLDS[a] RENTING BY THE			HIGHER-INCOME HOUSEHOLDS[b] RENTING BY THE	
	Week	**Month**	**Six Months**	**Month**	**Six Months**
(Number of households)	(7)	(18)	(14)	(15)	(12)
Housing characteristics					
Quality score[c]	1.5	1.8	1.9	2.5	2.1
Total habitable area (sq. meters)	4.1	4.7	5.2 **	5.2	5.7 *
Habitable area per adult	1.1	1.2	1.4 *	1.9	2.2
Total monthly rent	$6.20	$ 5.30	$ 3.15 **	$ 6.70	$ 3.45 ***
Monthly rent per adult	$1.90	$ 1.50	$ 0.85 ***	$ 2.30	$ 1.40 ***
Household characteristics					
Number of adults	3.7	4.5	4.4	3.3	2.9
Monthly income per adult	$7.90	$ 6.90	$ 5.80 **	$14.30	$16.30 *
Rent as % of income per adult	24.0%	21.7%	15.0%**	16.8%	9.0%***
Disposable income per adult after rent	$5.50	$ 5.50	$ 5.10	$12.20	$15.40 **
Income production characteristics					
% of households using market capital	83.0%	87.5%	78.6%	69.2%	54.5%
Amount of capital per household	$5.75	$21.40	$27.80	$28.00	$23.60 **
Earnings–capital ratio[d]	2.40	1.95	0.95 ***	2.65	2.10 **

Source: Fass (1987).

[a] See Note a, table 5.1.

[b] See Note b, table 5.1.

[c] See Note c, table 5.1.

[d] The ratio of monthly net earnings from trade and manufacturing to the value of fixed and working capital used in the production of earnings.

* Difference between means shown in three columns for lower-income households, or two columns for higher-income households, is significant at the 10% level.

** Difference between means shown in three columns for lower-income households, or two columns for higher-income households, is significant at the 5% level.

*** Difference means shown in three columns for lower-income households, or two columns for higher-income households is significance at the 1% level.

sources. For many of these families, larger units, higher-quality units, or longer-term rental contracts apparently provided lower returns than maintenance of funds in market activities.

The pertinent variable sustaining this explanation was the earnings-capital ratio. Interpreting the ratio as an indicator of the relative profitability of household enterprises, and assuming, at risk of overestimation, that average and marginal returns were about the same, table 5.2 suggests that weekly renters had little incentive to invest in monthly housing because it was not profitable for them to do so. A dollar not used for market production was perhaps $2.40 in foregone monthly earnings, while investment in a month of housing could yield no more than a one-dollar monthly cost reduction. At the other end, one dollar not used by six-month renters in the market might have involved an earnings opportunity cost of $0.95 per month, while their investment in long-term housing paid a dividend of $2.15 each month. In between, monthly renters could use a dollar in the market to make $1.95, which was not that much different than the $2.15 lower cost associated with six-month rental.

These calculations exaggerate what the differences in marginal returns might have been, but the essential aspect remained that as long as households could generate more earnings by using funds in the market than cost savings by buying larger time-packages, then that was what they were likely to do. Also, the essential meaning of quality score differences ranging from 1.5 to 1.9 was that more of the roofs did not leak as much, and the meaning of a per adult space standard of 1.1 to 1.4 square meters was that people could sleep on the floor with a few more centimeters between them. Like firms, these lower-income households behaved as if they obtained offices, warehouses, stores, factories, and residences only up to the level required for efficient production of earnings, nutrition, health, and other essential outputs. In this respect they did not behave any differently than households on the streets.

Evidence concerning higher-income renters, shown in the fourth and fifth columns of table 5.2, was more ambiguous. Smaller proportions of these households derived earnings from use of capital in the market, and it may well have been the case that the final consumption effect for wage-earning families diluted the explanatory potential of the earnings-capital ratio. In this instance, as the notion of foregone final consumption would have it, monthly renters had less income than six-month renters. The ratio nevertheless remained as a statistically more significant variable than income, perhaps suggesting that the users of market capital among these renters behaved more like firms, while the wage-earning households made their decisions along the lines espoused by consumer theory.

In general, therefore, St. Martin offered a variety of sizes, qualities, and time packages through which renters could adapt housing to their circumstances and efficiency or consumption needs, but there were limits to how far poorer renters could go to optimize combinations of these three attributes and still remain in the neighborhood. The number of households with incomes generally well above the average for the neighborhood was increasing substantially in 1976, and as I noted earlier, many of them were bidding against poorer households for space in areas around the downtown zone. In much the same way that families seemed to be running out of room to maintain nutritional intake through substitution of foods with higher energy–cost ratios for those with lower ratios, many renters were running out of room to combine size, quality, and time packages in a way that could allow them to maintain residence in St. Martin. Market forces were pressuring them to shift from larger to smaller units, from higher to lower quality dwellings, from longer- to shorter-term rental contracts, and from the central area of the city further out to the periphery. House ownership might in theory have slowed the displacement process for them, but even owners were subject to displacement pressure.

Homeowners

Homeowners, as distinct from landowners, were families that rented land and built structures upon it. In St. Martin, 16 percent of households claimed homeownership, and fell into two groups of identical size (table 5.3). The first contained lower-income families (i.e., those with less than $9.80 per month) that began renting parcels averaging 34 square meters before 1966. After building one or more large structures on the parcels, they occupied 13 meters and rented the balance out to an average of four tenants. Their earlier entry into St. Martin made it possible for them to keep land rents at a low figure of $1.30 per month, about 3 percent of income, and to generate net rental revenues between $12.00 and $20.00 per month, or 25 to 45 percent of their total monthly incomes. The dwellings were old, and in combination with income levels that did not permit adequate maintenance and repair, $7.80 per month per adult, their physical condition left much to be desired.[10]

The second group rented land and built structures from 1972 onward and seemed to represent a new and accelerating wave of investment in the neighborhood. One household arrived in 1972, another in 1973, two in 1974, and three in 1975. They all had above-average incomes. Indeed, they had to have high incomes to become homeowners in St. Martin. Rental rates for newly available land, meaning acquisition of a parcel containing a structure in such state of disrepair that its previous owner could neither rent it out, live there, or rebuild it, were approaching $0.40 per square

TABLE 5.3
Owner-Occupied Housing and Household Characteristics in St. Martin, 1976

	Lower-Income Homeowners[a]	Higher-Income Homeowners[b]	Landowners
(Number of households)	(8)	(6)	(8)
Housing characteristics			
Quality score[c]	1.5	1.9	2.0
Total habitable area (sq. meters)	12.7	8.6 ***	14.3
Habitable area per adult	2.3	2.5	2.1
Total monthly rent	$1.30	$ 2.50 ***	—
Monthly rent per adult	$0.22	$ 0.75 ***	—
Household characteristics			
Number of adults	5.6	3.3 ***	7.4
Monthly income per adult	$7.80	$15.00 **	$8.20
Rent as % of income per adult	3.2%	5.5%**	—
Disposable income after rent	$7.55	$14.20 **	$8.20
Years of residence in dwelling	15.8	2.1 ***	11.5
Total dwelling area owned (sq. meters)[d]	33.8	16.0 ***	26.4

Source: Data from author's survey in St. Martin.
[a] See Note a, table 5.1.
[b] See Note b, table 5.1.
[c] See Note c, table 5.1.
[d] Excludes areas providing income from land rent.
** Difference between means for homeowners is significant at the 5% level.
*** Difference between means for homeowners is significant at the 1% level.

meter in 1976. Rental of a 16 meter parcel upon which to construct a structure providing 8.6 meters for owner–occupancy and 7.4 meters for rental to tenants, the typical distribution of space used by new house owners, cost $6.40 per month. A household also needed to have $400.00 to construct the structure.[11] New house owners had to be relatively well–off and, with disposable monthly income after rent of $14.20 per adult indicated in table 5.3, they were indeed well–off by neighborhood standards.

The appearance of their houses were generally the same as those of house renters, and only of slightly higher quality than for older house owners. The new owners had sought to minimize construction costs by purchasing as much salvageable building material from the owners they replaced as possible, and this was the main reason that new houses resembled older ones. Similarly, new owners occupied about the same amount of space (per adult) as older owners, preferring to supplement income with rent earnings rather than occupy all the space they owned, thus earning about $4.35 per month in net rents.

St. Martin ran out of vacant parcels of appropriate size and shape to construct new dwellings long before 1976. New building occurred, as I implied above, when a structure reached the end of its useful economic life. At that point, homeowners were obliged to make important decisions concerning their assets. If they had adequate resources and saw no higher returns from using them for other purposes, they could rebuild the structure. If they pursued such a course, landlords (i.e., property owners) raised the land rents. In 1976 this meant a fourfold increase, from $0.10 to $0.40 per square meter.

A rent increase was due even if an owner did not have resources to rebuild. The end of a structure's economic life signaled the moment to raise rents. In this circumstance, an owner with a 34 meter parcel had to increase payments from $3.40 to $13.60 per month. Because the structure was no longer habitable, the owner's average monthly income would have fallen from the $7.80 shown in table 5.3 to around $5.70. At this stage, land rent, $2.45 per adult (i.e., $13.60 divided by 5.6 adults), would consume 40 percent of household income and drive disposable income per adult to a very low level of $3.25 per month. Depending on their resources, homeowners had to abandon all or part of the land they occupied. For example, they might retain half the land, sell half the salvageable materials from the existing structure, and then use the proceeds to have workers build another structure with remaining materials. Alternatively, they could sell all the materials, collect somewhere between $200 and $250, and move elsewhere.

Many older owners did not have the wherewithal to reconstruct, and the result of wear and tear on structures was that the way was opened for new investment by other households that necessarily had substantially more resources. St. Martin was undergoing a process of residential transformation in which houses designed for useful lives of ten to twenty years, depending on maintenance and durability of original construction, were expiring and making it possible for younger and smaller families with higher incomes to invest in the neighborhood. Such investment was profitable. At 1976 prices it provided an immediate return of 30 percent in the first year, and if rents continued to rise at their recent real rate of 6 percent, sizable increases in the return in future years.[12]

Homeownership was changing hands, shifting gradually from lower– to higher–income households in much the same manner as seemed to be happening in the case of house renters, and the principal beneficiaries of this process were the landowners.

Landowners

As in many developing countries, claims of landownership were often uncertain. For St. Martin, a research effort by the EPPLS, the government's housing agency, suggested that about 30 percent of the land was state–owned, that 50 percent of the balance belonged to perhaps ten individuals, at least four of whom were the neighborhood's principal Macoutes, and that the remaining 20 percent belonged to families holding small plots scattered across the area (EPPLS, communication, December 1984).

In 1976, 9 percent of families in St. Martin claimed to own small plots. Two–thirds of them reported making land purchases between 1950 and 1966, and the others between 1972 and 1975. The quality of their homes was comparable to that of higher–income homeowners, as was their average space consumption standard of 2.1 square meters per adult (table 5.3). Half the landowners occupied all the land they owned, an average of 19 square meters, and collected no rents. The other half occupied 12 meters of dwelling space, collected $8 per month from long–term rental of an additional 22 meters of dwelling space, and $14 per month in land rents from another 70 square meters.

Both groups of landowners were very wealthy by neighborhood standards. Households in the first group, with 19 meters, held land with a 1976 value of $380 and salvageable construction materials worth $240. Families in the second group held $2100 in land and $420 in materials. Together with many homeowners, they were part of the city's middle class. And even with substantially more wealth than the majority of people in St. Martin, members of the class in the neighborhood at that time did not seem moved by the need to consume much more space or higher quality than households with lower incomes. They too seemed to perceive more useful things to do with resources than squander it on consumption of housing attributes beyond the point at which such attributes could provide tangible returns.

One of these more useful things was investment in improvements to dwellings and to their surroundings in ways that could increase the attractiveness of the neighborhood to higher–income renters of land and houses. Although increasing demand for space in the neighborhood allowed owners to raise rents at an average real rate of 6 percent annually without requiring investment, this rate of rental income growth was acceptable only in the absence of means to raise it further. From about 1972 onwards increasing demand presented owners with such means. In theory, demolition of an older homeowner's dwelling to make room for a new land renter, thus permitting an immediate 400 percent rise in rents, was profitable over the short term. Profitable over the longer term was demolition of small, low–quality dwellings to make way for larger, higher–quality dwellings. A concrete block unit offering 10 square meters cost about $400 to construct, and on a monthly basis could yield rent of $200 to $270 per year, or 50 to 100 percent more per square meter than possible with existing structures. Such investments were not worthwhile as long as St. Martin remained unattractive to middle–class families willing and able to pay the higher rents, but in 1976 the neighborhood was becoming more attractive to them, and landowners were beginning to make the investments required to help the process along.

This process of economic displacement was not unique to St. Martin or Port–au–Prince. It took place in most cities undergoing rapid growth. The problem it presented to many low–income households was that the process was exacerbating difficulties caused by rising food and water prices and adding more downward pressure on their efficiency and income through increases in the cost of production. Areas such as La Saline and Poste Marchand were also undergoing displacement processes, and possibilities for relocation near the downtown area were becoming scarce. The same was happening to the south of downtown. The Brooklyn area, the closest zone to downtown where rents were low and stable, was the destination of most low–income households unable to compete for space anywhere else.

There was not much that these ordinary people could do except move, and not much interest by government to interfere with the process. In St. Martin almost all the landowners were Macoutes, or if not Macoutes, then affiliated with the party in some fashion. Guns, flags, signs, or denim uniforms about their homes left no doubt on this matter. Similarly, there was little doubt that at least 40 percent of the house owners, including most of the ones collecting rent, were attached to the party. Excluding women supported by ranking Macoutes to serve, among other functions, as informants, at least 15 percent of St. Martin households contained an individual playing some kind of active or passive role in one of the neighborhood's four principal party factions.

Ownership of land or housing in St. Martin, and in all neighborhoods like it, was imbued with political character. Party membership was not a prerequisite for purchase of land or investment in construction on rented land. However, if an individual had the means to invest and was not already a member, there was a high probability that he or she would eventually receive an invitation to join. Even if the individual did not share the same political perspective, acceptance of the invitation was almost mandatory because the seller of land or the landlord was likely to be a member, and because in the absence of legal documentation concerning title transfers or long-term land leases, only the party had power to protect property rights. The rising middle class seeking advantages of ownership was automatically expanding and strengthening party control of the city, and since the class and party were still principal constituents of the regime in 1976, government had no particular need to interfere in a process that provided constituents with benefits.

Politics

Official government action with respect to shelter followed three strategies. The first, for such people as public enterprise workers, midlevel government employees, soldiers, Macoutes, and others of consequence in the middle-class component of the political class, involved sale or rent of dwellings constructed by the state. After it regained control of the treasury from U.S. occupiers in 1934, the Vincent administration (1930–41) provided a series of low-priced dwellings for workers. The Magloire administration (1950–56) followed with two planned neighborhood projects containing a total of 600 units (Moore, 1972: 187). François Duvalier added about 1200 dwellings at Cité Simone (now Cité Soleil) through 1971. After increasing his father's project by 130 units in 1975, Jean-Claude introduced another 1100 near the airport in 1981 (Godard, 1983: 276). These various undertakings constituted about 2.2 percent of the city's total housing stock in 1982 and about 10 percent of the middle-class supply. The actions, which excluded dwellings built by public enterprises for their workers, had some political significance.

The second strategy, a traditional method of dealing with ordinary people, provided unserviced blocks of peripheral land to groups displaced by urban development projects or by planned and accidental fires. The Estimé government (1946–50) cleared a waterfront area in 1948 to make room for the city's Bicentennial Exposition and moved several hundred families onto an agricultural field and cemetery on the northern fringe of the city.

The field was St. Martin and the displaced families its first settlers. Similarly, a clearance project near La Saline to make room for port expansion in 1976 and 1977 moved 5000 people to Boston, a rapidly growing area next to Brooklyn (World Bank, 1979: 43). In neither case did government find it necessary to pay damages or relocation costs to more than a few important individuals in the cleared areas. What relocatees did receive was first priority to rent plots upon which they could build their homes.

These efforts had the advantage of a small amount of advance planning. Most efforts, the ones resulting from fire, had less. A major blaze in La Saline in 1967 sent 8000 people to colonize Brooklyn (Godard, 1983: 83). Another sent 6000 more to Brooklyn in 1972, and a third fire near La Saline sent 5000 to colonize Boston in 1975. Government action with respect to ordinary people took the form of a series of projects that provided 25,000 to 30,000 of them with what the World Bank called "sites without services" schemes (World Bank, 1979: 43).

For the most part these schemes transferred families to public land, and in principle, each family obtained the right to rent it from the state. In practice, army personnel in charge of the relocation process, joined after 1957 by Macoutes, claimed first rights of rental (i.e., de facto ownership). These beneficiaries of state patronage, in turn, leased or gave smaller parcels to junior officers, family, friends, or other close supporters in supplementary iterations of the patronage process. After complete subdivision of a tract by the pecking order of beneficiaries, each further subdivided his or her area into small lots for sale, land rental, or, after investment in construction, for dwelling rental to additional family, friends, and supporters. Displaced families not party to this process rented land and dwellings from households that were party to it.

This geopolitical strategy compensated high-ranking loyalists for their service to the state and lower-ranking loyalists for their services to the beneficiaries of state patronage. After 1967 it also permitted the party to spread benefits further afield to class members and some ordinary people choosing to live on the tracts and to exercise control in the new neighborhoods.

While maintaining political control, the state ceded certain parts of the Brooklyn–Boston area to the Catholic church. Starting in 1969, a group of Salesian Fathers who had worked with the population in La Saline, and who followed the displaced families after the first fire, introduced a program of high-cost housing. With support from Belgium, Canada, and the EEC, they completed 400 units by 1983 (Godard, 1983: 277). This effort improved the housing of 1.3 percent of the estimated 120,000 people living in the zone at that time (Fass, 1986: 253).

The Salesian action was part of the government's third strategy, which was to work with or to allow independent foreign assistance to undertake projects. These projects were supposed to address housing issues for ordinary people, but because foreigners could not easily distinguish between ordinary and extraordinary people, and because ordinary people such as the ones in St. Martin did not have housing "problems" of the types foreigners and Haitians of the political class assumed they should have, the projects often benefited the middle–class more than they did the intended beneficiaries.

An early foreign entrant, at least in terms of words, was USAID. In 1961 a visitor from the agency's Office of Housing noted that government did not place a priority on shelter, and because urban slums were breeders of disease, crime, discontent, and political unrest, recommended that the agency help alleviate the problem by supporting a mortgage bank (Dodge, 1961). Another visitor pursued the idea by developing the outline of a housing loan guarantee program in 1968 (Luiton, 1968). A third consultant refined the proposal, recommending a $3 million fund to finance $3000 to $6000 homes in 1972 (USAID, 1972). The OAS then entered the scene, helped the government establish a mortgage bank on paper in 1974, and pursued fruitless negotiations over the next few years to transform the legal entity into a functioning institution. Finally, in 1984, USAID provided a $1.8 million grant as initial capitalization for a private mortgage facility that, after additional capital subscriptions of $1.5 million and projected deposits of $6.5 million, would permit annual disbursement of about 250 loans averaging $3000 each (USAID, 1984f). The explicit target for the facility was the middle class, and ordinary people would benefit indirectly from an increased rate of conversion of urban land into residential use. They would also benefit from the facility's financing of low–income housing projects, at least in principle. Although its capital was oversubscribed in 1984, in 1986 the facility had yet to make a loan or lay out ideas for low–income housing.

Showing more evidence of effect in 1986 were efforts by the UN, World Bank, and Germany to develop "slum–upgrading" and low–cost shelter schemes. Simple in conception, during implementation the schemes became complex and yielded processes and outcomes that did not coincide exactly with original intent, as happened when fortune beckoned St. Martin to present itself as the target for a UN–assisted "upgrading" effort.

The St. Martin Project

Our UNCHBP technical assistance project proposed an improvement effort for St. Martin in 1976. There being no public institution with experience in designing or implementing this type of scheme—the National

Housing Office (ONL) did little but collect rents from occupants of the public housing units I identified earlier—we elected to restrict the proposal to what looked like a relatively simple undertaking. It included only two elements. The first was provision of basic infrastructure services to reduce health, fire, flooding, and other related risks. The second was provision of land tenure to residents, in order to stabilize neighborhood occupancy and thereby minimize economic displacement associated with higher land values and rents resulting from the physical improvements. Simplicity seemed appropriate for purposes of spreading limited public resources to as many neighborhoods as possible, of allowing maximum cost recovery commensurate with the ability of beneficiaries to pay, and of permitting the ONL to accumulate expertise before embarking on more complex ventures later on.

The proposal envisaged expenditure of $400,000, or about $20.00 per inhabitant, for construction of unpaved access roads for fire–fighting and garbage–collection vehicles (as well as to serve as firebreaks), ten public fountains, five fire hydrants, a community center to house social and health services, and 200 semifinished dwelling units on adjoining lands for families displaced by construction (to be sold at $10.00 per month for fifteen years) (Haiti, 1976c). The drainage canal and its tributaries were to be improved with separate financing by the IDB as part of an overall urban drainage improvement program already in progress. The pivotal component of the proposal was government acquisition of whatever lands it did not already own in the neighborhood, and subsequent resale to residents at a cost-recovery price of $1.20 a month for fifteen years. Once the process of land transfer was underway, we envisaged the possibility of creating a construction materials credit fund that would permit households to gradually upgrade their dwellings whenever circumstances permitted such investment.

The design seemed technically appropriate in 1976. It was relatively modest in terms of cost and in terms of managerial competency required to implement it. It also seemed sensible in terms of trying to keep dislocation to a minimum. What we did not appreciate at the time was the extreme difficulty of urban land reform in an area where claims of ownership were supported not only with guns and other sources of influence rather than with legal titles, but also where revenue from rent of land and dwellings was itself a basis of local political power linked to state and political class control. There was a price at which claimants to land would willingly give up their parcels, but it was much higher than the $20.00 per square meter that we estimated from the $1.00 to $1.50 per square meter in monthly rent.

In any event, after the UNCHBP project ended, one of its Haitian directors had a chance meeting in 1976 with a senior official of the United Nations Capital Development Fund (UNCDF) who expressed interest in doing "something" in Haiti. A few months later, after receiving a copy of the St. Martin proposal, the UNCDF signed a formal agreement to assist the government with the scheme.

The first activity called for expatriate technical assistance to design the project in greater detail, and a consultant's effort in this matter raised the project's estimated cost to $1.3 million in early 1977 (FCH, 1977). The additional $900,000 stemmed primarily from increases in estimated land acquisition costs, addition of a large construction credit and mortgage fund, and higher (expatriate) project management costs. The consultant's report also recommended a land tenure and household survey because there were no available data upon which to assess the consequences of improvements upon landowners and renters, and addition of a community development cooperative component to allow broad-based participation in the improvement effort.

The World Bank mission that I mentioned in chapter 4 with respect to the politics of water, reported in 1977 that project costs had risen to over $3 million (World Bank, 1979: 179). The further increase derived from a doubling of infrastructure costs (i.e., widening and paving proposed access roads), construction of an additional 500 housing units for families displaced as a result of the road widening, a shift in building standards for the new housing from semifinished units to completely finished units, introduction of the community development component, and a $1 million addition in project management expenses.

Bank mission staff thought the cost high. Concerned with things like cost-recovery and replicability, they noted that at an investment of $160 per person, the project would find it difficult to recover a significant proportion of costs from beneficaries, and the revenue shortfall would make it difficult for government to duplicate the project in other areas of the city. They also thought the project too complex for the management capabilities of the ONL, and returned to Washington in early 1978 unenthused about short-term prospects for Bank involvement in urban shelter schemes.

Project implementation began in March 1979. The ONL became responsible for overall management of the project, including within its mandate organization of the community development component, preparation and supervision of public works and house construction, financial management, coordination with public service agencies (e.g., water supply, garbage collection, public health), household relocation, expropriation, and rent/mortgage payment collection. The ONL had never held responsibilities of this kind, and the government seconded technicians and administrators from other ministries to strengthen it, including several who had been with the UNCHBP program, but they too had had limited exposure to such tasks. The UNCDF, in collaboration with the United Nations Development Program (UNDP), retained a foreign consulting firm to add greater technical and managerial experience to the project. A few of the firm's seven expatriates had been involved in project design work since 1977, but none of them had implementation experience in the country. The project would therefore constitute a learning experience of one kind or another for all project participants, as some of us at the UNCHBP in 1976 surmised that it would.

A progress report noted in October 1979 that implementation started earlier than planned in 1977 because government and the UNCDF were anxious to move forward quickly (FCH, 1979). Physical works were therefore beginning without the benefit of basic data to suggest what the impact of the project might be on the housing market, on residents, or on project personnel capabilities. Of more concern, households were being displaced by construction while the ONL had not yet secured replacement housing for them and had not yet begun to identify property owners or to acquire land from them. In addition, disruptions being caused by construction and displacement were making it difficult to begin the community development component of the project.

A review in October 1981 reported that several Macoutes, hoping or assuming that the project would be implemented through them, or that they would at least have an important role in it, established a project office containing ONL maps and plans for St. Martin (Mason, 1981). When they learned that they would not have a role, and that at the same time the ONL intended to take away their land rights, they opposed the project. The confrontation between the Macoute and ONL factions made it difficult for residents to take sides. On one hand, Macoutes had controlled the community for almost twenty–five years, and their powers of retribution were well known. On the other hand was the government (i.e., the ONL), whose historical record in matters of indemnification, relocation, and urban "improvement" did not bode well for residents. During the stalemate, communication and information about what the project would or would not do became confused. Messages from Macoutes said one thing, those from the ONL said the contrary, and different ONL administrators, including the expatriates, said different things to different residents. Temporary jailing of a leading Macoute made the government's position clearer and broke the deadlock, as did a decision by another important Macoute to participate in the project in order to maintain the support of his constituents.

But resolution of the political confrontation did not end the project's difficulties. In 1981 they included: demolition running ahead of housing construction; initial housing cost overruns; inability of CAMEP to provide water to completed public standpipes for more than a few hours a week; attempts by low–ranking Macoutes to divert water destined for the standpipes into private reservoirs during these hours and then to sell it at $0.10 per bucket; inadequate garbage collection; lack of motivation by community development workers; and lengthy delays in decision–making by the ONL and other public agencies. The only apparent positive sign, aside from progress in infrastructure construction, was that a fire that destroyed 160 houses in August 1981 had catalyzed a small communal effort at reconstruction. For a change, families displaced by fire were able to return and reclaim their space.

At the end of July 1982, the project met most of its construction objectives (FCH, 1982). In "new" St. Martin, the area in which the project provided housing for those displaced by physical works in "old" (i.e., the original) St. Martin, 670 of 700 planned units were complete and were being occupied by 3600 people. Thirteen public standpipes were also complete, but since water service was restricted to six hours per week, most families still relied on vendors. Garbage disposal facilities were falling into disuse for lack of collection services.

In old St. Martin, where the population had grown to 26,000, or 2,000 people per hectare, lack of supply to four new standpipes built by the project meant that over 90 percent of residents continued to depend on vendors (Haiti, 1982). The average price of water had risen to about $0.08 per bucket, and household water expenditures still hovered around an average of 15 percent of income. Lack of supply also meant that four new fire hydrants were unreliable.

Some 65 new housing units were added to partially replace the 160 destroyed by the 1981 fire, but only 21 additional units were built by means of self–help financed through the project's construction credit fund. About 3 percent of families had received land tenure by this time, and average rent for the whole area reached $12 per month. Progress in garbage collection was much the same as in new St. Martin, but widening and deepening of the drainage canal permitted residents to use it as a garbage dump without fear of creating dams and contributing to flooding (see figure 5.7).

Other aspects of the project were at a standstill. The community development cooperative was in place, but its inability to tend to water supply and garbage collection problems undermined its credibility with the population. Credibility was low in any case because the cooperative's initial appointed leadership came from the indigenous, Macoute–organized political structure, because at least one cooperative administrator had diverted monies from the construction credit fund, and because the ONL had made the cooperative responsible for collecting rent–mortgage payments from residents.

The ONL's credibility was also low. Property owners were still upset at the agency's recurrent attempts to acquire their land, and the ONL's failure to make progress on this matter frustrated residents in old St. Martin who were anticipating tenure but who in the interim were facing accelerating rental increases. This also frustrated local and expatriate staff of the ONL who worried about displacement and who wanted to get the building fund moving. Residents of new St. Martin did not think much of the ONL either. The agency's initial demand for a $130 down payment did not sit well with dislocated families who had $30 or so in savings or working capital. They were also concerned by the ONL's inability to provide them with official documents validating home ownership.

A fire in August 1982 added further confusion. Fire hydrants had failed to perform, but the widened access roads did contain the spread of flames. The fire nevertheless consumed 1400 dwelling units housing 7000 people in old St. Martin (figure 5.9). As was the case in the small fire a year earlier, almost all affected families were back the next day to rebuild some semblance of shelter with corrugated roofing materials left behind by the fire (figure 5.10). Traders and manufacturers had lost the wherewithal to generate income and any assets that they or other households could use as collateral for borrowing to reestablish their working capital or to rebuild their houses. They nevertheless returned because land rents of $5 to $10 per year were considerably less than the annual dwelling unit rents of $60 to $120 that they paid before the fire, and because the project still held out the promise of eventual land tenure. Indeed, within two months the population of the burned area climbed to 1800 families, with new households moving in to take advantage of low rents, and, they hoped, the promise of land tenure.

After spurning a $500,000 offer of reconstruction assistance from USAID, and another of $100,000 from the UNDP, the government decided to reallocate some project funds, primarily from the dormant construction fund, to erect 140 replacement houses. Several months later it accepted a $3 million offer from the German Reconstruction Loan Corporation (KFW) to rebuild the burned area, and expatriate KFW personnel, some already in Haiti to work on other shelter schemes, began to plan the task with the ONL.

A neighborhood census in July 1983 indicated that there were now 2400 families living in the burned area, and that the size of the area had grown smaller since 1982. Over the previous two years, especially after government had shown itself unable or unwilling to make rapid progress in land acquisition, property owners gradually tore down their wooden houses and began to replace them with larger concrete structures after rental agreements expired or after indemnifying occupants for premature departure.

FIGURE 5.9
Aerial View of St. Martin, 1982

New Housing

Community, Health, and Education Facilities

Area Destroyed in Fire of 1982

FIGURE 5.10
Retrogression and Progress in St. Martin, 1982

Old St. Martin After The Fire

New St. Martin Under Construction

The fire made it possible for this process to move ahead more rapidly because there was less need for extensive demolition or indemnity payments. In these expanding "redevelopment" zones, the original, ordinary population of St. Martin was being replaced more rapidly by higher–income households who could afford the rents that project improvement efforts engendered.

The increase in numbers of families living in the ever–decreasing burned area was partly a result of this displacement process, and partly the result of migration from other parts of the city. In principle, maintaining or acquiring residence in the area might still result in land tenure, or at least in another indemnity once the KFW project started moving. However, by the end of 1983, benefits of the proposed KFW undertaking were becoming less certain. The German technicians found that the burned area was so small that two– or three–story houses were required to accommodate the 2400 households, and that the households in question could not possibly afford to rent or buy such units. By the end of 1984, private redevelopment, and construction of KFW housing units had reduced the burned area still further, and many of the families that had been in metal tents at the end of 1983 were gone. Old St. Martin was well on its way to becoming a neighborhood of the middle class.

The process was already complete in new St. Martin. By international standards of comparison, housing design in the new area was quite modest. Residential density was a substantial 800 people per hectare, well above the 200 to 400 range in other countries (Grimes, 1976: 69). Similarly, the design standard allowing only 12 square meters of interior space in most dwellings, shown in table 5.4, was substantially less than the apparent minimum of 20 square meters in "sites and services" projects implemented in various countries with World Bank assistance. And for the quality and space provided by these houses, making allowance for a 100 percent increase in the consumer price index for housing between 1976 and 1984, the monthly unit prices of $0.60 per square meter for small dwellings and $0.40 for large ones were quite reasonable. Nothing comparable could be had in St. Martin at such prices.

But for many relocatees, monthly rent–purchase payments of $7.35 or $11.55 were apparently too high relative to what they were willing to spend. Making the very optimistic assumption that they had been able to keep up with inflation, that they were willing to spend the same share of income for housing as they did in 1976, and that the population of relocatees had general characteristics similar to those in tables 5.1, 5.2, and 5.3, perhaps a third were unwilling to spend as much as $7.35 per month.

The price would not have constituted a problem for any of them had the project provided houses with more than one entry door, or with the pos-

TABLE 5.4
Characteristics of UNCDF Project Housing in St. Martin, 1984

	Small Dwellings	Large Dwellings
Number of Units	705	200
Gross floor area per unit (sq. meters)	16.4	32.8
Internal floor area per unit (sq. meters)[a]	12.0	28.4
Total construction cost	$630.00	$985.00
Construction cost per gross sq. meter	$ 38.50	$ 30.00
Total monthly payment[b]	$ 7.35	$ 11.55
Monthly payment per internal sq. meter	$ 0.60	$ 0.40

Source: UNCDF (1984).

[a] Excluding open porch of 4.4 sq. meters in front of each dwelling which is included in the gross area figure.

[b] Scheduled to rise at a rate of 5% a year for an indeterminate period. The rate is based on a 12%, 15-year term for construction cost recovery only.

sibility of introducing doors in exterior walls at a later stage. Such designs would have permitted households to subdivide small units into two or three dwellings offering 4 to 6 square meters each, and large units into five to seven dwellings offering similar amounts of space. At the limit, the 900 dwellings of new St. Martin housing 5000 people could have become 3500 dwellings housing almost 20,000 people. Notwithstanding the "substandard" character that such an outcome might have presented to project planners and others of the political class concerned with standards of space consumption and residential density, it would have been appropriate from the perspective of ordinary households. Indeed, it would have proven a windfall benefit to them. Average rent in those parts of old St. Martin not destroyed by fire or by the redevelopment process was $15 per month in 1984. At that price the relocated households could occupy one part of a small subdivided house and generate $15 to $30 per month from tenants in the other one or two units, or $60 to $90 from a large subdivided house. Or they could have moved elsewhere, become absentee landlords, and collected an even larger rental income.

Unfortunately, except for end units, all the new houses were of a row house design, with common walls on three sides (figure 5.10). Not surprisingly, by the time most houses were ready for occupancy in 1982, one-third of the relocatees elected not to move into them. Some sold their rights to the houses for $150 well before the buildings were complete. Others waited for completion and then sold out at prices ranging from $800 to $1000, a practice leading to much confusion when buyers found out that they still had to pay the monthly rent–purchase charge for the next fifteen years. Still others became absentee landlords, but faced with the impossibility of subdivision were able to collect only $100 to $130 in semiannual rent prepayments for the units, netting $65 to $85 every six months after meeting their rent–purchase obligations. A random survey of thirty of the dwellings I conducted in late 1985 indicated that twelve households paid rent to absentee landlords, most of whom had moved back to or had never left old St. Martin, and six were new owners who claimed to have purchased the houses from previous ones.[13] Within four years of having been assigned new housing, perhaps 60 percent of the 900 original relocatees were no longer in them.

However modest by international standards, new St. Martin did not conform to the economic circumstances of most of its intended beneficiaries. Some of the relocatees who sold or rented their homes to others may have left because they did not have money to pay the monthly installments. But most had enough money in hand and therefore left for other reasons. Those reasons may have included a desire for production efficiency. They could not afford to stay because of the opportunity cost of foregone production of higher earnings. Occupancy meant tying up resources in a relatively nonproductive enterprise. Departure meant receipt of $65 to $85 twice a year, which might do wonders in trade, manufacturing, or some other market activity and thereby raise the household's level of consumption across a wide spectrum of goods and services, including housing. And sale of the house for $800 to $1000, among other things, represented instant passage to Miami or New York. This was perhaps the most productive investment a household could make and was, in fact, what several of them did (St. Martin project staff, personal communication, December 1984).

The new–housing component of the project generated few harmful effects upon its 900 intended beneficiary households. What most of them did with their houses was not what project planners had anticipated or wanted, but almost every one of the households gained something. For the 40 percent who elected to ccupy and remain in the houses assigned to them, the majority of whom were presumably like the higher–income groups in tables 5.2 and 5.3, the benefit took the form of better quality, more space, and the promise of ultimate ownership at a monthly price well below what they could have ever imagined possible (figure 5.11). For the rest, largely lower–income households, the benefit was the windfall gain of an asset that some held onto as a productive source of rental revenue, or that others disposed of in order to transfer its value to more productive uses and/or to the production of higher consumption of other things.

Institutional Progress

Whether the project improved the circumstances of original residents who tried to stay in old St. Martin was harder to determine. Property

FIGURE 5.11
Images of New St. Martin, 1986

owners and the 3 or 4 percent of renters who obtained tenure certainly benefited from an increase in the value of their assets. To the extent that for the first time in long memory a fire did not result in immediate displacement to the marshes, even the families who had lost their homes and possessions "gained" something. And the creation of an institutional self–interest to introduce a new faction into traditional neighborhood politics and to indirectly act on behalf of the interests of ordinary people was important. At minimum it meant that few if any residents of the burned area would get thrown out prematurely by property owners seeking higher rents or room for redevelopment without receiving some sort of indemnity payment. And all residents able to remain in the area benefited from the new canal and its service in preventing flooding and removing garbage.

Offsetting these gains was the indisputable fact that many ordinary residents, like those of 1976, had been pushed or had bought their way out of the neighborhood. The process started before 1976, but the project accelerated it. Still, although project planners did not achieve all originally intended objectives, they accomplished something of some value to some ordinary people. In Port–au–Prince this was a definite sign of progress.

Another sign of progress was the development over the decade of an urban shelter agency that, while containing many weaknesses, held considerable promise for the future at the end of 1985. With prompting from the World Bank, the government reorganized and strengthened the ONL in 1982, renaming it the Public Social Housing Promotion Corporation (EPPLS). With $1 million in technical support grants from the Bank and integration into it of Bank, KFW, and UNDP expatriate assistants, the new agency was in the process of administering $20 million in shelter projects at the end of 1985, including 1100 Bank–financed units in Linthau, 1600 KFW units in St. Martin, a separate KFW "sites and services" and environmental improvement scheme in Linthau, and 1000 units at Drouillard being supported by the UNCDF and UNDP as an extension of the St. Martin project (see figure 2.1) (Fass, 1986: 249). These efforts were much too small and costly to permit direct or indirect benefit by many ordinary people in the short term. But the agency and its activities at least offered the hope of tangible improvement in the long term.

But perhaps the most significant element of institutional progress, paralleling my arguments in chapter 2 with respect to PVO efforts and craft exports, was the direct involvement of at least a few components of the political class with the circumstances of a few components of the ordinary class. The upscaling of the project from $400,000 to over $3 million, among other things, reflected a bureaucratic desire by the UNCDF to spend an available block of funds, a desire to make the project more profitable for the foreign consulting firm, a desire by expatriate advisers to include congenial components that they believed would benefit the project, and a desire by public officials to maximize physical works and thereby show something "concrete" while giving construction contracts and jobs to the middle class. These were perhaps wasteful of scarce resources, but in some respects one could suggest that the project might never have taken place without them. They were essential to the self–interests and to the survival of individuals and organizations responsible for design and implementation. Project results, like the PVO efforts, were ambiguous, to say the least.

The key, however, was that the course of implementation was a significant political event that introduced many Haitians and expatriates directly into the economic and political circumstances of the ordinary class. Collectively they might not lobby as hard as PVOs on behalf of what they believed were ordinary class interests, but the process permitted at least a few more people to glimpse certain salient aspects of life in places like St. Martin, and more people of the political class to do so through similar experiences in Linthau, Drouillard, and projects in other towns. And in the process of fighting off the claims of the Macoutes, an interest stemming from a basic desire by project planners to protect their own interests and reputations, the event had the interesting side effect of revealing that there were times when survival needs of the political class could be consistent with certain survival needs of the ordinary class.

Political Progress

This course of institutional progess came to a halt in 1986. The departure of Duvalier precipitated a purge of senior EPPLS administrators, and encouraged junior army officers to lead invasions of almost–complete dwellings of Linthau, Drouillard, and KFW buildings in St. Martin. Homes destined for ordinary families, and the prospect of windfall gains from their abandonment, were in the hands of a newly rising middle class faction of the political class. It would take some time before the process begun in 1976 could regain momentum.

In the greater scheme of things the invasion of public housing was of little consequence. More than anything else what happened to the St. Martin project pointed out that opinions, assumptions, and concepts implicit in the well–intentioned efforts of the political class were often more consistent with middle–class than with ordinary realities. Ordinary people did not seem to have housing problems. They seemed to have survival and income–production problems in which simple shelters at strategic locations served particularly important functions within particular circumstances. Some nonhoused people could find dwellings helpful, and the lot of housed people could be improved by units that were more proximate to sources of input supply and to output markets. Their lives could also be improved by obtaining shelters that were slightly larger or more secure than those they already had. But by and large, what they already had was all that they required. To have substantially more, such as the new houses in St. Martin, was inefficient even if their budgets allowed them to pay for it. Acquisition of more food, investment in old or new market activities, travel to Miami, and several other items were much more productive in yielding improvement than occupancy of "improved" houses. The decision by 60 percent of the relocated families to dispose of their homes and move back to old St. Martin or other similar areas was a fundamental expression of the priorities that reality imposed upon them. Real earnings increases, and food and water price decreases, had a long way to go before many ordinary people could find themselves faced with housing problems.

Nor would the UNCHBP's notion of land tenure have helped, even if politics had permitted implementation of the idea. In principle, had families received 5 square meters suitable for one dwelling, they would have acquired a $100 asset (at 1976 land prices). Many ordinary people had more productive uses for such resources, and in all likelihood occupancy of most parcels would have passed to higher-income groups in the same way as the houses.

Even such simple ideas as providing water for fire protection, which with tragic results the St. Martin project did not do; of building roads for garbage collection and firebreaks; and of widening the drainage canal, were in perverse ways antithetic to the interests of many ordinary people. In Port-au-Prince environmental inadequacy was a form of limited protection against competition for space by those with higher incomes, largely members of the middle class. The good intentions of local and foreign agencies in bringing environmental improvements to Lintau, Brooklyn, Drouillard, and nearby areas were engendering the same kinds of displacement effects in 1985 as similar efforts had had in St. Martin. Such effects were unavoidable as long as ordinary family economic realities did not permit investment in relatively nonproductive land, as long as there remained a major reservoir of unsatisfied middle-class demand for land and housing in neighborhoods that in relative terms were or could be made environmentally acceptable, and as long as the overall supply of residential land did not increase in response to demand. Indeed, in many respects the heart of the aggregate problem of shelter was land.

For in addition to the three official government strategies with respect to shelter that I outlined earlier, there was a fourth, unofficial strategy that controlled land supply: organized squatting. Almost all of the city's rapid growth had occurred under the Duvaliers, and therefore under political control of the Macoutes and the party. The Macoutes were not only masters of built–up areas, but also the principal protectors of public land and private property rights. They were paid or otherwise encouraged by major property owners in good standing with the regime to make sure that vacant parcels stayed vacant. "Spontaneous" squatting did not exist.

Because the party was not a unified organization, and because "development" of new private land offered a rapid path to wealth, Macoutes did not always provide reliable protection. A faction sometimes turned against an owner if it perceived a weakening of the owner's political standing, or stronger factions sometimes led successful invasions of properties protected by weaker factions. These kinds of operations were more uncommon than official encouragement of Macoutes, army officers, and others to claim parcels expropriated from exiles or others of the traditional elite in disfavor, on behalf of the state, and to develop them along the lines I described earlier for public lands. A sizable segment of land on the city's fringes came into residential use through such processes. The quantity was nevertheless small, and the parcels so dispersed that pockets of high density could often be surrounded by vast open spaces.

Colonization of new lands seemed to gather greater importance after Duvalier's marriage in 1980 shifted state patronage away from party members, further weakening the link between the party and the family to which it swore allegiance. Party factions were increasingly on their own, and after unheard–of events like the jailing of St. Martin's leading Macoute, took initiative in invading properties of nonexiles who happened to live abroad, and resident landowners considered too weak to raise meaningful opposition. Invasion expanded very quickly in 1986. Unorganized squatting, a process that landlords found difficulty opposing without Macoute help, finally gained a foothold. But because disbanding of the Macoutes did not alter the basic structure of the party, because erstwhile rival factions were cooperating in mutual defense, because the army was not only preoccupied with maintaining order on the streets but also still composed of party loyalists, and because many landowners had aligned themselves with the provisional government and "progressive" parties and therefore represented a political opposition worthy of attack, much of the growth in squatting remained of an organized variety.

Expansion of this land development industry after 1980 may or may not have contributed to the 15 percent decline in the consumer price index for housing between 1983 and 1984, the first drop in over a decade. But the appearance of this industry was long overdue, and by increasing the rate of supply of land, it was accomplishing the basic things that had meaning to ordinary people as far as shelter was concerned: reducing the level of competition for scarce land; reducing the rate of increase in housing prices;

and in certain instances, reducing the price. These things were improvements that mattered.

Whether the provisional or subsequent governments would move against the industry was difficult to ascertain. Respect for property rights was important in maintaining a "business climate" attractive to private local and foreign investment and in maintaining support of property owners and other believers in the principle. Popular support required that the process be permitted to run its course. The issue, as for such others as the minimum wage, put political leaders in a difficult position. But that too was as it should be. Politics and political solvency were not supposed to be easy.

Whatever current or future governments would or would not choose to do, such improvements as the industry might engender in the time fortune allowed it to persist were small. Shelter, however offensive actual characteristics may have appeared to bourgeois aesthetic sentiments, was not yet as fundamental to the survival of most ordinary people as food and water. By logical extension, the act of sending children to school should not have been an important factor of survival either. But following the seemingly illogical ways by which extreme poverty inverted the meaning of simple things, and by which the self–interests of the political class yielded outcomes, schooling in Port–au–Prince was indeed vital to a great many of the ordinary class.

Notes

1. These units provided 0.8 square meters per adult or less.
2. Abrams (1964: 6) reported the figures for Kingston, Panama and Bombay; Hake (1977: 98) for Nairobi; and Dwyer (1975: 36, 37) for Calcutta and Hong Kong.
3. This estimate came from a subsample of respondents among monthly and six–month renters who had lived in their homes since 1972 and 1973. Rents did not change appreciably between 1972 and 1973, but thereafter followed an almost exponential growth pattern.
4. Burns and Grebler (1977: 15, 16), for example, noted that cooking and storage were among the important services provided by housing. Abrams (1964: 109) mentioned use of houses by tailors, dressmakers, and storekeepers. Dwyer (1975: 40) noted heavy use of houses for industrial and commercial purposes. McGee (1979: 12–21) went to great lengths to relate housing to hawker activities.
5. Burns (1966: 3–21) summarized the pro– and antihousing arguments very succinctly.
6. Population estimated from a one–week survey of downtown streets by Department of Public Works staff in 1975.
7. Data concerning street people is from a survey of 145 households that I conducted in 1975 as one of several pretests for the St. Martin survey.

8. The food and water expenditure of $0.25 per day per person meant that the individuals consumed more than 1500 calories per day. The storage fee of $1.50 resulted from their paying for a full stock the first night, or $1.00, and for half the stock remaining the second night, or $0.50.
9. My attempts to derive an indicator of "quality" from such specific elements as roofing material, flooring, and wall composition came to naught. What households meant by quality was the relative protection a house provided. Thus the density of holes in roofs and walls, the presence of shutters and doors with solid padlocks, and the type and height of interior partitions separating dwellings within a structure combined to present an image of higher or lower quality relative to what an "average-looking" dwelling provided. Thus a below-average quality score of 1 meant that the protection was quite poor, while an above-average score of 3 meant that the roof had no leaks, the walls had no openings other than windows and doors, interior partitions went up as high as the rafters, and the hardware to lock windows and doors was sturdy. I asked respondents whether they believed their units were relatively "good" or relatively "bad" compared to others in the area, and their responses usually coincided with my rating system.
10. They did make periodic repairs, but none of the respondents reported having made such expenditures during the preceeding six months.
11. Construction with scrap cost $25 per square meter in 1976, 67 percent for materials and 33 percent for labor (Haiti, 1976b: 20–28).
12. Land rent for a 16 meter parcel, for example, cost $6.40 per month. If their basis of comparison was long-term rental of an 8.6 meter dwelling costing $0.70 per square meter, or $6.00 per month, the rent saving was $0.40. Earnings from renting out the remaining 7.4 meters on a monthly basis for $1.40 per square meter might provide $10.40 per month. The total benefit was therefore $10.80 per month, a first-year return of $130.00 or 30 percent on $400.00 invested in construction.
13. I conducted this survey in December 1985.

6

Schooling

If the political class could lay claim to having undertaken serious efforts to broaden access to one seemingly important "thing" since Haiti's independence in 1804, it was primary schooling. Self–interests guiding such efforts flowed logically from political dynamics within the class. Parents inside the class valued education for their offspring and demanded schools and educators. Parents on the margins of the class, valuing education as a means for their offspring to move into the class, added to the demand. Educators, valuing the service they provided, and in alliance with parents, demanded more resources for existing schools, for new schools, and for additional teachers. More generally, "progressive" elements of the class concerned with doing good and spreading enlightenment to the "backward masses" of the ordinary class could see no harm and much potential good in expanding popular access to schooling.

For these and other reasons, proponents of education constituted a natural, broad–based faction within the political class. Unopposed until relatively recently by competing factions demanding resources for agriculture, industry, or public health, the proponents exerted considerable political influence over much of the last 180 years, especially after 1950. Along the way, although falling short on issues of quality raised by the proponents, Haiti gradually moved from having no schools at independence to having one of the highest rates of primary school enrollment relative to comparable developing countries. This movement was important to ordinary families, for some because of the opportunities for learning and upward socioeconomic mobility it provided their children, for most because of the social insurance and income that schooling contributed to their efforts to survive.

Evolution of the Schooling System

Though largely illiterate, most leaders of the newly–liberated country put establishment of an extensive public education system high on their list of goals warranting achievement. From 1804 to the incorporation of the principle of compulsory education in the revised Constitution of 1874, they and their successors produced a continuous stream of constitutions, laws, decrees, and circulars that affirmed and reaffirmed the value of education, underscored the need to expand it, and introduced various remedies and reforms to improve it.[1] Words and actions rarely coincided, however, and expansion of the educational system proceeded forward in short spurts between periods of retrogression.

In the north of the country, Emperor Henri Christophe established seven primary schools and one secondary school between 1804 and 1820. The schools were of such quality that English visitors could report that they were comparable to the best in their home country, though they probably neglected to ask themselves whether a good English school was good for Haiti. In the south, President-for-Life Pétion established eight primary schools and one secondary school, the constitutional principle of free primary education (though only one school was actually free at his death in 1818), and a school for girls. These efforts were small relative to current standards of progress, but quite substantial relative to circumstances of the time.

Under Boyer (1818–43) education in unified Haiti lost ground. Explanations for this retrogression included propositions to the effect that Boyer believed ignorant subjects less troublesome than educated ones; that in the absence of demand his inclination toward laissez-faire governance provided him little motive to maintain the system; and that because a squadron of warships in Port-au-Prince harbor forced Haiti to pay Charles X of France a substantial indemnity to reimburse mostly long-dead colonists for seizure of their assets, Boyer's government had better things to do with the funds that remained. In 1828 there were ten public primary schools and one secondary school left, and by 1843 a visitor sadly observed that out of a population of 700,000, only 1,000 pupils attended the primary schools, that each school had only one teacher, that the schools had no writing materials or books, and that the government was making no effort to print more of them.

Oscillation between expansion and contraction of secular public education became as routine as changes in government, but the forward movement was dominant. The ten urban schools of 1843 grew to forty-five in 1860, and on to about two hundred in 1895. In the process, governments of Haiti expanded public education at a pace comparable to that of other countries, and in quality and quantity were reported to have exceeded achievements in Puerto Rico, the Philippines, and in several southern states of the United States.

Helping them along was the Catholic church, which, after the Concordat of 1860, placed its educational resources at the service of the government, particularly with respect to schooling of girls. Under the 1862 supplement to the Concordat, Catholic schools became nonsecular public schools, funded jointly by the state and the Vatican.[2] Their number grew from two in 1864 to fifty–two in 1895, and eventually to eighty–two by 1905. Guided by Brothers and Sisters from France, these schools were the very best in Haiti, often providing instruction comparable to that received by pupils in Paris.

Preceding the Catholic church in the matter of education were the Protestants. Under the first of Haiti's constitutions, everyone had the right to teach, a legacy apparently carried forward from the tradition of private tutors in the colonial era, and few governments had ever interfered with this right, or the right of free worship. Such an open–door policy was irresistable to missionaries, and they came in. First were the African Methodists and the Baptists in 1824, followed by English Wesleyans in 1843, and then the Episcopals in 1861. By 1895 these mission schools represented a small proportion of the total 102 secular and nonsecular private schools in Haiti, but they constituted the core of quality within the private system.

Enrollment in public and private schools peaked at 45,000 pupils, or about 15 percent of the school–age population, between 1895 and 1910. With increasing political instability after 1900, the educational system collapsed. Enrollment dropped to 27,000 in 1904 before rising again to about 47,000 in 1913, but by then population growth had pushed the enrollment ratio down to around 10 to 12 percent of the school age population.[3]

In the turbulent years leading up to the U.S. occupation in 1915, discussions about education turned upon matters that would captivate all future discussants. One was the appropriateness of curricula. According to some critics of the system, curricula put too much emphasis on literature and classics and not enough on vocational training in the trades and manual arts. The result for graduates, according to other critics, was a life without productive usefulness, which put pressure on the state to employ them. Otherwise they would join with opposition forces to bring down governments in the hope that once the forces took power their support would be rewarded with a job.

Then, as later, the presumed problem of the educated unemployed had no easy solution. Trade skills and manual arts could be obtained without formal education, and in the French tradition the purpose of schooling was to bring enlightenment, intellectuality, and culture to individuals who had no other means of acquiring them. More specifically, education was a means to an end in which graduates would not have to earn their livelihoods in manual work. It was a path to joining or rising in the political class. The discussion placed in fundamental opposition a minority of education experts who believed that there was or should be a direct correspondence between formal education and specific future job prospects, a belief reinforced by the political turmoil of the times and the part in that turmoil ascribed to the educated unemployed, and a majority of parents and students who believed in a direct correspondence between education and avoidance of equally specific occupational prospects. Educational policy being perhaps the most democratic and participatory area of public decision making, at least with respect to the population in the political class with children already at school, majority opinion won the day, and would continue to do so for another sixty years. Some private and Catholic public schools introduced vocational programs, but they were few and far between.

Implicit in the issue of curricula was a second matter of considerable dispute, that of language of instruction. The language was French. Although many or most of the students in school before 1915 were already familiar with the language before enrollment, the rest of the school–age population was not. Their language was Creole. Teachers did speak Creole in class, but used French texts. The great challenge for such children was to learn a new language, used only in school, at a speed sufficient to maintain academic progress in mastering reading, writing, numbers, history, and other classroom subjects. Most of them did not succeed, and language served not only as an obstacle to literacy and the acquisition of other knowledge during the few years that such a child might struggle to remain in school, but also as a powerful filtering device to limit whatever benefits education had to offer to the small elite of the political class whose children learned to speak and understand French at home (Lundahl, 1979: 484–88).

Naturally enough, and independent of curricula, critics bemoaned a system that seemed to present more barriers to educational attainment than pathways to knowledge, and that could not even endow children with rudiments of reading and writing after they had spent several years in the classroom. But parents, even those who were illiterate, often saw little purpose in a conversion to Creole as language of instruction. Literacy in Creole meant nothing because there was little if anything to read in that language, not even an agreed–upon system of writing. More important, language was indeed, like curricula, supposed to be a filtering device that was to help children move into higher social strata and economic positions. Even when biased against their children, if parents believed that the key to advancement lay in moving through the filter of French and a difficult classical curriculum rather than obtention of "knowledge," they had every reason to support traditional education rather than a reformed version. Some Protestant and Catholic schools experimented with Creole instruction, but by and large, critics of the system had little impact before 1915, and would continue to have limited impact through 1976.

A third matter concerned teachers. Some in the public system qualified for the role with advanced training, and in 1905 received what must have been a very handsome remuneration of about $100 per month, comparing favorably with the $100 (in current $ terms) obtained by their successors in 1986. Others qualified by having completed enough years of primary school to justify an effort by some personal or family connection in higher reaches of government to find them a post. Often incompetent as instructors as well as illiterate, they also received $100.

This matter was less subject to debate than others, but nonetheless usually resulted in only limited public action. Reformers demanded improvements in teacher qualifications, either through stricter enforcement of hiring standards or through retraining, and higher salaries to attract and retain more competent individuals. Some parents could agree with the reformers, but not all. Salary rises unaccompanied by larger budgetary outlays would result in reduced enrollments and reduced opportunities for schooling. Better to have an incompetent instructor teaching an irrelevant curriculum in a language foreign to both teachers and pupils than nothing.

Reduction in the number of teachers also presented the prospect of pupils being unable to find appropriate jobs upon graduation. Although turnover in the ranks of the 2000 public and private teachers in 1913 could absorb only a small share of the 1500 to 2000 primary school graduates that year, there were enough new teaching opportunities to make schooling seem worthwhile. From a government's perspective, maintenance of political support and control of forces fueling opposition required stretching the national budget, particularly the highly labor–intensive educational budget, across as large a segment as possible of the politically relevant population. Schooled people, however incompetent at what they did, were usually relevant.

Finally, and largely a side effect of necessities surrounding optimum political allocation of limited budgetary resources, critics complained about the number of outdoor schools with classes under trees; the number of dilapidated school buildings without windows or other means of lighting and ventilation; the seemingly endless list of things lacking, such as chairs, desks, books, writing materials, didactic equipment, and so on. Here too, the critics found governments unwilling or unable to undertake major improvements.

Recurrent failure of efforts at curriculum and language reform, at improvements in teacher quality, and at upgrading facilities and equipment were to accompany education throughout the century. Imprecision about causal factors in learning may partly explain the almost universal propensity of educators to call for change and improvement in every conceivable aspect of primary schooling.[4] But failure of Haitian reformers did not seem to stem from any irrelevancy in their suggestions. Insufficient numbers of chairs and desks might not have been important, but illiteracy of teachers seemed somewhat fundamental.

Their frustrations, and the frustrations of many well-intentioned Haitians and foreigners that succeeded them, may have stemmed in part from their inability to step beyond the relatively narrow boundaries of the teaching profession to look at the broader set of meanings attaching themselves to education and to grasp the politics and policies that flowed from them. Had they done so, they might not have advanced their causes any further than they did but they might have developed a clearer sense that what they were trying to reform was not the education system but a vital element of the structure of Haitian social and economic organization. Sensible governments attuned to the prerequisites of solvency and survival did not tamper with such things. The U.S. colonial administration during the 1915–34 occupation was not sensible.

Though it is difficult to guess about how the evolution of the educational system might have proceeded without the occupation, or with an occupation similar to that taking place in other U.S. colonies at the time, evidence suggests that the occupiers did education much less of a service than they could have. Superimposing a U.S. vocational training model upon the ideas of Haitian reformers, the occupiers established a program of agricultural and industrial schooling in which enrollment grew from 825 in 1924 to 11,400 in 1929. In matters of quantity the program contained everything a reformer might have hoped for: buildings, equipment, books, good salaries, qualified teachers instructing in Creole (albeit translating from English texts), and a healthy recurrent budget expending $55 per student per year in 1929. The Haitian treasury bore the entire cost of the occupation, and under a colonial administration that could see no useful purpose served by what it called "academic" education, the price of vocational training was strangulation of resources devoted to all other public schools. Enrollment in those schools grew from 67,000 in 1924 to 96,000 in 1929, but with an allocation of $4.50 per year per pupil for recurrent costs, the general character of public education for most students was little different than it had been prior to 1915. In the meantime, U.S. occupiers in Puerto Rico had pushed public school enrollment from 30,000 in 1900 to 213,000 in 1927 (and illiteracy from 83 to 40 percent in the process), and in the Philippines increased enrollment from 228,000 in 1904 to 1.1 million by 1928. A similar approach in Haiti might conceivably have resulted in an enrollment of between 320,000 and 475,000 pupils by 1930, and perhaps a public school enrollment ratio between 0.45 and 0.65 rather than 0.13.[5]

Apparently moved by fear that funds reserved for scholarships would go for salaries of more U.S. training experts, and that the experts would fill some of the vacancies for which they were being trained, students at the vocational school in Port-au-Prince went on strike in October 1929, starting a chain of events that included the shooting by Marines of two dozen farmers in Cayes in December and the departure of the occupiers ahead of schedule five years later (Lundahl, 1979: 465). This standard revolutionary procedure, initiated by some sort of random but meaningful catalyst pushing students to extraordinary behavior, had helped unseat governments before 1915, and, in Gonaives and other towns after a false start, precipitated by food shortages in May 1983, would build around diesel fuel shortages in November 1985 to contribute to the disposal of Duvalier the younger in early 1986. Boyer may have ignored education for reasons other than the political problem posed by a schooled population, but had he believed it, his judgment would most certainly have been wise.

In any event, freed at last from the shackles of foreign administration, public education resumed its historical course of movement. Under Vincent (1930–41), Lescot (1941–46), and Estimé (1946–50), primary school enrollment grew at an average annual rate of 1.7 percent from 1930 to 1950, and urban enrollment at 1.2 percent. Urban and rural schools resumed the tradition of identical classical curricula notwithstanding efforts by many Haitian and expatriate scholars and technicians, including the UN mission of 1949 and the UNESCO social scientists of 1948–53, to convince governments to make education more relevant to something other than what it was already relevant to. What they and later scholars and technicians said about language, teachers, curricula, facilities, and equipment added little to what had been said since at least as far back as 1895.

Entering the development era under Magloire (1950–56) and François Duvalier (1957–71), the characteristics of Haitian primary education began to change more rapidly. The most dramatic change was the rise in primary school enrollment. Urban enrollments in the public sector during 1950–55, 1955–61, and 1961–67 expanded at average annual rates of 6.5, 4.4, and 4.1 percent respectively (table 6.1). Though the two governments both placed a high value on expanding access to public education, declining budgetary resources under Duvalier made it difficult to sustain earlier growth rates. Political conditions at the time also made it difficult for many teachers to remain on the payroll (or in the country). Less-qualified instructors with connections to the regime quickly replaced them, perhaps causing a drop in quality of instruction.[6] But in the continuing expansion, schools were

TABLE 6.1
Urban Primary School Enrollments, 1930–84

		STUDENTS IN PUBLIC SCHOOLS[a]		STUDENTS IN PRIVATE SCHOOLS[b]		TOTAL	
		Number (Thousands)	% of Total	Number (Thousands)	% of Total	Number (Thousands)	Enrollment Ratio[c]
All urban areas							
Totals	1930	40.1	81.2	9.4	18.8	49.4	n.a.
	1950	49.5	80.1	12.3	19.9	61.8	0.47
	1955	67.8	72.4	26.0	27.6	93.7	0.61
	1961	88.0	66.4	44.6	33.6	132.6	0.71
	1967	112.0	72.5	42.5	27.5	154.5	0.68
Annual Increase (in %)	1930–50	1.0	—	1.3	—	1.2	—
	1950–55	6.5	—	16.0	—	8.6	—
	1955–61	4.4	—	9.4	—	6.0	—
	1961–67	4.1	—	−0.8	—	2.6	—
Port-au-Prince							
Totals	1972	37.5	41.4	53.0	58.6	90.5	0.61
	1976	43.1	40.8	62.5	59.2	105.6	0.63
	1981	37.3	29.8	88.0	70.2	125.3	0.64
	1984	47.9	31.3	105.2	68.7	153.1	0.72

Annual Increase (in %)	1972–76	4.4	—	4.2	—	4.3	—
	1976-81	−2.9	—	7.1	—	3.5	—
	1981–84	8.7	—	6.1	—	6.9	—
	1976–84	1.3	—	6.7	—	4.7	—

Sources: Rotberg (1971), De Ronceray (1979), and author's estimates based on 1950, 1971, and 1982 census data (IHS, 1973; IHSI, 1982), and on unpublished annual statistics prepared by the Ministry of Education from 1974 to 1984.

[a] State secular and state-subsidized Catholic schools.

[b] For-profit lay schools, community schools, Protestant Mission schools, and nonsubsidized Catholic schools.

[c] The ratio of primary students to the population between five and sixteen years of age. This is a "gross" ratio that exaggerates the share of age-specific groups actually in school. The "net" ratio is about 67% of the gross in Haiti.

opening their doors to a broader segment of the population than had been the case earlier. The process was part of the social transformation, the creation of a larger middle class, that Duvalier promised along the road to the presidency.[7]

More dramatic was the rise of enrollment in the private sector. Corresponding to the rates of 6.5, 4.4, and 4.1 percent in public schools, growth in private institutions was 16.0, 9.4, and –0.8 percent. The decline in 1961–67 resulted from suppression of several private schools and teachers, a hostile environment for the establishment of new facilities, the sending of students abroad by wealthier parents, and emigration by families with means to travel. These served to lower the overall rate of enrollment expansion from 8.6 percent in 1950–55 and 6.0 percent in 1955–61 to 2.6 percent in 1961–67.

With social barriers to education lowered and government suppression of private education removed, enrollment moved ahead in Port-au-Prince at a rate of 4.3 percent per year from 1972 to 1976. This rise was largely due to resurgence of private enrollments, which in 1976 contained almost 60 percent of the total in the city. The increase was slightly ahead of the rate of growth of the school-age population, and the enrollment ratio rose from 0.61 to 0.63 during the period.

The ratio overstated the proportion of children at school because the school-age population in the denominator excluded those under six and over sixteen who were in primary school, and because enrollments on the first day of class were usually higher than average attendance rates during the academic term. But even if the 0.63 enrollment ratio in 1976 was a third off the mark, a 0.40 ratio remained remarkable in a city where perhaps half of all households earned barely enough to meet essential survival requirements. That almost 60 percent of children were going to private school, in principle more costly than public school, was very odd.

The evolution of enrollment after 1976 was even more so. The economy supposedly continued its upswing through 1981, and thereafter regressed. The growth of total enrollment from 1976 to 1981 slipped to 3.5 percent per year, primarily as a result of a shift of public school resources to rural areas.[8] This explained the drop in public enrollment. It could not explain how parents were able to shift students from low-cost public schools to supposedly higher-cost private ones. Then, with the economy in a downturn after 1981, total enrollment surged once more at a rate of 6.9 percent per year, pushing the enrollment ratio up to a bewildering 0.72 in 1984. In this instance the government's decision to revert back to an urban emphasis, adding 300 urban teachers while keeping rural personnel at 1981 levels, might have explained the 8.7 percent annual rise in public enrollment from 1981 to 1984. But again, it could not explain the 6.1 percent yearly increase in private schooling. A contracting economy, especially the contraction of a very poor one, was supposed to lower aggregate demand for education. It was not supposed to generate an acceleration in enrollment growth.

One attempt to estimate individual economic returns to urban primary school completion, prepared in 1985 by the Institute for International Research (IIR), indicated that returns could vary from a low of 9 percent for relatively high-cost private schools, through 14 percent for low-cost private schools, to 25 percent for public schools.[9] The public-private differential was helpful in suggesting why public schools filled up as soon as supply increased, as in 1981–84. But the issue remained that if the rate of return model had explanatory significance, lifetime returns of 9 to 25 percent were much too low to justify educational expenditures by most low-income families in Port-au-Prince. Their time horizons were generally quite short, and investments that yielded returns in seven or eight years were subject to heavy discounting. In 1976 at least, families could generate much more than 25 percent in many of their daily market and nonmarket activities. The IIR estimate might explain why some parents sent children to school, but not why as many of them did so during the last two decades, nor why most invested their children in private schools where returns supposedly ranged from 9 to 14 percent. The rate of return, actual or perceived, had to be much higher than proposed by the IIR.

Studies in countries similar to Haiti indicated that individual returns to primary school completion, relative to illiteracy, ranged from 25 to 35 percent between 1966 and 1972 (and from 14 to 33 percent for secondary school completion relative to primary school).[10] Also, estimates of the average addition to future income resulting from one extra year of education (after the first three or four), varied between 8 and 16 percent.[11] The IIR estimate was therefore somewhat lower than for other countries. But from the perspective of poor families, the difference between a 25 percent rate and a 35 percent rate was insignificant, as was an 8 to 16 percent rise in income several years in the future. If the IIR figures or estimates from other countries were correct, enrollments seemed to have no business being as high as they were. If enrollment figures were correct, rates of return seemed to have no business being so low. Indeed, the problem was with the calculations, not because of computational error, but rather because the actual characteristics of demand and supply for schooling in Haiti, the economics of quantity, did not conform exactly to the characteristics presumed for purposes of the calculations.

Economics of Quantity

Guesses about what the rate of return was supposed to be in order to provide families with incentive to school their children, and guesses about what aggregate demand was or was not supposed to do in response to changes in the urban economy, depended on several presuppositions. One was that costs of schooling relative to income, if not constant over time, were at least positive. That is, schooling would always incur net direct and opportunity costs to families in a fashion that permitted calculation of a rate of return and that served as a barrier to prevent those with incomes below a certain threshold range from sending children to school.

Another assumption was that perceived benefits of schooling rose and fell primarily in response to changes in domestic economic conditions. A third assumption was that what schools provided was "education." Parents therefore perceived the benefits of schooling primarily in terms of higher future earnings resulting from current investment in education of children.[12]

Characteristics of schooling in the city did not invalidate these suppositions, but changes in the characteristics from about 1950 onward served to limit the share of the population to which they applied. The key changes included: substantial declines in the cost of schooling, often to zero or less; rapid expansion in demand for (schooled) labor exports; and a massive broadening of the purpose of schools to include not only education but also income maintenance and social insurance. With these changes, an ever–increasing number of low–income families could not help but behave as if they perceived a rate of return approaching infinity (if one insisted on this method of explaining behavior) and could not help but increase their demand for schooling.

These factors went far toward explaining the remarkable rise in primary enrollments. For many, sending children to school was an investment in survival no different than investments in food and water. As for all things in which survival or other rationales gave rise to almost unlimited demand, scarcity of supply shaped a schooling industry offering excellent prospects for extraction of intermediation commissions and profits by individuals with productive skills and connections. Although the industry was to expand rapidly over the next decade, its essential features, and several of the factors explaining the rise in enrollment, were already evident in the characteristics of schooling costs and benefits in St. Martin during 1976.

Costs

Slightly more than half the households in St. Martin with school–age children enrolled them in primary school in 1976.[13] The significant difference between families that did and did not send children to school was income. Those with students earned $10.10 per month per adult, and those without students earned $8.00 (table 6.2). The difference in average incomes, 25 percent, was large, and implied that the costs of schooling appeared heavy from the perspective of households earning $8.00 or less.

First among these costs was the price of uniforms and shoes. These items had little bearing on knowledge acquisition, but every child was required to have them for attendance at a regular school. This admission charge was $6.00 to $8.00 per set, and because younger children grew out of them quickly, families usually purchased a new set every year. They could save something by handing down old uniforms and shoes to younger children or by selling them in the used–clothing section of the downtown market. In either event, the items represented a significant recurrent expenditure. Also, uniforms had to be clean. Biweekly laundering after school hours maintained this standard during the dry season, but not during the rainy season. Attending school in damp clothing meant running the risk of being sent home by schoolmasters, not to mention catching cold. Families with means therefore purchased two uniforms per child. In St. Martin, 40 percent had at least two uniforms and most of the rest one.

Uniforms and shoes may have appeared to be unnecessary barriers to education, but they were vital to certain sectors of the political economy. In 1976 there were about 500,000 children enrolled in primary school in Haiti.[14] Making allowance for trade in used clothing and shoes and shifting of these items from older to younger children, annual demand for cotton textiles may have been of the order of 400,000 yards and demand for new shoes on the order of 150,000 pairs. Total production by import–substitution firms in 1976 was two million yards of textiles and 220,000 pairs of shoes (see table 1.7). The dress code was therefore essential to their profits. Unfortunately, production inefficiencies kept domestic retail prices for these goods at approximately a 30 to 40 percent higher level than equivalent prices for imports at the time, thereby imposing an indirect tax of perhaps $1.00 on each new purchase to subsidize several hundred factory workers and owners.[15]

Teachers and schoolmasters in public and private schools sometimes imposed further taxes by purchasing an obscure color or pattern and then obliging parents to buy the required material from them, or by simply making purchase of materials from them a registration prerequisite. In these instances, the personal tax was about $0.50 per student. In the aggregate, $15.00 went to the teacher with a class of fifty, and $40.00 to $60.00 to the schoolmaster with four to six classes and teachers under his or her command. Conversely, some schools purchased large quantities of materials in order to sell them at cost to parents. Here the approximate saving was $0.25 per uniform.

Whatever the price paid, textiles required transformation into uniforms and shoes required maintenance. The schooling industry therefore formed

TABLE 6.2
Characteristics of Households with Children in Primary School in St. Martin, 1976

Type of Schooling	Number of Households	Number of Students	Students per Household	Enrollment Ratio[a]	Household Size[b]	MONTHLY INCOME[c] Per Adult (U.S. $)	MONTHLY INCOME[c] Total (U.S. $)	MONTHLY SCHOOL EXPENDITURE Amount[d] (U.S. $)	MONTHLY SCHOOL EXPENDITURE as % of income
Public	9	25	2.8	0.89	4.4	10.35	45.65	4.20	9.2
Private: regular	13	25	1.9	0.51	4.8	11.90	56.50	6.85	12.1
home lessons	3	6	0.2	1.00	4.2	8.65	36.10	2.40	6.6
sponsorship	4	12	0.3	0.92	6.0	4.85	29.30	2.10	7.2
TOTAL (average)	29	68	(2.3)	(0.73)	(4.7)	(10.10)	(47.30)	(4.90)	(10.4)
Households with school-age children, not sending any to school[e]:					3.9	8.00	31.50	—	—

Source: Data from author's survey in St. Martin.

[a] The ratio between children in school and the school-age population of the group.

[b] Measured in adult-equivalent units.

[c] The difference in the means between public and regular private schooling is not statistically significant. Differences between either of these and home lessons or sponsorship, between home lessons and sponsorship, and between the averages for all households sending children to school and households not sending any to school are significant at the 1% level.

[d] The differences in the means between public, regular private, and either home lessons or sponsorship are significant at the 1% level. The difference between home lessons and sponsorship is not significant.

[e] N = 26

a significant basis of demand for tailoring, dressmaking, shoemaking, and shoe repair services of small manufacturers, not to mention traders who specialized in selling cloth and shoes. The dress code was not essential to education but was a very important component of the urban economy.

Registration fees, the next hurdle, averaged $1.00 per year in public schools and $4.00 for private schools. Although schools could have disposed of such downpayments and raised monthly tuition rates slightly, the registration fee, equivalent to 25 percent of tuition, was a useful protective measure. Having already expended a sizable share of schooling expenditures for the fee, parents were likely to think twice before transferring a child to another school during the academic year. The fee also protected school finances from the effects of high dropout rates and the corresponding loss in monthly tuition revenues. But the effect, as for the dress code, was to erect a relatively high barrier to schooling. There were many families that could afford to pay monthly tuition of $0.50 in public schools and $2.20 in private schools, but the frontend cost of $7.00 to $12.00 for dress and registration requirements was often an insurmountable obstacle. Saving such amounts over the course of a year was not impossible, but investing in schooling when there were so many competing and more productive alternative uses for the funds did not always appear to be the wisest course of action.

Depending on grade level and school, complete sets of books and writing equipment cost $3.00 to $8.00 per year. These were not prerequisites for school enrollment, and therefore did not act as barriers to attendance. Half the households in St. Martin reported that their children had all essential books and equipment and a third had most or some. The rest went without books, parents arguing that children could at least learn something from teachers, and that they could share books with others in the class.

And then there was the opportunity cost. Beside costs associated with alternative use of funds, there was the matter of foregoing earnings and unpaid but nevertheless useful labor of children. A five- or six-year-old might not be adept at market activities or chores about the home, but from seven years of age onward could prove helpful earning money in such things as car washing or watching, assisting in the trade, manufacturing, or service activities of older household members, or in care of infants, home surveillance, shopping, and so forth.[16] The older a child the greater its capacity to contribute productively to the family economy and the higher the opportunity cost of keeping it in school. Not surprisingly, the enrollment ratio of six- to eleven-year-olds in St. Martin, 63 percent, was substantially higher than the ratio of 43 percent among twelve- to sixteen-year-olds.

Leaving aside supplementary uniforms and shoes, books, and opportunity costs, and spreading the cost of one uniform, a pair of shoes, and registration fees over the eight-month academic term, the average price in St. Martin of sending a child to a public school was $1.50 per month, and to a regular accredited private school, $3.60.

Parents in St. Martin were almost unanimous in their opinion that public schools were better than private schools. Public schools may have provided superior instruction, but the price advantage could not have been inconsequential in shaping parental opinion. Families able to find openings in public facilities spent 9 percent of monthly income to school 90 percent of school-age children (table 6.2). In contrast, families with roughly the same income but unable to secure similar openings spent 12 percent of earnings to send 51 percent of school-age children to the more costly regular private schools. Competition for access to scarce public school places was therefore quite keen, but only 37 percent of St. Martin students, close to the city average of 41 percent shown in table 6.1, were able to benefit from the luck and connections that their parents said were prerequisites for entry.

As for all important things in short supply, connections were available for purchase on the market. The structure of finder's fees, when the finder was not a Macoute, was a simple payment. When the finder was a Macoute, an implicit pledge of loyalty and a previously untarnished political record was necessary in addition to the payment. The structure of bribes, which a finder had to share with a public schoolmaster, teacher, or Ministry of Education clerk, was $10 without guarantees, $20 for assured placement in a secular establishment, and up to $35 for a slot in a relatively prestigious public Catholic school. Several parents in households that did not appear to be Macoute affiliated claimed to have paid these fees at some point during the previous three years.

As regards the Macoute-affiliated households, almost every school-age child in them was at a public school. Moreover, half of these students, or 13 percent of the total, had been sent by parents living outside the city to stay with (Macoute-affiliated) relatives while attending a public school to which their hosts had been able to arrange entry for them. The cost of schooling was low once a child enrolled in a public school, but the political and economic barrier to public enrollment often made private schools the less costly method of producing education.

A $20 to $35 bribe was recoverable within a year or two on tuition savings alone, but even among higher-income families who could pay for uniforms, shoes, and registration fees, additional amounts of such magnitude imposed severe short-term opportunity costs in terms of foregone production and consumption. Paying an extra $2 or $3 per month to school half as many children was not cost-effective, but it was apparently more efficient than drawing funds away from market capital, rent payments, food, or, in the case of education, from purchase of books.

But whether schooling cost more or less, most households usually needed above-average incomes before finding themselves in positions to expend as much as 9 to 12 percent of income for it. Families with lesser means had to find lower-cost solutions. One approach, pursued by 10 percent of households with 9 percent of all students, was to send children to the homes of teachers in and around the neighborhood after regular school hours. Here students needed shoes but not uniforms or registration fees, and tuition was $1.30 per month. With a class size of thirty to forty, teachers could double their earnings by establishing irregular schools of this type, and at the same time offer economies of scale and organization that allowed families to educate all their children for 6.6 percent of income.

A disadvantage of this irregular schooling was that students who progressed to completion might not be able to obtain a certificate of primary studies issued by the Ministry of Education. A teacher might be able to get one issued through the regular school where he or she taught earlier in the day, but even with a bribe, the outcome was uncertain. A more serious disadvantage was the inability of students to receive credit for their time at lessons. Transferring to a regular public or private school when means allowed required that the child start all over again. Parents reported, however, that teachers seemed to be making progress in having their homes accredited as private schools. Although accreditation would demand the meeting of dress requirements, it would not necessarily increase tuition. This kind of school might therefore remain relatively inexpensive. And even if the parents could not pay for uniforms, they could at least obtain a document stating that their child had attended (what would later become) a legitimate place of instruction before dropping out.

Another approach, relatively new in 1976, was to have children adopted by one or more of several foster parents' sponsorship programs. A small number of families had succeeded in getting almost all their children "adopted" into programs being implemented by the Salvation Army, Salesian Fathers, Church of the Nazarene, and other schools in the area. These programs paid for uniforms, shoes, books, registration fees, and two-thirds of tuition, bringing the direct cost of schooling to $0.70 per student per month, the lowest price available.

Many families with children already in school, as well as those keeping them at home, had placed their childrens' names on various program waiting lists. Rumor had it that for $10 a name could move to a higher position, shortening the waiting period by a year or more, and that $50 could guarantee adoption within a year. But parents had no tangible evidence of such bribes obtaining successful outcomes. From what they could determine, only the very poorest families qualified for sponsorship, a hypothesis supported strongly by the $4.85 per adult average monthly income of families with children in the programs. These were the very poorest people in St. Martin. Under the circumstances, families with higher income preferred to wait rather than pay in 1976. By 1985, however, intermediation services were more reliable, and the market for them was quite lively.[17]

Benefits

With high costs relative to income acting as a barrier, the observation that higher– rather than lower–income families in St. Martin schooled their children found a straightforward explanation. Similarly, the effect of lower cost in public schools on the household enrollment ratio, and of home lessons and sponsorship on access to education by lower–income families, highlighted the important influence of the cost–income relationship on the structure of demand for schooling. Presumably, such benefits as schooling could produce were more or less the same for all families. All that mattered was the relationship between benefits and the costs of producing them.

However, there was an anomaly in the data. Where the cost of 1500 calories was $4.80 per month per adult, poorest households earning $4.85 per month in table 6.2 had no rational reason to spend 7 percent of income for something like schooling. It had to offer more, much more than a 25 percent lifetime return.

The possibility that Haitians ascribed more to education than might normally be subsumed within the concept of tangible income was not strongly evident. Intellectuality, advanced degrees, and certain liberal professions reportedly carried prestige in elite circles (Lobb, 1940: 30). But the value of education for most was closely associated with maintaining or increasing individual and family wealth, directly through access to occupations and economic sectors with higher earnings, and indirectly through the making of potentially useful interpersonal connections with members of higher social and economic strata (Wingfield and Parenton, 1965: 344; De Ronceray, 1979: 51–57). Even if all Haitians attached status to education, such benefits could not increase the return by very much for low-income people. A family with $4.85 did not pay 7 percent of it for status enhancement.

One factor excluded from the IIR analysis of primary education, and from most calculations of returns to primary education in developing countries, was the potential effect of returns resulting from emigration. With enough schooling, an individual could pass quality–control checks and thereby obtain a visa. Even if it fell short of requisite quality, some education was nevertheless helpful in securing illegal passage to and work in the Bahamas or the United States. In such a context, especially after 1970 when the composition of the flow of emigrants broadened to include a wide spectrum of income groups, the perceived return from school expenditures could have risen very appreciably. With the addition of $1000 in direct costs for passport and exit taxes, bribes necessary to expedite these, as well as for foreign entry visas and air or sea travel, and assuming a lifetime earnings stream equal to the U.S. minimum wage, the IIR's calculus could yield returns several multiples beyond 25 percent, depending on when an individual reached the U.S. after graduation.[18] Discounting for the probability of actually reaching a foreign country, and for completing enough primary years of schooling to make a difference in export potential, the rate of return would have been less. But if emigration figured in how families viewed the value of education, the rate would still not have been high enough to convince a great many very low income households to spend for it. However, it might have been enough to convince some, and in this respect schools constituted an industry for the production of labor not only for domestic use, but also for export. Export rather than domestic demand was the primary source of urban economic growth up to 1976, and the rising output of the schooling industry may well have reflected this fact. But prospects for emigration still did not explain the interest in schooling among families with $4.85 in monthly earnings.

Perhaps the explanation lay outside the rate of return concept. Certain benefits of schooling were instantaneous and had nothing directly to do with education. One such benefit was day-care service. If parents valued the productive benefits of time free from the responsibility of supervising children at more than the cost of the service, which in 1976 ranged from 1.5 to 3.6 cents per hour per child, then schooling was a useful expenditure.[19] In households in which market participation rates of adults, adolescents, and older preadolescents were high, and in which distractions from work could yield a lowering of earnings, schooling offered the possibility of rendering a household's economy more efficient for at least half the day. If the distraction effect of boisterous five- to seven-year-olds was constant, then a lowering of the price for the service, as in a sponsorship program, could increase demand for it.

Still, the 1.5 to 3.6 cents-an-hour range, equivalent to 140 to 340 daily calories of corn or a half-bucket of water, was expensive. Those with relatively adequate intakes of food and water might have found the service useful, but for very low income families the opportunity cost must have outweighed the potential gain in earnings. Also, such day-care benefits as schools could provide declined as children grew older and learned to care for themselves. The enrollment ratio of twelve- to sixteen-year-olds, 43 percent, meant that children were in school well beyond the time that parents could extract any day–care benefits from further expenditure. If the service justified outlays, it could do so only for the first few grades, and only for families with more means than the very poorest.

A second instantaneous benefit of schooling, perhaps the most important of all from the perspective of the very poor, was the income effect of school feeding programs. Supported with grants of surplus commodities, primarily from the USAID Title II program, and with cash grants from PVOs for the construction of canteens and wages of cooks, the number of private schools offering meals was increasing rapidly. In 1972 there were about five school canteens in the whole northern section of Port–au–Prince (De Ronceray, 1979: 68). By 1976 the number exceeded twenty. Several served St. Martin, and the students listed in table 6.2 who were being sponsored in private schools took meals there.

The average canteen ration was about 800 calories and 40 grams of protein, what a 70 percent–30 percent mixture of corn and beans could provide (without cooking) for 8.5 cents at prevailing retail market prices.[20] Without shadow pricing the value of meals, each child received $1.70 per month in food, and the average household with three children in school earned $5.10. The $29.30 mean income of these families shown in table 6.2 consisted of $24.20 in cash and $5.10 in meals. Therefore, by paying $2.10 for tuition each month they were able to raise income by a net value of $3.00, or 12.4 percent more than the sums received from all other sources. They did not in fact pay 7.2 percent of income for schooling as suggested in table 6.2. There were no direct costs, only benefits.

For very poor families, the combination of sponsorship and meals was a powerful incentive to send children to school, at least until such time as the child grew old enough to earn more outside school than inside, and the poorer the family, the greater the incentive. The educational aspect of schooling in such instances may have been completely irrelevant compared to the income aspect. In any event, presented with the possibility of sponsorship and meals, a low–income family would have been irrational not to send as many children to school as possible. More generally, the $1.70 per month per child in food income could substantially lower the direct cost of schooling for any family fortunate enough to have a student enrolled in a facility with a canteen. Had the children in public school shown in table 6.2 received meals, monthly school expenditures would have been zero, and in the case of private regular schools, it would have been $3.60 rather than $6.85. As outlays and indirect costs approached zero, the rate of return, in theory, approached infinity. For the half of families in St. Martin with children in sponsorship programs or with children not at school, that is with incomes averaging $8.00 or less, rates of return had to be in the neighborhood of infinity to justify expenditures for schooling.[21]

Growth

Processes structuring the schooling industry in 1976 expanded rapidly over the next decade. Emigration, especially to the United States, increased substantially. Besides the incentive foreign opportunities may have provided to parents, there was the matter of remittances. Such remittances were insignificant to families in St. Martin in 1976, but may have increased afterward as the structure of emigration broadened to include ever lower income groups. With a firm connection to a family member abroad, using a portion of the remittances to prepare another member for eventual export was likely to have been perceived as a potentially productive investment.

School feeding programs, initiated with U.S. surplus commodities in 1958, expanded at an average annual rate of 12 percent from 1976 to 1984. In 1976 about 35 percent of all Haitian primary students received such meals. The proportion in 1984 was 58 percent and approached 65 percent in 1986.[22] Making allowance for additional support from EEC countries and purchases by philanthropic organizations, the proportion in 1986 could have been around 75 percent. The children of the poor were targets of these efforts, and the rise in enrollments of such children was not unrelated to this factor.

Complementing these processes was a rapid increase in the supply of low–cost private school spaces. Together with food, low–cost facilities very often reduced school expenditures to zero, or to less than zero. One source of this increase in supply was expansion of the number of PVOs establishing themselves in Haiti. Largely composed of Protestant missions covering a wide range of denominations, their first activity after constructing a church was to attach a school, a requirement imposed upon them by government from about 1970 onward, and to hire individuals with enough training to convince parents (and government school inspectors) that they qualified as teachers.[23] Tuition in these schools in 1985 was heavily subsidized, averaging about $2.00 per student per month within a range of $0.20 to $4.00, making a larger proportion of private schools price competitive with public facilities.[24]

A second source of growth was expansion of child sponsorship programs, which usually channeled funds through old and new PVOs, particularly the Protestant missions. Of every dollar spent by a North American or European foster parent, $0.65 to $0.75 went toward subsidizing a school's recurrent costs. Beyond overhead of about 10 percent, the balance covered uniforms, shoes, registration fees, books, and two-thirds of tuition for the adopted child. Reasons for the almost exclusive focus on education varied among the different programs. In some instances it was a question of default. If foster parents were to be convinced that their money was being put to good use on behalf of a specific child, there was no obvious place to put the money except education. In other instances, program administrators actually believed that sponsoring education was a good thing to do, either because it might raise the future earnings of the child, or in the case of several Protestant evangelical groups, because schools were more effective than churches in bringing the word of God to children and their families.

Whatever the reasons on the supply side, on the demand side sponsorship meant not only a lowered cost of education to parents but also access to a limited social insurance scheme. If parents faced distress which might cause a student to drop out of school, they could seek relief from social assistants attached to the sponsoring organization, especially for such things as medical crises, burial costs, and housing emergencies resulting from flood or fire. Parents had much interest in keeping children in school for as long as feasible even if meals were not available.

Compassion International, a major sponsor, arrived in Haiti in 1972, and by 1984 was sponsoring 17,000 students through several denominational missions. Foster Parents Plan International followed in 1973, covering 15,000 families and 30,000 students by 1984. World Vision, after a hasty departure from Vietnam in 1975, expanded its operations in Haiti in 1978 and reached 12,500 students five years later. Similar programs by World Missionary Action, the Baptist Mission, Salesian Fathers, Save the Children, Seventh Day Adventists, Church of God, and several others may have added another 15,000. By 1984–85 at least 75,000 primary students in Haiti, or 10 percent of the national total, were adoptees. Almost 25,000 of these students may have been in Port-au-Prince. In addition, because sponsorship programs usually covered no more than one-third of students within particular schools, the number of city students in sponsor-subsidized facilities may have been around 75,000, or 7 percent of total enrollment in private schools.[25] Many parents would have sent their children to school without the incentive of meals, sponsorship, or subsidized costs, but enrollment growth would not have been nearly as high.

Prospects for further expansion of enrollments were slim, however. Several of the PVOs became disillusioned with education as a means to address poverty. Foster Parents Plan, as I note in chapter 7, began to reorient its program toward family economic development in 1981. World Vision began to shift resource use towards community economic development in

1983. The Christian Children's Fund, destined to become one of the largest sponsorship programs by 1990 after starting up in 1986, was following the lead of World Vision. Although other sponsorship programs were not about to abandon education, none were planning major budgetary increases in Haiti. Private school enrollments were therefore likely to remain stable, or decrease, after 1986.

Prospects for growth in the public sector were also slight. The provisional government was not in a position in 1986 to expand the public school system. Satisfaction of teacher wage demands, noted in chapter 2, meant no growth in the number of teachers, and perhaps a policy of retrenchment through attrition. But whether or not the schooling industry would continue to expand, its historical evolution presented a very basic question: What was a school in Haiti?

While they may compete for explanatory dominance, productivity-enhancement, social filtering, behavior modification, credentialization, or other similar hypotheses presume that schools have to do with greater or lesser learning about something that one way or another will make a difference to future income.[26] Children have remarkable capacities to learn from whatever they do wherever they happen to be. Something like "education" invariably takes place in a school. But what also took place in or through Haitian schools, especially in recent times, was an important transfer of wealth from other countries to low-income families in Haiti. Schooling served to mitigate the effects of very low income by providing a vehicle for income growth or maintenance through meals, and in some instances by providing a limited social insurance program. In this sense the sending of children to school by the very poor fortunate enough to connect with the transfer process was an investment in survival no less important than any of the other things they did.

This transfer process was not efficient. Bribes to place children into low-cost public schools, into schools with canteens, into low-cost private schools, or into sponsorship programs (not an issue in 1976 but very much so later), were perhaps unavoidable in a situation in which demand outstripped supply. The dress code, however, conditioned by protective barriers to imports and high inefficiency in import-substitution industries, did little except transfer a sizable share of income received by low-income families to high-income factory owners and workers. More important perhaps, most of the transfer through sponsorship programs accrued primarily to self-styled teachers or schoolmasters who in many instances were not engaged in education. Often they were administrators of feeding and/or evangelical programs. Here education was a gloss that made use of resources much less cost-effective than it could have been.[27]

In this context the processing efficiency of the primary schooling industry was difficult to determine. According to the IIR, 45 percent of all students entering the first grade did not get into second grade after up to four years of repetition, and 45 percent of those entering the second grade were unlikely to progress to completion of the sixth and last grade even after ten or more years in school (table 6.3). If the purpose of the industry was social filtering, then it was proving technologically very effective. Less than one–third of all students entering the first grade would graduate from primary school. However, if the purpose was reinforcement of the existing structure of social stratification, it was not efficient. A 31 percent school completion rate, or a 22 percent rate if one made allowance for the fact that about 70 percent of the eligible population actually entered the first grade, was too high to maintain the status quo. Over half of primary school completers were likely to finish secondary and vocational studies. The addition to the population of such a large number of people with primary completion or with some secondary studies, unless disposed of through emigration, would more likely have the effect of altering rather than reinforcing a structure in which, according to the World Bank, less than 5 percent of the urban population controlled 75 percent of its wealth in 1976. Schooling industry growth was having a destabilizing influence on social structure.

At first glance, the industry also seemed inefficient if its purpose was productivity enhancement. Assuming no gains to productivity for the first four years of schooling, less than half of all entering students were likely to learn anything that might have long term productive value, including the

TABLE 6.3
Primary School Promotion, Retention, and Dropout Rates in Haiti, 1985

Grade	Cohort Progression to Next Grade[a]	Annual Promotion Rate (%)	Annual Retention Rate (%)	Annual Dropout Rate (%)
1. (CP1)	1000	41	27	33
2. (CP2)	533	70	18	12
3. (CE1)	472	72	20	8
4. (CE2)	423	73	18	9
5. (CM1)	374	74	12	14
6. (CM2)	313	96	4	0

Source: IIR (1985).

[a]Of 1000 children entering the first grade, 553 will, after no more than four years of repetition, move to the second grade. Of these 553, 472 will eventually move on to the third grade. Ultimately, 313 will enter the sixth grade, though some, in theory, will have taken twenty years to get there, and 227 will enter secondary school. The balance of 74 promoted from the sixth grade will not proceed further.

ability to read and write. Maybe the industry could do no better than add value to less than half its inputs, but it seemed low. Alternatively, if food intake of young children from poor families had significant long-term productivity-enhancing properties, then perhaps the lack of an alternative mechanism for accomplishing this end made the industry much more effective in achieving its purpose than one might deduce from pass rates alone.

But one thing was clear. By 1986 the share of the school-age population of Port-au-Prince sitting in buildings called schools was larger than in most other cities with comparable per capita incomes. Pétion could not have imagined the process by which primary schooling would eventually become free, and the producers of the Constitution of 1874 could not have imagined the circumstances under which schooling would become compulsory, but Haiti was never closer to their dreams than in 1986. Quantity of urban schooling was no longer pertinent. What needed attention was the quality of that which happened in schools.

Politics of Quality

Historical politics of school quality, which I described in the first section of this chapter, turned on matters pertaining to the appropriateness of curricula and language; teacher quality; and the perennial inadequacy of school facilities, equipment, teaching materials, and student books. As for most children in the country, students in St. Martin were attending classes in which the substance of what they learned, if they learned anything of substance, had not changed very much since the early part of the nineteenth century. Had the characteristics of primary schooling been different, perhaps the circumstances of the country and city might have been better than they were in 1976. Or, given the nebulous nature of education and the difficulty in ascribing causal properties to it, circumstances might have been the same or worse. But whatever the nature of conjectures about what might have been, 1976 seemed to mark a turning point in the qualitative evolution of Haitian primary schooling.

In that year reformers gained the upper hand in beginning a process that might eventually lead to fundamental change in the quality attributes of basic education. Outward manifestations of the impact of the process were hard to discern in 1986, but there was no mistaking that a process was indeed underway. If sustained for a generation or more, processes redirecting the historical course of curricula and language, and of teacher quality, might or might not alter the economic circumstances of the country, but they would most definitely make of Haiti, or more particularly, the population of Haiti, something substantially different from what they were and are.

Curricula and Language

Until alliances between local and foreign reformers in 1976 began to succeed in moving government away from traditional curricula in French, the characteristics of public primary instruction remained much as they had always been, and private instruction generally followed the same model. But processes of change were well underway long before 1976.

One process was the establishment in 1943 of public adult literacy programs. Available data indicate that 1.1 million people participated in these programs between 1962 and 1980, and that 375,000 learned to read and write in Creole (IIR, 1985: 11.4–7). Critics, believing that the number of literates was an exaggeration, that a conversion rate from participation to literacy of 35 percent was too low, and that twenty years of effort to make less than 10 percent of the population literate was not a serious effort, decried the entire enterprise (Lundahl, 1979: 478). Although achievements were less than critics might have preferred, the programs did two important things. They created things to read in Creole, and they created a readership sizable enough to prove of commercial value. Books, pamphlets, periodicals, and newspapers in Creole were almost nonexistent in 1960. But by the 1980s they became a thriving subcomponent of the publishing industry. Moreover, radio and television programming and printed commercial advertisements were dominated by Creole. French was still the official language, but Creole was fast overtaking it in terms of visibility. Indeed, it was the language of the 1985–86 rebellion.[28]

In addition to government programs, at least fifty of the major PVOs were also conducting adult literacy campaigns in the 1970s and 1980s.[29] The Catholic church, fully Haitianized under François Duvalier, took a leading role in promoting literacy in Creole. Depending on whether a diocese was under the hierarchical control of a conservative or liberal archbishop, promotional efforts could be either limited in geographical scope and oriented to straightforward reading and writing, or they could cover wide areas and combine literacy with liberation theology, consciousness raising, creation of cooperatives, and leadership development. Expansion of the liberal movement introduced strains within the Church hierarchy, and between the Church and the government, but the Church kept gaining ground. In areas where the movement operated freely, literacy rates of 80 to 90 percent became common. The influence of the liberal elements of the Church, which also worked its way through public primary and secondary schools run by the Church, was not so much to increase the number of Creole readers and writers, but to give the language semiofficial sanction as a valid language. Church leaders, however, did not dispute the position of French as the ideal pathway to enlightenment. They too were part of Haiti's political class.

These processes yielded what many reformers saw as a politically valid constituency that would support their arguments for a change in the language of instruction, and for a change in the substance of curricula. Early off the mark was an effort in 1976 by the IDB to work with the Ministry of Agriculture, then in charge of rural education, in introducing a vocationally oriented curriculum to public primary schools in rural areas. The incentive was a $9.6 million loan, primarily for construction and rehabilitation of schools. This effort quickly went nowhere. The proposed curriculum, reminiscent of the U.S. occupation, was unpopular within the ministry.[30] In 1978 the government transferred authority for rural education to the Ministry of Education, which for the previous two years had been working with the UN family, particularly the World Bank, in developing new educational strategies. With the World Bank assuming foreign-assistance dominion over the Ministry of Education, and through the ministry over primary education, the IDB withdrew from matters of curriculum and refocused attention on financing facilities, equipment, and materials. With about $1 million unaccounted for of $3 million disbursed by 1984, the IDB project came to a grinding halt as it tried to develop means of lending that would result in a less than 33 percent rate of fund disappearance.[31]

The World Bank was somewhat more successful. Linking with reformist tendencies within the Ministry of Education in 1976, it embarked the government on an ambitious twelve-year, $55 million program to completely reorient the direction of primary education (IIR, 1985: 5.85–88). In the first of four stages (1976–82), schools were built and UNESCO and the UNDP provided assistance in the matter of statistics and administration. During the second stage (1978–83), more schools were built and teacher training, development of materials, evaluation exercises, and radio education supported. Attention during the third phase (1983–86) was shifted to curriculum development, teacher training, supervision, and other direct pedagogical elements. The largest component of plans for the fourth stage (1985–88), was to finance the spread of change over the whole country.

This program had four essential features (De Regt, 1984: 126–30). One was integration of public education under one roof. As mentioned, this happened in 1978. A second feature was a law making Creole the principal language of primary instruction. This also was implemented in 1978. A third was development and testing of new curricula between 1978 and 1982, and the fourth was implementation and diffusion of the new educational system beginning in 1982. The attributes of the new system included a curriculum stressing only four subjects in early grades (reading, writing, numbers, and environmental science); automatic promotion from grade one to two and three to four; introduction of a teacher charter giving professional status to instructors; new teaching methods; and improved school supervision and inspection.

All this was supposed to make the primary schooling industry more effective in using resources to produce higher promotion and graduation rates. Automatic promotion, for example, would almost certainly assure lower dropout rates after grades one and three, and increases in the numbers of students receiving at least two or four years of progressive instruction. Also, where language rather than teacher quality was the primary barrier to learning, levels of knowledge absorption would rise. Even if students did not progress beyond grades two or four, a much higher proportion of them would become literate in Creole before dropping out than under the old curriculum. The Teacher Charter, about which I will say more later, teacher training, and improved supervision and inspection were all to make the industry even more effective. Books, however, remained the responsibility of parents, and the dress code remained in place as a principal method of keeping demand in check.

This "Reform" as it was called, covering both public and private instruction, was in scale and proposed speed nothing less than revolutionary. No change of such magnitude potentially affecting so many students had ever been contemplated, let alone implemented, in Haitian education. The undertaking ran into numerous technical, financial, managerial, and human difficulties (i.e., principally teacher and student motivation) that, as happened with most large-scale projects in Haiti, slowed intended progress on all fronts (De Regt, 1984: 130–34). Duplicating the experience of the IDB, these difficulties included $2 to $3 million of $12 million loaned by the Bank having somehow gone astray by 1985.[32] But the pedagogical characteristics of schooling were unlikely to return to their previous states.

The most pertinent difficulty was caused by factional politics. The tendency of governments in Haiti to make declarations without necessarily intending to implement them was sufficiently engrained in popular belief that, when Creole became the official language of instruction in 1978, the matter caused only a minor stir. Actual implementation in 1982 became the subject of intense debate. Some parties to the debate suggested that it transcended pedagogy (De Regt, 1984: 132). The debate supposedly had to do with the effect of Creole, as the language of instruction, upon the existing social and economic order. In their view, opponents of the Reform wished to maintain the social filtering and stratification-maintenance functions of schooling, while proponents wished to break down these functions and thereby improve chances of social and economic mobility to a wider spectrum of the population. This interpretation may have been valid. Certainly there were many concerned educators and parents with high and low incomes who worried that the Reform would create a two-tiered schooling system in which traditional instruction would remain for schools serving the wealthy while the new curriculum served everyone else.[33] They opposed the Reform because it seemed to reinforce rather than erode the existing order. As far as they were concerned, mastery of French was the only demonstrated road to progress, and Creole, historically, led nowhere. Belief in the historical order of things was very strong and permeated all segments of society. In a sense, many of the people who were supposed to benefit from the Reform were the ones who opposed it. In this context, the Ministry of Education had to promise, without conviction since there was no proof to sustain the claim, that introduction of Creole in grades one to four would lead to a "passage" to French in later grades.[34]

But the debate had other dimensions as well. The 1978–82 testing period for the new curriculum was very short. Outcomes in terms of how students might fare in later grades, or what their chances to enter secondary schools (as yet unaffected by the Reform) might be, or what they might accomplish in the world of work after completing all or some grades of primary school, were unknown. The traditional system gave each child a one in three chance of completing primary studies, a one in five chance of entering secondary school, and a one in seven chance of completing secondary school. Low as they were, these probabilities were higher than the lottery. Notwithstanding all the promises made by reformers about the utility of literacy and numeracy, probabilities associated with the Reform were not yet calculable. The risk reformers were asking parents to take were enormous, and parents, especially those with limited resources, were naturally resistant to acceptance of an untried and untested technology.

Educators, even reform-minded ones, shared the reticence of parents. In addition, they objected to the lack of democratic practice in an area that had traditionally been democratic, at least inside the political class. The basic elements of the Reform had been devised by a handful of local and expatriate educational experts, had been discussed within the Ministry of Education among the experts, public administrators, and World Bank, UNESCO, and UNDP technicians, and had then been thrust upon society in an authoritarian manner. Teachers, schoolmasters, school-system administrators, and parents were never party to formulation of the Reform. The traditional education system at least had a central theme that allowed each school some latitude for implementation based on teacher quality and experience, differences among students, availability of resources, and so on. The Reform had no such flexibility. It was a technocratic–bureaucratic concoction that still needed considerable revision and testing.

These and other sources of resistance slowed progress, but the Reform proceeded apace with objectors resigning themselves to having to come to terms with it. But at the end of 1985, the debate heated up once more. The first cohort of students in schools reformed in 1982–83 were entering the fourth grade, and the government for the first time published textbooks for the fifth and sixth grades. The new books were extensions of fourth-grade texts, and nowhere in them was there evidence of the beginning of the promised "passage" to French. Government deceit, common in other areas, was uncommon in matters of education. Many in the middle class that had brought François Duvalier to power, that had subsequently benefited from broadened access for their children to public education, and that had grown in size and influence over thirty years, were now convinced that the regime no longer attended to their interests. The Reform, or, more precisely, the method by which the government introduced it, may not have been a decisive factor in ending the Duvalier administration but it was certainly one of the more serious of the family's many political blunders in the 1980s.

An interesting latecomer to matters of school quality was USAID. Aside from support for a short-lived effort in the mid-1950s to improve rural schools, for school feeding programs, for preschool nutrition and education programs, and for research on the relative learning rates of rural children in traditional French and new Creole classes (which showed the superiority of the latter), the U.S. government generally stayed out of Haitian education until 1984 (USAID, 1982a: 55–58; 1984a: 10). Reasons for lack of interest may have included the belief that assistance to education might prove politically sensitive, given the experience of the occupation, that U.S. expertise was ill-adapted to addressing curricula steeped in the French tradition, that involvement of the IDB, World Bank, UNESCO, UNDP, OAS, France, and Canada left little scope for additional intervention, or that education was not a productive way to use foreign aid. Whatever the source of prior lack of interest, or new interest, in 1984 USAID commissioned a study of the entire educational structure with a view toward perhaps doing more in the area of primary schooling, through such action to have an impact on the country's high rate of illiteracy, and through such impact to render the agency's long-term assistance strategy for poverty alleviation more effective.

The study's pertinent findings were that most primary schooling was private, that most private schools were neither supporting nor adopting the Reform, and that they had little tangible incentive to do so (IIR, 1985: 1.3–4). The study's basic implication was that USAID was in an ideal position to provide necessary incentives and thereby assist in the diffusion of the presumed benefits of the Reform. USAID's unique position with respect to private schooling stemmed in part from its established relationship with the schools through feeding programs, and in part from the new U.S. foreign–aid policy putting emphasis on support for private–sector development. Other multilateral and bilateral assistance organizations could not or would not deal with private schools on a large–scale basis except through the government. Conservative creators of the private–sector emphasis in Washington could not have imagined that in Haiti it would mean direct assistance to Protestant and Catholic schools, or to support of the liberal, antiimperialist, anticapitalist, and antiDuvalier movement in the Catholic church, but that is what happened.

The time period between initial dissemination of the study's principal findings in December 1984 to initiation of support for the first group of private schools in June 1986 was a remarkably short eighteen months.[35] The political processes at work during those eighteen months were even more remarkable. One important process had to do with creating an institutional framework for the assistance project. Private schools operated as independent units or as independent groups attached to different Protestant denominations, different dioceses, and different Catholic orders.[36] Somehow or other these various clusters had to come together in some organized fashion. The Protestants organized themselves very quickly into an association with a board representing the most important and interested denominations. The Catholics were slower. Hierarchical decision making within the Church was cumbersome, and this tended to delay its response to USAID's request for a statement of interest in project participation and for an organizational framework through which to design and implement the project.

But other factors were equally important. Certain church leaders were busy unseating the government, addressing internal dissent caused by the unseating effort, responding to government demands to cease and desist from sedition, and struggling to make ends meet as the government countered with cutbacks in subsidies to public Catholic schools in which students and teachers were leading the assault on the regime. Dealing with USAID was low on the list of their priorities. There was also a matter of suspicion. In general, Church leaders believed that USAID was a pro–Protestant agency which not only gave preferential service to non–Catholic schools in its school feeding program, but also supported Protestant efforts at evangelization that not only undermined Catholicism but also supposedly steered the population away from transformative social action. More to the point, the U.S. government sustained the Duvaliers, the most recent explicit example having been suppression, through emergency deliveries of grain requested by the government, of popular unrest catalyzed by food shortages in 1983. Was it not curious, they asked, that USAID should interest itself in Catholic education at the very moment that students and teachers in Catholic schools were once again at the forefront of political action and being shot as a result?[37] A good question.

Somehow, a combination of considerable legwork and discussion by two staff members of the USAID mission in Port–au–Prince and one visiting american consultant who spoke better French than most of the clergy overcame much of the resistance even before the fall of the government. The Catholics would participate in the project, and would organize themselves for this purpose.

An important element in cultivating both Catholic and Protestant involvement, a second political process of interest, was USAID's retreat from early notions concerning project design. On the matter of the Reform, for example, the original idea had been to provide incentives for adoption of the government's program. However, almost all the Protestant and Catholic participants in the discussions with USAID objected to the Reform for the reasons outlined earlier. They wanted to collaborate in developing alternative methods of achieving the Reform's goals, including development of their own curricula, pedagogical methods, teacher training techniques, books, and so forth. In particular, they asserted that the immediate issue with respect to primary school quality was not language or curriculum, but rather the abilities and motivations of teachers with respect to instruction of any subject.[38]

USAID eventually backed away from almost all its early ideas, and replaced them with conditions concerning acceptable and unacceptable uses of funds, and anticipated outcomes of any combination of expenditures. That is, the way in which private schools might choose to use funds was, within limits, up to the Protestant and Catholic organizations to decide in a democratic way. The organizations' contractual obligations to USAID in exchange for support were clear demonstration that participating schools would show substantial increases in promotion rates, decreases in retention and dropout rates, and measurable gains in literacy and other indicators of learning within five or six years.

Other processes included the making of decisions about the level of government involvement in the project, degrees of collaboration between Protestants and Catholics who did not have a history of close collaboration, allocation of resources between and within the two groups, selection criteria for schools, and several additional matters. The issues gradually sorted themselves out, and in June 1986 teams made up of one Protestant and one Catholic educator began to pick schools for assistance. The $20 million grant would provide support over six years for upgrading a total of perhaps 350 schools containing 1800 teachers and would affect about 70,000 students per year. The coverage of 15 percent of teachers and students was small, but if the experiment proved itself, USAID mission staff in

Port–au–Prince during 1986 believed that further support would be forthcoming. Besides implementation and financial control difficulties that would normally be expected to hamper progress, the only major foreseeable problems were what might happen if conservative tendencies in Washington caught wind of educational happenings in Haiti, and what attitude Haiti's new government might have toward its USAID ally while the ally was offering support to Protestants and Catholics who in many instances were only slightly less opposed to the new regime than they were to the old one.[39]

Teachers

The perceived problem about teachers, in 1985 as it was in 1895, was about their qualifications to teach. Many observers seemed to believe that only graduates of teacher training institutions, and perhaps upper secondary certificate holders, had whatever it took to make classroom instruction effective. Using this criterion, observers naturally lamented the fact that so few primary instructors were properly qualified, and the tendency for the share of such teachers to decline over time (e.g. Lundahl, 1979: 488–89). Thus, according to one recent report, quality of schooling had deteriorated because the share of qualified teachers in the country fell from 50 percent in 1975 to 27 percent in 1981 (De Regt, 1984: 123–24). The situation was better in urban areas, where 38.3 percent of public teachers and 28.5 percent of private ones met the grade of quality in 1983 (table 6.4). But even urban areas were subject to deterioration. The share of urban private teachers with qualification had been 31.5 percent in 1981, implying a 12 percent drop in quality in only two years.

Ideas about stemming and perhaps reversing this apparent degeneration of quality focused on three interventions. One was to ascribe professional status to the teaching profession. Tradition, as inscribed in Haiti's first Constitution, gave everyone the right to teach. Quality control was up to parents and schoolmasters, and rates of remuneration were left to market supply and demand conditions. But 150 years of pressure by many teachers and local and expatriate (particularly World Bank) reformers to reify the status of the occupation finally convinced government to produce a teacher charter in 1984 as part of the Reform. The charter made teaching a formally recognized profession, and spelled out explicit qualification requirements, procedures for recruitment, selection, posting, and promotion, and the duties and responsibilities of instructors. Under the charter, implicitly if not always explicitly, teachers were not supposed to take bribes to sell uniform textiles, or to subcontract others to fill in for them at half their salary while they took other jobs. In laying out a career path and a

TABLE 6.4
Educational Attainment of Urban Primary School Teachers, 1981 and 1983

	SHARE OF TEACHERS IN			
		Private Schools		
Educational Attainment	**Public Schools 1983 (%)**	**1983 (%)**	**1981 (%)**	**Teacher Salaries in Private Schools 1981 (U.S. $)**
Primary completion (CEP)	0.8	7.0	4.7	32
Lower secondary, one year (6iéme)	1.1	4.4	2.3	33
Lower secondary, two years (5iéme)	2.1	8.7	7.8	43
Lower secondary, three years (4iéme)	7.6	16.1	12.2	44
Lower secondary, four years (3iéme)	16.8	17.0	15.8	49
Lower secondary, certificate (B.E.)	20.0	7.3	11.4	58
Upper secondary, one year (2iéme)	13.3	11.0	14.3	48
Upper secondary, certificate (rheto/philo)[a]	15.8	22.4	26.7	62
Teacher training certificate (normale)[a]	22.5	6.1	4.8	50
TOTAL (average)	100.0	100.0	100.0	(51)
Total number of teachers	3,450	6,500	4,445	
Number of "qualified" teachers	1,320	1,855	1,400	
("qualified" as % of total)	(38.3)	(28.5)	(31.5)	

Sources: IIR (1985) and UNESCO (1981).

[a] Level of educational attainment assumed by government to qualify individuals as teachers.

salary structure differentiated by years of service and qualifications, the charter was also supposed to provide incentive for certified teachers to remain within the profession.

By drawing out the meaning of qualification, the Charter disqualified 75 to 80 percent of Haiti's teachers. In so doing it created a professional elite where none had existed before, and, for the majority of teachers, produced a status–related incentive for them to go back to school, a difficult thing to do when they had families to support and no schools to go to after working hours; or to leave the occupation, also difficult in an economy offering only limited opportunities for wages equivalent to those they received for half–days of work; or to lower their levels of motivation and effort in their teaching work. The charter might have the desired effect of increasing the share of certified instructors in the long term, but in the short term might yield a drop rather than a rise in quality.

The second intervention was to raise teacher salaries. The purpose of such action was to make earnings more competitive in the job market; to lower incentives for teachers to subcontract their jobs, to make extra money from parents, or to take second jobs in afternoons instead of preparing for class the next day (including teaching or running irregular schools); and to raise the opportunity costs associated with losing a teaching post for inadequate performance. In 1979 the government raised public school salaries to $100 per month, a rise of $10 to $40 per instructor. The Teacher Charter called for subsequent raises based on experience, but until 1986 salaries remained the same as in 1979. Although the new government found funds to raise teacher salaries in 1986, further increases in the near term without corresponding layoffs and a drop in the number of public school teachers seemed unlikely.

Salaries in the private sector were unaffected by the 1979 increase in public wages. In 1980 the monthly average salary of a private school teacher in urban areas was $51, considerably higher than the rural average of $38, but still only half the public rate (table 6.4). By 1985 the responsiveness of private schools to market pressures narrowed the public–private average differential to $20 to $30. But these teachers also wanted more, at least as much as public school teachers, and various groups attached to several Protestant missions began work stoppages in 1986. The missions, facing their own fiscal crises as sponsorship funds shifted out of education, were not in a good position to raise salaries without cutting down on numbers of teachers.

Lowering the number of public and private teachers was hard, however. It presented the potential political problem of perceived unemployment of educated people. It also presented the problem of parental protest if the consequence of teacher layoffs resulted in school closings. Therefore, even if some layoffs were to occur, the direction of forces seemed to be toward a decrease of teachers without a corresponding drop in enrollments, an increase in student–teacher ratios, and if such ratios influenced quality of instruction, a decrease in the quality of schooling, at least over the short term.

The third intervention to improve quality of instruction was in–service training of teachers. Such training was irregular and on the whole negligible before 1976. Implementation of the Reform demanded in–service training, and in 1981, with World Bank and OAS support the government launched itself into the formidable task of training 13,000 teachers by 1986. At the end of 1984, some 8000 teachers, for the most part public school instructors, had participated to some extent in training sessions (IIR, 1985: 7.8) Because the purpose of the training was to acquaint teachers with Reform principles and materials, the effort did little to add substance or motivation to their pedagogical skills. In 1984 the government began to experiment with a more intensive kind of training. Using radio during the academic term and in–house seminars during vacation periods, the new program was to permit teachers with at least ten years of schooling (which excluded about 15 percent of urban public and 40 percent of urban private teachers) to work toward obtaining a special teaching certificate. With such certificates teachers would be eligible for the rights and privileges of the Teacher Charter, and they therefore presumably had incentive to work hard and pass the qualifying examination. Unfortunately, trainers were not that much more qualified or motivated than trainees, and radio–dependent training had yet to prove itself a useful technology in Haiti. This program was more or less stagnant in 1986.

In the meantime, the USAID project was gradually gathering momentum with the private sector, and its organizers were beginning to select the first trainees for what was supposed to result in the retraining of 1800 teachers and schoolmasters by 1992. In this instance, whole schools qualified for support based on their prior performance. The planned incentive for teachers was a three–stage bribe. The first was payment of a "per diem" of $5 per day while they attended class. Teachers could usually manage to pocket $2 to $3 per day, and thus earn a substantial summer salary. The second was a "scholarship" of $100 paid upon satisfactory completion of all training requirements. The third was a "performance incentive grant" equal to 25 percent of their annual salaries and payable two and five years after training as an encouragement for the teachers to translate training into classroom practice that the project would monitor closely.

Besides the manner in which the project's "incentives" seemed to blend with the economic (and political) realities of teaching in Haiti, an interesting feature of the project's design was that selection for training depended on actual prior performance in the classroom rather than on a teacher's level of educational attainment. Evidence might later show that attainment and quality of instruction went hand in hand, but in the early stages of the project such association was not presumed.

For whatever length of time this project might be able to maintain a distinction between certification and quality, the making of the distinction was important because it was the first time that a major effort at educational upgrading did not insist that what made teachers good was complete or almost complete secondary education.[40]

This departure from locally accepted norms about criteria for measuring teacher quality was long overdue for several reasons. One was that the challenge facing a student in proceeding beyond the first grade was much more formidable than primary school completion, and primary completion was much more difficult than secondary school completion. Because of these difficulties, anyone with a grade–two education, or perhaps with primary completion, was likely to be as qualified to teach as a secondary school graduate.

A second reason was that if teaching quality was low in Haiti, certificate holders were presumably the product of prior low quality in primary and secondary schools. The difference between teachers with primary and secondary certificates was therefore four to six years of supposedly inadequate learning, which might or might not make any difference in upgrading instruction in the first grade and in increasing promotion rates to the second.

Similarly, a third reason was that historical biases in school promotion meant that most teachers with secondary certificates were products of urban higher–income strata, the political class. If similarity in social and economic backgrounds between teachers and students was conducive to learning, then most secondary school graduates were less appropriate in the classroom than primary graduates.

The general thrust of these arguments is that there was little evidence available to connect educational attainment of teachers with what happened in a classroom, with the probability of their taxing parents or accepting bribes to give preferential access to certain students, or with their frequent habit of subcontracting their teaching jobs to friends and relatives. But over and above such matters, a fourth reason was that the purpose of schooling remained ambiguous. Besides the unsettled matter of curricula, which by automatic promotion and Creolization temporarily removed clear measures of pedagogical achievement and rendered outcome measures of teacher performance very unclear, there was the question of whether a school was primarily or exclusively a feeding center, an evangelization center, a social insurance agency, a taxation mechanism, or a place where a child was supposed to learn something.

In this context the perceived decline in teacher quality in recent years may have been a fiction. For example, while the share of certified private teachers indicated in table 6.4 did drop from 31.5 percent in 1981 to 28.5 percent in 1983, the absolute number of such urban teachers rose by 32 percent, from 1400 to 1855. The mathematical problem was that the total number of teachers expanded by 46 percent during the same interval. If, for the sake of argument, half the schools were not schools, then half of all teachers were overqualified for their jobs. Or, more to the point, they were not teachers. The only way to determine the primary purpose of schools was to visit them with a predisposition not to say that they were of low quality, but rather with a predisposition to say that they were not schools. Until USAID project entered the scene, this predisposition was not widespread.

Futures

After thirty–five years of apparent overinvestment, primary schooling in 1986 was like an overinflated inner tube about to burst, or about to pop its valve and deflate less dramatically. Quantities of schools, teachers, and students exaggerated the level of domestic resources available to sustain them and for the most part seemed dependent on continued flows of food, remittances, PVO expenditures, and sponsorship program funds. Food support was not likely to decline in an imminent future, but curtailment of emigration, especially that of lower–income segments, and reorientation of PVO and sponsorship support, were unlikely to be counterbalanced by World Bank and USAID projects that, in any event, were financing qualitative rather than quantitative changes.

From a technological perspective, quality might now have a better chance of catching up to quantity, but from political and economic perspectives the circumstance of primary schooling was unstable. Depending on the speed of contraction, if in fact there was to be a contraction, political issues would turn on teachers becoming the "educated unemployed" that worried all governments of Haiti (except those that wisely chose to ignore education), on parents with students becoming frustrated at the closure of schools and loss of the one possibility they could hope for in terms of advancement of offspring, on parents without students but planning ahead similarly losing hope, on numbers of secondary school graduates unable to find work because of the end of the schooling industry's capacity to absorb a significant share of them, on numbers of primary school students forced to leave class and enter an already highly competitive labor market, and on the increased rate of labor market entry caused by diversion of younger age groups away from schools. Schooling had been a major industry in Port-au-Prince, growing by 6000 students annually in recent years, and thereby temporarily slowing the rate of growth of the urban labor force by perhaps 1000 to 2000 workers a year, or a reduction of about 10 percent of what the growth rate might have been without the industry's extraordinary expansion. Unless compensated for by expansion in other urban sectors, there was risk of noticeable intensification of labor market competition and downward pressure on earnings and income.

Foresight and hindsight being equally imprecise in matters of politics and economics, there was no telling how adjustments to industrial decline might act themselves out in the near future, or how quality improvements might contribute to more democratic practice, to expansion of the political class, or to economic growth in the longer term. A certain thing was that the decade had witnessed an important drama among various factions of the political class. Opinions, assumptions, and theories about education held by many Haitian reformers and expatriate experts, unlike the experiences of their counterparts concerned with issues of employment, food, water, and shelter, had been challenged by the indirect objects of their will. To be sure, these objects—parents, teachers, education system administrators, and others with vital self-interests in matters of education—were for the most part of the political class. But their resistance to the imperialism of individual and organizational expertise, a resistance based in large measure on arguments that seemed no less sound than those of the experts and reformers, was a resistance that appeared to reflect the interests of parents in the ordinary class who worried about the educational component of schooling. This was a rare moment of shared interest between resisting factions of the political class and the ordinary class; a coincidence of a natural sort flowing out of concerns by all parents for the well-being of their children.

Education being too ambiguous a concept and process to sustain claims of expertise in places like Haiti, questions about what the "correct" policies or programs should have been, or should be, were unimportant, perhaps even irrelevant. The essence of the drama was not about policy but rather about the political dynamics which constructed and reconstructed policy. In this context, one of the most important political events in the struggle among factions may have been the process by which the USAID project amended and adapted itself to political circumstances while still maintaining sight of its basic outcome objectives. That is, individual and organizational needs, including the need to maintain repute, credibility, and other variables entering the calculus of survival did not prohibit adaptation. The rare kind of expertise exhibited by USAID mission staff and consultants, an expertise desperately needed in matters of food and water, was for better or worse the capacity to listen, to devolve responsibility for appropriate knowledge to the Haitians and PVO expatriates directly involved with parents and students in the education process, and to accept the added personal and organizational risks that such a strategy entailed. Whatever might transpire in the project, it constituted a certain kind of empirical proof that the dubious behaviors of the political class, as I have described them in the last four chapters, were not absolute necessities.

For the present, however, for all the drama of a decade or more of substantial change in the matter of schooling, the situation of ordinary families such as those in St. Martin were much the same in 1986 as they had been in 1976. Uniforms and shoes needed buying. Payments to schoolmasters, teachers, ex–Macoutes, and to the replacements of defrocked Macoutes were still required for access to cheap schools, food, and foster parents. The taxes remained, and together with the constant need to purchase all manner of other things basic to survival, what also remained was reliance on credit as a means to pay for them when circumstances demanded.

Notes

1. This introductory material, through the end of the U.S. occupation of Haiti, extracts names, dates, data, and to a lesser extent, interpretation, from Logan (1930).
2. The Church therefore operated two types of schools. One, heavily supported with public funds, were state or public schools. The other, supported to a lesser extent or not at all by the state, were private Catholic schools.
3. The enrollment ratio, expressed either as a decimalized number (0.10) or as a percentage (10 percent), is the ratio of students to the school–age population theoretically supposed to be in a certain level of schooling. This "gross" ratio, because it neglects the age structure of students, tends to overestimate the share of the school–age population actually in school (e.g., it includes students who are younger or older than the bracket specified by the school–age group). A "net" ratio divides students in specific age groups by the population in the same age group, and thereby arrives at a more accurate indication of enrollment. In recent years estimates have suggested that for Haitian primary education the net ratio is about 67 percent of the gross ratio.
4. That is, reformers did not have evidence to indicate which of the proposed changes in language, curricula, teachers, facilities, or equipment would in fact make a difference in learning achievement. Their reform suggestions were about inputs unrelated to probable outcomes.
5. The enrollment ratio of 0.13 for 1930 is from Rotberg (1971: 310).
6. The allocation of new teaching positions, as for all government jobs, was always a part of the political patronage system in Haiti. How patronage affected the overall marginal quality of teaching is unknown. It could as readily lead to an improvement in quality as to a decline, depending on the characteristics of new

appointees relative to the existing teaching force. Turnover under Duvalier was apparently so extensive that even if new appointees had training similar to outgoing teachers, the loss of experienced teachers would have implied a drop in quality.

7. Since the essence of the transformation was to create a Black elite or middle class, education for current and prospective members of that group was essential (Wingfield and Parenton, 1965: 343).
8. According to government statistics in IIR (1985: 5.48), numbers of urban public primary teachers in 1976, 1981, and 1983 were 3310, 3191, and 3448, and for public rural teachers, 1760, 2168, and 2195. Although there may have been some movement in teachers from urban to rural areas, the decrease in urban and increase in rural instructors was largely the effect of shifting resources. In urban areas teachers who retired or left their jobs were not always replaced, while in rural areas there was an increase in the rate of new appointments. These shifts in resources were part of the government's obligations with respect to IDB and World Bank projects in support of expanded rural education.
9. IIR (1985: 2.150). "Individual" rates of return refer to "private" as distinct from "social" returns.
10. Psacharopoulos (1980: 84) reported these returns for Ethiopia, Ghana, Kenya, and Nigeria.
11. Psacharopoulos (1980: 89) for Ethiopia and Kenya.
12. This assumption did not necessarily mean that parents had to believe that the substance of instruction would influence future earnings. The hypothesis that children with more years of school attendance will generally obtain higher incomes in their later lives than children with fewer years, supported by considerable evidence like that in Psacharopoulos (1980), was all that was required. Whether the cause of this association was "human" capitalization or productivity enhancement resulting from acquisition of tangible "knowledge," social filtering and screening, creation of monopoly rents for limited-entry occupations and certificate holders, of inculcation of marketable behavior patterns, or of other similar interpretations reviewed briefly by Lundahl (1979: 453–55), was immaterial. All that was required was that parents not believe that education was a mechanism for maintaining or reinforcing existing systems of social stratification. In this case, the filter was impermeable and education was irrelevant since school achievement and future earnings depended entirely on the prior social and economic status of parents.
13. Three adolescents in two families were in secondary school.
14. Government statistics in IIR (1985: 5.4). The number rose to 770,000 in 1984.
15. The cost structure for a $7.00 outlay for uniforms and shoes in Port-au-Prince, with comparable retail prices (net of duties) for Chinese products that I inquired about in Canada in 1976, was as follows: shoes $2.50 (Canada price $1.75); textile $3.50 (Canada price $2.30); and tailoring $1.00. The share of marketing costs in Canadian retail prices was considerably higher than in Haiti. On the other hand, the larger volume of imports to Canada would have lowered landed costs relative to Haiti. The $1.95 differential in prices for shoes and textiles might therefore have exaggerated the size of the implicit tax for inefficiency. But an estimate of $1.00 in tax would not have been too far off the mark.
16. Since a young child consumed less food than an adult, its earning or contribution to earning of $0.05 to $0.10 per day would have been a productive use of labor.

17. Intermediation prices, perhaps reflecting strong competition among intermediaries, were relatively low in 1985. In two areas I visited, assured adoption could be had for $20 to $30 if a family qualified under selection criteria used by sponsorship programs.
18. The IIR (1985: 2.149–52) used the short–form or shortcut method of calculating the rate of return. For a brief review of this method, see Psacharopoulos (1980: 80–82).
19. Schools operated for twenty days per month and five hours per day, or a total of 100 hours per month. The monthly cost of $1.50 per child in public schools and $3.60 in private schools therefore yielded the 1.5 to 3.6 cents–per–hour range.
20. In theory, the ration increased to 900–950 calories by 1986.
21. That is, a rate of return approaching infinity for the first two or three years of schooling when income effects of food and sponsorship exceeded opportunity costs of foregone earnings of a child. Actually, when costs are zero or less, the rate of return model is inapplicable.
22. Data obtained from the USAID mission in Port–au–Prince.
23. See chapter 1 for discussion of PVOs in Haiti.
24. Tuition data and data concerning sponsorship programs come from interviews I conducted and unpublished material I collected at the end of 1985.
25. This did not include students in schools subsidized by private means other than child sponsorship.
26. See note 12, above.
27. This is not to suggest that feeding or evangelization were inappropriate. The pertinent issue was whether uniforms, books, teachers, bribes, and so forth were really necessary where the purpose of the activity was eating or praying.
28. Most of the tracts and pamphlets in circulation denouncing the government in 1985 and 1986 were in Creole.
29. Data from an unpublished USAID survey conducted in 1985.
30. In 1976 I worked with the Interamerican Institute of Agricultural Sciences (IICA) to prepare this project for the IDB. Unpopularity was only partially related to historical experience within the country. Educators in the ministry often waved copies of scholarly works like that of Foster (1966) to counter the claims of IICA planners that what Haiti needed was an all–out, massive effort at vocational training. Following Foster's suggestion, they preferred a range of small–scale experiments to test what different changes could do before undertaking a full–scale reform. They also pointed out, as did Lockheed, Jamison, and Lau (1980: 61) with more in the way of empirical support several years later, that vocational training oriented to agricultural development was not likely to yield results in the absence of "modernizing" agricultural environments. All that the IDB's curriculum might accomplish was an increase in out–migration from rural areas.
31. The disappearance, according to IDB informants, was partly graft, in the form of billings for materials and labor never supplied but paid for in any event, partly theft of materials and overbillings connected with kickbacks, and partly poor accounting for legitimate disbursements. The IDB must have resolved the problem, or decided that it was not the Bank's problem since the government would eventually have to reimburse the loan no matter what the destination of funds. It announced an $11.9 million revised loan in 1985 (IDB, 1985).
32. The disappearance, according to the World Bank project's staff in Haiti, was of the same character as I described for the IDB in note 31, above.

33. This description of various objections to the Reform builds on interviews I held, and on meetings I attended, in which educators spelled them out in considerable detail.
34. Few objected to the general principles of the Reform syllabus. The emphasis on reading, writing, numbers, and science, as an introduction to what was supposed to become a general education, was fine. The problem was that unless a student progressed to French (or English), prospects for a general education later on were slim because books in Creole were extremely scarce. Parents and educators always looked at the long term even though probabilities that many students would stay in school for a long time were not high.
35. This description of the private–sector schooling assistance project flows from my participation in it during 1985, and from subsequent discussions with key participants in 1986.
36. For–profit lay or secular schools and nonprofit community schools, were scheduled for support in the early days of project design, but the idea was postponed because of the complexity of organizing even the supposedly "organized" Protestant and Catholic schools.
37. The death of three students, killed by security forces at their school in Gonaives in November 1985, rekindled a wave of student protest that eventually expanded to other segments of the urban population and contributed to the departure of the Duvaliers. Many of the key meetings between USAID and the Church were held in November and December 1985.
38. Attempting to strengthen their arguments about the relative unimportance of language in roundabout fashion, some educators referred to a World Bank review of language choice in primary education that showed beyond a shadow of doubt that relationships between first or second languages in school and educational achievement were absolutely uncertain (i.e., Dutcher, 1982).
39. The principal coordinator of the Protestant association working with USAID on the project became minister of education in the new government during 1986. But officials in government and regimes in control of government are separable entities in Haiti.
40. Heynemann and Loxley (1983) provided substantial support for the hypothesis that school and teacher quality can make a significant difference in learning achievement in developing countries. Although educational attainment proved useful as one indicator of teacher quality in some countries, there were many other indicators that often seemed equally or more important. These included years of experience, proximity of teacher's place of origin to a school, teacher's work enthusiasm, use of in–class discussion, level of homework assignments, time spent on class preparation, teacher's age, and so on.

7

Credit

Ordinary people in rural and urban areas of Haiti had what appeared to be a very good sense of the tangible difference between productive and nonproductive uses of available resources, and of the considerable importance of emphasizing the former relative to the latter for purposes of maximizing earnings and survival. Women operating the country's agricultural marketing system, for example, held the concept of (productive) capital in such high regard that they gave it a special name, "mother money." They also followed an explicit code of conduct with respect to its management. One of the code's five principles required that labor substitute for capital whenever possible. A second called for traders to maximize the share of resources used productively relative to the share used nonproductively in financing final consumption. A third principle required them to maintain capital in use, that is, to never keep resources idle or trapped in uses that were less than fully productive. Fourth, traders should strive to maximize capital accumulation, not for the purpose of eventually financing consumption, but rather for the purpose of increasing their shares of market demand. Finally, they should be vigilant and persistent in directing and redirecting capital to areas of greatest scarcity in order to maximize returns (Mintz, 1964: 261–65). The behavior of traders and manufacturers in St. Martin also seemed to conform to this code. In fact, almost all households in the neighborhood conformed to it in their daily activities whether or not the activities were market-oriented.

This kind of capitalist consciousness was an important property of the urban economy because it meant that at any given moment the vicissitudes of life and business, such as capturing a fleeting opportunity or defending against misfortune, could cause large numbers of people to actively search for capital as a means of producing either gain or protection.[1] With potential gains from investment being high under conditions of acute poverty, as I have emphasized in chapters 2 to 6, with survival often pushing perceived rates of return toward infinity, and with seekers of capital willing to pay any price for credit so long as it was lower than the advantage to be derived from its use, others with resources and no immediately available methods of generating higher returns, following the principle of directing resources to areas of greatest scarcity, would find advantage in renting some or all of it to the seekers. At another moment, money market roles would reverse, with erstwhile demanders turning into suppliers, and suppliers into demanders.

With modes of capitalist behavior embedded in the culture, resources could flow more or less freely from wherever they happened to be to wherever they could obtain highest known returns.[2] Because such returns could stem as readily from market as from nonmarket production activities, this free competitive market for credit was equally vital to expansion and efficiency enhancement of trade and manufacturing, to more general household economic growth and productivity, and to survival. In this last respect, the credit market served as a private insurance mechanism of last resort. What mattered was not the appearance of the activity to be financed, an issue having to do with inputs and therefore irrelevant, but rather the anticipated rate of return, or outcome of the investment activity.[3]

Demand and Supply

Where family resources were often low relative to the cost of adequate quantities of food, water, pots, buckets, and roofs, and where peculiarities of supply made uniforms, shoes, tuition, and other school requirements short–term investments in survival, rates of return to small increases in one or more of these essential factors could be high. Families in such circumstances were not likely to hold idle cash for long because, in the form of cash, it was much less productive than the inputs for which the families could have exchanged it.[4] At the limit, a penny earned by someone on the street was a penny saved for an hour or two before being invested in a glass or water or a piece of bread. Similarly, returns to marginal additions of capital in trade or manufacturing could sometimes be extraordinarily high when the amount already in use was small relative to labor.

Possibilities for continuous reinvestment of earnings in market and nonmarket production made it improbable that lower–income families would find themselves with cash in hand to meet financing requirements imposed by newfound opportunities to increase efficiency or earnings, or by untoward events such as illness. If the cost of borrowing was less than the opportunity cost of disposing of a productive household asset, of shifting working capital out of current use, or of lowering consumption, these families would have had considerable interest in borrowing to meet financing requirements. Indeed, almost 80 percent of St. Martin households borrowed money during the six–month period preceding my interviews, at interest rates ranging from 15 to 95 percent per month.

In places like St. Martin, the probability of encountering situations demanding such financing were high, and the propensity for families to borrow seemed to reflect not only the frequency of the situations but also perceived costs of borrowing that were lower than alternative methods of financing. Conversely, if the cost of borrowing was lower than alternatives, returns to lending, by extension, were lower than putting it to other uses. Therefore, the lower the level of income available to a family, the more likely it was that it would not hold idle savings for long and that it would borrow, and the less likely that it would lend.

In higher–income families, which in St. Martin meant those with more capital in trade and manufacturing; more wage and other sources of income; adequate levels of food, water, and shelter; sufficient numbers of pots and buckets; and high proportions of children in school, returns to further investment in any of these things were likely to be less than for lower–income households. They were in positions in which further expenditures would seem more like final consumption than productive consumption, in which further investment in market activities would yield relatively small additions to income and productive capacity, and in which the process of making decisions about how to spend income took more time. These families would tend to hold idle cash for longer periods than lower–income households, and although they might also borrow as circumstance warranted, they were often in positions to lend when returns from lending seemed higher than returns from other uses, or from holding idle cash.

My discussions with twenty–seven higher–income households holding cash savings ranging from $2 to over $50 suggested several reasons for the existence of such idle resources. In some cases family members had specific investment project objectives such as wholesale purchase of stocks, tools, longer–term housing, or school uniforms. They were accumulating resources to meet necessary investment thresholds and were keeping them in the form of cash because they had no obvious place to put the funds.[5] In other cases, the presence of cash was transitional. Earnings built up during the peak business period were in use to carry households through a slack season, and again, these families reported that they could not think of more productive ways to use money at the moment. These fund accumulators, cash–flow flow equalizers, and others also said that some of the cash was a precaution against unpredictable events. Borrowing, in their opinion, was expensive, and since the cost of holding cash in the absence of better things to do with it was low, it might eventually serve as a useful cushion for emergencies or as a useful reserve fund for taking advantage of an opportunity. In principle, they had a precautionary demand for money and held cash for that purpose.

In most cases, however, the existence of cash was accidental. Families had recently received spurts of income that exceeded their habitual or permanent patterns of expenditure and had not yet decided what to do with the transitory funds. Cash sat idle as a result of indecision. In the absence of immediately obvious investment possibilities, the opportunity cost of holding it was perhaps the price individuals believed they had to pay in exchange for the time required to obtain adequate information upon which to select an appropriate course of action. Here savings were side effects of time lags between resource receipt and allocation decisions, or more generally, of temporary ignorance lasting from a few days to a few weeks. These families indicated that they might be willing to lend some of the cash for short periods if they could think of no better use for it, and if they knew the borrower well enough to judge whether he or she could repay it. They did lend money from time to time.

Whatever the causes and durations of such savings, at any given moment there existed a pool of relatively unproductive cash scattered across St. Martin awaiting use, while at the same time there was substantial demand to borrow it. Part of the demand derived from the circumstances of lower-income families outlined above. Part of it also derived from higher-income families whose savings were inadequate to meet particular needs, and more commonly, whose needs had arisen after prior savings were already allocated to specific purposes. With sources of supply and sources of demand located next to each other in one area, St. Martin fulfilled the basic prerequisites for establishment of a market for money.[6]

However, in order for the market to have been as active as it was in 1976, to have permitted almost 80 percent of families to borrow within the preceding six months, the price of credit had to be relatively low. In order for the price to appear low there had to have been a large number of competing suppliers who saw the price as attractive for lending. In fact, 34 percent of all credit transactions, and 47 percent of the total value of the transactions, were conducted between families wanting to rent resources and families with temporarily idle resources. Professional moneylenders took care of the balance. In either instance the price of credit was a monthly real interest rate averaging 50 percent for unsecured or large loans, and 20 to 25 percent for secured or small loans. These prices, reflecting scarcity of resources in a very poor region of the economy, were high in comparison to other places. But because scarcity was also the cause of high returns from almost every conceivable area of expenditure, prices were quite reasonable in the context.

The Price of Credit

The price of credit in St. Martin ranged from 15 to 95 percent per month, simple interest. Loan terms, fourteen to ninety days, appeared short but were in fact renewable by mutual consent of borrowers and lenders for periods that could sometimes extend for up to a year.

Although interest rates were somewhat dispersed, they clustered around characteristic means associated with different types of credit sources. One source, carrying a high average rate of 50 percent, was what people called a "usurer." The term was not so much a pejorative as a reference to a commercial moneylender. Loans from usurers were large, averaging $20, and individuals tended to make use of them when alternative sources of such sums were unavailable (table 7.1). Ten percent of the households that had borrowed money relied on usurers, and in all cases they used the loans for specific investment projects in trade or manufacturing. In all but one case households reimbursed the usurer according to the original terms of their contract. In the exceptional case the loan was extended for a month and then repaid with full interest.

Households that relied on usurers, relative to households using other means of credit, had several distinguishing features. Their incomes derived entirely from self-employment earnings. The seasonal variability of income, as measured by the ratio of earnings in the peak season of the annual business cycle to earnings in the slack season, was high. The level of slack season income was quite low, as was the earnings–capital ratio, implying that individual members used relatively large amounts of market capital. This kind of borrowing was recurrent, with traders and manufacturers apparently using a line of credit every season to smooth their production cycles.

Borrowing at 50 percent per month made commercial sense to a household not only when slack season income or other factors made accumulation of savings difficult but also when variations in income caused them to consume part of their capital, or "dissave," for a portion of the year. With a $20 loan, for example, a borrower with a monthly earnings–capital ratio of 1.0 in self-employment could generate a net earning of $20 at the end of a month, return the principal and an interest payment of $10, and still have $10 in retained earnings.[7]

A more common source of unsecured loans was the "friend" (that is, other families with resources on hand). The only apparent differences between a usurer and a friend were that the latter was not a professional moneylender, and that the size of loan tended to be smaller. Whereas usurer credit was based almost exclusively on an assessment of the finan-

TABLE 7.1
Commercial Credit in St. Martin, 1976

	SOURCE OF LOAN				
	"Usurer"[a]	"Friend"[b]	Pawnshop[c]	Borrowers	Nonborrowers
(Number of households)	(7)	(23)	(39)	(69)	(19)
Loan characteristics					
Amount borrowed (U.S. $)	20.00***	10.90***	4.00***	7.90	—
Monthly interest rate (%)	50***	33	25***	30	—
Household income characteristics					
Monthly wage earnings (U.S. $)	0	13.30	19.50	17.25	33.30***
Share of wage earnings in income (%)[d]	0	39**	57**	49	84***
Seasonal income ratio[e]	2.6 **	2.1 **	1.8 **	2.0	1.4 ***
Earnings–capital ratio[f]	1.0 ***	1.5 ***	2.2 ***	1.7	1.3 ***
Low season income (U.S. $)[g]	16.00***	27.00	28.00***	25.50	34.30***
Monthly income per adult (U.S. $)	8.60	9.40	10.40	9.70	11.20

Source: Data from author's survey in St. Martin.

[a] Unsecured loans.

[b] Unsecured loans.

[c] Secured loans.

[d] Household income received from regular wages as share of total income from all sources.

[e] Ratio of average income received in peak season to average income received in slack season.

[f] Ratio of monthly net earnings from trade and manufacturing to value of fixed and working capital used in production of earnings.

[g] Minimum level of monthly income received in slack season.

** Differences between means for indicated sources, or between means of borrowers and nonborrowers, is significant at the 5% level.

***Differences between means for indicated sources, or between means for borrowers and nonborrowers, is significant at the 1% level.

cial viability of proposed investments and a historical record of mutually satisfactory transactions between borrower and lender, credit from friends had the additional property of involving a prior, personal, noncommercial relationship between them.

Loans from a friend generally cost less than usurer loans, 33 percent per month. However, there was a dual credit structure within this category. Larger loans averaging $15.00 carried the same price as usurer loans, 50 percent, while smaller loans averaging $8.50 cost about 25 percent. The difference in the average size of loans, suggesting that demand for larger units of credit was greater relative to supply than smaller units, the constraint on supply being not only a scarcity of lenders with large amounts to loan but also a higher default risk to the lender of larger loans, may have explained the difference in interest rates.

Households borrowing from a friend derived a considerable share of income from regular wages, 39 percent; had lower seasonal variation in income; a higher slack season income than families borrowing from usurers; and a higher earnings–capital ratio, suggesting use of smaller amounts of market capital by individual members. By and large, their earnings streams were more regular, permitting easier management of resources and therefore less recourse to large loans. The purposes for which they borrowed were quite varied. Larger loans seemed closely associated with specific market investments in trade or manufacturing. The purposes of smaller loans, in addition to market investments, included partial finance of such things as additional or replacement cooking pots, buckets, and utensils; advances for monthly rent payments; house repairs; purchase of textiles, shoes, books or other schooling expenditures; medical expenses; burial and marriage expenses; and sending money to relatives for emergencies. Borrowing for these purposes rather than using internal resources made eminent sense. The price of credit for small loans, 25 percent, was inexpensive relative to the financial gains to be derived from most of the investments and, more important, was less than the opportunity cost of drawing resources out of current use. Lowered food consumption, for example, was not an attractive option, and drawing from market resources providing an average earnings–capital ratio of, say, 1.5, or $1.50 per month in net earnings for every dollar in use, would have been irrational when credit was only $0.25 per dollar.

Borrowing from a friend had one disadvantage. It took time to find one with enough money to lend, and more time to come to an agreement on terms. Demand for credit was often instantaneous, and the most common form of credit was a secured loan from a pawnbroker. As a method limiting not only risk but also the use of their services as goods–to–cash conversion facilities, pawnbrokers imposed high collateral requirements. The market value of goods on deposit was almost universally equal to three times the value of loans. Families in St. Martin did not have much in the way of possessions, and loans from pawnbrokers were therefore quite small. They averaged $4, and in half the cases were $2 or less. Things put down as collateral included eating utensils, watches, jewelery, radios, clocks, and other goods with no inherent productive value. Cooking pots, buckets, tools, trade goods, shoes, or books almost never appeared as collateral. The attraction of a relatively low interest rate of 25 percent, a rate paid by almost all borrowers, was not sufficient to offset the decline in production efficiency that loss of inherently useful factors like pots and tools might engender. Families with no possessions other than pots or buckets would not offer them up unless compelled by extremely dire circumstances. At that level it was better to beg than to borrow.[8]

Although table 7.1 suggests that there were some differences between users of pawnshops and users of friends in terms of the share of wages in income, the ratio of peak to slack season income, and the earnings–capital ratio, all of which implied that demand for large loans would not be extensive, the basic difference was that users of pawnshops were not as well connected to acquaintances with money available to lend when they needed it. Borrowing from pawnshops seemed to have touches of urgency attached to it. The most common purpose of borrowing in these instances was for medical costs, principally pharmaceuticals, followed by additions to trade stocks or raw materials. In these latter cases, individuals used pawnshops to finance investments when opportunities presented themselves at short notice or, conversely, when some inopportune market transaction caused an erosion of market capital and a corresponding need for capital replenishment. The last significant use of funds was purchase of larger amounts of grain or charcoal destined for family consumption. In these instances, the interest rate of 25 percent seemed less than the opportunity costs of using internal resources and less than the productive gains to be had from lower unit prices.

However, the collateral requirement that transferred the burden of risk from the lender to the borrower carried a potentially high interest rate. For example, if an individual put up a $15.00 watch as collateral for a $5.00 loan, an act that presumably incurred a relatively low opportunity cost of foregone production, if the loan increased trade capital from $20.00 to $25.00, and if at the same time the average monthly earnings–capital ratio fell from, say, 1.4 to 1.3 (see figure 2.2), the net gain in earnings at the end of one month, $4.50, would be substantial.[9] The individual could combine this gain with $1.75 of the borrowed capital, put together $6.25 in principal and interest to retrieve the watch, and still be left with $23.25, or a 6 percent increase in market capital. But as I discussed in relation to traders and manufacturers in chapter 2, possibilities for quickly increasing sales were limited. Borrowing $5.00 entailed risk because there was the possibility of sales remaining constant, in which case the earnings–capital ratio with $25.00 in use would fall to 1.1. With earnings constant the only way to retrieve the watch without curtailing consumption would be to extract $1.25 from original capital, lowering this last by 6 percent, from $20.00 to $18.75, adding it to the $5.00 in borrowed funds, and then reimbursing the pawnbroker. If the individual failed to collect the watch, the loss of a $15.00 asset in exchange for the $5.00 loan represented an interest rate of 200 percent.

The loss of 6 percent of capital for someone working with $20.00 was not particularly serious. But for the one–third of traders and manufacturers working with $6.00 or less (see table 2.4), a $1.25 erosion of capital caused by an ill–advised $5.00 loan could have meant a disastrous 20 to 40 percent drop in earnings. Loans from pawnbrokers may have been small because many families did not have much in the way of non–productive assets useful for collateral, but the substantial financial risk of borrowing could not have been an insignificant factor.

Credit mechanisms in St. Martin, as elsewhere, were biased against borrowers who did not have the capacity or luck to use funds productively in market or non–market activities. In terms of access to loan amounts consistent with usual recurrent needs, the mechanisms did not discriminate by income. Non–borrowers, those who did not use credit within the preceding six months, differed from borrowers by having higher regular wage incomes, a larger share of wages in total income, lower seasonal variation in income, higher slack season income, and a lower earnings–capital ratio implying the presence of household members with large amounts of market capital. In general, their income income–production characteristics were more stable over time, generating less frequent demand for credit. There were no significant differences in household income between borrowers and nonborrowers, or between users of different sources of credit. Even the very poorest families unable to produce collateral for pawnshop loans seemed able to find friends when they needed them.

In this kind of environment, reports by traders, manufacturers, and others that resources were generally available for investment, or to meet recurrent shortfalls in household income, seemed substantiated by facts concerning the credit market. However, credit was available only within a restricted range that matched supply with demonstrated ability to reimburse it. The collateral requirement meant that pawnbroker loans were a direct function of prior productivity in accumulating low–yield, disposable assets.[10] Families without such assets, meaning that they had assets that provided higher marginal returns in use than as collateral, were ineligible for loans. For such families the costs of pawnbroker borrowing were very high, not because of the interest rate or the risk, but because of the opportunity cost of production foregone through loss of the asset for a period of time.[11] Although friends did not impose a collateral constraint, the sizes and terms of most loans seemed well adapted to the circumstances of the borrower. That is, the friend loaned on the basis of his or her assessment of the ability of the borrower to repay it, as did the usurer. The credit market was conservative.

As a result, the market seemed to lack a higher–risk venture capital component that could direct resources to individuals working well below their productive potential, for example, the 5 percent or so of traders and manufacturers I mentioned in chapter 2 who seemed to be good candidates for capital infusions.[12] By extension, it also lacked a mechanism to finance recovery from disasters like hospitalization needs, loss of capital goods through fire or flooding, and so on. But for ordinary marginal financing requirements, credit seemed to work reasonably well at the time. Making allowance for risks incurred for unsecured loans, and for large versus small ones, the interest rate differential seemed logical, and relative to the productive properties of capital in use, both rates seemed reasonable. Or, if such prices were not reasonable, they were at least consistent with rates of 1.5 to 100 percent per month reported for rural areas of Haiti.[13]

They were not consistent with reported rates for other developing countries, however. In other countries, the upper end of the rate schedule typically lay in the 5 to 12 percent range, and might exceptionally reach 30 percent.[14] They were also inconsistent with the premise of a single economy–wide rate of return to investment, often assumed to lie in the range of 0.7 to 1.3 percent per month, that is, annual returns of 8 to 15 percent (Gittinger, 1982: 314). By such standards interest rates in St. Martin seemed quite high.

In what may be the only attempt to explain prevailing rates in Haiti, Lundahl (1979: 503–55) used the theory of interest as a function of time preferences to explain why farmers might be willing to borrow money at rates substantially higher than the 1 percent that he seemed to believe was the real opportunity cost of moneylending. He arrived at a theoretical conclusion that under certain circumstances farmers would pay up to 12 percent per month.[15] Looking at the perspective of lenders, Lundahl noted that monopoly profits and administration (or transaction) costs were unlikely to have much influence on rates, and therefore deduced that the causes of high asking rates were risk premiums to protect lenders from default.[16] Assuming that a lender wished to obtain a "normal" interest of 4 percent per month, and that the default rate was 50 percent on all outstanding loans, the rate that a lender would have to charge, the maximum that Lundahl could envisage, was 17 percent per month.[17]

This approach could also explain interest rates in St. Martin. The time preference of low-income families for present rather than future consumption was evident in the efforts they made to obtain food, water, shelter, and, if one chooses to define it as consumption, schooling. The number of individuals who could lose their jobs or capital, fall ill, or give birth, also suggested that lending could entail some risk. The large number of lending families and pawnbrokers indicated that the possibility of monopoly profits was remote. And the acquaintanceship of lenders and borrowers, and pawnbroker collateral, implied low administration costs. But even after incorporating all these factors, one would be very hard-pressed to guess how time preferences and risk could explain more than a fraction of the difference between Lundahl's maximum rates of 12 to 17 percent per month and actual real rates of 25 to 50 percent. Moreover, while credit did entail some risk, lending by friends kept it to a minimum as a result of their prior knowledge of the characteristics of borrowers, as did usurers from earlier successful transactions, and pawnbrokers passed the burden of risk to borrowers. Even if risk explained the 25–50 percent differential, the lower rate could not have contained much of a risk premium. Finally, interest rates for each type of loan were essentially the same whether paid by the very poorest or the very wealthiest individuals. That is, the price of credit seemed no more the result of individual negotiation than the price of any other market commodity. Bargaining might add or subtract a few percentage points, but the basic prices of secured and unsecured loans, and of large and small ones, seemed dictated by aggregate forces in the market.

Others have suggested that perhaps the problem of understanding interest rates in places like St. Martin lay in the premises rather than in the observations. One line of reasoning argued that the assumption of homogeneous capital of uniform productivity may not be entirely appropriate. In a "fragmented" economy in which firms and households are so isolated that they face different prices for labor, capital, and commodities, and in which they do not have access to the same technologies, there is likely to be a fragmented capital market (McKinnon, 1973: 10). In such a market, an entrepreneur's own capital, particular productive opportunity, and market opportunities for lending or borrowing are badly correlated, resulting in a dispersion of real rates of return. Observations of high interest rates are therefore observations associated with fragmentation or disorganization of the market. St. Martin, however, did not itself have a fragmented capital market. There were no large-scale institutions to accumulate savings and reallocate them, but there were savings and a market that appeared to function efficiently to move them to investors.

Another line of reasoning argued that capital did in fact have homogenous productivity within countries, but that demand and supply factors in different countries could, under conditions of scarcity, raise productivity to an unusually high level (Tun Wai, 1957: 123–24). There were few cities where scarcity of almost everything was as acute as in Port–au–Prince, and there may have been few places where productivity of capital, and hence its price, was as high. Therefore, if the basic, essentially risk–free interest rate was 25 percent per month in 1976, it was because the opportunity cost of capital, internal rates of return, or other indicators of the productive value of things that resources could buy were such as to warrant it. This line of reasoning, set in a context in which the most essential market and non-market production activities were extraordinarily labor–intensive, and in which almost any appropriate investment in marginal additions of capital could yield increases in income as well as productive capacity, seemed to make sense. But it did not explain why rates in St. Martin should have differed so much from regulated or "modern" sector bank rates of 1 percent per month at the time.[18]

While neither of the two lines of reasoning seemed able to explain interest rates within the neighborhood, or between the neighborhood and other regions of the economy, in combination with each other they presented a plausible argument. That is, although the market in St. Martin was not itself fragmented, it was one of several internally homogeneous components that together constituted an urban economy fragmented into different components. Households within each component faced a characteristic distribution of relative prices. These prices influenced their choice of technologies for producing income (or survival), which in turn yielded a specific range of productivities of capital, subject as always to decreasing returns to scale. The matter of whether or not to invest in cooking pots or buckets, for example, was dictated by the structure of relative prices faced by households in that particular labor–intensive component. And as I described in chapters 3 and 4, productivities of such capital additions were very high.

In the poorest neighborhoods of the city, such as Brooklyn, interest rates in 1976 were 5 to 10 percent per day, the equivalent of 150 to 300 percent per month. The expectation of borrowers and lenders was that $1.00 invested at dawn in trade, a dominant occupation in the neighborhood, should have yielded a total revenue of $1.30 by dusk.[19] The lender retrieved $1.05 or $1.10, and left $0.20 to $0.25 to the borrower. The process would repeat itself the next morning. The only capital engaged in trade was the daily loan.

Passing from this component of the urban economy, where capital per worker was $1, very scarce, and highly productive, to St. Martin where it was about $18, the rate moved to the 25 to 50 percent range. Beyond St. Martin, in areas where capital per worker was $1000 to $5000, the rate declined to a 3 to 20 percent range (Haggblade, Defay, and Pitman, 1979:

70–71). In wealthier components of the economy with access to regulated bank lending, the unregulated range outside banks was around 2 to 5 percent. And, finally, there were the regulated bank rates of 1 to 1.5 percent.

Information and resources, or at least those resources left behind after various tax machines collected their dues, did not flow easily from one fragment of the economy to another. Such savings as residents of each component accumulated circulated within it, and the prices of credit reflected aggregate demand and supply within the component. In those components where capital was a fundamental factor of survival, as in the situation of day–to–day credit in Brooklyn, demand was likely to be extremely intense, supply correspondingly low, and prices and returns were likely to reflect the component's circumstances. An interest rate of 150 to 300 percent per month in Brooklyn was therefore neither higher or lower than 1 percent in another component relative to the productivity of capital in each. The basic implication of this line of reasoning was that problems of credit had little to do with interest rates.

Projects

Problems of credit for ordinary households in Port–au–Prince were problems of poverty, and to the extent that poverty was to a certain extent a function of political class behaviors that intentionally or unintentionally imposed implicit or explicit taxes on tools, raw materials, food, water, shelter, and schooling, problems of credit were to the same extent problems of politics. There was cause to wonder in 1976, and in 1986, about how much lower demand for credit, and therefore interest rates, might have been, and how much higher savings and supply of credit, if factional activities and the fortunes of factional struggles had somehow conspired to offer small traders and manufacturers the same advantages received by their counterparts inside the political class; to make corn, rice, flour, and cooking oil prices consistent with world prices; to press water prices toward the range of reason; to encourage expansion in supply of land for shelter; to permit importation of shoes, textiles, and other restricted essentials, and free entry into import and export trade; and to abolish the school dress code.

Had the forces of history conspired to allow these and other vital changes, there was also cause to wonder whether saving among the wealthier of Port–au–Prince before 1986 would have been in such excess supply that they could find few better methods of using it than to send it abroad or place it with banks paying them 0.5 percent per month in 1976, which in turn could find nothing better to do with it than lend it at about 1 percent to investors wanting to finance import–export trade and import–

substitution industry in order to renew and expand their private taxation of the general populace. Habit compelled some analysts to call credit markets like the one in St. Martin "informal" or "unorganized," and to refer to banks as "formal" or "organized." Not that any of these labels made much difference to facts, but by rights the market in St. Martin deserved the label "organized," since it operated according to formal principles of demand, supply, and efficiency, and banks deserved the title "disorganized," since they operated according to imported custom having little to do with the basic attributes of the general society and its economy.[20]

But most members of the political class were not in the habit of wondering about such things. To them, problems of credit were mostly about credit and not about the political economy of which it was a part. So defined, issues of policy revolved around certain inadequacies of banks, and projects around the difficulty of access to bank-like credit by borrowers usually working with nonbank credit mechanisms.

With respect to banks, as I mentioned in chapter 1, a dominant theme was the apparent absence of longer-term lending, particularly for industrial investment. It did not seem to matter that almost all the sizable investments in import-substitution and export manufacturing had managed to occur and expand without such credit. In practice, this often meant that banks offering short-term loans rolled them over when they became due, or that increases in the size and frequency of short-term loans to finance international trade allowed borrowers to divert previously encumbered personal funds to their own industrial investments, or to personal lending to other investing "friends" in a manner not different from that in St. Martin.[21] It also meant that monopoly profits allowed what might have been popular savings to accrue directly to investors, obviating the need for institutionalized financial intermediation, and in sufficient quantity to permit longer-term investment. But premises about inadequacy of long-term finance were dominant, and the IDB, World Bank, and USAID industrial credit schemes I described in chapter 1 flowed out of them. Depending on interpretation, these schemes had accomplished either a great deal or nothing.

A 1985 World Bank review of banking identified several presumed problems in addition to the shortage of long-term lending (World Bank, 1985: 54–55). One was (another kind of) fragmentation, meaning that there were too many financial institutions and that there was no central, strong institution to assess the viability of projects seeking loans. A second was the lack of appropriate security on the part of new entrepreneurs and the difficulties faced by banks in enforcing debt collection or seizing collateral. A third was the presence of "high" interest rates that tended to make long-term financing difficult, and the absence of long–term deposit interest rates high enough to attract new savings.

This was a boilerplate review of the standard form I described for small manufacturing in chapter 2 that had little to do with Haiti. Haiti required more, not fewer, institutions in order to introduce something resembling serious competition in attracting deposits from different components of the economy, in seeking investment opportunities, and in establishing an interest rate structure that more accurately reflected scarcity and actual rates of return in the country (as opposed to returns in the fragment). The last thing Haiti required, if one judged by the Bank's own credit scheme that reportedly squandered its resources, or its management of the education project funds which disappeared, was centralized control of resources.

With regard to projects desgined to move bank–like credit to enterprises that normally would not have recourse to banks, USAID assisted in the creation of the Haitian Development Foundation (HDF) in 1979. The purpose of the HDF was to extend short–term loans (i.e., long–term from the perspective of borrowers) at commercial bank rates.[22] Target beneficiaries were firms of the types documented by Michigan State University in a 1979 survey of small businesses, that is, capitalized at $900 or more and therefore several leagues removed from the scale of operation in St. Martin.[23] This was a very ambitious undertaking, at one time envisaging growth of the loan fund to $5 million over five years, and an active portfolio containing perhaps 1500 borrowers (USAID, 1982: 164). Nothing similar in scale had ever been attempted on behalf of small business in Haiti. Except for grants and loans from USAID, the IDB, and the World Bank, the HDF was an entirely private venture, with a board containing notable members of the Haitian business community and a local professional staff supplemented by one or two expatriate assistants.

Early reviews of the project commented about the low interest rate, which could not possibly cover administration expenses or protect the fund from risks of default, about the high costs associated with processing and administering loans averaging $2200 at the time, about the absence in borrower selection criteria of assessments concerning investment outcomes, about the wisdom of extensive lending to trade and service activities where large capital additions were unlikely to yield increases in earnings or productive capacity, and about the delay of fifty days between loan approval and disbursement caused by HDF's insistance that borrowers needed management training prior to taking out loans (USAID, 1982: 159–61). The firms had reached where they were without the need for formal training, and the possibility that HDF's trainers might know more about management than the entrepreneurs was remote.

An evaluation in 1982, by which time the HDF had lent out more than $540,000 to 215 borrowers, showed no change in the 14 percent interest rate or in loan processing time (Garcia–Zamor, 1982). The HDF did, however, increase average loan size to $3000 and did shift more toward lending to manufacturers. The arrears rate was less than 10 percent, and the evaluators lauded the work of the HDF and the method by which the project's accountant was keeping accurate records.

During 1983, lending expanded beyond $1 million, the interest rate climbed to 18 percent, and the accountant left HDF. At that point things apparently began to go wrong. By the time USAID became aware that resignations by some board members were intended to communicate a message of things amiss, causing it to audit HDF in early 1984, perhaps $900,000 could no longer be accounted for. Following forced and voluntary resignations of HDF's board, local and expatriate staff, and USAID's own personnel responsible for project supervision, lending came to a standstill. There was some talk about cancelling the effort, but eventually convinced that the goals were worthwhile, USAID, the IDB, and the World Bank began to slowly reconstitute HDF, and it resumed operations in 1986.

Moving beyond people like those in St. Martin to the very poorest of the city's poor in Brooklyn, Foster Parents Plan International began to shift resources towards what it called a "Family Development Plan" program in 1983. The idea was to provide about five thousand households sponsored by the agency with training in basic planning and budgeting skills, to help them cope more effectively with circumstances many degrees worse than those found in St. Martin, and with small loans to implement the plans. Work with the families in 1984 produced 9800 requests for money to be used for specific purposes, including financing capital for trade (40 percent of all requests); payment of school fees (15 percent); house repairs (10 percent); house construction (7 percent); purchase of sewing machines (4 percent); medical treatment (4 percent); house purchase (3 percent); long–term rent payment (3 percent); latrine construction (3 percent); literacy training (3 percent); and purchase of tools and raw materials (2 percent) (Greenidge, 1984). Priorities in Brooklyn in 1984 were similar to those in St. Martin in 1976.

The agency's preliminary assessment of its program, after 160 families completed training, yielded three conclusions. With respect to the premise that training in management and planning could help families improve their lot, one conclusion was that this hypothesis was not yet proven. With respect to the assumption that the agency's staff would have the ability and motivation to train families, the second conclusion was that indications seemed to be positive, but no definitive assessments were possible yet. Regarding the whole idea of the program, the third conclusion was that it was definitely superior to the alternative of providing monthly family allowances, not because there was any proof of superior outcomes, but because staff and families believed it was better.

Finally, beginning in 1986, Mennonite Economic Development Associates (MEDA) initiated a small loan and technical assistance project that was to attempt to address the financial and technological difficulties faced by traders and manufacturers like those in St. Martin. With $60,000 available, project accomplishments were likely to be limited in terms of scale, but it represented an interesting beginning by a PVO that had a tradition of doing things well in Haiti.

In the matter of credit, the bases upon which statements were made and projects initiated by different elements of the political class were little different from the bases I described in earlier chapters with respect to other issues. Standard paragraphs of expertise to fill space in reports and mask ignorance; standard industrial credit projects flowing from the theoretical underpinnings of presumed expertise (e.g., Who would suggest that credit is not a problem in poor countries?) and from organizational compulsion (e.g, What does a World Bank or IDB do except offer credit?); and small enterprise credit/technical assistance schemes flowing from notions about entrepreneurship, employment–generation, self–help, appropriate technology, family economic development, and several other themes all have sufficiently familiar origins that they require no repetition here. Behaviors of the political class are for the most part predictable.

This is not to imply that writings and actions were necessarily irrelevant or inappropriate. Maybe the World Bank's analysis of banking problems was accurate. Notwithstanding difficulties of implementation, perhaps the World Bank, IDB, and USAID industrial credit schemes were helpful in contributing to export expansion. Similarly, a reconstituted HDF and the new Foster Parents Plan and MEDA projects might also generate outcomes useful for ordinary people. One could suppose that efforts stemming from a philosophy of "nothing ventured, nothing gained" might yield some good without causing direct harm along the way, as happened in the housing project in St. Martin.

But insofar as ordinary people were concerned, such efforts could only prove helpful if the problem of credit was a credit problem. Where daily middle–income earnings averaged $0.32 per adult per day, where food, water, and space consumption averaged 1500 calories, 12 lad and 2.0 square meters, and where circumstances created insurance and feeding facilities from schools, a range of monthly interest rates between 25 and 50 percent did not suggest a credit problem. The range suggested a problem of extreme poverty that traced its basic source to the political class, and to 500 years of sustained bankruptcy of that class.

Notes

1. This kind of consciousness distinguishes an economy like Port-au-Prince from what Coats and Khatkhate (1980: 5) defined as a subsistence economy in which savers and investors tend to be identical. The city had a fully monetized capitalist economy.
2. Voluntary direction of resources cannot, by definition, flow beyond the boundaries of the "known" environment. Highest returns within the boundary of knowns may therefore be lower than possible beyond it.
3. The focus on outcomes was especially important in Haiti because, as I noted with regard to food consumption in chapter 3, what seemed to be productive investment was sometimes nonproductive final consumption, and what seemed to be final consumption could often be highly productive.
4. Some economists, for example, Khatkhate (1980: 133), have pointed out that where incomes are low, the average propensity to consume is too high to permit families to set aside savings. This seemed true in St. Martin, but while economists tend to interpret the consumption as final consumption, evidence I have put forward suggests that it may sometimes be productive consumption. In this instance it is the propensity to produce in situations offering exceptionally high returns to investment that limits savings.
5. Banks, according to respondents, were not interested in keeping their money because the amounts they could deposit were too small.
6. Coats and Khatkhate (1980: 5) argued that if the only known use for savings is self-investment or lending in a limited neighborhood market, returns are likely to be unattractive and households are likely to save less than if rates are more attractive. Financial assets in such an environment are scarce and illiquid. To the extent that savings will always be less where returns are relatively low, the argument is irrefutable. In the case of Port-au-Prince, however, there were only a few destitute neighborhoods where returns were higher than in St. Martin. Savings and lending were scarce relative to demand precisely because returns to self-investment were exceptionally high.
7. Typical borrowers in this instance had an average of about $40 in owned capital producing $16 per month in the slack season, or an earnings-capital ratio of 0.4, implying that they were working below their productive capacity. In the peak season they borrowed $20 and produced $60 per month with $60 in capital. Without borrowing they could have produced no more than $40. The additional $10 in net earnings after the interest payment represented a 25 percent gain in monthly earnings. Borrowing more than $20 would have been impractical because at $60 they were working at full capacity.
8. Suppose that an individual with $2.00 in trade placed a bucket as collateral for a $1.00 loan. Suppose also that in moving from $2.00 to $3.00 in market capital the monthly earnings-capital ratio dropped from 5.2 to 3.8, yielding an increase in monthly earnings from $10.40 to $11.40, or $0.75 after paying the $0.25 in interest. Offsetting this not inconsequential gain of 7.2 percent in earnings was the increased cost of buying water. With a bucket an individual could consume 18 lad (one bucketful) at a cost of $0.04 per day or $1.20 per month. Maintaining the same level of water intake without a bucket, in theory, required purchase of glassfuls at $0.01 per liter, or $0.18 per day and $5.40 per month. Alternatively, it required travel time to find a drink at a standpipe, which would incur loss of valuable selling time. An hour per day for this

purpose represented a 12 percent drop in selling time and in earnings. Under these conditions buckets were too valuable to use as collateral.

9. At $20.00, an earnings–capital ratio of 1.4 would yield a net earning of $28.00; and $25.00 at a ratio of 1.3 would yield $32.50. The differential of $4.50 resulted from the addition of the $5.00 loan.
10. That is, access to pawnbroker loans demanded prior accumulation of "useless" assets, meaning in the case of traders and manufacturers that returns to further additions of market capital were low enough to warrant purchases of final consumption items. Making allowance for the presence of wage and other income, the squared correlation coefficient (r^2) of 0.33 between value of fixed and working capital in households and value of collateral they used for borrowing seemed somewhat significant. The F value was 4.9, significant at the 1 percent level. With access to pawnbrokers so dependent on collateral, and with pawnbroker loans looking very much like insurance mechanisms, one could wonder whether the assets were really "useless" methods of final consumption. They may have been insurance premiums, and therefore part of a household's overhead production cost.
11. See note 8, above.
12. The market offered them small amounts consistent with their current states, but what they might have needed were what McKinnon (1973: 12) defined as discrete, indivisible increases to propel them more quickly to their full productive capacities. Loans of $100 or more, for example, were very difficult to find for workers using $20 or less, and loans of $10 equally difficult for those with $1 or $2.
13. Moral (1961: 247) and OAS (1962: 37) reported rates of 20 to 50 percent per year, and Métraux (1951: 130) the equivalent of 1200 percent.
14. A review of rates in thirty–four developing countries by Tun Wai (1980: 180) showed only four instances where rates exceeded 300 percent per year, which he regarded as exceptional. The typical upper end of the rate schedule was 60 to 145 percent. Nisbet (1971: 74) and Long (1968: 284) reported similar rates, with a maximum according to Nisbet (1967: 77) of 360 percent, or 30 percent per month.
15. Lundahl applied Fischer's (1930) theory of interest. He arrived at the figure of 12 percent, or 140 percent per year, by assuming a one–month loan for an asset yielding a return of 20 percent per year.
16. That is, by a process of elimination, Lundahl deduced that of the three factors that he assumed could push rates beyond the presumed opportunity cost of capital, monopoly profits, transaction costs, and risks, only the last factor could possibly explain the rates. Lundahl did not provide strong evidence to sustain this hypothesis.
17. The maximum could have been higher. Lundahl used Tun Wai's (1957: 110) table showing the relationship of defaults and normal interest rates to rates that lenders would have to charge. The table did not extend beyond a normal interest rate of 50 percent per year.
18. Bank lending rates in 1976 were 11 to 15 percent per year (World Bank, 1985: 178).
19. Lenders in many of these instances were traders with stocks who sold goods on credit to others without stocks. The lending transaction was in–kind. The data on nonbank lending rates comes from small but detailed surveys carried out in the central market in 1975 by some of my colleagues at the UNCHBP, from a

more cursory survey I conducted in 1981 at the Brooklyn market, and from discussions with bankers and business people that I held in 1983 in connection with a USAID assessment of Haiti's industrial investment climate.

20. To be fairer to banks, one could say that every society has a financial system appropriate to it. In developing countries like Haiti, where there are more than one society (i.e., fragment) within national boundaries, there should be several financial systems. The formal–informal dichotomy touches this aspect, but because it suggests that banks are more "formal" than other systems, and perhaps "better," the dichotomy can be misleading.
21. Banks operated as "friends" to customers with long traditions of interaction between them. Bank behavior in this respect tended to be quite "informal," especially with respect to well–established families. Banks operated more like usurers, in the sense of looking carefully at the purpose of a loan, and as pawnbrokers, in the sense of demanding sizable collateral, when loan applicants were new.
22. As in most projects of this type, the determination of the interest rate pitted proponents of three differing views against each other. One group, the smallest, argued in favor of interest rates that reflected rates of return in the fragment, that is, monthly rates slightly below actual rates of 3 to 20 percent. A larger group argued for a rate that could at least cover administration costs, some risk, and the costs of borrowing to the HDF, or 2 to 4 percent. The majority, arguing that the purpose was to integrate borrowers into the "modern" banking sector and thereby provide them relief from usurious interest rates, claimed that even current bank rates were too high. The compromise was the legal bank rate.
23. Haggblade, Defay, and Pitman (1979). Their study indicated that credit did not seem to be a major problem for small enterprises.

8

Conclusion: The Devil's Hand

On a Venetian map dated 1436, there is a land called Antilla to the west of the Canary Islands, and to the north of this land an "Isola de la Man Satanaxio," the island of the devil's hand (Barros, 1984: 840). Later cartographers attached Hispaniola, Saint Domingue, and Haiti to Antilla, but the history of unnecessary human suffering might more accurately have attached them to the island.

From at least 1492 onward Haiti was a very productive country. It provided wealth to the buccaneers and the Spanish, and approaching 1804 had the distinction of being France's most prosperous territory. Lauded as the "Pearl of the Antilles," it outranked all colonial possessions in contributing to the economic growth of mother countries. It was the wealthiest European outpost in the New World, and by and large retained this type of honor through 1986. Public and private profits from international trade remain high. Although falling on the import side, coffee still provides greater exporter profit per kilogram than almost any other country in the New World, and export of assembled and other similar manufactured goods do the same. All of this wealth was and is the product of cheapened labor. With the advent of foreign assistance, which had as its basic objective making labor more expensive, fortune called upon Haiti to become one of the leading outposts of external aid receipt in 1986 (on a per capita basis), and to thereby permit increased public and private profit to Haitians and expatriates associated with the industry.

From 1492 onward Haiti was also a desperately poor country. Most or all of the indigenous Caribs died within twenty years of Columbus's arrival. The slaves from Africa that worked the land for the next 280 years, and their "liberated" descendants who worked at it and other things for another 195, did not live well. But fortune could not abandon them so completely as it did the Caribs. Haiti's prosperity demanded that they be very poor, but it also demanded that they remain alive to produce profit for others and to eventually provide justification for foreign aid and the profit attendant on it. As a result, life expectancy is very high. A visitor to the city in 1833 reported an encounter with a twisted beggar who dragged his lifeless legs behind as he crawled on hands and knees seeking alms (Chateaubriand, cited by Barros, 1984: 818). I met the same beggar in 1974, used him as a respondent in surveys of housholds residing on the streets in 1975, and again as an informant on the cost of living in 1986. The beggar was at least 200, maybe almost 500 years old. What useful purpose he might have served in 1833 or before is uncertain, but from 1974 to 1986 he was critical to that segment of the foreign-assistance and development scholarship industries that provided me with livelihood and other types of tangible and intangible profit.

Perhaps, as one recent expatriate scholar put it, the great lesson of Haiti is to demonstrate how national and international egoisms, organized as aggression against the common interest and as brute force against justice can lead a nation to paralysis (Barros, 1984: 843). Perhaps, as a scholar–manufacturer resident in St. Martin concluded a decade ago, it was just the bad luck of living in the devil's hand.

Much as I am tempted to agree with my colleague in St. Martin, and to therefore treat Haiti as an example of extraordinary bad luck, I cannot easily accept his hypothesis that there are no identifiable causes traceable to human volition. Insofar as the political class is concerned, there is certainly little in the evidence I have presented to refute the expatriate scholar's argument, or to extend it by means of a systematic reversal of every accusation of abnormality that the class has ever leveled at ordinary people. With respect to the 1968 opinion of the minister of finance that I mentioned in chapter 2, one could suggest that as a result of inertia, ignorance, attitude, and the low value placed on science, the political class, and not the ordinary class, is hostile to progress. If there is a need for labeling, then terms like subsistence, informal, marginal, backward, traditional, artisanal, petty, unorganized, unregulated, irregular, casual, and scrounging are apt characterizations of a great many activities of the political class. Adopting the definition of underemployment as that situation in which the removal of a worker from the market does not result in a drop in production output, then many or most members of the political class are underemployed in low–productivity and non–productive activities. Their activities are predominantly of the type that could be construed as "dissaving" or as acts of "final" consumption. The class is the inappropriate technology in Haiti that desperately needs treatment with a "policy" or some other change to render its political economy more competitive, more efficient, and more productive. Transmitted intergenerationally for 500 years, the political class, and not the ordinary class, can be said to be the locus of Haiti's "culture of poverty."

Useful as this exercise in accusatory reversal may be in highlighting the mystification of language and in implying an inherent sameness in the behaviors of members of both classes, the labels and concepts explain no more about political class behaviors and how they may have influenced the course of history, than they do about the ordinary class. To explain certain aspects of the behavior of ordinary people in their relationship to simple things, I found it useful to depend on microeconomic theory. This choice necessarily incurred the high cost of sacrificing all other formal and informal procedures of social and psychological understanding. But when joined with the notion that the ultimate meaning of profitability (or utility) is corporeal survival, adoption of a theory admirably suited to, indeed, derived precisely from, the study of people and tangible things, the gain in insight and explanatory potential seemed well worth the price paid to obtain them. The essence of the resulting explanation for the behavior of this class was, at the lower limit, reproduction of bare survival, and further away from the limit, sustained effort to promote individual and household economic growth.

Against this setting, the behavior of certain elements of the political class with respect to the same simple things, and particularly with respect to what often appeared to be an unwillingness or incapacity of individual or group behavior in the class to yield actions and outcomes that might conceivably prove helpful to ordinary people, can be explained in several ways. One approach, implicitly presuming that in whole or in part the political class is by some divine instruction supposed to care about the circumstances of ordinary people, might have it that too many individuals and organizations in the class are hypocritical and therefore uncaring, that they are insensitive to the implications of what they say and do, that they suffer from cognitive problems and are therefore unaware of the "truth," or that they may simply be incompetent. But this is not a satisfactory approach to explanation. It implies that such individuals "should" or "ought" to be less hypocritical, more sensitive, more aware, and more competent. But without a self-evident "truth" or common consciousnesses to sustain either the accusations or the implications, the approach carries little meaning even if accusations of hypocrisy, insensitivity, ignorance, and incompetence seem appropriate. Members of the class, like most people, believe that what they say and do are correct and valid, or if not correct and valid, then they believe that there is sound justification for incorrectness and invalidity; which then makes their behavior acceptable in their own eyes.

In retrospect I have had many second thoughts about the things I have said and done, such as my position with respect to what our UNCHBP reports should contain in regard to the informal sector. In prospect I am certain to have second thoughts about the opinions, assumptions, and theories that through this book I join with all the others already in circulation within the political class. But I rarely doubted that my ideas and actions of the moment were anything but correct and valid, and I do not doubt it at this moment. My behavior was and remains normal. The behaviors of all the others I have criticized explicitly or implicitly were equally valid, equally normal.

Leading toward a similar conclusion, a second approach to explanation (which still retains the premise that the political class has a mandate to assist the ordinary class) might suggest that data of the type I have assembled in this book were not available to members of the class. It may well have been the case that many of the sources I have drawn upon were not readily at hand. Suppression of the UNCHBP reports by government, and suppression of most World Bank reports with white, green, or grey covers, for example, rendered access to certain potentially important documents difficult. The St. Martin data, however, were widely available for several years. The ILO, UNDP, World Bank, USAID, and the Ministry of Finance received them in 1977. USAID's publication and distribution in 1980 of several hundred copies of a research report containing rudimentary versions of chapters 2 through 7 (Fass, 1980), made them accessible to almost everyone interested in the subject matter.

In the course of events, some individuals found the material interesting, but discounted the usefulness of the work for intervention purposes because the sample was too small and therefore not only potentially nonrepresentative of the urban population but also of questionable statistical validity on its own terms. Some discounted it because of what they believed was an incorrect application of the theory of the firm to analyze household consumption. Some simply disagreed with my conclusions. Others thought the work very useful. For the ILO, it was helpful in describing the characteristics of the informal sector and the problem of underemployment, and it served similar purposes for the World Bank. At USAID it played a part in decision making leading to creation of the HDF and in eroding the premise at the beginning of the private primary education project that all schools were educational facilities. At the Ministry of Social Affairs, at that time working in collaboration with UNICEF, it contributed to thought and then a program to complement the St. Martin project's physical works with health, education, and social work services. For Foster Parents Plan, my notation of the concept of family economic development helped guide the agency to the decision to shift from providing monthly allowances and toward using resources more strategically as credit to invest in economic mobility.

I had and have a natural inclination to disagree not only with those who discounted the work but also with those who used it for the very purposes that I hoped the data would oppose, such as reinforcement of the informal sector and underemployment concepts, introduction of social work, and creation of credit programs. But the discounting of the data and the various uses to which they were put by individuals and organizations were also normal. Only unbridled arrogance can sustain a claim that every datum in the earlier works and this book, and every interpretation therein, are correct in any absolute sense, or that they are anything more than one person's opinions. There is, as I noted above, no truth here. It would be equally arrogant to claim that the data were instrumental in altering the behavior of any of the individuals and organizations I mention. Availability of the data allowed them to be used for processes already in motion. In this sense, lack of data, or more generally, of a certain kind of documented knowledge, is not a satisfactory basis for explaining political class behaviors.

The difficulty with these two approaches to explanation, as would be the case for any approaches that implicitly or explicitly attached different motives to different imputed categories of what remains the same human species, is that in whole or in part they reify the political class—they make the class abnormal. For if one assumes that some parts of the political class are supposed to care about the circumstances of the ordinary class, analytical consistency would demand an imputation to the effect that some parts of the ordinary class are supposed to care about the circumstances of the political class. The record of five centuries shows strong evidence that the ordinary class has done much better in helping the political class than the other way around. If a class must be reified on the basis of actual rather than presumed performance, then ordinary people are more deserving of such treatment. And if explanations and recommendations need finding, the search would necessarily focus on the reasons that ordinary people have been so self-sacrificing and benevolent, and on methods to encourage them towards a more proper level of selfishness. The point, however, is that if this reasoning about ordinary selflessness seems to make little sense, it makes no more sense to apply it to the political class.

For this and other reasons, I had little choice but to presume that if microeconomic theory was useful in explaining some aspects of ordinary behavior, something akin to the theory must also serve to explain some behaviors of the political class. The concept of self-interest being only a rephrasing of the concepts of utility and profitability, and corporate survival being as close an approximation for most members of the political class as the corporeal variety was for ordinary people, the joining of self-interest and corporate survival to define the lower limit, and of self-interest and tangible "growth" further away from the limit, served the purposes of basic causal explanation. This approach also incurred a heavy cost in sacrificing other potentially useful procedures, with much less certainty about whether the price paid was worth the benefit. But at the very least it permitted, or rather, demanded a premise that the behavior of individuals and organizations of the political class be identical in substance to the behavior of individuals and households in St. Martin.

Whether in government, foreign assistance, trade, or industry, whether Haitian or expatriate, whether leaders, administrators, technicians, consultants, scholars, or other professionals, whether affiliated with the Macoutes or not, individuals of the political class unable to conceive of altering their methods of doing things, even when outcomes of their efforts are in their own eyes of dubious merit, are no different from traders who cannot conceive of changing their stocks of goods in the face of declining margins. Those able to conceive of change in thoughts and practices but unwilling to risk doing so are no different from traders who worry about the consequences of shifting out of their commodity and locational niches in the market.

The tangible and intangible things that individuals and organizations produce and reproduce for themselves include political solvency, power, influence, recognized expertise, professional standing, career security, consulting fees, salaries, public and private taxes, profits, organizational repute, capital accumulation, "doing good," and other essential survival and growth benefits. No matter if some others (or the individuals and organizations in question) might interpret the inputs required to produce the benefits as corruption, favoritism, terrorism, conceptual abuse, intellectual inappropriateness, documentary decoration, boilerplating, numerical fabrication, deference to social acceptability of numbers, adherence to absurd standards, counterproductive programs, or irrelevant projects, the iron law of supply and demand compels the production of such inputs. Manufacturers did not produce for nonexistent markets. Macoutes did not extort for trivial purposes. Casuistries, or moral accounting, did not concern the manufacturers or the Macoutes very much. They cannot and do not concern the political class very much.

Following similar lines, if production skill, technology, and capital resources available for survival and growth are so specialized that they can only yield one type of final good or service, such as housing, schooling, or credit projects, then the question of whether or not a market exists for them is irrelevant. Survival requires that demand be created for the goods and services through strenuous efforts at marketing. Along the way, if the opportunity costs of foregone time and resources useful for production and consumption of other things in the short term seem to outweigh the (unknown and unpredictable) benefits of research and development, then the logic guiding St. Martin manufacturers to delay their efforts in this regard is the same as that which delayed similar efforts by several segments of the political class.

If somewhere in these processes one can find no explanation consistent with theory to interpret certain events, a temporary detour around the limitations of theory to suggest that there are individuals and organizations who seem evil, inept, incompetent, or just plain stupid in the manner in which they behave, or that certain things elude explanation of any sort except through resort to acts of providence, they all had their counterparts in St. Martin. And, still outside the theory, pure, unadulterated altruism, if one can admit to the possibility of such a concept, is no more prevalent in the political class than in the ordinary class. Through the income transfer process, many families in St. Martin gave up considerable comfort to sustain others for reasons having apparently nothing to do with personal gain. They still do.

Imputation of normalcy to the behaviors of the political class means that the historical bankruptcy of the class was and remains a normal attribute of the class. To summarize a very large and complex subject into one sentence, this is the tragedy of Haiti.

For Columbus and his colonial successors it was perfectly normal to think of the Caribs and Africans as slaves and perfectly normal to act upon this premise. It would have been abnormal for them to ask the Caribs or Africans their opinions about the concept or about the policies that flowed from it. The dominant consciousness of the political class at the time, and the political economy to which it was attached, did not provide scope for such questions. Following independence, auto–colonial masters found it perfectly normal to think of liberated citizens as producers of extractable surplus, to tax exports of their production and imports of their consumption, to return nothing to the producers except what was required to reproduce the surplus, and to refrain from asking opinions. With the advent of the armed foreign intervention era, it was normal for the masters of France and Germany to claim shares of the surplus as indemnity for their own citizens, and for masters in the United States to claim shares in payment for occupational assistance.

Under unarmed foreign–aid intervention, it is normal to think of ordinary people as the inexpert (ignorant) poor who can and must be helped, to think that the help cannot but come through expert (knowledgeable) assistance, and to think that methods of assistance can take no form but unilaterally devised reports, recommendations, policies, programs, projects, and prayers. Conversely, the notion that ordinary people are expert at what they do, that they can help themselves without inexpert assistants and inexpert documents and actions, and that the only coherent policy required is that the self-proclaimed assistants leave them alone, is abnormal. Such a notion is inconsistent with dominant contemporary consciousness about public and private missionary work from abroad (or, such as it is, from domestic charity), and the political economies attendant to them. Similarly, and by extension, normalcy demands not only that half or more of aid be claimed by missionaries for pursuit of their hobbies, but also that a share of already extracted surplus, or additional surplus, be taken in the form of counterpart financing or community contributions to humor the assistants and their organizations. And it is no more normal today than in 1492 for the assistants, missionaries, helpers, and their organizations to inquire about the opinions of the objects of their attentions on these or other matters. The politics and economics of foreign aid, development, beautification of the small, or whatever names one chooses to give these various forms of secular and nonsecular evangelism, require such opinions no more than did the politics and economics of slavery. Actors change. Rationales change. Criteria for normalcy change. Procedures of the political class remain constant.

If all these things are normal, it is also normal to expect that the ILO and similarly preoccupied agencies will continue to measure and discuss an unemployment problem for which no amount of measurement or discussion can by themselves provide a solution; that the World Bank will continue to waste the writing time of its missionaries, and the time of readers by producing standard and universally meaningless paragraphs; that many PVO and USAID personnel will continue to search for inappropriate technologies everywhere but in the one place where it can be found, a mirror; that USAID will dawdle about wheat until 1990 or beyond; that the IMF will continue to complain each time the government expends money on imports even if the matter at hand is starvation; that the IDB and PAHO will continue to pursue their little political exercise with CAMEP and the government while water remains the scarcest of scarce commodities; that the UNCDF, KFW, World Bank, USAID, and EPPLS will continue to spend millions on a basic need that is not basic; that the World Bank, UNESCO, Canada, France, USAID, PVOs, and the Ministry of Education will spend more millions on training personnel and providing facilities for use as cafeterias; and that the IDB, World Bank, USAID, Foster Parents Plan and the Mennonites will continue to provide loans for purposes that are not at all evident.

Against these normalcies, the political class will continue to regard as abnormal the efforts of ordinary people to escape, and will find it normal for the U.S. Coast Guard, Haitian army, and Dominican frontier patrols to serve as keepers of this half-island prison. Also abnormal and requiring armed force to sooner or later correct will be smuggling of cheaper producer and consumer goods, popular raids on food-storage facilities, breaking of water pipes, and land invasions. Indeed, any spontaneous or organized actions emanating from the ordinary class, or any general "anarchy" as the political class was wont to call deviations from its standard of tranquility in 1983 and 1986, is abnormal. Slaves were not supposed to establish unilateral communication of their own making. Ordinary people in 1986 are not supposed to do such things either. They are supposed to vote in the next election.

"Progressives" in the class will therefore find it abnormal that few may vote, and that of those who do, a great many will likely vote in favor of "regressives." Their sense of normalcy cannot embrace the possibility that ordinary people may be so deprived of means of producing and reproducing survival that concrete realities permit no time for attending meetings, participating in organization building, demonstrating, or voting. An hour in political activity is an hour not at work, a 12 percent drop in daily earnings, a lowering of consumption, and an extra expenditure of calories and water to find a voting station. The act of voting for many ordinary people, like everything else, is something that they must produce. In a country where political class behaviors are constant no matter who controls the administrative apparatus, and where voting does not alter the composition of the foreign-assistance shadow government, political actions such as voting are final consumption luxuries that most cannot afford unless remunerated for the opportunity cost involved. This is perhaps one of the more salient factors in maintaining the oppressive success of the political class, and perhaps also why, in recent times, regressives can pay such people to show political support for even further oppression. Ordinary people caught up in commercial politics are not necessarily misled. They can appreciate the long-term impact upon themselves of supporting repressive factions, but their circumstances do not permit them to discount long-term disbenefits at a rate lower than long-term benefits of any investment of their time and resources. The calculus of survival is about *now,* and the benefits of producing a vote (or a revolt), like the benefits of schooling, must be apparent *now* as well.

Because it is also normal for the political class in Haiti and elsewhere to think of time and historical movement in relatively short terms, these variations on a theme about normalcy, to the progressive mind, can provoke pessimism and a sense of deep despair about the evolution of the future. But for much the same reasons that I could not impute different behavioral motives to different categorizations of the same species, consistency demands that a temporal horizon for the future be consistent with the past. If it took 500 years for Haiti to become what it is, the measure of the future may also require a 500-year horizon. In that kind of abnormal time span, there is no particular reason to despair. More important, however, if the concept, myth, or fairy tale about the capacity of human volition to alter the destiny of civilization is to continue to breathe life into that most heroic and arrogant enterprise called "development," then there is no place for pessimism. There is hope because in a place like Haiti there is no hope without it, and because ordinary people, who by my method of definition cannot shape their own destinies, deserve that much from at least a few members of the political class who can and do shape their destinies. If not to the people of St. Martin, wherever they may now be, then I owe it to the beggar.

In this context, I see progress in Haiti because I choose to look for it among processes and actions that appear both normal and abnormal, and both significant and insignificant. One matter is the expansion and diversification of the political class through the dynamics of economic change in Haiti and the rest of the world. This includes fifty years of slow evolution out of the ordinary class of a middle class with varied self-interests that sometimes coincide with ordinary interests, and twenty years of evolution (or seventy years if one includes the U.S. occupation) of public and private assistance with even more varied self-interests. In St. Martin I could not find more than 5 percent or so of traders or manufacturers whom I thought had the capacity to rapidly proceed beyond their actual states. I doubt that more than 5 percent of the individuals and organizations of the political class, or even the progressive elements of the class, can readily move beyond their present states either. But a constant share of an increasing class population still leaves scope for some increase in beneficial outcomes of class thoughts, actions, and struggles.

More tangibly, for however long it lasts, the destruction of several public and private tax machines was good. For once, change in government did not result exclusively in a transfer of ownership in the machinery. Growth in assembly exports was good, in part because of the immediate benefits it provided, in part because it gave proof that sustained and concerted efforts by the UN, World Bank, IDB, USAID, private businessmen, and government to produce something out of nothing were possible in a place where anything like it, by rights, should have been impossible. PVO and bilateral agency efforts to export crafts were good, for reasons similar to those for assembly exports, and also because they introduced several of the political class to some aspects of the daily struggle of the ordinary class. In this respect, actions of USAID with respect to credit in the HDF, of Foster Parents Plan, and of the Mennonites were also good no matter what the measurable outcomes might turn out to be. For if the problem of credit was not a credit problem, the proof lay in the doing and not the saying. Good also were USAID's initiation of a food-consumption survey and World

Bank involvement in the general subject, the collaboration of efforts to make CAMEP better and to prepare for an improvement in water supply that might actually register as an improvement one day, the evolution of an institutional capacity in matters of shelter, and the gradual democratization of the schooling intervention process.

In suggesting that such limited and sometimes seemingly insignificant things are signs of progress and symbols for hope, I do not mean to imply that it is useful to regard a half-empty glass as half-full. These things are much more important in historical perspective than a matter of interpretation. For a long time in Haiti the glass was empty, and for an even longer time, there was no glass and no water to pour into it. Haiti still needs a table for the glass, a room for the table, a house for the room, a neighborhood for the house, a city for the neighborhood, and a country for the city. It is normal for those of the political class concerned with such things to bemoan the lack of country, and it is abnormal for them to give thanks for the glass and the bit of water at the bottom of it. In the opinion of ordinary people of Port-au-Prince, thankful always for the water, such behavior is difficult to understand. In my opinion the behavior is easy to understand. It is the expression of moral bankruptcy. It is nonsense.

Appendix A

Manufacturers in St. Martin: Ten Case Studies

Manufacturers included in table 2.5 of the text produced over thirty different products. They worked with different factors of production, different combinations of labor and capital, and at different scales of production. Also, they operated in different raw material supply and product output markets requiring different marketing skills under varying conditions of demand. This heterogeneity, and the complexity that accompanied it, was not revealed in chapter 2. It is a complexity worthy of description, and the following ten cases, selected at random from the table, serve to present it. The descriptions are based on my interviews in St. Martin, and generally cover the history, current accounts, production characteristics, and constraints of each enterprise. Levels of detail vary from case to case because dynamics during each interview did not always permit me to pose all my questions, nor to receive answers to all the ones I did pose. The information nevertheless highlights the difficulties and challenges associated with making a living from activities that, to uninitiated observers at least, may appear relatively simple. The activities were indeed simple, but extracting livelihoods from them was not.

Before proceeding to the cases, a matter warranting some emphasis is that the language of each case description is a translation from the language of each interview. This does not mean transformation of Creole into English, but rather translation from an informal dialogue in a language largely devoid of economic categories to a language of description heavily imbued with such terminology, both explicitly and implicitly. Several of the cases, for example, mention "risks" or "opportunity costs." These words never entered the dialogues. In the course of discussions in Creole, I recorded such expressions as, "it isn't worth the effort." If that was the reply to a query about why a respondent did not do something or other, it would mark the beginning of what usually turned out to be a long series of questions concerning "why" the something or other was not "worth the effort." In almost all instances, the answers seemed to be very cogent reasons that I could later translate into a formal abstraction as perceived risk or opportunity cost. This matter warrants emphasis because the descriptions portray the manufacturers as highly astute actors working as best they were able within the limits of their knowledge, capabilities, and circumstances. I believe that such a portrayal is accurate. It might not be as apparent to an observer unwilling to work with respondents for several hours to develop it.

Doormats

A matmaker first came to the city with his wife in 1959. The wife's earnings from trade supported them for the first two years because he could not find steady work. In addition to trade in dry goods, the wife made sisal braids as a sideline. Around 1962 she was finding that craftsmen were buying her braids as fast as she could make them. She asked her husband to help her, which he did, and soon afterward they were earning more from selling braids than from her ongoing trade. The husband did not like braiding because it was a woman's occupation. She then taught him how to make carpets with the braids, a man's occupation that she had acquired from her father, and their income rose still further. The wife died in 1964. At the same time, the husband found that rug sales were falling off, that he could not make ends meet without his wife's income, and that he could not find other work. He returned to his village of origin and rejoined his brothers in their fishing activities.

The man remarried in 1971 and moved to St. Martin with his second wife in 1973. As before, he could not find steady work, but did manage to feed his family by selling carpets of the type that he made ten years earlier. In the course of his first year back in the city, he discovered that a new and smaller rug design was more marketable as a doormat than the carpet he was producing. Through his network of acquaintances in the business he gradually learned where to find materials appropriate for the new design (e.g., sisal squares, dyes, etc.), and how to make the product. By 1974 he had mastered the new technique and business became quite brisk. The production accounting for one mat was:

Input costs:	sisal braids	$0.20
	sisal squares	0.24
	twine	0.20
	transportation	0.01
	aniline dye	0.01
	water	0.01
	subtotal	$0.67
Price		0.80
Net revenue		$0.13

The production cycle began with a one–day visit to a market 12 kilometers north of the city, where the man usually purchased enough braids to make about fifty mats, or a one–week supply of material. He did not bother to take a bus because the return fare represented almost 10 percent of the cash he had for the material, and the three–hour travel time savings was not important. It would take him five or six hours to look for the quality braids he needed and to haggle over their price; after this he would be too tired to produce or to sell. The time savings was worth less than the money savings, and a weekly walk to the country was always pleasant. He did not make braids because it was still a woman's job, because neither he nor his wife could produce the required quality, and because his time was better spent on production and sales. He did not buy in the central market because the price was too high and the required quality was harder to find.

Twice a month the mat maker would take a 30 kilometer bus ride to a town where a group of craftsmen spiraled sisal into squares that formed the center of his carpets and that he did not know how to make. He usually bought a two–week supply. He took a bus in this instance because the weight and bulk of the quantity he bought were not practical to carry on foot and because he did not want to lose a full day of work unnecessarily.

Combining the braids and squares with dye and twine obtained at the central market every few days, he and his wife used two dozen large nails, a hammer, an awl, and a metal pan to produce up to a maximum of twenty–four mats a day. At the usual selling price of $0.80 each, or as low as $0.70 if need be, they could obtain a net revenue of $0.13 per mat and, theoretically, a combined daily earning of $3.12. Maximum production, however, left no time for selling. The most they ever made was eighteen mats per day. The husband had to spend a part of each afternoon wandering the streets in search of customers. The wife did not market because she had two infants to look after and because consumers seemed to prefer buying them from a man. If pressed for money while at the same time having a large inventory, she would leave the children with an aunt and try to market in areas not covered by her husband.

When business was good the couple could sell 100 mats a week, earning them $13.00. When business was off they might earn $1.30 from selling 10. On average they sold 40 to 45 a week, and each individual earned about $0.45 per day.

Looking ahead, the man indicated that what he really would like was a long–term contract with an exporter. Such an arrangement would allow him to focus his time on production, would stabilize his earnings, and might even raise his income. He had approached several exporters who told him that his products were not suitable for their purposes. The producer was nevertheless optimistic. It was only a question of time until he found out where to obtain the particular braids, squares, and dyes that exporters seemed to want, and to learn how to assemble them in the appropriate patterns and colors. In the meantime, the couple had to eat, and so would continue making the mats that they knew would keep them going.

Carpets

Two brothers made sisal carpets that were similar to the type made by the husband in the previous case before he shifted to mats in 1974. The carpets differed from the mats in several respects. They were four times larger, used a thicker and lower–quality braid, did not incorporate dyes, and instead of preassembled squares in the center surrounded by a few loops of braid, consisted of a single strand of braid wound in an oval pattern from the center out to the perimeter. The manufacturing account for each carpet was:

Input costs:	sisal braids	$0.40
	twine	0.67
	transportation	0.11
	subtotal	$1.18
Price range		1.40-2.00
Net revenue range		$0.22-0.82

The brothers could, theoretically, produce about forty carpets a week but had never come close to that level. When business was very good the best they could manage was three sales a week at the price of $2.00 per carpet, and thus divide a weekly net earning of $2.46, equivalent to a daily earning of $0.21 per individual. When business was slow they might drop the price to $1.40, but still sell only one carpet a week. At that rate each brother would earn a daily amount of $0.02. On average some combination of price and sales rate would earn each of them about $0.15 per day.

They perceived their basic business problem as competition from rural producers who made their own braids, and who perhaps also produced their own sisal. How else could it be, they asked, that carpets of the same size were selling for $0.90 to $1.00 in the downtown market? Such a price made sense only if their competitors did not have to purchase braids. Everyone had to pay for twine and for transportation to the city.

The competition had forced them to focus their marketing attention toward tourists and foreign residents of the city. These were the only kind of potential customers who probably did not know the going market price, and who probably did not care that much about whether they paid one dollar or two. Even then, competition to attract the attention of visitors on the street was severe. The brothers thought that their ability to find visiting individuals and groups who walked along on their own was good, but that their skill in converting a contact into a sale needed improvement.

An acquaintance once told them that the heart of the matter was courage and patience. One had to be willing to accompany and talk to a visitor up to the critical point where the potential client seemed to get angry, at which point the moment had arrived to break off contact. Even if customers did not really want carpets, there were always a few who would eventually buy one simply to end the transaction. A visitor who seemed upset was not likely to buy. The trick, up to that critical moment, was to resist the temptation of concluding that a sale was not possible and that one should search for another potential customer.

After trying this method, the brothers had concluded that what sounded like a good idea in theory was not as good in practice. They did not have the courage required to test the limits of a visitor's patience. This was not proper practice in trade between Haitians and did not seem appropriate with foreigners either. The brothers did not believe that improved salesmanship would really help them. They had to drop out of the business and find some other kind of work, but they could not predict when that might happen.

Baskets

Prior to moving to the city with his family six months earlier, a basket maker farmed his father's land in the southern peninsula. He had started making banana–leaf baskets when he was a boy, and in recent years, after meeting, in rural markets, commercial buyers who offered him regular purchase contracts, was finding that he earned much more from this trade than from his agricultural pursuits. During certain periods of the year he had found it difficult to make baskets and farm at the same time. On a visit to the city in 1973 he discovered that he could obtain double the price for his baskets by selling them directly to exporters and tourist shops. However, the potential gain in earnings was largely offset by the costs of transporting the bulky baskets, and the cost of staying in the city overnight on each trip. This suggested to him that he ought to consider moving to the city.

He weighed the advantages and disadvantages of such a move for almost a year. One advantage was the prospect of higher prices for his output. A second advantage, resulting from his divestiture of agricultural activities and from being closer to customers, was an increase in the availability of time for production and sales. Less direct but nonetheless important further advantages were that his children might have a better chance of going to school, and that his brother, who knew only farming and had a large family, could generate a higher income by taking over the basketmaker's plots. Disadvantages included loss of farm income (e.g., cash from produce sales, imputed rent, and auto consumption), higher raw material costs (i.e., he would have to pay for banana leaves), and higher overhead household costs for housing, food, and other essentials. During his year of indecision he used his visits to the city to carry out research on food and production costs, on housing rents in various parts of the city, and on urban transportation costs. This information seemed to suggest that the move would be worthwhile if he could sell at least two dozen baskets a month. He was not sure whether he could sell that many but, since he could return to farming if his sales objective fell short, he decided that he could afford the risk of moving. He chose St. Martin as his first place of residence in the city because the rent of $7.00 per month, double what he would have to pay in other locations, and the high cost of water were offset by the higher time and money costs of commuting between home, where he produced, and downtown, where he purchased banana leaves and sold his baskets.

His accounting for production of a dozen baskets was as follows:

Input costs:	banana leaves	$ 7.60
	paid labor	2.30
	subtotal	$ 9.90
Price		22.00
Net revenue		$12.10

The production cycle started with visits to potential customers. If they wanted baskets, they placed an order together with a 20 percent down payment, or $4.40 per dozen baskets. With the order in hand the basket maker would go to the central market to buy leaves from wholesale traders who used them as protective covering during transport of bananas to the city. The search for raw material could use up considerable time, primarily in finding leaves of acceptable quality and then bargaining down the price. Manufacturing, which required two and one–half days for a dozen baskets, took place at home with the help of a knife and an employee receiving a piecework rate equivalent to $0.90 per day. The last step was delivery of the baskets to customers, at which time the producer sought out new orders. A complete cycle therefore took three days per dozen baskets and generated a net revenue of $4.00 per day if the producer worked at maximum capacity. The producer then set $1.85 of this amount aside as working capital, and used the balance to meet household requirements.

Demand for baskets tended to fluctuate considerably, and the producer did not always work at peak capacity. He nevertheless believed that his business was a good one, enabling him to pocket a minimum of $6 to $8 per week, and to be proud to say that no one else in his eight–member family had to work.

The price of his baskets in tourist shops was $60 per dozen (and $220 to $290 in the United States at that time). Responding to my question about why he did not try to sell directly to tourists, at least when business was slow, his reply mentioned complete lack of foreign language skill, including French, and his lack of experience in bargaining prices with tourists. This was not an insurmountable difficulty. All he needed was practice. A greater difficulty was the risk involved in producing a somewhat perishable product for a marketing process that would take time to master. He usually kept about $6 on hand as his working capital for a dozen baskets, which, together with down payments, was enough to finance each production cycle. In order to produce two baskets for potential sale to tourists, he would have to buy leaves at a "retail" price (i.e., a higher unit cost for a lesser quantity), and this would mean a $1 investment. Selling a pair of baskets to tourists within a few days at a price of $5 each would certainly provide a handsome return if the time required for wandering the streets in search of tourists did not interfere with obtaining contracts and producing for his regular customers. However, as the sun and heat reduced the moisture content of the leaves, the price he could ask for the baskets would fall. At the end of two weeks, the baskets would be worthless and he would find himself $1 (or 17 percent) short on working capital.

If he then obtained a regular contract, he would have to borrow a dollar from relatives, from commercial lenders, or from household savings (which were earmarked for sending one child to school). He already had more or less steady work, and did not see the need to risk time, capital, and inconvenience in learning how to sell to tourists. He also reported that his customers usually had to throw away half the baskets they bought since only fresh ones were marketable. The customers who sold baskets for $60 per dozen were really getting closer to $30 for each set they purchased, or a net revenue of $8 that they had to use for rent, salaries, electricity, and so on. The customers were in a better position to take risks than he was.

If regular sales fell off considerably, the basket maker would more seriously consider selling directly to tourists. For the moment the only significant problem was that he had the capacity to generate a net revenue of $4 per day, but demand was not high enough to keep him at peak production for as long as he wished.

Bead Curtains

A young couple had moved to the city from a farming area two years before. When they married the husband's father offered him a plot to work on. The plot was large enough to support two people, but too small for a larger family. Also, the offer meant that the father would probably not have enough land to support the rest of his household. The couple decided to move to the city to look for work and to establish themselves before having children. The first year was difficult, and they got by with odd jobs and money sent by their parents.

One of these odd jobs was a request by a jobber that they make bead curtains composed of alternating strings of beads and wood chips. The jobber provided them with a drill, drill bit, saw, materials, and one afternoon of training. He was satisfied with their work and paid them one dollar each for their labor in producing six dozen strings per day. The contract lasted one month, after which the jobber took back the drill, saw, and remaining materials.

The couple had no further work for the next two months. They then learned from an acquaintance that an exporter was looking for producers of bead curtains almost identical to the ones they had made for the jobber. They contacted the exporter, who told them that if they could indeed make the curtains according to specifications he would purchase them at $1.00 per dozen strings. He would not, however, provide them with equipment and materials.

With savings left over from the jobber's contract, they purchased an old drill bit of the right size that had been discarded by a factory. It cost them $4.00. With another dollar they bought enough materials to make two dozen strings. The exporter liked them and they had been busy ever since. Their accounting for production of one dozen strings was:

Input costs:	beads	$0.10
	wood	0.07
	metal wire	0.23
	aniline dye	0.08
	water	0.02
	subtotal	$0.50
Price		1.00
Net revenue		$0.50

During the first eight months of production, they cut wood with a kitchen knife and drilled holes by turning the bit with their fingers. They could not find a used crank–type drill, and could not afford the $20 that a new one cost. As a result, their combined production rate was two dozen strings per day, earning each of them a net daily earning of $0.50. They nevertheless managed to accumulate some savings and, when a used drill appeared on the market, they borrowed money and bought it, together with a saw and two new bits, for $12. Since this purchase they had increased production to six dozen strings per day, earning each $1.50 in daily net revenues. During the two–month period of increased production, they sent $20 to their parents to repay the sacrifices the latter had made in helping them through the first year, and lent $3 to the wife's sister so that she could quit her job as a domestic servant and enter into trade activities.

They still had $37 in savings accumulated during the two months, but had not yet decided what to do with it. One possibility was to buy another drill and hire two workers, either from their own families or strangers. This could earn the couple another $20 to $25 per month if the workers were good. But they were not certain how much longer the exporter would buy from them. A second possibility was to lease a house in St. Martin for $30 a year. Their current monthly rent was $5 and so a lease would only save them $30. However, if they ran out of work in a near future, they would not have to worry about housing for at least twelve months. Assuming they could earn enough to eat, their current savings would carry them for seven months, and if they bought another drill they would have enough for only four months. A related option was to lease another dwelling unit, or at least one where water was more readily available, further away from downtown, but the couple had not yet researched this avenue. The final possibility they had thought about was to lend $35 to the wife's brother who wanted to lease a parcel for growing beans. The brother promised to repay them $80 at harvest, four months after he received the loan, but the couple was not sure whether the price of beans would permit him to pay them that much. In any event, they were quite busy for the moment. They said that the important thing was to keep saving money. Sooner or later they would arrive at a decision, or be forced into one as a result of losing their work, having a child, or accommodating another relative who might want to move in with them.

Buckets

A maker of 5– and 8–gallon buckets lived in St. Martin for many years. He learned the trade from his father, manufactured buckets for as long as he could remember, and still used the hammer, shears, and workblade that he inherited when his father passed away. The only equipment that he had added to his inheritance was a wooden forming block, which required replacement every two or three years.

His basic raw material was metal sheets that he purchased from an importer in the central market. The sheets were destined originally for production of carbonated beverage cans (e.g., beer, soft drinks) in the Dominican Republic or the United States, but substandard metal quality or label misprints led to their disposal and eventual export to Haiti. The bucket–maker was, in effect, recycling discarded manufacturing inputs. His production accounting for three dozen buckets was as follows:

Input costs:	metal sheeting	$14.00
	transportation	2.00
	subtotal	$16.00
Price		20.00
Net revenue		$ 4.00

Although production of three dozen buckets in front of his home took an average of only three days, he usually needed six days to sell them. Two days were used in traveling to and from a rice–growing region north of the city where he sold the buckets in regional markets, and he needed an average of four days to sell the buckets. His average net revenue per day, after deducting the $2.00 cost of public transportation between the city and the markets, was therefore $0.44. Although he kept his overhead food and housing costs down by staying with friends and family while on the road, he did spend a small portion of the $0.44 in buying small gifts of appreciation for the households that offered him accommodation. However, his principal method of returning the kindness of meals and lodging was to carry mail, messages, and certain small goods between city and country on behalf of his hosts.

Demand was stable throughout the year. The buckets were flimsy, did not last long, and therefore forced customers to replace them every three or four months. The manufacturer indicated that he was not sensing much competition from factory–made buckets. Such buckets could remain functional for up to five years, and at a price of $4.00 to $5.00 each could save customers anywhere from $3.00 to $6.00 over the five–year period by eliminating the need for constant replacement of the flimsier ones. His customers, however, were farmers who were not prepared to invest a large proportion of relatively scarce resources for the long–term investment purpose implicit in buying a factory–made bucket. Buckets were helpful but were not particularly productive from a farmer's point of view. Buying a bucket with an operational life of five years made as much sense as buying enough seed to plant for five years. Farmers worked out their expenditures on a seasonal basis, and a $0.55 bucket that would last one season made more sense than a $5.00 expenditure that would last longer, especially since the farmer would still have $4.45 in hand for other purposes. The only people who bought factory–made buckets, according to the manufacturer, were farmers with considerably more land and other forms of wealth than his customers. The manufacturer did not worry about the possibility that farmers would grow wealthier and shift their purchase to factory–made buckets. This kind of trend in income and expenditure patterns was not evident. If anything, the trends were in an opposite direction. He was, after all, selling more buckets in 1976 than he did in 1973.

His prime concern was what would happen if the price of competing buckets fell. Before thin metal appeared on the market, he had made buckets with the same heavier–gauge galvanized steel as used in factory products. His buckets were not as sturdy as factory ones, but the price difference between them assured him a market. When the price of the factory buckets dropped, sales fell off and he had to develop the new thin metal product. The new product sold more easily than the previous one, but he still had to compete with plastic buckets that sold for about the same price. For reasons which he did not fully understand, the price of plastic buckets rose quickly in 1974 and 1975, and still seemed to be rising in 1976.[1] His sales increased significantly when this happened. He was afraid that they would decrease if the price of plastic or factory metal buckets declined. If that happened he might have to struggle to develop yet another new product if he wished to remain in the business, and was not sure that he could develop such a product again.

Since the producer seemed to be working at full capacity, I asked him why he did not obtain equipment to speed up his rate of production, and why he did not sell wholesale to traders in the city so that he could shift part of his time from selling to manufacturing. His reply to the first question was that hand–cranked rolling machines that he had once seen in a vocational training workshop seemed to save considerable time in shaping heavy–gauge metal, but saved very little when it came to thin metal. Hand methods were almost as fast as machine methods, and the $50.00 to $60.00 cost of the machine did not seem worth it, especially since he would have to borrow the money and perhaps pay $25.00 to $30.00 a month in interest. In order to pay the interest, let alone the principal, the machine would have to help him at least triple his rate of production. Such an increase was not apparent.

In reply to the second question, he said that he could indeed make more money by selling to local traders. Their offer in the downtown market was currently $16.00 per three dozen. Nine days of production could therefore give him a gross sale of $48.00, and net earnings of $6.00 after paying for the metal. This would raise his monthly earnings by 50 percent, from $12.00 to $18.00. He then noted that the additional $6.00 per month looked like a gain only because my accounting was still incomplete. Before each of his return trips he used the proceeds from sale of buckets to purchase two sixty–pound sacks of rice in the rural market. He then sold them at about a 10 percent margin to a friend in the central market, who always bought the rice because it was 5 to 10 percent cheaper than the current central market price. For example, on the most recent trip he bought two sacks for $21.60, and sold them for $23.70, or a profit of $2.10. He made three trips a month so his total margin at this rate would be $6.30. Responding to my observation that the extra $0.30 did not seem worth all the trouble he went through in traveling back and forth and in carrying 120 pounds of rice, he agreed that is was hard work, but the opportunity to spend most of his time outside St. Martin was well worth the effort.

Castings

A man who manufactured lead castings for use as ornaments on coffins used his St. Martin dwelling unit as a workshop. He slept in it four nights a week, and employed a housekeeper to maintain it and to watch over the equipment and materials he stored there. He had worked in a bakery until 1972 when he left the job to earn more in production and sale of castings. He made so much more that he soon earned enough to purchase a house. Not finding a decent property in or around St. Martin, he bought one on the periphery of the city and moved his family to it in 1974. He nevertheless continued to work in St. Martin. Although the rent ($0.20 per day), the housekeeper's salary ($0.10 per day), and the additional cost of food for himself and the housekeeper came to more than the $0.18 cost of commuting between his home and downtown once a day, the nature of his business often required several daily trips downtown to buy materials. He actually saved an average of $0.06 per day by keeping the workshop and sleeping in it.

His production account for 12 dozen, or 1 gross of castings, was:

Input costs:	auto batteries	$0.40
	screws	1.20
	charcoal	0.10
	rent	0.10
	housekeeper	0.20
	subtotal	$2.00
Price		3.00
Net revenue		$1.00

This accounting excluded the cost of commuting between home and workshop two days a week (i.e., $0.06 per gross), and depreciation of a small pot, a heater, and plaster molds that constituted his capital equipment.

The production cycle began with purchase of discarded auto and bus batteries from which he extracted lead to make 1–inch diameter star–shaped castings, and metal screws to which he attached the castings. He would then melt the lead and pour it into plaster molds that he made at least once a year with a prototype imported ornament he bought at a funeral parlor in 1972. The process of making a gross of castings took one complete day.

Funeral parlors in the city bought the castings at $3.00 per gross, providing him with a net revenue of $1.00 per gross. He also sold the ornaments to buyers in the town of Jacmel, about 60 kilometers away, once every two months. The price in Jacmel was $4.00 per gross, but since he traveled there with 4 gross at a time and paid a fare of $4.40, his net revenue from sales outside the city was $0.90.

The market for castings was stable throughout the year, although sales transactions occurred infrequently. A buyer purchased four weeks of production the previous month, and another customer had bought six weeks of production during the current month. The producer tried to build up his inventory so that he could spend more time with his family, but usually found himself in the position of clearing it in one transaction, thus forcing him to continue manufacturing without a break. Since he sold everything he produced and usually worked twenty–eight days a month, his daily earning was around $1.00 a day.

In an effort to increase earnings, the producer tried as often as possible to raise his price. Sometimes he would notice that the result was a drop in sales, and his earnings would be the same or less than before the price change. If less he would return to the original price and sales seemed to pick up again. At other times a price increase did not result in fewer sales, but the gain in earnings would not last long because the cost of batteries, screws, and charcoal would gradually increase. Increasing cost was, in fact, his major problem. In 1974 his price was $2.50 and his costs were about $1.50 per gross. Since his margin in 1976 was still $1.00, and since a dollar did not buy as much as before, his income was really lower in 1976 than in 1974.

The producer indicated that what he earnestly wanted to do was to increase his rate of production. That seemed the only way to increase earnings. If, for example, he could find a worker able to produce 1 gross per day, he could pay the individual $0.60 per gross, and thus make an additional $0.40 per day. There were plenty of experienced people willing to work for him at $0.60 per day, and he had often tried to hire and train them. Unfortunately, each time he did this he lost money. Workers who did quality work could not produce even half a gross per day after a month of trying, and quit their jobs after the producer told them that their production rates warranted payment of only $0.40 per day. He had also tried to get apprentices who were willing to assist him at $0.15 to $0.25 per day. But their work required so much constant supervision to make sure they did not ruin materials and equipment that his own rate of production would drop to half its normal level. The lowering of his production rate invariably extended for too long a period to make the apprenticeship program worthwhile, and he abandoned it. It was hard, he said, to find good workers in the city.

Noticing that the slowest part of the production process was extraction of the casting from the plaster mold, a task that had to be done carefully in order not to damage the mold or the ornament, I asked the producer whether he had looked into obtaining a metal mold that did not require as much care in handling and that might therefore increase the rate of production. He replied that he had never seen such a mold, and that I should tell him where he might have a chance to look at one. Although I hadn't seen one either, and, although I kept my eyes open for a mold for several months, I never did come across a good example before leaving Haiti.

Purses

A man who made leather purses learned his craft while working in a factory in 1967. He operated a punch press cutting figure–eight shaped pieces of leather about 4 inches in length. Women working behind him then assembled the pieces into purses, and he had the opportunity to watch how they worked. The factory paid him $1.00 per day, a great deal of money in those days, but he nevertheless believed he could do better working independently.[2] His opportunity came when, after replacing the worn cutting blade on his press, the factory foreman threw the old one into a trash bin. The pursemaker retrieved it and a few weeks later quit his job to strike out on his own. The timing of blade replacement was a stroke of luck because the factory shut down for a year in 1968, and without the blade he would have found more difficulty in earning a living.

His production accounting for one purse was:

Input costs:	leather	$0.13
	paid labor	0.20
	subtotal	$0.33
Price		1.00
Net revenue		$0.67

The manufacturing process was relatively simple. The producer bought scrap leather from factory supervisors in the industrial area just north of St. Martin, where he invariably found a varied selection of finishes, colors, and thicknesses with which to respond to changing consumer preferences. He would then punch out the appropriately shaped pieces by putting the leather on a wood block and hitting the blade through the material with a hammer. While he did this, a worker that he had trained would assemble the purses. Working together, the two men produced three bags a day. The pursemaker's spouse, whom he married after he divorced his first wife in 1973, would help out whenever the worker failed to show up. She was not as quick because every little while she had to stop working to attend to their two infant children. The couple could rarely make as many as two bags a day, and that was the reason for hiring a worker. Perhaps, if they had no further children, the wife might take over from the worker when the infants became old enough to take care of themselves.

In 1970 the purses sold for $3.00 each. Competition from other manufacturers had forced the producer to gradually bring the price down to $1.00, and his net revenue to $0.67 per purse. Earnings, however, had not declined. Scrap leather of the appropriate quality was hard to find in 1970, and also quite expensive. At that time he paid $1.80 to $2.00 for enough material to make a purse, giving him a margin of about a dollar. On average he might sell three purses every two days, and thus earn $1.50 per day. Currently sales ranged from two purses a day in the off–season, earning $1.35 per day, to three in the high season, earning $2.00 per day. The pursemaker believed that he was still better off with the business than with a factory job.

He indicated that there was not much he could do to increase off–season earnings, or to use the period for building up inventory for the high season when the market took everything he produced. His cash–flow situation demanded that he spend all his non–production time in the off–season trying to make the average of two sales per day. The more basic dilemma was finding a means to increase production in the high season. The problem was that he still used the same cutting blade as in 1967. He sharpened it periodically, but it was so worn down that the punching of each piece of leather took much more time than before. A new blade could easily increase his production to four or five purses a day because he would spend less time punching and more time assembling. Indeed, even with another used blade he could hire two more workers, and perhaps make six or seven purses. He had already done his calculations, and figured out that selling that many purses could net close to $4.00 per day after paying the workers.

Over the preceding nine years he had tried to find a second blade, but to no avail. Metalsmiths had offered to make him one for about $30, but the metal was very soft and he doubted that such a blade could serve more than a week, not long enough to pay a monthly interest of perhaps $15 that an unsecured $30 loan would require. He also visited factories to see if they had any blades for sale. All of them had discontinued the pattern and had already sold the blades to his competitors. Importers said they could get a blade for about $50. However, they wanted a 40 percent deposit and could not give him a precise date for delivery except to say that it would be within three to six months. If it took six months, the producer would have a debt of over $100, consisting of an initial $20 for the deposit, $60 in interest on the $20, and then another $30 when it came time to pick up the blade. At that point he would be facing a monthly interest payment obligation of $25 (i.e., $10 on the first loan of $20 and $15 on the second loan of $30). As long as the lender did not ask for repayment of principal right away, the figures were acceptable. However, they were only acceptable if delivery took no longer than six months and if he could indeed sell six or seven purses a day. Neither of these factors were certain, and so large a debt in the face of such uncertainty was worrisome.

The manufacturer was nonetheless optimistic. He had taken the blade to a photographer six months earlier and, together with a note prepared for him by a letter writer near the post office, sent the photograph to a cousin working as a maid near Miami. She came to Haiti once a year with various things that relatives asked for, and he hoped that she would be able to find the blade and bring it on her next visit. In the meantime he was doing well. His customers were traders who seemed to sell purses primarily to tourists, and from what the customers told him, the number of tourists was increasing.

Handbags

A young couple had arrived in St. Martin two months earlier. He was from the southern peninsula, and she from the northwestern peninsula. They had met on a night boat to the Bahamas in 1974, and married several weeks later.[3] Independently of each other, they had paid $80 and $120 respectively to labor agents who promised to get them to places in the Bahamas where they could work. They eventually ended up in a workshop outside Nassau where they received only food and lodging for the first month and a half. During this period, the workshop foreman, also a Haitian, taught them how to make handbags out of palm bark, cardboard, and sisal. When they were able to produce ten satisfactory handbags a day without supervision, the workshop paid them the equivalent of $0.40 per bag, or $2.00 per day per person, and still provided them with food and lodging. Work was not too steady. Sometimes they made ten bags per day, at other times the foreman would ask them to make only five. Still, they estimated that during their year in Nassau they together earned almost $1,000, which they had sent to their parents in cash via the labor agents who visited the workshop about once a month. The agents charged each of them $2.50 per trip for the service, the same fee as for everyone else they knew, and proved very reliable. Their parents received exactly what the couple sent them, usually within three weeks.

In 1975 the foreman told them that they should leave as soon as possible because the police were in the area looking for Haitians without work permits. If they were caught they would have to pay a fine before being sent back to Haiti. If they did not have enough to pay the fine they might be put in jail as an example to others. The couple took the next boat back, paying $50.00 of their last month's earnings for the trip. They said that they were unhappy to leave. The lodging, food, and money were better than anything they had experienced in Haiti before they left, and their neighborhood in Nassau was "a hundred times better" than St. Martin.

After spending two weeks with their respective families, they collected some of the money they had sent from the Bahamas and established themselves in St. Martin. During their first week in the city they went from one tourist shop to another showing examples of the handbags that they brought with them from Nassau. Every shop offered to buy as many as they could produce. They selected the shop that offered them the highest price: $0.60 per handbag.

The price was higher than in Nassau in terms of cash, but earnings were lower because the tourist shop, unlike the Bahamian workshop, did not provide them with any of the necessary materials. Their accounting for one handbag was:

Input costs:	sisal braid	$0.13
	aniline dye	0.04
	cardboard	0.03
	palm bark	0.12
	transportation	0.04
	water	0.01
	subtotal	$0.37
Price		0.60
Net revenue		$0.23

The production process, which required use of a knife, a pair of scissors, and an enamel mixing bowl, began with purchase of sisal braid, cardboard, and dye in the central market, and with monthly trips to one of two coastal towns 20 kilometers north and west of the city to purchase palm bark. Including time necessary to purchase these inputs, the couple produced four bags per day, or 40 percent of their production rate in the Bahamas. Their daily net earnings as a result were $0.46 per person.

The tourist shop sold the handbags either without modification or with the names Haiti, Trinidad, St. Maarten, or other islands of the region affixed in brightly–colored sisal twine to each side. Employees in a workshop at the rear of the shop made the modification. The retail price to local consumers and tourists for the unmodified version was $2.50 each, and for the modified version with the word "Haiti," $5.00.[4] The couple noted, however, that the shop did not seem to sell many bags directly to consumers at these retail prices. A large number of traders, perhaps forty, each bought one to five bags at wholesale prices ranging from $1.00 to $1.75. These traders covered the city's main markets and tourist areas, and were the ones who made sales to final consumers. Depending on the circumstances and talents of the trader, the retail price could be less than, equal to, or greater than the wholesale price (my subsequent investigation indicated that handbags with the names of other islands on them sold for an F.O.B. export price of $60.00 per four dozen, or $1.25 each).

Responding to my question about why they did not try to earn more money by selling directly to traders, local consumers, or tourists, they replied that the process would take too long. The more time they spent selling, the less time they had to make the handbags. When delivering products to the shop, they always met one or two traders who were there to obtain a new supply of bags. In discussions with these traders they had learned that selling retail was a slow and difficult process. Traders told them that, by and large, selling five bags at a margin of $0.50 each constituted a good week. The couple estimated that even if they could obtain a margin of $0.90, they would need to sell at least six bags to equal their current earnings. Production would take up a day and a half, leaving only four and a half days to sell six bags. Their sales rate would have to be 1.33 bags per day, or 60 percent higher than the traders' rate of 0.83 bags per day. They were much less experienced in selling than the traders, and did not think they would do well in retail marketing.[5]

The couple also indicated that their understanding with the shop was that the latter would buy everything they produced on condition that the couple not compete with it by also selling to traders or consumers in the city. Although they did sell a few bags each month to acquaintances in St. Martin whom they trusted, the couple believed that the network of traders who bought from the shop were not reliable. The shop's traders covered the city and would soon know if the couple was competing with them by selling to consumers or to other traders and would inform the shop. If the couple sold to members of the network, the shop would not be long in discovering it. The couple believed that the risk involved in losing a sure customer outweighed any hope they had of increasing earnings through direct marketing.

Processed Peanuts

A woman who processed peanuts learned how to sell them from her mother, and had been a trader for most of her life. When she married in 1970, her husband gave her $4.00 to add to her own capital of $2.00, and this made it possible for her to shift away from retail selling, to buy wholesale, and to concentrate her time on processing. Her weekly accounting was:

Input costs:	peanuts	$10.00
	water	0.25
	charcoal	0.75
	subtotal	$11.00
Gross revenue		13.00
Net revenue		$ 2.00

The production cycle began on Monday mornings when she bought raw nuts from an importer. She started shelling them by hand on Monday afternoons and continued this operation through Wednesdays. On Thursdays she washed and dried the nuts in the sun, and on Fridays roasted them in a large pan. She spent from dawn to late evening on Saturdays selling in the central market, and generally earned a gross revenue of $13.00 each time. This was a $2.00 net revenue, providing her with an average daily earning of $0.33.

According to her estimates, about a third of her supply was bought by final consumers who spent $0.02 or $0.05 for a smaller or larger cup of nuts. She sold the rest to a regular clientele of mobile traders who circulated in the market and who generally purchased five or ten large cups at a time (i.e., in lots of $0.25 or $0.50). Her customers' margins were 100 percent early in the day and 50 percent or less toward the end of the day. They could usually sell at least one lot and thus earn $0.20 to $0.40 for their labor. The difference in earnings, according to the processor, reflected the difference in the traders' working capital, and the difference in capital reflected differences in the traders' selling skills and household circumstances. She knew several good traders who started with only a penny or two and who managed to build up to a dollar within a few months. Often, however, such things as the birth of a child or an illness would prevent capital from rising further, and would sometimes cause it to decline or disappear.

I remarked to her that since she had accumulated a sizable working capital of $11.00, retail sales at a 50 percent margin might bring her $5.50 instead of $2.00. She replied that it was absolutely impossible for one person to sell such an amount in one day. Besides the added cost of hiring someone to carry the heavy sack behind her as she searched for customers, one seller could not contact as many retail buyers as necessary to dispose of $11.00 in stock. Even if each transaction was for a large cup (i.e., $0.05), she would need to make 260 sales in a twelve–hour period. Nobody could make a sale every three minutes. She might be able to sell $2.00 in a day, but this would only give her a net of $1.00 for the week compared to the $2.00 she was already earning.

Replying to my confusion about her focus on only one day of the week, Saturday, she explained that most peanut sales took place on the principal market day. A good retail trader would be lucky to sell even $0.50 to ten to twenty–five customers a day during the rest of the week. If she did that, she would not have time to process, would have to buy at a higher price, and might then earn perhaps $0.20 a day from Monday to Friday. Adding a dollar in earnings for Saturdays, she noted that she would still come out with $2.00, and would have had to put in much more effort to do so in comparison to her current activity. Wholesale was better than retail.

Her main concern was the havoc caused to her production schedule during the rainy season. Rain or overcast skies on Thursdays would force her to work all day and night fanning heat from the charcoal burner across a metal pan in which she placed small quantities of nuts every five or ten minutes. Roasting without proper drying changed the flavor and made sales more difficult. Her customers trusted her quality and she could not afford to disappoint them. The extra effort and $0.75 in charcoal that this method of drying required was essential for business.

At that point I showed her how to make a dryer from flattened beverage cans that, according to a UNIDO report I had read a few months before, promised a substantial reduction in charcoal and drying–time requirements.[6] She was quite skeptical about this proposed invention. About two weeks later, she came to interrupt another interview I was conducting not too far from her house, and asked me to come by when the interview finished. When I did so she showed me the new drier which her husband had commissioned from a metalworker for $2.00. She said it was expensive, but after trying it out believed that she could earn it back during the next rainy season. She was now quite pleased and gave me a large cup of nuts to take home.

Soup

The peanut processor's weekly cycle could sometimes compress itself into a single day. A woman who did embroidery work at home for a factory until 1971 decided that her earnings of no more than $3.00 per week would not lead her anywhere. With $0.40 in capital she entered trade in foodstuffs. She did well enough to build up a capital of $2.00 in a year, but was not satisfied with her progress. She still earned less than from her earlier embroidery work. During this period, her neighbors would increasingly ask her to sell them a soup that she made for special family occasions. Although some neighbors wanted it because they had no time to cook, she believed that the basic reason was her unique recipe. She made the soup only once or twice a month because it required several hours of shopping and of cooking, and she needed the time for her trade. If convenience was the reason for demand, why was it that the neighbors would place orders with her several weeks in advance?

She eventually calculated that a day of soupmaking would earn her more than a day of trade if she could increase the number of customers. There weren't enough customers where she lived because most of them ate lunch near their work. Her market was downtown, which was also where she purchased her ingredients. For a while she tried to produce the soup in the central market, but found the cost too high. She needed to hire someone to help her carry charcoal, a heater, a large pot, a wooden bowl, and a large pestle between home and the market twice a day. This was expensive because she lived 4 kilometers from downtown. She had to hire someone else to watch over her equipment while she looked for ingredients, and the price of water was very high in the market. She then tried to make the soup at home, but the time required to get ingredients, return home, and then go back to the market used up too many of the best hours for selling food. She eventually convinced her husband that the only way to earn more from this activity was to move closer to the market. The higher rent that such a move might entail would be offset by lower production costs and a superior time frame for selling. They moved to St. Martin in 1973, and her daily production accounting for 1976 was:

Input costs:	ingredients	$ 9.00
	water	0.40
	charcoal	0.40
	paid labor	0.20
	subtotal	$10.00
Gross revenue		12.00
Net revenue		$ 2.00

The soupmaker's day began at 4:00 A.M. when she left home to purchase roots, crab, pork, goat meat, beef, and vegetables. She returned home at 6:00 A.M. to crush the roots for an hour, and then to add them to the other ingredients already simmering in water. Cooking was done by 10:00 A.M., and she hired a porter to carry the product to the market, arriving there no later than 10:30 A.M. At 3:00 P.M. she was usually sold out. In peak periods following harvests the flow of money in the market was high and she could always earn a net of $2.00 per day. She earned less when the flow of money ebbed, but still obtained at least $1.00 per day.

Her present problem was finding a way to increase her earnings. Costs were as low as she could make them without compromising her recipe, and raising her price would only push consumers to other food suppliers. She had the $15.00 required for another pot and charcoal heater, but since she could not sell out until 3:00 P.M., and since there were hardly any sales after that time, she doubted that she could sell a second pot at the same location. She had once reduced her price to see what would happen, but the rate of selling did not increase very much. What she needed was a trustworthy person (who would not skim off money or steal her recipe) to manage sales of a second pot at another place in the market. Her husband, a shoemaker who did not earn very much, was out of the question because even if he were willing to sell food, no one bought this kind of meal from a man. Her daughter was too young. She hoped that one day soon her sister in Cap Haitien would accept her standing invitation to come and work with her. In the meantime she would wait.

Notes

1. The rise in plastic bucket prices may have been associated with the rise in oil prices in 1973 and afterwards, and/or with changes in import duties.
2. One dollar in 1967 was equivalent to about $1.90 in 1976.
3. They were early "boatpeople" who worked in the Bahamas illegally.
4. The shop provided me with this price later in the week. The producers did not know it when I spoke to them.
5. Here, as elsewhere, rates are based on the assumption of a six-day week. In this instance, the producers had not calculated comparative sales rates. They only stated that they would have less time for selling and would need to sell faster than professional traders.
6. The report was Kherdekar (1976).

Appendix B

The Evolution of a Carpet Export Enterprise

The ten case studies presented in Appendix A, although they contain certain recollections about the history and evolution of each business, are static portrayals. They capture manufacturers at one moment in time. In various ways each description treats aspects concerning credit and investment, raw material supply, production organization, marketing and research, profitability, and sometimes, either explicitly or implicitly, touches upon such environmental conditions as aggregate domestic or export demand. So organized, the cases may imply that there exist possibilities for program and project intervention to "help" some manufacturers in matters of credit, materials procurement, technological advice, management training, and marketing. Such help may be possible, but static portrayals do not provide particularly useful bases for deciding upon which types of assistance, if any, may be appropriate. For this purpose the portrayals lack at least two important elements.

One missing element is the "assistant." Although it may seem relatively straightforward to ascribe a demand for helpful services, there is always the matter of whether the characteristics of supply of such services are commensurate with the task. For in the logic of things there is no perfection, and no reason to believe that the assistant is necessarily more capable than the proposed beneficiary in overcoming "obstacles" to progress, or that the assistant does not also require help. And the assistant's assistant, by extension, may also require assistance, ad infinitum.

The second missing element is time. There is little constant in economic or other dimensions of life, and vicissitudes in the flow events have an unfortunate habit of superannuating the validity of conclusions extracted from observations of the moment. So it may appear on a certain day that a manufacturer has a credit problem, and on another day that the credit problem has shifted to raw materials supply. Time presents problems and solutions as sequences of issues of greater or lesser importance that conspire to yield an uncertainty regarding what is appropriate or inappropriate in matters of assistance.

I had the fortune to stumble across the infancy of a sisal carpet export undertaking being organized in 1976 by COHAN, a major PVO, to follow its course through 1986, and to record certain particulars about its history. The telling of its story, organized explicitly in terms of origins, credit and investment, raw materials, production, marketing and research, politics, and outcomes highlights the influence that the two elements may have on certainties about assistance and its effect.

With regard to the assistant component, the story works at two levels. One has to do with the efforts of COHAN to assist people very much like those who lived in St. Martin. The other has to do with indirect or direct efforts by multilateral and bilateral agencies to act as assistants to COHAN's assistance enterprise. With regard to the time component, the story simply highlights the difficulty that streams of worldwide and local change have upon determination of problems and solutions, and upon causes and effects.

On both accounts, there is nothing special about the case. Any story about any organization, any public or private enterprise, any manufacturer in St. Martin, any household or any individual in Haiti or elsewhere will have similar properties because it is a story about (corporate) survival, about profits, and, in general, about the course of life.

Origins

The start of the project was fortuitous. In 1976 a manufacturer of the type who worked in St. Martin wandered into the offices of COHAN in search of sales for a sisal doormat. At that moment, as for other PVOs, COHAN was seeking to establish income–generating projects as a way to assist the urban and rural poor beyond the limits of the resources it had available for relief and educational programs. It was spending about $375,000 a year in foreign grants, but because these appeared as social transfers rather than income–producing investments, COHAN's resources depended entirely on external decision making. Income–generating projects offered the possibility of self–sustaining activities that could provide benefits independent of annual allocations from abroad and, if profitable, a source of additional revenue to supplement other programs. COHAN was already having some modest success in agricultural projects such as coffee marketing cooperatives and in such nonagricultural projects as sale of paintings and sculptures to visitors through an outlet it established in its offices.

COHAN's director reasoned that if the organization could market the doormats in Europe, workers like the manufacturer could obtain higher earnings, and COHAN could obtain a marketing margin. COHAN therefore began a small marketing effort in the Netherlands. This produced no sales. What it did produce two months later was a visit by a Dutch businessman who had traveled regularly between Haiti and Europe for many years and who imported natural fiber products from an export firm in the city.

The businessman had already noticed the doormats and similar sisal products for sale on city streets and believed that with a few design changes, quality improvements, expansion of the mats into carpets, and with volume production to keep costs competitive, the product would find a market in Europe. What he required was a supplier willing and able to make necessary changes and to provide timely deliveries at an acceptable price.

He contacted his supplier in the city and offered a one–year contract for delivery at $10,000 per month if it could supply his needs. The supplier was hesitant to take the offer because it would have required a relatively large investment in organizing a quality–controlled subcontractual system with independent manufacturers, or in training a large number of workers in hand production methods within its factory building, or in searching for and acquiring machinery unknown in Haiti and then training a lesser number of workers in their use. Each of these combinations of production techniques required substantial preinvestment and, since the Dutch importer offered no assurances that he would make purchases until satisfied with sample products, or that he would extend the contract beyond one year, a sizable risk. Under the best of circumstances the contract could not yield a margin to the supplier of more than about 20 percent, and this did not seem high enough to offset the risk.[1] Faced with this hesistance, the importer approached COHAN to explore possibilities. The PVO's staff had little experience in organizing industrial production or in volume export, but had learned from previous experiences in small craft projects that it would not be wise to launch an undertaking that did not have a clearly defined market for its output. Running a project at a small loss requiring subsidies was less than ideal, but it was distinctly superior to social programs that required constant subsidy of all costs. In COHAN's perspective, a decision regarding whether or not to proceed with an undertaking would also have to revolve around the calculation of margins, but unlike the situation of commercial exporters, the margin did not have to be measured entirely in terms of profits. A sizable reduction in subsidy per unit of benefit would constitute a distinct economic advantage. COHAN staff decided that they would try to supply the Dutch importer.

Credit and Investment

COHAN's operating budget could absorb some of the recurrent costs associated with the project, such as administrative staff salaries and fuel, but it did not have enough resources to command all the means of production that starting the project demanded. It needed a loan. Commercial bank loans required collateral, which COHAN was not prepared to provide. The IDB–supported Agricultural and Industrial Development Institute's public credit facility had the necessary funds available but access to them required a lengthy processing period, too long for COHAN's purposes. COHAN then applied for and quickly received a $12,000 short-term loan from the Netherlands government, which it used to lease a house with a large yard, to build a workshed in the yard, to buy a van, and to create a working capital fund.

Before acquiring the house, located in the middle of the city and costing $1,400 per year, COHAN explored the possibility of leasing factory space in the IDB–financed industrial park. The park was located near the airport, and had reliable water and electrical service. However, even after accounting for workshed construction, COHAN found that space in the park was eight times more costly than the house. The park's pricing policies were not intended for undertakings of the type COHAN envisaged.

Raw Material

COHAN's securing of a reliable supply of high–grade sisal at an acceptable price was straightforward. Materials available in the city from commodity speculators were unsatisfactory. Their stocks contained inferior sisal destined eventually for rope production, and the price of $0.60 per kilogram seemed high in relation to the average farmgate price of $0.21 per kilogram which COHAN's field extension agents were reporting from rural areas. Since COHAN had a network of field agents already in place for social and agricultural programs, it could circumvent the regular trade system and purchase directly from producers with little or no additional expenditures for information or transportation costs. It offered the farmers $0.25 per kilogram, 20 percent more than they were receiving from other buyers, and they accepted the price. This direct purchase, together with a $0.05 per kilogram transportation cost, provided COHAN with what it needed for $0.30 per kilogram.

Production

The manufacture of carpets required a sequence of six steps. The first was to purchase or make high–quality twine from low–grade sisal. The second was to wash and dry high–grade sisal obtained from rural producers. The third was to convert this sisal into long braids. After dyeing, the fifth step was to spiral the braids into 4–, 6– or 12–inch modular squares, held in place with the high–quality twine. The last step involved assembling the carpets by sewing the modules to each other with the twine. The end product could have any rectangular dimension, and thus serve various purposes including coasters, hot plates, table mats, wall hangings, small throw rugs, and wall–to–wall carpeting. Twining, braiding, dyeing, spiraling, and sewing assembly were not new to Haiti. What was new was the particular way these tasks had to be combined to respond to European consumer tastes.

COHAN, at least in principle, had to choose one of two general production strategies alluded to earlier. One strategy could entail purchase of relatively simple machinery for one or all tasks. The difficulty here was that, except for twine making, such equipment was unknown in Haiti. Finding each piece of machinery and training workers in their use would take time. Moreover, the approach would also entail a higher initial investment in machines and training that, even if it lowered production costs, offered little assurance of being able to produce the desired quality. The investment seemed large in relation to the size of the contract. This strategy had too high a level of risk.

A second strategy could entail subcontracting to jobbers or directly to independent producers. Labor costs, including producer margins, seemed low enough relative to the importer's price to leave COHAN with a comfortable margin. This kind of approach also made sense to COHAN because it would maximize use of the one productive factor that Haiti seemed overly endowed with, labor, and would spread the direct benefits of export revenues to a larger number of people than would be the case with use of machines. However, a pure subcontracting approach also entailed risks. Quality control and timely delivery among subcontractors, and between the contractors and COHAN, would be difficult to manage if spread all over the city. Losses resulting from poor workmanship of the raw material that COHAN intended to supply, for example, could be substantial.

After a period of trial–and–error production experiments, during which COHAN sent samples to the importer for his appraisal, the method of production evolved as a modified version of the second strategy. COHAN subcontracted twine making and braiding to outside producers who seemed able to deliver quality and quantity with minimal supervision, and hired wage employees for washing, drying, dyeing, and carpet assembly inside the workshed. The workshed also housed craftsmen responsible for spiraling braids into square modules. As for outside producers, the craftsmen received piecework rates. One could have called them independent subcontractors as well. However, workers in many of the city's factories who were generally regarded as wage employees also received piecework rates. One could as readily have called the craftsmen wage employees. The distinction was irrelevant. What mattered was that COHAN, like most of the city's light–manufacturing enterprises, organized a new combination of means of production by combining already available goods and producer services in a different way. The process of developing the new combination was not, however, as simple as the foregoing might imply.

Twine production was the easiest step. About one hundred of the farmers who had contracted for delivery of high–grade sisal were skilled at transforming low–grade material into twine with characteristics superior to machine–made twine, and to hand–made twine being produced in the city. Prices for twine being similar, the only apparent disadvantage of buying from farmers was quality control and timely delivery. However, since COHAN was already about to use its network of rural extension agents to assure quality and timely delivery of raw sisal, the same network could suffice for twine. Besides, buying twine from farmers would serve the useful purpose of spreading the benefits of "industrialization" into rural areas. The 100 farmers would eventually receive a piecework rate equivalent to one dollar for each day of work, including $0.20 for the low–grade sisal and $0.80 for their labor. Their returns from an average of five working days per month would be small in absolute terms, about $60.00 per year, but if their real annual household incomes were near the estimated average of $500.00 per year for rural inhabitants in 1976, they would obtain an income increase of 12 percent.[2]

With regard to braiding, COHAN invited several hundred women with braiding experience to collect sisal at the workshop and then to return with samples of their work. Braiding, like twine making, was a common skill, and COHAN used its network of social workers and teachers in the city to put out word that it was looking for this expertise. Assessment of samples yielded 200 women with requisite skill, most of whom were traders and vendors of prepared food. COHAN promised them a piecework rate that they found acceptable. It also demanded production and delivery rates that did not interfere with the women's other obligations. Most of the women could braid at home or during slack periods in their trade activities and still meet production deadlines. Those that were too busy subcontracted production to friends and family members and restricted themselves to intermediation and quality assurance. Women who did their own braiding earned an average of $7.00 per month, representing an earnings increase of between 25 and 50 percent and an average increase in household income of almost 20 percent.

Finding itself still short of qualified braiders, COHAN organized a six–week intensive training program for fifty young girls at two of its schools in the city, one of which was adjacent to St. Martin. This program proved successful. Less successful was COHAN's effort to also teach twine making to the girls. Acquisition of this skill took much longer than six weeks. COHAN could not spare teachers for longer than that and abandoned this line of training.

From among the women who presented themselves as braiding sub-contractors, but who did not have requisite skill, COHAN hired three without other occupations for washing and drying, paying each $40.00 per month, and another ten at $30.00 per month for assembling the carpets in the workshed. COHAN trained these women on the job. It also hired a driver/transportation clerk and two managers at rates of $80.00 per month, and seconded an accountant and an overall coordinator from its own staff to serve the project on a part–time basis.

Completion of COHAN's production system demanded that it find thirty craftsmen to spiral the braids into squares. This presented some difficulty. There were many craftsmen in the city like the ones in St. Martin, but COHAN staff could not evaluate which ones would prove most adept at manufacturing a relatively new type of product. It therefore hired a master craftsman to serve as production manager (at $80.00 per month), and asked him to use his network of associates, competitors, and ex–apprentices to recruit suitable candidates. He found only eleven individuals. COHAN then increased its piecework rate offer by 20 percent in an effort to entice workers away from the export firm mentioned earlier. Four workers left the factory before the firm raised its rates to retain those who remained. The problem seemed to be that COHAN and the export firm required a total of fifty–five qualified workers, but there were apparently less than forty individuals available in the city. Because these craftsmen constituted 25 percent of total labor costs, a piecework price war could only reduce the price competitiveness of the carpets. COHAN therefore decided to undertake another training program. The decision also had a diplomatic rationale. If pressed, the export firm's owners might demand government intervention to protect them from unfair competition. As a nonprofit organization COHAN benefited from several administrative and tax advantages that the factory did not have and that COHAN did not want to lose.[3] Also, the owners had well–established connections with foreign importers that through sub–contracting from the factory, COHAN's project might one day find useful.

For purposes of training COHAN could not rely on formal instruction of the kind that seemed to work for the fifty girls. The only valid teachers it had were the fifteen craftsmen in its employ. The situation required a modified apprenticeship program. For this purpose COHAN asked each of the skilled craftsmen to work with and provide on–the–job training to one less–skilled individual. Two months later COHAN had the full complement of thirty craftsmen, with each one earning an average of $40.00 per month. This was a 20 to 30 percent increase for the four individuals enticed away from the factory, a 150 to 200 percent increase for the eleven craftsmen previously engaged as independent manufacturers, and a 500 to 600 percent increase for the fifteen men who previously worked as employees or apprentices of independent producers.

Organization of the full production system took about six months, although COHAN had a contract and was exporting within three months of the importer's departure. The process cost COHAN, in addition to the $12,000 loan, some $33,000 in administrative salaries and other recurrent costs.

Strictly speaking, the project directly created forty–seven "new" jobs within COHAN's factory (i.e., thirty craftsmen, ten assemblers, three washers and dryers, two managers, a driver and a production supervisor). This implied a fixed capital investment of $255 per worker. There were, however, another 350 individuals engaged outside in subcontractual twine making and braiding. Their addition provided the project with a total, full–time equivalent workforce of about 130 people, therefore implying investment of about $92 per worker. Inclusion of COHAN's administrative costs would have raised this last figure to $346. All of these estimates were much higher than in St. Martin. But they appeared almost ridiculously low in comparison to the OAS's fixed cost estimates for the textile sector in 1963 ($1570 per worker), to an IDB handicraft project proposal in 1976 ($2700), to a similar USAID project proposal in 1977 ($7100), and to a World Bank estimate of minimum investment per worker of $1920 in its worldwide lending operations up to 1978.[4] Assuming that these figures were comparable, COHAN's relatively low cost seemed to stem principally from the fact that circumstances in 1976 did not require it to substitute capital for labor.[5] From an economic standpoint, a new combination of existing labor–intensive methods was sufficiently appropriate to yield a price–competitive product, the direct benefits of which, excluding sisal producers, flowed to 450 workers and to another 1,800 people who lived with them.[6]

Marketing and Research

Small as the project seemed to be, it was important not only to workers but also to the economy. COHAN's initial contract constituted 40 percent of the $300,000 increase in carpet exports between 1975 and 1976, and 9 percent of the $1.34 million increase in Haiti's total net exports of light manufactured goods in the same period. A modest investment combined with luck and hard work could go a long way. Unfortunately, faced with limited resources and changes in the world market working to its detriment, COHAN found it difficult to sustain initial momentum.

In 1977 COHAN decided that the cooperative was too dependent on a single customer and on a single line of products. Survival, let alone growth, demanded diversification. Until this decision COHAN had managed to put together a production system that, while new, did not extend too far beyond the boundaries of the agency's prior experience. Export marketing and "research and development," however, were absolutely new to COHAN. It did not know exactly how to implement the decision.

Being in the United States at this time, and hence able to obtain market information at lower cost than COHAN staff could, I spent a few days on the agency's behalf talking with business people in the interior design and craft import trades. What they said tempered my initial optimism about COHAN's future export prospects. First, although they noted that the COHAN's carpets were unique, the U.S. market was already saturated with similar products made in Pakistan, the Philippines, India, China, Tanzania, Angola, and Mexico. Second, demand for natural fiber carpets had flattened out, and coupled with increasing supply, was exercising downward pressure on prices. Third, countries such as Pakistan and India were able to withstand lower prices because they used simple machinery that not only reduced production costs, but also yielded better quality than pure, handmade products like COHAN's. Fourth, the rise in oil prices after 1973 had shifted demand from polymer twine and rope to natural fibers and this shift still seemed to be pushing the price of jute, sisal, and similar materials upwards.[7] Chinese producers, in addition to having the advantage of machinery, were able to adapt to the rise in material prices by shifting from jute and sisal to seaweed. There was a stable and relatively inelastic market for certain sisal products, notably floor and wall coverings for acoustical, institutional, and industrial applications, but production of the coverings required use of complex weaving equipment and highly trained workers. Firms in Belgium, Holland, and Switzerland dominated the market for such coverings.

Translated into operational terms, these general observations only confirmed what COHAN already knew. It had to assure that its products maintained a discernable degree of uniqueness, and that production costs stayed low enough to maintain a competitive price. The problem of husbanding resources to accomplish these tasks remained, and in the opinion of the U.S. importers, it was a problem of monumental proportions relative to COHAN's scale of operation.

According to them, the costs of marketing, including market and product research, generally absorbed 80 percent of the retail price of carpets. In 1977 the retail price of COHAN's carpets could not exceed about $0.80 per square foot, implying that production costs had to be $0.16 or less with the balance spread over various parts of the international marketing chain.

Because COHAN's carpets were unknown in the United States, the importers guessed that, at least initially, the agency would have to bear a disproportionate share of wholesale marketing and research costs, and suggested a figure of $50,000 as a serious investment in the first year. This was equivalent to $0.25 per square foot at COHAN's level of production at the time. Unfortunately, COHAN's production cost was already $0.54 per square foot (delivering at an F.O.B. price of $0.60 per square foot). Even if COHAN could extend its extraordinary stroke of luck by continuing to market so costly a product at existing rates of sale, the most it could generate for marketing investment was $12,000 a year.

COHAN was in a difficult position. It could use credit to introduce cost-saving technologies, but minimizing risks associated with the loan required advance knowledge of the capabilities of new technology and some assurance of a market. However, it would also have to resort to credit in order to find out about technologies and about whether or not there was indeed a market. Such a loan, if COHAN could find one, would expose the agency to inordinate risk. This kind of exposure for a PVO, let alone a business, was too high. COHAN would have to make do with its own limited resources, and with whatever opportunities fortune might continue to provide it.

Back in Haiti at the end of 1977, I met a Swiss technician from UNCTAD's International Trade Center. He was on assignment to write a report on Haitian export promotion and, after learning of COHAN's dilemma, volunteered to help as best he could in an unofficial capacity. He provided several European addresses for COHAN to write to, and the result was a considerable volume of information about new uses and product designs for sisal, new production techniques, improved inputs like dyes, and a list of major product distributors. Some of this information would later prove valuable.

In the meantime, carpet exports from Haiti fell significantly from an all-time high of $930,000 in 1976 to $370,000 in 1978 and then rose again to $660,000 in 1980 (see table 1.8). In parallel, COHAN's sales to the single Dutch importer fell to less than $50,000 in 1978, and climbed to $68,000 in 1980. The project was at least maintaining its export share of 10 to 12 percent of carpet exports. It now had a second customer in Holland, developed from the UNCTAD expert's list.

In 1980 COHAN invested $7,000 in a research and development effort aimed at discovering new products and new color combinations. A large portion of this outlay covered installation, in a closet, of a small laboratory in which to mix dyes. A dye supplier contacted by COHAN in 1978, also through the UNCTAD expert's address list, provided technical assistance in setting up the laboratory and training in its use. The investments proved timely. In 1981, and now working with its erstwhile competitor, the local exporter, COHAN participated in trade shows in Frankfurt and Berlin. The trip was sponsored by the government's Office of Industrial Promotion (ONAPI) with financial and technical assistance from the German foreign-aid agency, GTZ.

The result, between the spring of 1981 and the spring of 1982, were sales of $140,000 to seven customers in Holland, Germany, Belgium, Canada, and the United States. These sales, which represented about 18 percent of Haiti's carpet exports for the period, provided COHAN with its first profit, amounting to $33,000 before deducting indirect administrative costs, and $700 after deducting these costs. Part of this success was a technological breakthrough in 1980 and 1981 that provided the product with the uniqueness that it lacked earlier. Whereas COHAN had been producing 1-foot square modules made up of submodules no smaller than 16 square inches (i.e. nine modules per square foot), the research phase had succeeded in producing submodules of 9 square inches (or sixteen modules per square foot). This was important. The scale of detail could not be reproduced by machines and therefore required that foreign competitors also resort to the pure labor-intensive methods in which Haiti had a decided comparative cost advantage at the time.

This progress, unfortunately, was soon offset by a production loss of 65,000 square feet of carpet. COHAN hired a GTZ expatriate to assist in reorganizing production methods. He proved helpful in introducing more efficient and less costly methods to produce carpets. Unfortunately, production proceeded far ahead of actual orders, and when later combined with cancellation of an order from Germany for which COHAN had already begun production, the project had to absorb a $50,000 loss.

Sales dropped off during 1982, compelling COHAN to sell below cost in order to dispose of inventory and to keep a skeletal work force on the job, and continued to decline through 1983. Four factors seemed to conspire to force this turn of events. One was declining demand for consumer durables associated with the worldwide recession. Second was a 36 percent increase in the price of sisal between 1981, when the price was already 62 percent above the 1977 level, and 1982.[8] Third was deterioration in Haiti's terms of trade. Haitian currency was pegged to the U.S. dollar. The dollar was continuing to rise in value against most European currencies, and a number of competitor countries, notably Mexico, were devaluating their currencies. COHAN's principal cost advantage, relatively inexpensive labor, had largely disappeared. Fourth, in 1982 and 1983 COHAN was in no better position, at least not financially, than it found itself in 1977 with respect to obtaining labor-saving machinery.

In late 1983, USAID invited COHAN and nine other craft producers to participate in a project leading to an exhibit the following summer at the Atlanta Market Center's "Caribbean Gift Show." The invitation came after a USAID–sponsored team of marketing and design experts had appraised the marketability of crafts produced by fifty local manufacturers (Brinkerhoff, 1984). COHAN's carpets struck the experts as promising. A second team followed in early 1984. It made suggestions for certain design changes, and provided basic information about pricing, packaging, and shipping requirements. Later, USAID brought the ten producers to Atlanta for a seminar on marketing. Finally, in midsummer, COHAN and the other producers showed their products over a four–day period. Combined sales of the Haiti contingent were $48,000, but COHAN's share was only $1,700 (Chalden, Robinson, and Lockridge, 1984).

USAID personnel suggested at the end of 1984 that COHAN's products were attractive and still unique. The poor outcome in Atlanta, in their opinion, resulted from COHAN's failure to send an experienced salesperson fluent in English to the show. This could certainly have been a factor, although COHAN did send the same Haitian who had been responsible for sales since 1976, and who had done quite well in Frankfurt and Berlin speaking Dutch, French, German, and enough English to sign contracts with U.S. and Canadian importers. Of greater interest in this retrospective causal ascription was that USAID consultants could have overlooked so simple a matter as language proficiency requirements in the course of expending $60,000 to assist Haitian producers in key aspects of international marketing. If language was a factor, it seemed inappropriate to lay the blame entirely at COHAN's doorstep.

In any event, there were other technological difficulties associated with marketing to the United States that USAID did not anticipate. While COHAN did not make sales at the Atlanta exposition, it made several useful contacts wanting to order carpets. Unfortunately, the major contacts were sizable wholesalers who passed the burden of risk on new products to suppliers. They would not carry stocks of the carpets, and at the same time wanted guarantees that COHAN could maintain inventory and production schedules that, over the period of a year, could assure delivery of up to 1000 carpets. This scale of operation, and the risk, was too high for COHAN. At the same time, several U.S. retailers also wanted to order rugs. However, unlike their European counterparts who saw few difficulties in ordering abroad and then importing products themselves, the U.S. firms wanted COHAN to stock a warehouse in the U.S., which COHAN was also not prepared to do.

But these were difficulties of 1984. In 1985 COHAN participated at another trade show in Berlin, and with the drop in exchange rate of the U.S. dollar, found new orders from Germany and Egypt. Sales to a U.S.

firm in New York were also increasing, and local sales to residents and tourists from the COHAN outlet in Port-au-Prince were turning random purchases for personal use into small commercial orders brought back by travelers.

At the end of 1985, the project was gathering momentum quickly, rehiring craftsmen and other workers who had been laid off, and subcontracting again with farmers and women to produce braids. There was hope that 1986 would bring a recurrence of the one thing that had eluded COHAN for most of the decade: profits.

Politics

The fall of Duvalier, as noted in chapter 1, was followed quickly by worker-induced purges of factory and sometimes office managers and supervisors. The process did not discriminate between public or private enterprise, or between foreign and local ones. COHAN did not escape this treatment, and in the course of events lost an assistant director who had doubled as the carpet project's manager and who had done most of the research, marketing, and production organization since 1976. The momentum was lost, and mid-1986 found COHAN struggling to adjust itself to the new political circumstances, and as many other factories were doing at the same time, fighting to meet production and delivery deadlines in order to retain contract orders and to do all the other things required to keep the investment and progress of a decade alive. Profits were unlikely in 1986, but that was the least of COHAN's worries at that moment.

Outcomes

Whatever might happen in the future, the project had accomplished several things of considerable worth during the decade. Like several manufacturers in St. Martin who left factory employment before 1976 with newly acquired skills and product ideas in order to enter independent enterprise, many craftsmen had left the project over the decade and in 1986 were making carpets very similar to the ones they once made for COHAN; they were buying braids and twine from tradeswomen and rural producers they had met and were selling to tourists, tourist shops, exporters, and local consumers in the manner they were long familiar with. The project had helped diffuse a new product and a new "appropriate technology."

Also, over the span of the decade, COHAN's project generated an average of about $60,000 a year in income flows to urban and rural areas at an average annual loss of $10,000. Spending $70,000 to generate $60,000, or a net cost of $0.17 per dollar of income, fell short of the margin profit-seeking firms would have found acceptable, and to some extent showed the rationality of not accepting the Dutch importer's offer in 1976. But what might have been irrational for a firm turned out to be perfectly rational for COHAN. Prior to the project it generated almost no income. Every dollar of expenditure was a dollar in subsidy. Moreover, COHAN's performance appeared superior to some other PVO efforts. USAID's Atlanta project spent \$60,000 to generate \$48,000 in the short–term, or \$0.25 per dollar of income, and other PVO undertakings, such as the HACHO/CARE operation mentioned in chapter 2, apparently spent \$4.00 per dollar of income (Brinkerhoff, Fotzo, and Ormond, 1983:16).

These were appreciable results, and COHAN staff had to surmount many more hurdles than described by the foregoing, simplified case history. There were administrative and legal acrobatics to go through before the project could obtain duty–free import and export privileges that the government allowed as a matter of policy but that it implemented more grudgingly. Staff had to learn about and adapt to the convoluted system of payments to self–proclaimed "expediters" inside and outside government service in order to move dyes and carpets through customs more quickly. There were recurrent power and water outages that stymied production at critical moments. There were serious inconveniences when several staff members found themselves manhandled by Macoutes and others during a human rights gathering in 1980. The list of large and small vicissitudes that touched the project during its ten–year life was quite long. In the relative scheme of things, COHAN staff did well. With that kind of history, there was no particular reason to believe that the difficulties of 1986 would necessarily have to prove more insurmountable than all the other difficulties that had looked insurmountable every day and week and month from 1976 to 1986.

And as for the various kinds of assistance that passed by COHAN, such as IDB credit and place in the industrial park, or passed into and through it, such as production and research/contact help from individuals attached to the GTZ and UNCTAD, and the more formalized help from the GTZ and USAID in matters of marketing, there were moments in which some of these actions seemed hopeless and irrelevant, and there were later moments when most appeared quite helpful in retrospect. They were small parts of the flow of events that did punctual things at particular moments. The fellow from the GTZ was helpful, but was not responsible for overproduction and contract cancellation that accompanied his departure. GTZ marketing support for European trade fairs had no control over the exchange rate of the U.S. dollar. USAID assistance for Atlanta would have been hard–pressed to know so much about everything that they would be able to prepare for a cultural habit of refusal by many U.S. retailers to import directly. And the confluence of a declining dollar, technological breakthroughs, cultivation of market contacts, and adoption of lower–cost production methods that presented prospects of major advance in 1986 could not anticipate political change. All things "might have" been done differently by the various actors, but indications that ultimate outcomes in 1986 "would have" been different were not evident. In the accumulation of events over a decade, COHAN's assistants also seemed to have done well.

Notes

1. Haitian firms, or at least those I interviewed in 1983, generally believed that they needed a minimum margin of 20 percent to justify an undertaking. Their discount rate for risk, however, tended to be 50 percent or more per year. Therefore, on paper, a project had to show a minimum margin of 40 percent before it began to appear interesting.
2. Estimate of rural income in 1976 from World Bank (1978b: 27).
3. COHAN adopted a nonprofit "cooperative" status for the project that enabled it to obtain government designation as an organization having "public utility." This designation presented the project with several administrative and tax advantages not available to other export firms. For example, COHAN did not need to have a nurse on its premises or provide for doctor services, and did not have to pay social security or workmen's compensation charges. It provided equivalent services through its ongoing social service programs. It also did not have to pay income or corporate taxes, leaving it, at least in principle, with a larger profit for reinvestment or for supporting its social service activities around the country.
4. Figures reported in OAS (1972: 311), IDB (1976), USAID (1977), and World Bank (1978c: 83).
5. COHAN's costs were not too far out of line with those of other firms in Haiti. Average investment per worker in electronics assembly in 1982 was as low as $785 per worker, or about $490 in 1976 dollar terms (Haiti, 1983: 38). Electronics assembly was much more capital–intensive than COHAN's carpet assembly.
6. The estimate of 1,800 additional beneficiaries assumes that each worker lived in a different household, and that each household contained an average of five individuals.
7. The price of sisal in 1977 was actually 20 percent lower than in 1973 in current dollar terms, but would rise significantly thereafter (World Bank, 1978b: 41).
8. Sisal prices per ton were: $309 in 1977, $500 in 1981, and $680 in 1982 (IMF, 1983: 85; World Bank, 1982: 118).

References

Abrams, C. 1964. *Man's Struggle For Shelter in an Urbanizing World.* Cambridge, Mass.: M.I.T. Press.

ADIH. 1981. *The Industrial Sector in Haiti: Situation, Prospects and Policies.* Study prepared for the Association des Industries D'Haiti (ADIH), by Capital Consult S.A. and Dr. Serge Tardieu. Port-au-Prince, March.

Ahlers, T.H. 1978. *Haitian Rural-Urban Migration: A Case Study of Four Small Towns.* Report No. 46ZL/H-78. Port-au-Prince: Interamerican Institute of Agricultural Sciences, June.

Alderman, H. 1984. *The Effect of Income and Food Price Changes on the Acquisition of Food by Low-Income Households.* Washington, D.C.: International Food Policy Research Institute, October.

Alderman, H., and von Braun, J. 1984. *The Effects of the Egyptian Food Ration and Subsidy System on Income Distribution and Consumption.* Research Report No. 45. Washington, D.C.: International Food Policy Research Institute, July.

Allman, J. 1982. "Haitian Migration: 30 Years Assessed." *Migration Today.* 10(1): 6–12.

Alvarez, M.D., and Murray, G.F. 1981. *Specialization for Scarcity: Child Feeding Beliefs and Practices in a Haitian Village.* Report prepared for the United States Agency for International Development, Port-au-Prince, August.

Aristide, A. 1978. *Culture, Civilisation et Développement.* Port-au-Prince: Henri Deschamps.

Baldwin, R.E., and Weisbrod, B.A. 1974. "Disease and Labor Productivity." *Economic Development and Cultural Change* 22: 414–35.

Barros, J. 1984. *Haiti de 1804 à nos jours.* Paris: Editions L'Harmattan.

Bartkowiak, C.S. 1967. *Rapport au Gouvernement de La République d'Haiti sur la commercialisation des produits agricoles et l'artisanat en Haiti et l'établissement d'un centre d'études de commercialisation.* Port-au-Prince: United Nations Development Program.

Bates, R.H. 1983. "Governments and Agricultural Markets in Africa." In *The Role of Markets in the World Food Economy,* ed. D.G. Johnson and G. E. Schuh. Boulder: Westview Press.

Beardsley, J.R. 1981. *Trading With the Third World.* Washington, D.C.: Office of Urban Development, Bureau for Development Support. U.S. Agency for International Development.

Beghin, I.D., Fougère, W., and King, K.W. 1970. *L'alimentation et la nutrition en Haiti.* Paris: Presses Universitaires de France.

Bellegarde, D. 1941. *Haiti et Ses Problèmes.* Montréal: Bernard Valiquette.

Belli, P. 1971. "The Economic Implications of Malnutrition: The Dismal Science Revisited." *Economic Development and Cultural Change* 20: 1–23.

Berg, A. 1981. *Malnourished People.* Washington, D.C.: World Bank, June.

Berry, B.J.L., and Sierra, K. 1978. *Public Works Investment Strategy in a Developing Country: Urban Water Supply in Indonesia.* Research Report R78–3. Cambridge, Mass.: Department of City and Regional Planning, Harvard University, December.

Bienefield, M. 1975. "The Informal Sector and Peripheral Capitalism: The Case of Tanzania." In *Human Resources Research,* ed. J. Oxenham. Bulletin 6:3. Sussex: University of Sussex, Institute of Development Studies.

Binswanger, H.P., and Rosenzweig, M.R., eds. 1984. *Contractual Arrangements, Employment and Wages in Rural Labor Markets in Asia.* New Haven: Yale University Press.

BNB. 1958. Banco de Noreste do Brasil. *Aspectos Economicos do Artesenato Nordestin.* Fortaleza–Ceara.

Borsdorf, R., and Foster, K. 1985. *A Compilation of Market Price Data for Cereals and Beans, Haiti.* Report prepared for the U.S. Agency for International Development by the Food and Feed Grain Institute, Kansas State University, Manhattan, Kansas.

Boulos, C. 1978. *Enquête Sur Le Statut Socio–Economique des Ménages de Boston.* Port–au–Prince. Mimeographed.

Brecht, B. 1972. *Collected Plays.* Vol. 5. New York: Vintage Press.

Brinkerhoff, D.W., Fotzo, P.T., and Ormond, B.J. 1983. *Haiti: HACHO Rural Community Development.* Project Impact Evaluation Report No. 49. U.S. Agency for International Development, Washington, D.C., November.

Brinkerhoff, M.C. 1984. *Export Promotion in the Handicraft Sector: A Report on Haiti's Experience at the Atlanta Market Center's Caribbean Exhibit During the July 1984 AMC Gift Show.* U.S. Agency for International Development, Office of Private Enterprise Development, Port–au–Prince, August.

Brown, D.G. 1968. *Action.* Toronto: University of Toronto Press.

Buchanan, S.H. 1982. *Haitian Emigration: The Perspective from South Florida and Haiti.* Report submitted to the U.S. Agency for International Development, Port–au–Prince.

Buck, J.M. 1982. *Plan for the Improvement of Tax Administration in Haiti.* Washington, D.C.: Development Alternatives Inc., June.

Burns, L.S. 1966. "Housing as Social Overhead Capital." In *Essays in Urban Land Economics,* ed. J. Gillies. Los Angeles: University of California Real Estate Research Program.

Burns, L.S., and Grebler, L. 1977. *The Housing of Nations.* New York: John Wiley.

Cairncross, A.K. 1958. "Economic Schizophrenia." *Scottish Journal of Political Economy,* February.

Chalden, J.H., Robinson, A.J., and Lockridge, E. 1984. *Summary Report: Atlanta Market Center Gift/Handicraft Project in Six Caribbean Basin Countries.* Washington, D.C.: U.S. Agency for International Development, August.

Chambers, R. 1980. *Rural Poverty Unperceived: Problems and Remedies.* Institute of Development Studies, University of Sussex, March. Mimeographed.

Coats, W.L., and Khatkhate, D.R. 1980. "Monetary Policy Formulation and Objectives." In *Money and Monetary Policy in Less Developed Countries,* ed. W. L. Coats and D. R. Khatkhate. New York: Pergamon.

Comhaire–Sylvain, S., and Comhaire–Sylvain, J., 1964. "A Statistical Note on the Kenscoff Market System." *Social and Economic Studies* 13: 397–404.

Corvington, G. 1974. *Port–au–Prince au Cours des Ans: 1804–1888.* Port–au–Prince: Henri Deschamps.

_____. 1977. *Port-au-Prince au Cours des Ans: 1888–1915.* Port-au-Prince: Henri Deschamps.

_____. 1984. *Port-au-Prince au Cours des Ans: 1915–1922.* Port-au-Prince: Henri Deschamps.

Dasgupta, B. 1973. "Calcutta's Informal Sector." *Institute of Development Studies Bulletin* 5:2/3, 53–75. Sussex: University of Sussex.

Delatour, L. 1983. *Structure and Performance of the Haitian Coffee Industry, 1950–1982.* Report prepared for Capital Consult, S.A., Port-au-Prince, January.

Delatour, L., and Voltaire, K. 1980. *International Sub-Contracting Activities in Haiti.* Case study prepared for the UNCTAD–UNDP North–South Complementary Intra-Industry Trade Project. Washington, D.C.: Brookings Institution, May. Mimeographed.

De Jesus, C.M. 1962. *Child of the Dark.* New York: Mentor Books.

Delince, K. 1979. *Armée et Politique en Haiti.* Paris: Editions L'Harmattan.

De Regt, J.P. 1984. "Basic Education in Haiti." In *Haiti—Today and Tommorrow,* ed. C. R. Foster and A. Valdman. Lanham, Md: University Press of America.

De Ronceray, H. 1979. *Sociologie du Fait Haitien.* Québec: Les Presses de L'Université du Québec.

DEWIT, Inc. 1976. *Informal Small-Scale Enterprise Sector of the Urban Economy: Problems and Suggested Approaches.* Report prepared for the Office of Urban Development, Bureau of Technical Assistance, U.S. Agency for International Development, Washington, D.C.

Diegues, H. 1966. "Urban Employment in Brazil." *International Labour Review* 93(6): 643–57.

Dodge, J. 1961. *Memorandum to the Director of USOM in Haiti.* Report prepared by the Director, Division of Documentation, Office of International Housing, Port-au-Prince, April. Mimeographed.

Donas, S. 1978. *Precio de Los Alimentos Y Costo de Nutrientes en Puerto Principe, Haiti.* Port-au-Prince: Pan American Health Organization, April.

Downs, A. 1957. *An Economic Theory of Democracy.* New York: Harper & Row.

Duchon, J. 1986. "Baisse des Prix Pour Une Répartition Equitable des Pertes," *Le Matin* (25 Mars): 1,5.

Duplan, V., and LaGra, J. 1974. *Analyse du Système de Taxation Des Produits Agricoles Dans Les Marchés Haitiens.* Port-au-Prince: Interamerican Institute of Agricultural Sciences, September.

_____. *Transport des Produits Agricoles Vers Port-au-Prince.* Port-au-Prince: Interamerican Institute of Agricultural Sciences, June.

Durand, R. 1979. *Penser le Développement.* Port-au-Prince: Editions Jardin.

Dutcher, N. 1982. *The Use of First and Second Languages in Primary Education: Selected Case Studies.* World Bank Staff Working Paper No. 504. Washington, D.C.: World Bank, January.

Dwyer, D.J. 1975. *People and Housing in Third World Cities.* New York: Longman.

Early, E. 1937. *Ports of the Sun.* Boston: Houghton Mifflin.

ECLA. 1965. Economic Commission for Latin America. *La Progression d'Industrialisation en Amerique Latine.* (Statistical Annex). Santiago.

Economist. 1982. *World Business Cycles.* London: The Economist Newspaper Ltd.

Elkan, W. 1959, "Criteria for Industrial Development in Uganda." *East African Economic Review* 5: 52–57.

English, E.P. 1984. *Canadian Development Assistance to Haiti.* Ottawa: North–South Institute.

Evenson, R.E. 1976. "On the New Household Economics." *Journal of Agricultural Economics and Development* 6: 87–103.

Evenson, R.E., Popkin, B.M., and Quizon, E.K. 1980. "Nutrition, Work and Demographic Behavior in Rural Philippine Households." In *Rural Household Studies in Asia.* ed. H.P. Binswanger, R.E. Evenson, C.A. Florenci, and B.N.F. White. Singapore: Singapore University Press.

Fass, S.M. 1978. "Port-au-Prince: Awakening to the Urban Crisis." In *Metropolitan Latin America: The Challenge and the Response,* ed. W.A. Cornelius, and R.V. Kemper. Beverly Hills: Sage Publications.

———. 1980. *The Economics of Survival.* Washington, D.C.: Office of Urban Development, U.S. Agency for International Development, October.

———. 1982. "Water and Politics: The Process of Meeting a Basic Need in Haiti." *Development and Change* 13(3): 347–364.

———. 1986. "The St. Martin Project: A Decade of Pain and Progress in the Evolution of an Urban Development Institution." In *Politics, Projects and People: Institutional Development in Haiti,* ed. D.W. Brinkerhoff and J.C. Garcia-Zamor. New York: Praeger.

———. 1987. "Housing The Ultra-Poor: Theory and Practice in Haiti." *Journal of the American Planning Association* 53(2): 193–212.

Fass, S.M., and Alderman, H.H. 1985. *Design for an Expenditure and Consumption Survey Project in Haiti.* Report prepared for the U.S. Agency for International Development, Port-au-Prince, March.

FCH. 1977. Foundation for Cooperative Housing, Inc. *Assessment Report to the United Nations Capital Development Fund on Proposed Sites and Services and Slum Rehabilitation Programs in Port-au-Prince.* Washington, D.C., March.

———. 1979. Foundation for Cooperative Housing, Inc. *Rapport d'Avancement des Travaux, Avril-Sept. 1979.* Port-au-Prince, October.

———. 1982. Foundation for Cooperative Housing, Inc. *Rehabilitation of St. Martin Quarter and Les Drouillards Sites and Services Project of Technical Assistance, Final Report.* Washington, D.C., September.

Feyerabend, P. 1975. *Against Method: An Outline of an Anarchistic Theory of Knowledge.* London.

Fischer, I. 1930. *The Theory of Interest.* New York: Macmillan.

Folsom, R.S. 1953. *The Haitian Economy.* Port-au-Prince. Draft Mimeograph.

Fontaine, R. 1986. "Hanging On to a Fragile Leadership." *Insight* (30 June): 25.

Foster, P.J. 1966. "The Vocational School Fallacy in Development Planning." In *Education and Economic Development,* ed. C.A. Anderson and M.J. Bowman. Chicago: Aldine Publishing.

Francisque, E. 1968. *Perspectives du Développement Economique en Haiti.* Port-au-Prince: Henri Deschamps.

Friedman, M. 1952. "A Method for Comparing Income of Families Differing in Composition." Conference on Research in Income and Wealth. *Studies in Income and Wealth* 15: 9–24.

Garcia-Zamor, J.C. 1982. *Evaluation of the Haitian Development Foundation.* Report prepared for the Pan American Development Foundation and the U.S. Agency for International Development, Port-au-Prince.

Girault, C.A. 1978. "Tourisme et Dépendance en Haiti." *Cahiers des Ameriques Latines* 17: 23–56.

———. 1981. *Le Commerce du Café en Haiti: Habitants, Spéculateurs et Exportateurs.* Paris: Centre Nationale de Recherche Sociale.

Gittinger, J.P. 1982. *Economic Analysis of Agricultural Projects.* Baltimore: Johns Hopkins University Press.

Godard, H.R. 1983. *Port-au-Prince: Les Mutations Urbaines Dans Le Cadre d'Une Croissance Rapide et Incontrôlée.* Ph.D. dissertation, Université de Bordeaux III.

Grant, F.W., and Groom, D. 1958. "A Dietary Study of Haiti." *Journal of the American Dietetic Association* 34: 708–16.

Grasmuck, S. 1982. "Migration within the Periphery: Haitian Labor in the Dominican Sugar and Coffee Industries." *International Migration Review* 16(2): 365–77.

Gray, C.W. 1982. *Food Consumption Parameters for Brazil and Their Application to Food Policy.* Research Report No. 32. Washington, D.C.: International Food Policy Research Institute, September.

Greenidge, J. 1984. *Mid-Year Program Report.* Port-au-Prince: Foster Parents Plan International.

Grimes, Jr., O.F. 1976. *Housing for Low-Income Urban Families.* Baltimore: Johns Hopkins University Press.

Grootaert, C., and Cheung, K.F. 1984. *Household Expenditure Surveys.* Living Standards Measurement Study, Working Paper No. 22. Washington, D.C.: World Bank.

Grunwald, J., Delatour, L., and Voltaire, K. 1985. "Foreign Assembly in Haiti." In *The Global Factory,* ed. J. Grunwald and K. Flamm. Washington, D.C.: The Brookings Institution.

Grunwald, J., and Flamm, K. 1985. *The Global Factory.* Washington, D.C.: The Brookings Institution.

Guest, I. 1982. "End of the Line for Fiscal Reform." *MacLean's,* (2 August): 24–25.

Haggblade, S., Defay, J., and Pitman, B. 1979. *Small Manufacturing and Repair Enterprises in Haiti: Survey Results.* Department of Agricultural Economics, Michigan State University, Working Paper No. 4, East Lansing, Michigan.

Haiti. 1974. *Plan de Développement de Port-au-Prince et de Sa Zone Métropolitaine, Phase I: Stratègie de Développement de Port-au-Prince et de Sa Zone Métropolitaine Dans le Cadre d'un Schéma de Développement National.* Projet Conjoint Nations-Unies, CONADEP, TPTC HAI/SD 0970. Port-au-Prince, Octobre.

_____. 1975. *Plan de Développement de Port-au-Prince et de Sa Zone Métropolitaine, Phase II, Volume 1: Le Plan de Développement de La Region Métropolitaine.* Projet Conjoint Nations-Unies, CONADEP, TPTC HAI/SD 0970. Port-au-Prince, Mai.

_____. 1976a. *Plan de Développement de Port-au-Prince et de Sa Zone Métropolitaine, Phase III, Volume III (Première Série): Infrastructure.* Projet Conjoint Nations-Unies, CONADEP, TPTC HAI/SD 0970. Port-au-Prince, Février.

_____. 1976b. *Plan de Développement de Port-au-Prince et de Sa Zone Métropolitaine, Phase III, Volume V (Première Série): Habitat.* Projet Conjoint Nations-Unies, CONADEP, TPTC HAI/SD 0970. Port-au-Prince, Février.

_____. 1976c. *Plan de Développement de Port-au-Prince et de Sa Zone Métropolitaine, Phase III, Volume IV (Deuxième Série): La Réhabilitation du Quartier St. Martin.* Projet Conjoint Nations-Unies, CONADEP, TPTC HAI/SD 0970. Port-au-Prince, Février.

_____. 1977. *Plan de Développement de Port-au-Prince et de Sa Zone Métropolitaine, Phase III, Volume II (Première Série—Revisé): Infrastucture, Con-*

struction, Commerce, Services. Projet Conjoint Nations–Unies, CONADEP, TPTC HAI/74 R 40. Port–au–Prince, Novembre.

———. 1980. Secrétairerie d'Etat du Plan. *Diagnostic de la Situation Alimentaire et Nutritionelle de la Population Haitienne.* Port–au–Prince: Fardin.

———. 1982. *Etude de Factibilité du Quartier St. Martin.* Secrétairerie d'Etat des Affaires Sociales, Gouvernement Haitien. Port–au–Prince, Août.

———. 1983. *The Electrotechnical Industry of Haiti.* Study prepared by Capital Consult S.A. for the Investment Promotion Division, Ministry of Finance, Economy and Industry. Port–au–Prince.

———. 1984. *Stratègies et Plan Pour Une Production Alimentaire Stable.* Département du Plan, Unité de Planification Alimentaire et Nutrionnelle. Port–au–Prince.

———. 1985. Départment du Plan. *Planification et Développement, Revue Trimestrielle.* No. 1, Janvier–Mars.

Hake, A. 1977. *African Metropolis.* New York: St. Martin's Press.

Hart, K. 1970. "Small–Scale Entrepreneurs in Ghana and Development Planning." *Journal of Development Studies* 6(4): 104–20.

———. 1973. "Informal Income Opportunities and Urban Employment in Ghana." *Journal of Modern African Studies* 2(1): 61–89.

Herman, T. 1956. "The Role of Cottage and Small–Scale Industries in Asian Economic Development." *Economic Development and Cultural Change,* pp. 356–65.

Herskovits, M.J. 1971. *Life in a Haitian Valley.* Garden City, N.Y.: Doubleday.

HEW. 1975. U.S. Department of Health, Education and Welfare. *Syncresis: The Dynamics of Health, Vol. VI: Haiti (Revised).* Washington, D.C.: Public Health Service, Office of International Health.

Heyneman, S.P., and Loxley, W.A. 1983. "The Effect of Primary–School Quality on Academic Achievement Across Twenty–Nine High– and Low–Income Countries." *American Journal of Sociology* 88 (6): 1162–94.

Hippolyte–Manigat, M. 1980. *Haiti and the Caribbean Community.* Kingston: Institute of Social and Economic Research, University of the West Indies.

Ho, Y.M., and Huddle, D.L. 1973. *The Contribution of Traditional and Small Scale Culture Goods in International Trade and in Employment.* Houston, Texas: Rice University.

Honorat, J–J. 1974. *Enquête Sur Le Développement.* Port–au–Prince: Imprimerie Centrale.

———. 1980. *Le Manifeste du Dernier Monde.* Port–au–Prince: Henri Deschamps.

Horowitz, I.L. 1982. *Beyond Empire and Revolution.* New York: Oxford University Press.

Horton, S., and King, T. 1981. *Labor Productivity: Un Tour d'Horizon.* World Bank Staff Working Paper No. 497. Washington, D.C.: World Bank, October.

Hoselitz, B., ed. 1968. *The Role of Small Industry in the Process of Economic Growth.* The Hague, Netherlands: Mouton.

IDB. 1976. Interamerican Development Bank. *Draft Report of the IDB Mission to Haiti.* Prepared by Mrs. Ruth Dayan. Port–au–Prince, July.

———. 1977. Interamerican Development Bank. *Etude d'Une Système d'Eau Potable pour Petionville, Nouveau Port–au–Prince, Carrefour.* Rapport No. III. Port–au–Prince.

———. 1979. Interamerican Development Bank. *Opportunities for Industrial Investment in Haiti.* Industrial Economics and Infrastructure Section, Economic and Social Development Department, Washington, D.C., August.

———. 1985. Interamerican Development Bank. *Economic and Social Progress in Latin America.* Washington, D.C.: Interamerican Development Bank.

IHS. 1973. Institut Haitien de Statistique. *Resultats Préliminaires du Recensement Général (Septembre 1971).* Départment des Finances et des Affaires Economiques. Port-au-Prince.

———. 1974. Institut Haitien de Statistique. *Bulletin Trimestriel de Statistique No. 96.* Département des Finances et des Affaires Economiques. Port-au-Prince.

———. 1975. Institut Haitien de Statistique. *Enquête Socio-Economique (Avril 1970) Premiers Resultats.* Département des Finances et des Affaires Economiques. Port-au-Prince. Mai.

IHSI. 1982. Institut Haitien de Statistique et D'Informatique. *Résultats Anticipés du Recensement Général.* Ministère du Plan. Port-au-Prince.

———. 1983. Institut Haitien de Statistique et d'Informatique. *Indices de Prix à la Consommateur.* Ministère du Plan. Juin.

———. 1984. Institut Haitien de Statistique et d'Informatique. *La Population Active en 1982.* Ministère du Plan. Juillet.

IIR. 1985. Institute for International Research Inc. *Haiti: Education and Human Resources Sector Assessment.* Report prepared for The Florida State University, Improving the Efficiency of Educational Systems (IEES) Project. Tallahassee, Fla., June. Draft.

ILO. 1948. International Labor Office. "Industrial Homework." *International Labor Review,* pp. 735–40.

———. 1952. International Labor Office. *Report on Handicrafts and Small-Scale Industries in Iraq.* Geneva.

———. 1962. International Labor Office. *Small-Scale and Handicraft Industries in African Countries and ILO Activites in This Field.* Geneva. Mimeographed.

———. 1972. International Labor Office. *Employment, Incomes and Equality: A Strategy for Increasing Productive Employment in Kenya.* Geneva.

———. 1976. International Labor Office. *Problèmes de Main-D'Oeuvre et Emploi.* Programme de Nations-Unies Pour Le Développement et Organisation Internationale du Travail. Genève.

———. 1979. International Labor Office. *Enquête 1978–79 Sur L'Emploi Urbain Dans la République D'Haiti.* Rapport Technique No. 2, Projet HAI/FY/014. Programme des Nations-Unies Pour le Développement/Office International du Travail. Genève, Novembre.

———. 1981. International Labor Office. *Resultats de l'Enquête sur L'Emploi Industriel Realisée à Port-au-Prince et l'Aire Métropolitaine.* Port-au-Prince, Janvier.

IMF. 1983. International Monetary Fund. *Haiti: Recent Economic Developments, Background Paper to the Staff Report on the 1983 Article VI Consultation.* Report No. SM/83/209. Washington, D.C., October.

India. 1956. Planning Commission, Programme Evaluation Organization. *Study of Village Artisans.* New Delhi.

———. 1958. Development Commissioner for Small-Scale Industries. *Agricultural Implements.* Small-Scale Industry Analysis and Planning Report 14. New Delhi.

———. 1960. Ministry of Community Development and Cooperation. *Report of the Syllabus Committee on the Training of Rural Artisans in the Community Development Blocks.* New Delhi.

Jacques, R. 1986. "En Jetant Un Regard sur La Politique du Jour." *Petit Samedi Soir,* no. 626 (29 Mars–4 Avril).

Janvier, L.J. 1885. *Les Affaires d'Haiti (1883–1884).* Paris: Marpon et Flammarion.
———. 1886. *Les Constitutions d'Haiti.* Paris: Marpon et Flammarion.
Jean–Frantz, T. 1986. "Une Arrière–Goût de Déchoukage." *Petit Samedi Soir,* no. 626 (29 Mars–4 Avril): 13–17.
Joachim, B. 1979. *Les Racines du Sous–Développement en Haiti.* Port–au–Prince: Henri Deschamps.
Johnson, E.A.J. 1970. *The Organization of Space in Developing Countries.* Cambridge: Harvard University Press.
Johnson, J.L., and LaGra, J. 1975. *The Internal Agricultural Marketing System of Haiti: A Price Analysis.* Interamerican Institute for Agricultural Sciences. Port–au–Prince, November.
Jorgenson, D.W., and Lau, L.J. 1969. "An Econometric Theory of Agricultural Household Behavior." Paper presented at the Far Eastern Meeting of the Econometric Society, Tokyo.
Kalbermatten, J.M., De Anne, S.J., and Gunnerson, C.G. 1982. *Appropriate Sanitation Alternatives: A Technical and Economic Appraisal.* Baltimore: Johns Hopkins University Press.
Keliman, E. 1966. "Age Composition, Size of Household and the Interpretation of Per Capita Income." *Economic Development and Cultural Change* 15: 37–58.
Kennedy, P. 1976. "Cultural Factors Affecting Entrepreneurship and Development in the Informal Economy in Ghana." *Bulletin of the Institute of Development Studies* (University of Sussex)8(2): 17–21.
Khatkhate, D.R. 1980. "Monetary Policy Formulation and Objectives." In *Money and Monetary Policy in Less Developed Countries,* ed. W.L. Coats and D.R. Khatkhate, New York: Pergamon.
Kherdekar, D.N. 1976. *Integrated Programme for Local Development of Agricultural Machinery and Implements.* United Nations Industrial Development Organisation/United Nations Development Program, Port–au–Prince, January.
King, J.M. 1978. *Analyses and Compilation of Nutrition Data and Studies.* Port–au–Prince: Bureau of Nutrition, U.S. Agency for International Development, March.
King, K.W., Dominique, G., Uriodain, G., Fougère, W., and Beghin, I.D. 1968. "Food Patterns from Dietary Surveys in Rural Haiti." *Journal of the American Dietetic Association* 53(2): 114–18.
King, K.W., Fougère, W., Webb, R.E., Berggren, G., Berggren, W.L., and Hilaire, A. 1978. "Preventive and Therapeutic Benefits in Relation to Cost: Performance Over 10 Years of Mothercraft Centers in Haiti." *American Journal of Clinical Nutrition* 31(4): 679–89.
Krueger, A. 1974. "The Political Economy of the Rent–Seeking Society." *American Economic Review* 64: 291–303.
Kurien, CT. 1978. *Poverty, Planning and Social Transformation.* New Delhi: Allied Publishers.
Labrousse, B. 1978. *De L'Idéologie Dominée.* Montréal: Nouvelle Optique.
Latortue, G.R. 1972. "Haiti et les Institutions Economiques Caraibéennes." In *Culture et Développement en Haiti,* ed. E. Douyon. Ottawa: Leméac.
Lebert, J–P. 1966. "Aspects Extra–Economiques du Développement." *Griots,* no. 1, serie II (22 Sept.).
Leger, J.N. [1907] 1970. *Haiti: Her History and Her Detractors.* Westport: Negro Universities Press.
Le Matin. 1986. "Des Suggestions Concernant Service Immigration." *Le Matin* (25 Mars): 1–2.

Liggett, D.R. 1959. *Small Industry Development Organizations: A Worldwide Directory.* International Development Center, Stanford Research Institute. New York: Free Press.

Linn, J.F. 1983. *Cities in the Developing World.* New York: Oxford University Press.

Lipton, M. 1983. *Poverty, Undernutrition and Hunger.* World Bank Staff Working Paper No. 597. Washington, D.C.: World Bank.

Lobb, J. 1940. "Caste and Class in Haiti." *American Journal of Sociology* 46(1): 23–34.

Locher, U. 1974. *The Internal Marketing System for Agricultural Produce in Port-au-Prince.* Port-au-Prince: Interamerican Institute for Agricultural Sciences, November.

______. 1975. "The Market System of Port-au-Prince." In *Working Papers in Haitian Society and Culture,* ed. S.W. Mintz. New Haven: Yale University Press.

Lockheed, M.E., Jamison, D.T., and Lau, L.J. 1980. "Farmer Education and Farm Efficiency: A Survey." *Economic Development and Cultural Change* 29(1): 37–76.

Logan, R.W. 1930. "Education in Haiti." *Journal of Negro History* 15: 401–60.

Long, M.F. 1968. "Interest Rates and the Structure of Agricultural Credit Markets." *Oxford Economic Papers* 20(2): 275–88.

Lowenthal, I.P. 1984. "Labor, Sexuality and the Conjugal Contract in Rural Haiti." In *Haiti—Today and Tomorrow,* ed. C.R. Foster and A. Valdman. Lanham, Md.: University Press of America.

Luc, J. 1976. *Structures Economiques et Lutte Nationale Populaire en Haiti.* Montréal: Editions Nouvelle Optique.

Luiton, P.H. 1968. *Housing Development Program for the Republic of Haiti: Preliminary Site Selection.* Port-au-Prince: U.S. Agency for International Development, October.

Lundahl, M. 1979. *Peasants and Poverty: A Study of Haiti.* New York: St. Martin's Press.

______. 1983. *The Haitian Economy.* New York: St. Martin's Press.

Madsen, M. 1986. "Mise au Point de Huilerie Nationale S.A." *Petit Samedi Soir,* no. 626 (29 Mars–4 Avril): 18, 38.

Manigat, C., Moise, C., and Olivier, E. 1975. *Haiti, Quel Développement?* Montréal: Collectifs Paroles.

Marsden, K. 1975. "The Role of Small-Scale Industry in Development: Opportunities and Constraints." *Colloquium on Urban Poverty: A Comparison of the Latin American and the United States Experience.* Los Angeles, Calif.: University of California, School of Architecture and Urban Planning.

Marx, K. 1847. *The Poverty of Philosophy.* Moscow (undated publication).

Mason, J. 1981. *Miracle on Ave. St. Martin: A Lesson in Self-Help Housing from Port-au-Prince.* Port-au-Prince, October. Mimeographed.

Mathon, A. 1969. *Canevas Pour Une Doctrine.* Port-au-Prince. Mimeographed.

McGee, T.G. 1974. *The Persistence of the Proto-Proletariat: Occupational Structures and Planning for the Future of Third World Cities.* Los Angeles, Calif.: University of California, School of Architecture and Urban Planning.

______. 1979. "Urbanization, Housing and Hawkers: The Contest for Development Policy." In *Housing in Third World Countries,* ed. H.S. Murison and J.P. Lea, pp. 13–21. New York: St. Martin's Press.

McKinnon, R.I. 1973. *Money and Capital in Economic Development.* Washington, D.C.: The Brookings Institution.

Meier, G.M. 1970. *Leading Issues in Economic Development.* New York: Oxford University Press.

Métraux, A. 1951. *L'Homme et La Terre dans La Vallée de Marbial.* Paris, UNESCO.

Mintz, S.W. 1957. "The Role of the Middleman in the Internal Distribution System of a Caribbean Peasant Economy." *Human Organization* 15: 256–86.

———. 1960. "A Tentative Typology of Eight Haitian Marketplaces." *Revista de Ciencias Sociales* 4(2).

———. 1961. "Pratik: Haitian Personal and Economic Relationships." *Proceedings of the Annual Spring Meeting of the American Ethnological Society,* pp. 54–63.

———. 1964. "The Employment of Capital by Market Women in Haiti." In *Capital, Saving and Credit in Peasant Societies,* ed. R. Firth and B.S. Yamey. Chicago: Aldine Publishing.

———. 1971. "Men, Women and Trade." *Comparative Studies in Society and History* 13(2): 248.

———. 1974. *Caribbean Transformations.* Chicago: Aldine Publishing.

Mixson, W. 1981. *Report of the Florida Mission to Haiti.* Tallahassee, Fla., November.

Mondot-Bernard, J. 1981. *Satisfaction of Food Requirements and Agricultural Development.* Development Center of the Organisation for Economic Cooperation and Development. Paris.

Moore, E.O. 1972. *Haiti, Its Stagnant Society and Shackled Economy.* New York: Exposition Press.

Moral, P. 1961. *Le Paysan Haitien.* Paris: Maisonneuve et Larose.

Morrison, T.K. 1975. "Case Study of a Least Developed Country Successfully Exporting Manufactures: Haiti." *Inter-American Economic Affairs* 29(1): 21–31.

Murray, G.F., and Alvarez, A.D. 1973. *The Marketing of Beans in Haiti: An Exploratory Study.* Port-au-Prince: Institut Interamericain des Sciences Agricoles.

Nerlove, M. 1974. "Household and Economy: Toward a New Theory of Population and Economic Growth." *Journal of Political Economy* 82(2): 200–218.

Nicholls, D. 1979. *From Dessalines to Duvalier.* Cambridge: Cambridge University Press.

Nihan, G. 1976. *Projet de Recherches sur l'Education et l'Emploi: Formation, Emploi et Productivité dans le Secteur Non-Structuré Urbain.* World Employment Programme Research Working Papers. Geneva: International Labour Office.

Nisbet, C.T. 1967. "Interest Rates and Imperfect Competition in the Informal Credit Market of Rural Chile." *Economic Development and Cultural Change* 16(1): 73–90.

———. 1971. "Moneylending in Rural Areas of Latin America." *American Journal of Economics and Sociology* 30(1): 71–84.

Norwood, H.C. 1975. "Informal Industry in Developing Countries." *Town Planning Review* 46(1): 83–94.

OAS. 1962. Organisation of American States. *Rapport Général Présenté au Government de la République d'Haiti.* Mission Conjointe OEA–CEPAL–BID en Haiti. Washington, D.C., Decembre.

———. 1972. Organisation of American States. *Haiti: Mission d'Assistance Technique Integrée.* Washington, D.C.: Secrétariat Général.

Oshima, H.T. 1967. "Food Consumption, Nutrition, and Economic Development in Asian Countries." *Economic Development and Cultural Change* 15(4): 385–97.

Papanek, G.F. 1975. "The Poor of Jakarta." *Economic Development and Cultural Change* 24(1): 1–28.

Pierre–Charles, G. 1967. *L'Economie Haitienne et Sa Voie de Développement.* Paris: Maisonneuve et Larose.

Pinstrup–Anderson, P., de Londono, N.R., and Hoover, E. 1976. "The Impact of Increasing Food Supply on Human Nutrition: Implications for Commodity Priorities in Agricultural Research and Policy." *American Journal of Agricultural Economics* 58(2): May: 131–42.

Pitt, M. 1983. "Food Preferences and Nutrition in Rural Bangladesh." *Review of Economics and Statistics* 65(1): 105–14.

Pitt, M., and Rosenzwieg, M.R. 1984. *Agricultural Prices, Food Consumption and the Health and Productivity of Farmers.* Bulletin No. 84–1, Economic Development Center. Department of Economics, University of Minnesota, March.

Pragma Corporation. 1984. *Maximizing Development Assistance in the Caribbean Through AID–PVO Collaboration.* Report on the Quarterly Meeting of 17–20 June 1984 in Port–au–Prince, Haiti. U.S. Agency for International Development, Advisory Committee on Voluntary Foreign Aid. Washington, D.C., July.

Preeg, E.H. 1984. *Haiti and the CBI: Taiwan of the Caribbean?* Port–au–Prince. Mimeographed.

Psacharopoulos, G. 1980. "Returns to Education: An Updated International Comparison." In *Education and Income,* ed. T. King. World Bank Staff Working Paper No. 402, Washington, D.C.: World Bank, July.

Reid, M.G. 1934. *Economics of Household Production.* New York: John Wiley.

Reveco, L. 1984. *Bases et Critères Pour Une Politique Des Prix.* United Nations Development Program, Port–au–Prince, October.

Rogers, B.L. 1983. *The Internal Dynamics of Households: A Critical Factor in Development Policy.* Tufts University School of Nutrition. October. Mimeographed.

Rotberg, R.I. 1971. *The Politics of Squalor.* Boston: Houghton Mifflin.

Saunders, R.J., and Warford, J.J. 1976. *Village Water Supply.* Baltimore: Johns Hopkins University Press.

Schumacher, E.F. 1965. "Industrialization Through 'Intermediate Technology.'" In *Industrialization in Developing Countries,* ed. R. Robinson. Cambridge: Cambridge University Press.

Schumpeter, J.A. 1969. *The Theory of Economic Development.* London: Oxford University Press.

Segal, A. 1975. "Haiti." In *Population Policies in the Caribbean,* ed. A. Segal. Lexington, Mass.: Lexington Books.

Selowsky, M., and Taylor, L. 1973. "The Economics of Malnourished Children: An Example of Disinvestment in Human Capital." *Economic Development and Cultural Change* 22(1): 17–30.

Shetty, M.C. 1963. *Small–Scale and Household Industries in a Developing Economy: A Study of Their Rationale, Structure and Operative Conditions.* Bombay: Asia Publishing House.

Shoup, C.S. 1965. "Production from Consumption." *Public Finance* 20(1–2): 173–98.

Singh, B. 1961. *The Economics of Small–Scale Industries: A Case Study of Small–Scale Industrial Establishments of Moradabad.* Bombay: Asia Publishing House.

Sirinit, K., Abdel–Gamad, M.S., Ali, T.V.L., and King, K.W. 1965. "Nutritional Value of Haitian Cereal–Legume Blends." *Journal of Nutrition* 86(4): 415–23.

Smith, H.V. 1952. *American Market Posssibilities for Asian Handicrafts.* New York: United Nations Technical Assistance Administration.

Smith, N.R. 1962. *Review of Four Years of Public Administration Services to the Republic of Haiti.* Washington, D.C.: U.S. Agency for International Development, December.

Southerland, D. 1984. "Haitian Finance Officials Try to Plug Nation's Leaky Ledgers." *Christian Science Monitor* (2 October): 3,5.

SRI. 1958. *Notes on Small Industry and Handicraft Development in Mainland China.* Miscellaneous Paper No. 2 of the Research Program on Small Industry Development, Stanford Research Institute. Mimeographed.

Srinivasan, T.N. 1985. "Neoclassical Political Economy, the State and Economic Development." *Asian Development Review* 3: 38–58.

Staley, E., and Morse, R. 1965. *Modern Small Industry for Developing Countries.* New York: McGraw–Hill.

Standing, F. 1982. *Labor Force Participation and Development.* Geneva: International Labor Office.

Stepanek, J.E. 1960. *Small Industry Advisory Services: An International Study.* International Development Center of the Stanford Research Institute. New York: Free Press.

Stepick, A. 1984. "The Roots of Haitian Migration." In *Haiti—Today and Tomorrow,* ed. C.R. Foster and A. Valdman. Lanham, Md.: University Press of America.

Thacker, S.B., Music, S.I., and Pollard, R.A. 1980. "Acute Water Shortage and Health Problems in Haiti." *Lancet* 1(8166): 471–73.

Tillman, G. 1981. *Environmentally Sound Small-Scale Water Projects.* New York: CODEL.

Timmer, C.P., Falcon, W.P., and Pearson, S.R. 1983. *Food Policy Analysis.* Baltimore: Johns Hopkins University Press.

Trairatvorakul, P. 1984. *The Effects of Income Distribution and Nutrition of Alternative Rice Price Policies in Thailand.* Research Report 46, International Food Policy Research Institute. Washington, D.C., November.

Tun Wai, U. 1957. "Interest Rates Outside the Organized Money Markets of Underdeveloped Countries." *International Monetary Fund Staff Papers* 6(1): 80–144.

———. 1980. *Economic Essays on Developing Countries.* Rockville, Md.: Sijthoff & Noordhoff.

Turnier, A. 1955. *Les Etats–Unis et Le Marché Haitien.* Montréal: Washington.

U.N. 1949. United Nations. *Mission to Haiti.* New York.

———. 1955. United Nations. *Survey of Uttar Pradesh Handicrafts: Production and Export Market Possibilities.* New York: United Nations Technical Assistance Administration.

UNCDF. 1984. United Nations Capital Development Fund. *Evaluation Ex Post, Réhabilitation du Quartier St. Martin à Port–au–Prince.* New York, October.

UNCTAD. 1976. United Nations Conference on Trade and Development. *Le Secteur Externe d'Haiti: Analyse et Recommandations.* Rapport No. UNCTAD/RD/103. Rapport de Mission, Genève, Mars.

Underwood, F.W. 1960. *The Marketing System in Peasant Haiti.* Yale University Publication in Anthropology No. 6, Department of Anthropology, Yale University.

UNDP. 1977. United Nations Development Program. *Rapport Sur L'Assistance Externe en Haiti—1976.* Port–au–Prince.

_____. 1983. United Nations Development Program. *Rapport Sur L'Assistance Externe en Haiti—1983*. Port-au-Prince.

_____. 1984. United Nations Development Program. *Assistance en Haiti du Système des Nations-Unies Pendant La Période 1982-1986*. Port-au-Prince, Janvier.

_____. 1985. United Nations Development Program. *Rapport Sur L'Assistance Externe en Haiti—1984*. Port-au-Prince, Octobre.

UNESCO. 1981. United Nations Educational, Scientific and Cultural Organisation. *Résultats de L'Enquête Par Sondage Sur Les Ecoles de L'Enseignement Primaire, 1980-81*. Projet Haiti/PNUD/UNESCO/77/008, Décembre.

UNIDO. 1969. United Nations Industrial Development Organisation. *Rapport d'Une Mission de Services Industriels Spéciaux de l'ONUDI en Haiti*. Rapport No. id. 71-7660 UNIDO ref. TCD.63, Septembre 1971. Port-au-Prince, Mars.

_____. 1984. United Nations Industrial Development Organisation. *Assessment of Haiti's Competitive Position in Exports of Light Manufactures*. Report No. UC/HAI/83/034/M52/62.2.2. Report to the U.N. Industrial Development Organization, Vienna, April 30.

USAID. 1962. U.S. Agency for International Development. "Helping Honduran Industry." *International Development Review* 4:2.

_____. 1972. U.S. Agency for International Development. *Pre-Investment Survey Report: Housing Guarantee Program*. Washington, D.C., May.

_____. 1977. U.S. Agency for International Development. *Annual Budget Submission FY 1977*. Port-au-Prince, June.

_____. 1978a. U.S. Agency for International Development. *Project Paper, Haiti, Appropriate Technology*. Washington, D.C., January.

_____. 1978b. U.S. Agency for International Development. *Republic of Haiti: National Nutrition Survey*. Washington, D.C.: Development Support Bureau, Office of Nutrition.

_____. 1979. U.S. Agency for International Development. *Annual Budget Submission FY 1979*. Port-au-Prince, June.

_____.1980. U.S. Agency for International Development. *Country Development Strategy Statement, FY 1982, Haiti*. Washington, D.C., January.

_____. 1981. U.S. Agency for International Development. *Housing and Health: An Analysis for Use in the Planning, Design and Evaluation of Low-Income Housing Programs*. Washington, D.C.: Office of Housing and Urban Development, November.

_____. 1982a. U.S. Agency for International Development. *Country Development Strategy Statement, FY 1984, Haiti*. Washington, D.C., January.

_____. 1982b. U.S. Agency for International Development. *Food and Agriculture Sector Strategy for Haiti: Final Report*. Port-au-Prince, February.

_____. 1982c. U.S. Agency for International Development. *Project Paper: Development Finance Corporation*. Report No. AID/LAC/P-118, Washington, D.C., October.

_____. 1983. U.S. Agency for International Development. *Contradictions in the Investment Climate of Haiti*. White Paper prepared for the Government of the Republic of Haiti and the U.S. Agency for International Development, Port-au-Prince, September.

_____. 1984a. U.S. Agency for International Development. *Haiti Country Development Strategy Statement FY 1986*. Washington, D.C., January.

_____. 1984b. U.S. Agency for International Development. *Source Report on Hait-*

ian Factory Women: The Case of 24 Factory Women in the Light Assembly Industries in Port-au-Prince. Report prepared by F. Lewis, F. Lightfoot, B. Duval, and J. Salomon for the Office of Women in Development, U.S. Agency for International Development. Port-au-Prince, February.

———. 1984c. U.S. Agency for International Development. *Comparative Analysis of Investment Factors for Production Sharing Ventures.* Report prepared for USAID Latin America and Caribbean Regional Office by Production Sharing International and Free Zone Authority Services, 31 March.

———. 1984d. U.S. Agency for International Development. *Project Paper: Management and Productivity Center.* Port-au-Prince, December. Draft.

———. 1984e. U.S. Agency for International Development. *Quarterly Financial Status Report as of September 30, 1984.* Port-au-Prince, October.

———. 1984f. U.S. Agency for International Development. *Project Paper: Haiti National Mortgage Bank.* Washington, D.C., August.

———. 1984g. U.S. Agency for International Development. *Project Paper: Food for Development Program, PL-480 Title III, FY 1985–FY 1987.* Port-au-Prince, July.

USIS. 1986. United States Information Service. "Utilisez Immédiatement Cette Aide Americaine Pour Combattre Le Chômage." Press release in *Le Matin* (25 Mars): 1.

Walker, J.L. 1984. "Foreign Assistance and Haiti's Economic Development." In *Haiti—Today and Tomorrow,* ed. C.R. Foster and A. Valdman. Lanham, Md.: University Press of America.

Waterfield, C. 1985. "Disaggregating Food Consumption Parameters: Evolution of a Concept for Designing Targeted Nutritional Interventions." *Food Policy* (November): 337–51.

Weddell, K. 1960. *Aiding Small Industry Through Government Purchases.* Menlo Park, Calif.: Stanford Research Institute.

Wiese, H.J.C. 1976. "Maternal Nutrition and Traditional Food Behavior in Haiti." *Human Organization* 35(2): 193–200.

Willis, E.B. 1955. *Production and Export Market Possibilities for Taiwan Handicrafts.* New York: United Nations Technical Assistance Administration.

Wingfield, R., and Parenton, V.J. 1965. "Class Structure and Class Conflict in Haitian Society." In *Social Forces* 43(3): 338–47.

World Bank. 1976a. *Current Economic Position and Prospects of Haiti. Vol. 1, Main Report.* Report No. 1243–HA. Country Programs Department I, Latin America and the Caribbean, Washington, D.C, December.

———. 1976b. *Income Distribution and the Economy of the Urban Household: The Case of Belo Horizonte.* World Bank Staff Working Paper no. 237. Washington, D.C.

———. 1978a. *Current Economic Position and Prospects of Haiti. Vol. l, Main Report.* Report No. 2165–HA. Country Programs Department I, Latin America and the Caribbean, Washington, D.C., 22 December.

———. 1978b. *Current Economic Position and Prospects of Haiti. Vol. 2, Statistical Annex.* Report No. 2165–HA. Country Programs Department I, Latin America and the Caribbean, Washington, D.C., 22 December.

———. 1978c. *Employment and Development of Small Enterprises, Sector Policy Paper.* Washington, D.C., February.

———. 1979. *Haiti, Urban Sector Survey.* Report No. 2152–HA. Country Programs Department I, Latin America and the Caribbean, Washington, D.C., 19 April.

_____. 1980a. *Opportunities and Obstacles to the Development of the Private Sector in Haiti.* Task Force on Private Sector Activities of the Caribbean Group for Cooperation in Economic Development, Washington, D.C., 12 August.

_____. 1980b. *Water Supply and Waste Disposal.* Poverty and Basic Needs Series, Washington, D.C.: World Bank, September.

_____. 1981a. *Haiti: Economic Memorandum.* Report No. 3079–HA. Latin America and Caribbean Regional Office, Washington, D.C., 17 February.

_____. 1981b. *Memorandum of the Haitian Economy.* Report No. 3444–HA. Latin America and Caribbean Regional Office, Washington, D.C., 13 May.

_____. 1982. *Economic Memorandum on Haiti.* Report No. 3931–HA. Latin America and Caribbean Regional Office, Washington, D.C., 25 May.

_____. 1983a. *Economic Note for the Haitian Subgroup.* Prepared for the Caribbean Group for Cooperation in Economic Development by the Latin America and the Caribbean Regional Office, Washington, D.C., 23 November.

_____. 1983b. *World Development Report 1983.* New York: Oxford University Press.

_____. 1984a. *Haiti: Agricultural Sector Study. Vol. 1, Main Text.* Report No. 5375–HA. Projects Department, Latin America and the Caribbean Regional Office, Washington, D.C., 20 December.

_____. 1984b. *Haiti: Agricultural Sector Study. Vol. 2, Annexes A–G.* Report No. 5375–HA. Projects Department, Latin America and the Caribbean Regional Office, Washington, D.C., December.

_____. 1984c. *Haiti: Agricultural Sector Study. Vol. 3, Statistical Appendix.* Report No. 5375–HA. Projects Department, Latin America and the Caribbean Regional Office, Washington, D.C., 14 June 1985.

_____. 1985. *Haiti: Policy Proposals for Growth.* Report No. 5601–HA. Latin America and the Caribbean Regional Office, Washington, D.C., 10 June.

Zaidi, M.A. 1983. "Human Resource Development and the Unorganized Sector in the Developing Countries," pp. 137–50. *Proceedings of the International Industrial Relations Association's Sixth World Congress,* Kyoto, March.

Zuvekas, C. 1978. *Agricultural Development in Haiti.* Study Prepared for the U.S. Agency for International Development, Port–au–Prince, May.

Index